Betsy Bruce
John Ray

Sams **Teach Yourself**

Adobe®

Dreamweaver® CS4

in **24** Hours

SAMS   800 East 96th Street, Indianapolis, Indiana 46240 USA

Sams Teach Yourself Adobe Dreamweaver CS4 in 24 Hours

ISBN-13: 978-0-672-33040-7
ISBN-10: 0-672-33040-7

Library of Congress Cataloging-in-Publication Data

Bruce, Betsy.
 Sams teach yourself Adobe Dreamweaver CS4 in 24 hours / Betsy Bruce and John Ray.
   p. cm.
  ISBN 978-0-672-33040-7 (pbk.)
 1. Dreamweaver (Computer file) 2. Web sites—Authoring programs. 3. Web sites—Design. I. Ray, John, 1971- II. Title. III. Title: Adobe Dreamweaver CS4 in 24 hours. IV. Title: Dreamweaver CS4 in 24 hours.
 TK5105.8885.D74B782156 2007
 006.7'8—dc22

                              2008042137

Printed in the United States of America
First Printing November 2008

Trademarks

All terms mentioned in this book that are known to be trademarks or service marks have been appropriately capitalized. Sams Publishing cannot attest to the accuracy of this information. Use of a term in this book should not be regarded as affecting the validity of any trademark or service mark.

Warning and Disclaimer

Every effort has been made to make this book as complete and as accurate as possible, but no warranty or fitness is implied. The information provided is on an "as is" basis. The authors and the publisher shall have neither liability nor responsibility to any person or entity with respect to any loss or damages arising from the information contained in this book.

Bulk Sales

Sams Publishing offers excellent discounts on this book when ordered in quantity for bulk purchases or special sales. For more information, please contact

 U.S. Corporate and Government Sales
 1-800-382-3419
 corpsales@pearsontechgroup.com

For sales outside of the U.S., please contact

 International Sales
 international@pearson.com

Acquisitions Editor
Mark Taber

Development Editor
Songlin Qiu

Managing Editor
Kristy Hart

Project Editor
Anne Goebel

Copy Editor
Cheri Clark

Indexer
Erika Millen

Proofreader
Leslie Joseph

Technical Editor
Scott Antall

Publishing Coordinator
Vanessa Evans

Cover Designer
Gary Adair

Compositor
Jake McFarland

Contents

About the Authors

Betsy Bruce is a developer and consultant who specializes in creating eLearning applications using Dreamweaver, Authorware, Captivate, and Flash. She was lead developer at the Cobalt Group in Seattle, where her team won the 2003 Macromedia Innovation in eLearning award and was Manager of Technical Services at MediaPro, Inc., where her team won many awards for the projects it developed. She is an Adobe-certified trainer for Dreamweaver, Contribute, Flash, Captivate, and Authorware. Betsy received her B.S. degree from the University of Iowa and her M.A. degree in educational technology from San Diego State University. She is frequently a speaker at conferences on creating eLearning and using Dreamweaver. She is also the author of *eLearning with Dreamweaver MX: Creating Online Learning Applications* from New Riders Publishing. Born and raised in Iowa, Betsy lives in Seattle with her partner and two Siberian huskies. Her website is located at www.betsybruce.com.

John Ray is a Senior Business Analyst and leads the enterprise application development team for The Ohio State University Research Foundation. He has provided custom network, security, and programming solutions for clients across the country, including the National Regulatory Research Institute, the Brevard Metropolitan Planning Organization in Florida, and NEMO network partners at UC Davis and the University of Connecticut.

In his spare time, John has written a number of books, on topics ranging from IT security to operating systems and web development—including *Adobe CS3 All In One*, *Leopard All In One*, and *Maximum Linux Security*. He also serves as a course and textbook writer for many online institutions, such as ITT Technical Institute, and has authored classes in MIS, security, database development, and other advanced computing topics. John currently resides in Delaware, Ohio, with his fiancé (depending on when you read this), their two dogs, and a very large lawn that desperately needs mowing. John's website is located at http://www.johneray.com.

Dedication

This book is dedicated to my parents.

Acknowledgments

Many thanks to the group at Sams Publishing—Songlin Qiu, Mark Taber, and Scott Antall—for keeping the project under control and making sure that my words make sense!

As always, many thanks go to my friends and family for dealing with me as I worked on the project. There have been days when I started to think that I would suffer Vista burn-in on my retinas after taking so many screenshots!

Most of all, thanks to you, the reader, for being interested in taking up web development in Dreamweaver! You're about to venture into one of the most exciting, rewarding, and creative fields available to technology professionals today.

We Want to Hear from You!

As the reader of this book, *you* are our most important critic and commentator. We value your opinion and want to know what we're doing right, what we could do better, what areas you'd like to see us publish in, and any other words of wisdom you're willing to pass our way.

You can email or write me directly to let me know what you did or didn't like about this book—as well as what we can do to make our books stronger.

Please note that I cannot help you with technical problems related to the topic of this book, and that due to the high volume of mail I receive, I might not be able to reply to every message.

When you write, please be sure to include this book's title and author as well as your name and phone or email address. I will carefully review your comments and share them with the author and editors who worked on the book.

E-mail: graphics@samspublishing.com

Mail: Mark Taber
Associate Publisher
Sams Publishing
800 East 96th Street
Indianapolis, IN 46240 USA

Reader Services

Visit our website and register this book at informit.com/register for convenient access to any updates, downloads, or errata that might be available for this book.

Introduction

There was a time, not long ago, when the idea of using an application to develop websites was considered a travesty! The idea that an application could create code that would be clean, would be efficient, and would display properly in virtually any web browser seemed like pure fantasy.

Dreamweaver has forever changed how we think about web development. It is no longer the realm of the professional programmer. It is no longer a tangled mess of complicated codes and files. With the help of Dreamweaver, web development has become both a structured and a creative process. As a website development environment, it keeps your pages nice and neat and your links in working order. As a visual design tool, it frees you from the complexities of coding and allows you to focus on the content and look and feel of your site.

What is truly unique about Dreamweaver is that it can author virtually any type of website with any appearance. You may have heard someone say, "That site was made with such and such a tool." In Dreamweaver, the application helps you create your designs as you envision them, rather than trying to force you into a mold.

What Is Dreamweaver CS4?

Dreamweaver CS4 is the latest release of Adobe's award-winning HTML editor and web application development tool. Dreamweaver offers tools that can be adapted to a very design-centric environment, or a code-centric programming focus. The depth and maturity of the tools ensure that everyone, regardless of their skill level or needs, will be able to use Dreamweaver effectively.

Dreamweaver, like most Adobe products, is fully cross-platform. The Mac OS X and Windows versions of the software offer the same features, with very slight variations in look and feel. Projects that you create in Dreamweaver can easily be shared among Windows and Mac users alike.

Dreamweaver's openness doesn't end at the desktop—it extends to the servers it supports, as well. Using the built-in tools, you can create websites that are ready for almost any modern web server—and transfer them to your remote host without ever leaving the application.

Making use of the latest web technologies, Dreamweaver makes it simple to add design elements using Cascading Style Sheets, and dynamic interfaces with Spry AJAX components. These features can help you create a new, modern website, or transform an existing site into a compelling online experience featuring animation, drag-and-drop elements, drop-down menus, and much, much more!

What's New in This Edition?

In Dreamweaver CS4, Adobe has given Dreamweaver a much-needed spring-cleaning. The application is sleeker, is easier to navigate, and gets rid of older, problematic features. A few of the changes you'll find in this edition are listed here:

▶ An updated user interface with callouts for quick reference

▶ New CSS features for quickly assigning and working with styles

▶ Adobe Photoshop Smart Objects for embedding live Photoshop files in your designs

▶ Adobe Bridge, a central hub for managing CS4 suite resources

▶ Spry AJAX effects and other third-party AJAX options

▶ InContext Editing, Adobe's new hosted content management option

▶ Information on gathering web statistics from finished sites

▶ New "Try It Yourself" step-by-step guides for testing out some of the most interesting Dreamweaver CS4 features

Dreamweaver never ceases to amaze with the range of features it provides. This update makes those features even more accessible than ever before. As you work through the 24 hours in this book, you'll find information on everything from the basics of site file structures all the way to content management systems and version control.

Who Should Use Dreamweaver CS4?

One word: everyone. First-time web developers will love the ability to visually develop a site using tools that feel natural and provide instant feedback. Experienced developers may choose to start a layout visually and then switch to a code view to finish it off by hand. Dreamweaver gives you the flexibility to work the way you want, without getting in the way.

Who Should Use This Book?

This book is for anyone new to Dreamweaver CS4 and anyone already using the application who wants to take it to the next level. Beginners will quickly learn how to create new pages, create and manage CSS, and deploy websites. More experienced readers will find the tips and tricks they need in order to use the application to its fullest.

Conventions Used in This Book

This book uses several design elements and conventions to help you prioritize and reference the information it contains:

▶ New terms appear in a **semibold typeface**.

▶ When you are asked to type or enter text, that text appears in **bold**.

▶ Menu options are separated by a comma. For example, when you should open the File menu and choose the New Project menu option, the text says "Select File, New Project."

▶ A special `monospace` font is used on programming-related terms and language, and code.

▶ Placeholders—words or characters that represent the real words or characters you would type in code—appear in *`italic monospace`*.

▶ Some code statements presented in this book are too long to appear on a single line. In these cases, a line-continuation character is used to indicate that the following line is a continuation of the current statement.

HOUR 1
A World Wide Web of Dreamweaver Possibilities

The World Wide Web is a collection of interconnected documents created by people like you and me. This enormous network of information serves people all over the world. Today, researchers and students can find and share information with peers around the world without setting foot outside their homes, offices, and schools. Services like InformIT's Safari take traditional printed media (like this book) and make it available online. The World Wide Web is the world's new digital library, and you can contribute to it!

Maybe you dream of sharing information over the Web. For instance, you can share your portfolio, family pictures, creative writing, or genealogical research with friends, family, or the entire world! Or maybe you want to sell T-shirts, photos, cookie mixes, books, or note cards online. Perhaps you have to create a website for the company or public agency that employs you. These are all excellent applications for Adobe Dreamweaver.

I've received hundreds of emails from readers around the world who, like you, purchased this book to learn Dreamweaver. Some of these readers send me links to the websites they created using this book, and I'm thrilled to view them. Other readers are students who use this book in a course on HTML and web development. Please keep those links coming!

What Can You Do with Dreamweaver?

Dreamweaver is the most popular professional web creation tool, and you are in excellent company as a user of this exceptional software. Dreamweaver is integrated into the industry-standard Adobe Creative Suite. This makes Dreamweaver adoption a clean and effective addition

WHAT YOU'LL LEARN IN THIS HOUR:

▶ Types of web pages you can create with Dreamweaver

▶ Examples of text, images, hyperlinks, forms, multimedia, interactivity, and page layout design created in Dreamweaver

▶ How Dreamweaver can create reusable, updatable web pages and web page elements

▶ What the built-in file transfer tool can do

NOTE

Can Information on the Web Be Trusted?

The Web allows anyone to present information online—**anyone**. This openness means that as an information consumer, you need to be wary of what you read. Wikipedia, for example (http://www.wikipedia.org), provides a reader-contributed encyclopedia. Wikipedia articles are written and edited by the visitors themselves, people who may or may not be experts. Although Wikipedia provides some level of review, other sites may actively present information that is patently false. You need to be careful that you get information from a trusted and credible source.

NOTE

Should I Learn Dreamweaver or XHTML First?

This the-chicken-or-the-egg question comes up often when I speak with people who want to learn about web design and development. I think that it's best to learn a tool such as Dreamweaver first and then expand your knowledge of XHTML as you complete real-world projects. You will have more context for the XHTML you are learning after you have a basic understanding of Dreamweaver.

into a content publishing workflow. Many large corporations standardize on Dreamweaver as their web development tool of choice. Dreamweaver is also a popular tool for independent web developers who work on websites for their clients. As a cross-platform tool, Dreamweaver works virtually identically on Macintosh and Windows-based computers and is popular on both platforms.

Personally, I develop web applications in Dreamweaver. As the development team lead for a large university, I find that Dreamweaver enables me to quickly prototype application interfaces, then create the behind-the-scenes code using the built-in code editor and server behavior tools.

Defining the Technology

The foundation of Dreamweaver, and web development as a whole, is the Hypertext Markup Language (HTML), a language used to describe the structure of content so that it can be viewed over the Web in a web browser. In this book, we'll use the most modern version of HTML called XHTML (Extensible Hypertext Markup Language). Dreamweaver writes the XHTML for you, so you don't need to know how to write XHTML to get started using Dreamweaver. I suggest to all of my students and to you, the reader of this book, that learning some XHTML will help you become a more professional and flexible web page author. Hour 7, "Looking Under the Hood: Exploring XHTML," introduces you to viewing and editing XHTML in Dreamweaver.

If you are new to web development, you might not know some of the possibilities available to you in Dreamweaver. This hour explores examples of the types of elements you can add to your web pages no matter what its topic or purpose. Most people who are interested in creating web pages have spent some time looking at websites. Many of you are experts at navigating around and getting information on the Web! Now that you are learning Dreamweaver and XHTML, you'll begin to look at web pages differently: Instead of reading a column of text, you'll now think, *How can I create a column of text in Dreamweaver?*

One of the best ways to learn is by examining examples of web pages you find while browsing the Web. Most browser software has a Source or Page Source command (usually under the View menu) that enables you to view the HTML code of a web page. Even better, you can actually save a web page to your hard drive by selecting the Save Page As or the Save As command under the browser's File menu. After you save the web page, you can open the files in Dreamweaver and examine the page's structure. This is a great way to figure out how a web page author created an effect. If you are a beginner, you probably won't understand everything in the web page, but this is still a great way to learn by emulating others.

In this hour, I begin exposing you to some of the web terms and technologies that this book explores in depth. If you don't perfectly understand everything in this hour, don't worry; later hours cover all the concepts with step-by-step instructions so that you can follow along. This hour gives you an overview of the types of web pages you can create with Dreamweaver.

CAUTION

Copyright Laws and Content

Remember that there are copyright laws protecting the intellectual property of companies and individuals, including websites. You cannot copy the content (text, HTML, or images) from copyright-protected websites.

Dissecting Website Examples

FloraPhotographs.com—a popular flower site specializing in macro photography—serves as a point of reference for many examples throughout this book. FloraPhotographs.com uses a modern web design using the latest web technologies, such as a full CSS layout and dynamic AJAX elements. Don't know what that means? Don't worry—you'll be a web acronym expert by the end of the book! Best of all, FloraPhotographs.com was designed in Dreamweaver, so it is an example of the types of designs you can create yourself!

Basic Web Page Elements: Text, Images, and Hyperlinks

Most web pages have at least these three minimal elements:

▶ Text

▶ Images

▶ Hyperlinks

Figure 1.1 shows that the Flora Photographs **home page**, the web page that is the entry point for the website, contains only those elements, plus a search box in the upper-right corner of the page. Those three elements are the foundation of most websites, providing information (text) along with graphical support (images), plus a method to navigate to other pages (hyperlinks). Although Flora Photographs is a graphics-heavy site, it still includes obvious text and hyperlink elements so that users can find their bearings.

Text   Images   Hyperlinks

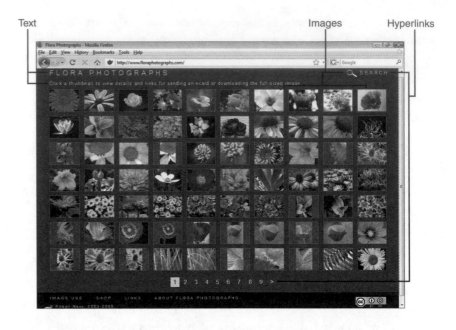

NOTE

Choosing Fonts

Fonts were traditionally developed for print, but several new fonts have been developed to be easy to read on a computer screen. Arial, Verdana, and Trebuchet are three popular screen fonts. You can find out more about web typography at http://webstyleguide.com/type/face.html.

Notice that there are several styles of text in Figure 1.1. The site title is larger and presented in a different color than the instructions and link text. Controlling the size and coloring of text is an effective way to guide your users' eyes where you want them on the page. Less important elements are smaller, whereas more significant navigation is frequently larger and highlighted.

Obviously, there are also many images in Figure 1.1. In web pages, images are always external image files. The XHTML tells the browser where the image should appear in the web page. In the Flora Photographs example, there are dozens of images onscreen. These are all separate references to image files within the site. The web browser must request and display each image separately when the page loads. Sometimes a single large image is broken into smaller pieces to improve page loading times and to give the designer additional flexibility in the layout. Dividing an image into smaller pieces is called slicing and is discussed in Hour 8, "Displaying Images." Images can also have transparent elements—such as the "lens" of the search magnifying glass in Figure 1.1. In this small icon, the lens portion is transparent, allowing the background color of the site to show through.

There are numerous hyperlinks in Figure 1.1. Clicking these hyperlinks takes you to different pages of flowers, a search screen, or other parts of the Flora Photographs site. By default, hyperlinks appear in blue text and are underlined, but you can change this using CSS. Flora Photographs, for example, removes the underline from links but adds a rollover effect so that the links highlight when your mouse cursor is over them. You'll learn about creating hyperlinks in Hour 5, "Adding Links: Hyperlinks, Anchors, and Mailto Links," and formatting them using CSS is covered in Hour 6, "Formatting Web Pages Using Cascading Style Sheets."

Dreamweaver can add a hyperlink to an image as well as text, as with the magnifying glass in Figure 1.1. You can even define just a small section of an image as a hyperlink by creating an imagemap. Hour 8 introduces you to image properties and the different types of images you can display in a web page, and shows you how to add image maps to web pages.

Page Layout

When creating web pages, you need to keep in mind that people will be viewing your design at different screen resolutions (for example, 800×600, 1024×768, 1280×1024) and might not have the browser window maximized to take up the whole screen. **Page layout**, the design and positioning of text and images on the web page, often requires a lot of thought, time, and experimentation.

The Flora Photographs website has a clean page style that makes it easy to view in browser windows of various sizes. The page layout for this website uses CSS, covered in Hour 6 and Hour 13, "Using CSS for Positioning." Figure 1.2 shows a page from Flora Photographs open in the Dreamweaver editor. The CSS Styles panel is open on the right side of the screen, displaying a list of the CSS rules applied to this website. The Dreamweaver interface and other items visible in Figure 1.2 are covered in depth throughout this book.

CSS enables you to format the way text appears, how various XHTML tags appear, and the positioning of various layout elements on the web page. Figure 1.2 displays the CSS Styles panel on the right side. All the CSS definitions are listed under the external style sheet name nav.css. An external style sheet enables all the pages in the site to share the same styles. And, best of all, the external style sheet enables the website developers to make a change to a single file to update the entire website.

CSS is the most recent language used to design page layouts for web pages, and it is still an evolving technology. The positioning and page layouts subset of the CSS language is sometimes called **CSS-P**. This subset defines page design essentials such as the widths and heights of elements, whether they float beside adjoining elements or break to a new line, and whether the elements stack on top of other elements.

TIP

Exporting from Page Layout Software

You can export web pages from most software programs, including Word, and then use Dreamweaver to clean up and edit the results. Test a representative page before you decide whether this method works for the content with which you are working.

FIGURE 1.2
FloraPhotographs.com uses CSS to stylize and lay out its web display.

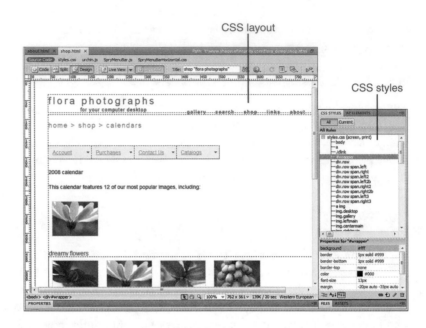

As more devices large and small incorporate web browsers, people might be viewing your web pages on a mobile phone or even in a flat-panel screen embedded in the refrigerator door! Figure 1.3 shows Adobe Device Central CS4, which installs with Dreamweaver CS4. You launch this application to emulate how different devices display a web page. It's important to test your page layout so that viewers using different devices have a pleasant viewing experience on your website. You'll further explore the emulator and mobile devices in Hour 14, "Creating CSS for Mobile Devices and Printing."

Forms: Collecting Data for E-Commerce, Newsletters, or Anything Else

Some websites have a business purpose for exchanging information with visitors, whether it be selling automobiles (http://www.acura.com), auctioning a ticket to a Barbra Streisand concert (http://www.ebay.com), planning a healthier diet (http://www.mypyramid.gov), or selling a design on a T-shirt, coffee mug, or mouse pad (http://www.cafepress.com). All these websites offer visitors the option of entering information into **forms** in order to purchase goods or receive information. Forms enable websites to become a two-way conduit as a visitor not only views information on the website but also can send information back.

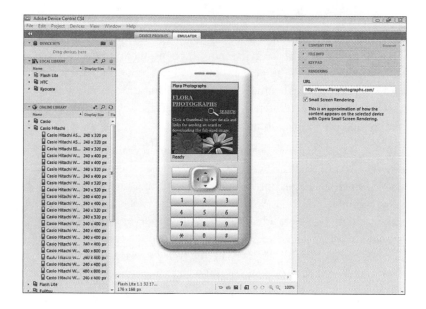

FIGURE 1.3
The Adobe Device Central CS4 emulator enables you to test your websites on various mobile and small-screen devices.

The Flora Photographs site uses web forms to collect user feedback and to provide an interactive search feature for users. The search form shown in Figure 1.4 consists of radio buttons, a drop-down menu, and a submit button, three of the form elements that are discussed in Hour 20, "Creating a Form and Collecting Data."

FIGURE 1.4
A search form enables the viewer to enter information and then submit it to a script that returns results.

Scripting for Forms

Although creating forms is easy, creating the scripts to make those forms function can be complicated. Don't assume that web design is the most difficult part of a web development project—sometimes the scripting work is an arduous process.

TIP

Easy Online Sales

As you grow your web presence and begin to consider possible online sales, Café Press can help! This online service allows you to create a wide variety of branded products and sell them with very little overhead and no additional programming for your website!

NOTE

Installed Player Applications

Often an operating system (such as Macintosh OS X or Windows Vista) comes with several popular multimedia player applications already installed. For instance, the Adobe Flash player comes installed on most computers. And players are included when you install the major browsers. Sometimes, however, computers in a corporate environment have players stripped out.

Creating scripts is an advanced topic that is beyond the scope of this book on Dreamweaver, but examples of scripting languages and locations to download scripts are discussed in Hour 21, "Sending and Reacting to Form Data." The Rick Steves' Europe website uses PHP, a popular and widely supported free scripting language. You can tell that the script is written for PHP because the file extension is .php. Creating a script to search a website is the tiny tip of the iceberg of what PHP can do.

FloraPhotographs.com also uses PHP to maintain its catalog of images and to generate e-cards that can be sent to other people. These **dynamic web pages**, in which the page content changes depending on the user's actions, can also be created in Dreamweaver. After you master the 24 hours in this book, you might decide to advance to learning a server application language such as PHP. It's perfectly realistic, however, to continue creating **static web pages** (the opposite of dynamic web pages), such as the ones described in this book, and be a successful web page author.

In an e-commerce site, such as the Flora Photographs CafePress.com site, an HTML form collects information about the purchaser.

Figure 1.5 displays a form that includes text fields and drop-down menus to collect address information. An asterisk (*) is a common way to signify that a text field must be filled out in order to submit the form. When you're creating your own forms, Dreamweaver provides a Validate Form behavior, scripted in JavaScript, to make sure that the visitor enters the correct type of information (see Hour 21).

Multimedia

Many websites include movies, audio, music, animations, 3D renderings, and other multimedia elements. These elements require that you download and install a player application, such as Flash (http://www.adobe.com/flash), QuickTime (http://apple.com/quicktime), Windows Media (http://microsoft.com/windows/windowsmedia), or RealPlayer (http://www.real.com/), to see or hear the multimedia files. Web pages created in Dreamweaver can automatically trigger the download of the appropriate player, making it easy for the website visitor. As more and more people have access to higher-bandwidth connections, a greater number of websites include multimedia files that require more transfer capacity.

Many pages, such as YouTube, have turned to Flash for creating completely cross-platform video and animation fields. Adobe TV provides a constant source of flash videos, as shown in Figure 1.6, for creative professionals.

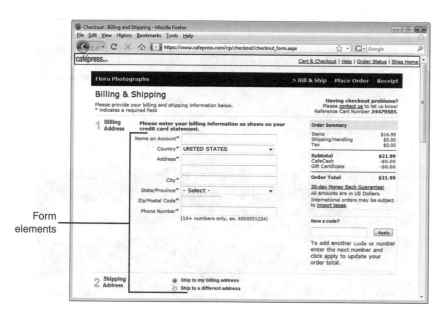

Form elements

FIGURE 1.5
This form collects information about the purchaser, and a script validates the form, making sure that all required information is entered before the form is processed.

In these cases, an Adobe Flash file containing video, audio, and animation effects plays when you initially load the web page...if you have the Flash player installed, that is! But the large majority of computers have the ever-present Flash player, so most viewers are capable of seeing Flash movies. Although Adobe Flash software is required to create Flash movies from scratch, Dreamweaver is capable of inserting, configuring, and previewing Flash movies. Hour 10, "Adding Flash and Other Multimedia to a Web Page," explains how to add Flash and other types of multimedia to a web page.

Interactivity

Dreamweaver can add JavaScript to a web page even if you don't know how to write JavaScript. Dreamweaver Behaviors add JavaScript to the page, enabling it to capture the user clicking on an image, rolling the cursor over an element, or many other events that the browser can detect, all using a point-and-click interface, as shown in Figure 1.7.

Dreamweaver behaviors can add interactivity without any programming experience! Hour 18, "Adding Interactivity with Behaviors," discusses and demonstrates behaviors. You might not have a need for some of the interactive capabilities of Dreamweaver, but others, such as the Swap Image behavior to create a rollover effect on an image, in which the image changes when the user rolls the cursor over it, can be helpful in creating a modern and attractive web design.

TIP

Creating Rollover Effects

You can use Dreamweaver's Swap Image behavior to create the effect in which an image changes when the user rolls the mouse over the image. You can also add the behavior by using Dreamweaver's Rollover Image object—it adds the behavior for you. There are often multiple ways to accomplish your goal in Dreamweaver.

FIGURE 1.6
Flash movies have gained in popularity and offer full cross-platform compatibility. http://tv.adobe.com is Adobe's flash video content site for creative professionals.

FIGURE 1.7
Dreamweaver makes it simple to react to browser events.

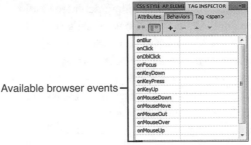

Available browser events

Dreamweaver also makes it possible to easily include JavaScript code that others have written. Let's take a look at a popular interactive behavior called a "lightbox":

1. Open the live Flora Photographs site in your browser: http://www.floraphotographs.com/.

2. Click the Search link.

   A "window" appears within the web page and the background dims in a smooth animation.

This animated effect, as shown in Figure 1.8 and called a lightbox, is preferred over creating pop-up windows. With Dreamweaver, you can download and use this same lightbox effect (called "lightview") without writing a line of code!

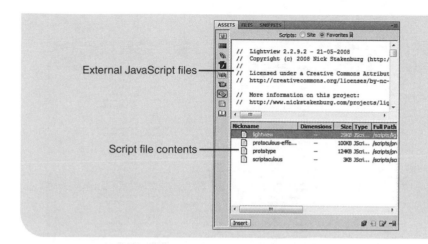

External JavaScript files

Script file contents

FIGURE 1.8
Dreamweaver can make use of external JavaScript behaviors, such as a lightbox effect.

Uploading a Website to the Web

You can create web pages for days, weeks, months, or even years, but eventually you'll either want or need to put them on a web server somewhere and share them with other people. You don't need another piece of software to accomplish this task: Dreamweaver has fully functional file transfer protocol (FTP) software built in, enabling you to connect to a remote web server and upload your files from Dreamweaver. Figure 1.9 shows Dreamweaver's expanded Files panel connected to a remote web server. The remote site files on the server are visible on the left, and the local files are visible on the right side of the screen.

Reusable Code and Files

Dreamweaver is an industrial-strength web development tool that enables you to work on individual web pages and on very large websites. Many websites, such as the Rick Steves' Europe website, have thousands of web pages. Managing all those pages, especially when a change is required, can be a daunting task. Dreamweaver has reusable and updatable pages, called **templates**, which you can use as the basis for a web page. Web pages created from a template maintain a link to the original template, so when the original is updated, the changes can be propagated to all the web pages based on the template. Dreamweaver templates are covered in Hour 15, "Creating Library Items and Templates."

Dreamweaver also offers another type of reusable element, called a **library item**, which inserts only a portion of a web page. Like templates, library items maintain a link to the parent library item and can be updated throughout an entire website. In the FloraPhotographs.com website, the

TIP

Finding Web Hosting

If you don't yet have a home for your remote, public website, you can find many websites rating the thousands of hosting companies vying for your business. You can type **"web hosting reviews"** into a search engine such as Google (http://www.google.com) or check out http://www.web-hosting-reviews.org. You need to specify the features you want on your website and what type of server you'd prefer (usually a choice of Windows or UNIX). You might want to wait to make your choice until you've finished this book so that you understand more of the possibilities of the Web.

FIGURE 1.9
Dreamweaver has built-in FTP software that enables the transfer of web pages to a web server.

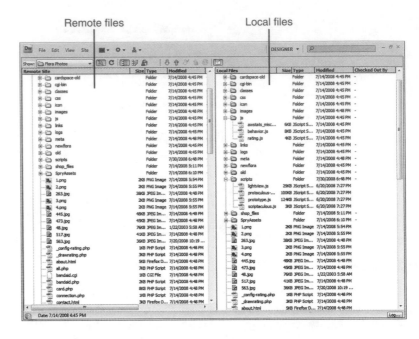

header and footer on each page are library items (shown in Figure 1.10). This enables the web developers to add additional information to the footer in the future, save the library item, and automatically update every page in the website without opening each web page.

FIGURE 1.10
You can insert Dreamweaver library items into web pages and update them later without opening each web page.

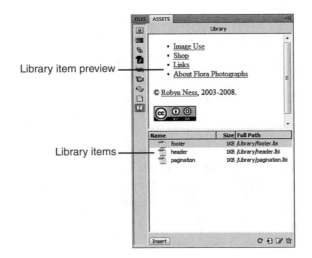

Summary

In this hour, you saw examples of both basic and advanced functionalities of Dreamweaver. You examined a photography web page, identifying text, images, and hyperlinks. You saw examples of forms and were introduced to how scripts work in the background to process what users enter into forms. You saw examples of multimedia either launched from a hyperlink on a web page or embedded directly into the web page. Examples of interactivity demonstrated what you can accomplish with Dreamweaver behaviors. And you were introduced to Dreamweaver file transfer capabilities and using reusable elements to help manage large websites.

Q&A

Q. Do I have to understand how to accomplish everything that Dreamweaver can do before I start working on a website?

A. You have to understand only the basics of Dreamweaver—that is, its interface and how to work with text, images, and hyperlinks. You'll also want to understand how to design a page layout for your web pages. Then you can learn some of the specialized functions that are necessary for the website you want to create. For instance, if you are creating an e-commerce website, you'll want to learn about forms (Hours 20 and 21). If you are interested in creating an interactive website, you'll want to understand Dreamweaver behaviors (Hour 18).

The best way to learn is by doing, so don't be afraid to dig in and create web pages in Dreamweaver. You can always improve or edit the pages later.

Q. I work with several programmers who say that Dreamweaver is a waste of money, and that I should just learn HTML and create web pages by typing HTML tags into a text editor. Is that really a better way to create web pages?

A. That might be the ideal way to create web pages for your programmer friends, but it takes a long time to learn HTML and even longer to learn how to program and write the JavaScript that Dreamweaver behaviors contain. I always recommend that after you master Dreamweaver, you take a look behind the scenes (which we'll do in this book!). There are always some things that will be easier to do in Dreamweaver, and some things that will be easier to do by hand.

Workshop

Quiz

1. What is the name of the web page element that a user clicks to navigate to another web page?

2. What is the name of the language used to style text and create web page layouts in Dreamweaver?

3. What is the Dreamweaver feature that enables you to add JavaScript and interactivity to your web pages?

Quiz Answers

1. A hyperlink is the web page element that navigates the user to another web page.

2. Cascading Style Sheets is an important style sheet language used to define both the structure and the presentation of web pages.

3. Dreamweaver behaviors enable you to add JavaScript and interactivity to your web pages.

Exercises

1. Visit a few of your favorite websites (stores, news sites, and so on). Look at the elements on each page and identify their functionality. Begin to consider how you would go about designing a similar page and what features of Dreamweaver you might need.

   Adobe occasionally redesigns its website, but these showcases should be available somewhere on the site.

2. Go to Web Pages That Suck (http://www.webpagesthatsuck.com) and read some of the articles and critiques of other web pages so that you know what to avoid!

3. Go to CSS Zen Garden (http://www.csszengarden.com) and click some of the design links on the right side of the home page. Do you notice that the content in each design's web page is the same? Only the CSS changes for each design. Pretty amazing!

HOUR 2
A Tour of Dreamweaver

I'm sure you are itching to begin creating dazzling and fun websites, the type that you'll show off to your friends, family members, and co-workers. Or maybe you've been assigned the task of creating a website in Dreamweaver for your job. First, however, you have to understand the Dreamweaver interface and the numerous functions that are going to help you be successful as a web developer. Understanding the Dreamweaver user interface enables you to understand the instructions in the rest of this book.

If you have used other Adobe tools, you'll recognize the standard Adobe user interface elements, such as Tab groups and inspectors. If you have used previous versions of Dreamweaver, you should quickly skim this hour to see what exciting changes and updates Adobe has made to the new version of Dreamweaver. This hour provides an important orientation to the concepts you'll use to create web pages in later hours.

Acquainting Yourself with Dreamweaver

Dreamweaver is a complete web development environment and Hypertext Markup Language (HTML) editor, an authoring tool, a dynamic web page development tool, and a website management tool, all rolled into one. Web pages are created using HTML, but you can do many things without ever laying your eyes on any HTML. If you want to produce professional-quality web pages, including scripting, Dreamweaver makes it easy to do so.

HTML is the language of web pages. It consists mainly of paired tags contained in angle brackets (<>). The tags surround objects on a web page, such as text, or stand on their own. For instance, the HTML code to make text

WHAT YOU'LL LEARN IN THIS HOUR:

▶ How to use the Dreamweaver user interface

▶ How to access commands

▶ How to manage panels, inspectors, and windows

▶ How to get help in Dreamweaver

bold looks like this: `<strong>bold text</strong>`; notice how the tags are paired, one before and one after the text they affect. The ending tag of the paired tag always begins with a forward slash. HTML also allows you to use single tags: `<img src="smile.gif">`. By default, Dreamweaver uses a stricter version of HTML called **XHTML** (Extensible Hypertext Markup Language), and all the examples in this book are in XHTML. XHTML requires the use of paired tags, so the earlier image tag example could look like this: `<img src="smile.gif"></img>`. The shortcut XHTML would look like this: `<img src="smile.gif" />`, where the closing slash is added to the end of the tag.

Dreamweaver is a **WYSIWYG** (what you see is what you get) web page editor that is extremely powerful while also being easy to use. You can create new websites by using Dreamweaver, and you can import and edit existing websites, too. Dreamweaver does not change or rearrange your code. One of Dreamweaver's most popular features has always been that it leaves existing sites intact; the folks at Adobe, the company that creates Dreamweaver, call this feature **Roundtrip HTML**. No conversion or importation process is necessary to work on any standard HTML, XHTML, or XML file in Dreamweaver. All you need to do is open the files and make your edits.

Dreamweaver is also an authoring tool. What do I mean by *authoring tool*? **Authoring tools** enable you to create a complete application that includes interactivity. Dreamweaver can be used as simply an HTML editor, but it can also be used to create multimedia applications. You can author an experience complete with audio, animation, video, and interactions for your viewers.

Exploring the Dreamweaver Work Area

Dreamweaver recognizes that different people have different web development roles and different uses for their software. Designers, for example, are mostly interested in the visual elements of a web page. Programmers, on the other hand, want to get their hands dirty in the underlying code. To make life easy for everyone, in Dreamweaver CS4, Adobe has created a handful of different workspaces that can accommodate almost every need.

By default, Dreamweaver places you in the "Designer" workspace mode, which is what we used when writing this book. To switch workspace modes, use the drop-down menu on the right side of the Dreamweaver Application bar. On the Mac, this is visible immediately following the other toolbar elements, while on Windows it is pushed to the far right. Alternatively, use the Workspace Layout menu under the Window menu.

The Welcome Screen

Before opening any files, Dreamweaver displays a box with a green bar across the top; this is the Welcome screen (shown in Figure 2.1). The Welcome screen lists common Dreamweaver tasks, such as Open a Recent Item, Create New, and Top Features. At the bottom of the Welcome screen are links to the Getting Started, New Features, and Resources pages on the Adobe website. Whenever you don't have web pages open in Dreamweaver, it displays the Welcome screen. My Welcome screen shown in Figure 2.1 probably looks different from yours because I have a list of files I've recently opened in the Open a Recent Item column. After you have opened files in Dreamweaver, this list offers a quick way to open them again.

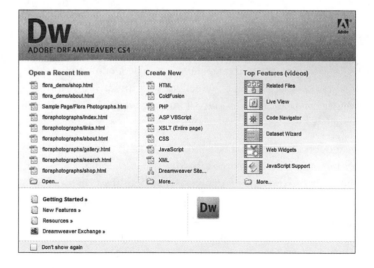

FIGURE 2.1
The Dreamweaver Welcome screen.

You can configure Dreamweaver not to display this Welcome screen by clicking Don't Show Again in the lower-left corner of the window (as shown in Figure 2.1). You can also toggle this preference by choosing Edit, Preferences, and then clicking the General category to display the Show

NOTE

Macintosh Preferences Under the Dreamweaver Menu

Dreamweaver's Macintosh version presents the Preferences command under the Dreamweaver menu, the first menu in the menu bar after the Apple menu, instead of under the Edit menu.

Welcome Screen setting, as shown in Figure 2.2. You explore many other Dreamweaver preferences throughout this book.

FIGURE 2.2
Turn on and off the Welcome screen
in the General category of
Dreamweaver preferences.

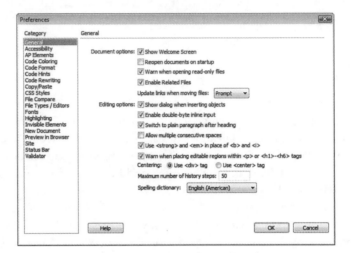

The Welcome screen appears in an important part of Dreamweaver called the **Document window**. The Document window displays a web page approximately as it will appear in a web browser. The Document window is bordered on the right by Tab groups (in the Designer workspace—panels are on the left in programmer-centric workspaces), as shown in Figure 2.3. These Tab groups contain the commands and lists you use to modify and organize web pages and web page elements. The Document window, the Tab groups, and other elements, which you explore in a few minutes, are grouped into an integrated interface if you are working in the Windows operating system.

When you open Dreamweaver CS4 for Macintosh, you see the Document window displaying the Welcome screen, as shown in Figure 2.4. The Macintosh version of Dreamweaver CS4 has panels that float on top of the Document window. You can move floating panels, launched from the Window menu, to any location on the desktop. The Mac and Windows versions of Dreamweaver look slightly different from each other but have the same features and functionality and produce fully compatible files.

The Menu Bar

Some people prefer to use menu commands and some people prefer to click icons (I like keyboard shortcuts). For the menu-liking crowd, this section

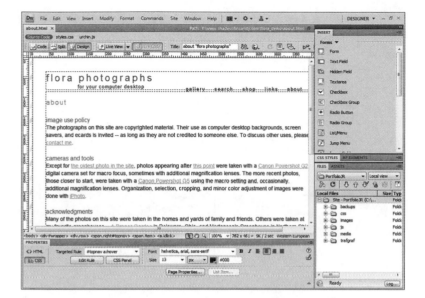

FIGURE 2.3
The Dreamweaver workspace contains the Document window along with integrated panels.

FIGURE 2.4
The Macintosh workspace includes the Document window with panels that float on top.

describes the organization of Dreamweaver's menus that make up the menu bar.

The File and Edit menus (see Figure 2.5) are standard in most programs. The File menu contains commands for opening, closing, saving, importing, exporting, and printing files. The Edit menu contains the Cut, Copy, and

Paste commands, along with the Find and Replace command and the Preferences command (in Windows). You can configure many elements of the Dreamweaver user interface and its operation with the Preferences options.

FIGURE 2.5
The File and Edit menus contain commands that are common to many applications, plus a few Dreamweaver-specific ones.

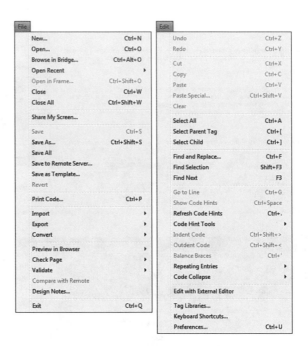

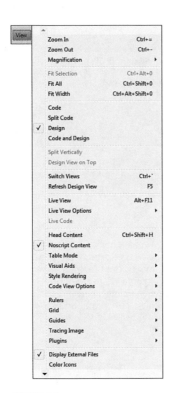

FIGURE 2.6
The View menu houses commands to turn interface elements on and off.

The View menu (see Figure 2.6) turns on and off the display of the head content; invisible elements; layer, table, and frame borders; image maps; and the status bar. A check mark signals that a feature is currently turned on. The View menu also has commands to turn on the ruler, the grid, and the guides; to play plug-ins; and to show a tracing image. It's okay if you don't understand what these commands enable you to do because you learn more about them in later hours.

The Insert menu (see Figure 2.7) is roughly equivalent to the Insert panel that you explore in a few minutes because you can add all the items available on the Insert panel by using this menu. If you prefer to click visual icons, use the Insert panel instead of the text commands in the Insert menu. The Modify menu (see Figure 2.7) enables you to modify properties of the currently selected object. After you've added an object to your web page, use the commands under the Modify menu to make it look and act the way you'd like.

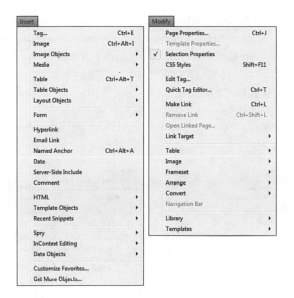

FIGURE 2.7
The Insert and Modify menus give you control over inserting objects and changing their attributes.

The Format menu (see Figure 2.8) gives you access to multiple ways of fine-tuning the appearance of the text in a web page. The Format menu mirrors many of the properties available in the Property inspector (you learn about that in a few minutes) when text is selected. You can use this menu to indent text, create a list, and modify font properties. The Commands menu (see Figure 2.8) offers useful commands such as Clean Up XHTML and Clean Up Word HTML. Most important to those of you who are questionable spellers, the Commands menu contains the Check Spelling command. You can also use this menu to format and sort a table, create a photo album, and optimize an image for the Web.

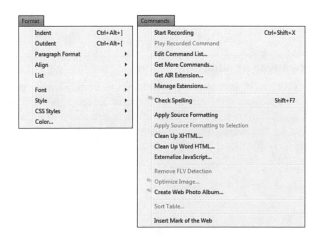

FIGURE 2.8
All the commands necessary to change text elements are in the Format menu. The Commands menu has commands to clean up HTML, optimize images, perform spell checking, and format and sort tables. Powerful stuff!

The Site menu (see Figure 2.9) presents the commands that have to do with an entire website. You explore Dreamweaver website management in Hour 3, "Setting Up a Website," Hour 22, "Uploading, Sharing, and Managing Website Projects," and Hour 23, "Maintaining a Website." The Window menu (see Figure 2.9) is important because it opens and closes all the Dreamweaver panels and inspectors that you learn about later in this hour. There's also a list of all the open files at the bottom of the menu.

FIGURE 2.9
The Site menu commands help you manage an entire website. The Window menu commands help you manage the Dreamweaver panels and inspectors.

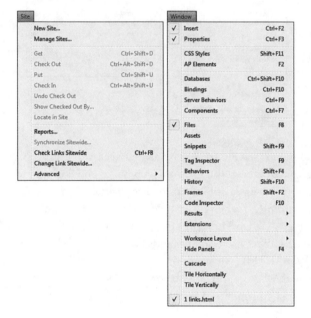

TIP

Open Panels from the Window Menu

You don't have to worry about finding a specific panel and re-membering which Tab group contains it because you can simply select the name of the panel from the Window menu. This Window menu enables you to quickly find and open all Dreamweaver's panels. You see a check mark next to the name of the panel if it is already open. You can even open and close the Insert panel (the Insert command) and the Property inspector (the Properties command) in the Window menu.

TIP

The Dreamweaver Application Menu

The Macintosh version of Dreamweaver includes the Dreamweaver menu in addition to the menus previously described. This menu contains the About Adobe Dreamweaver command that is available from the Help menu in the Windows version. It also gives you access to the Preferences command. The Keyboard Shortcuts command is in this menu instead of the Edit menu, as in the Windows version of Dreamweaver.

You learn about the help system later this hour. Along with providing links to the HTML-based help files, the Help menu, shown in Figure 2.10, contains the command to launch the Extension Manager (the Manage Extensions command). There are numerous links to Adobe resources, including the Dreamweaver Support Center on the Adobe website. Selecting the About Dreamweaver command is useful if you need to find out which version of Dreamweaver you are running. You want to keep an eye on the Adobe website in case the company releases an update for Dreamweaver later. It's always a good idea to keep your software as up-to-date as possible.

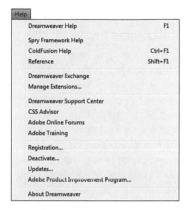

FIGURE 2.10
The Help menu gives you access to Dreamweaver's extensive help system.

The Application Bar

Directly to the right of the menus on Windows (and under the menus on the Macintosh) lives the Dreamweaver Application bar. This interface element contains four drop-down menus for managing layout, extensions, sites, and workspaces, as shown in Figure 2.11.

FIGURE 2.11
The customizable Application bar provides quick access to common tools.

All of these features are available in other menus, so this toolbar is offered as more of a convenience than a necessity. Of particular note is the quick access to the Workspace modes. As mentioned previously, you can use the workspace menu to choose between several predefined window layouts, or even choose New Workspace to save your existing screen layout as a new custom workspace.

To the right of the workspace menu is a search box that you can use to quickly launch a web search, just as in your favorite browser.

The Insert Panel

The Insert panel is located on the top right of the screen. It contains buttons for inserting web page elements, such as images, tables, forms, and hyperlinks. You can either click or drag a button's icon to insert that object into a web page. All the commands in the Insert panel are also accessible from the Insert menu. The Insert panel has the following categories:

TIP

Horizontal Insert Panel

In previous versions of Dreamweaver, the Insert panel was initially displayed horizontally at the top of the screen with each category in a tab. You can quickly switch to this old style of display by dragging the Insert panel (using the text "Insert" as a handle) up under the menu bar.

- ▶ Common
- ▶ Layout
- ▶ Forms
- ▶ Data
- ▶ Spry
- ▶ InContext Editing
- ▶ Text
- ▶ Favorites

The Insert panel has a drop-down menu at its top which enables you to choose from the eight available categories (see Figure 2.12). To display a category, drop down the menu and then select the category. By default, the Common category displays, but if you are working on forms, you might want to display the Forms category, and if you are working with text, you might want to display the Text category.

Some of the objects in the Insert panel are drop-down menus that organize a group of related objects. For instance, in the Common category, the Images object drops down a menu displaying Image, Image Placeholder, Rollover Image, Fireworks HTML, Navigation Bar, and other image-related commands. All these objects have to do with images, so they are grouped together in a single drop-down menu in the Insert panel.

Table 2.1 lists all the objects available in the Insert panel, with descriptions. The table briefly describes each of the objects in the Insert panel except those found in the Data tab because those objects are used for creating dynamic web pages and sites. While you read through this table, familiarize yourself with the types of objects and content you can add to a web page in Dreamweaver.

FIGURE 2.12
The Insert panel drop-down menu displays a list of the categories and Color Icons option to replace the black-and-white interface icons with color versions.

TABLE 2.1   Insert Panel Objects

Icon	Icon Name	Description
Common Category		
	Hyperlink	Inserts a hyperlink, including the text and the link location.
	Email Link	Adds a hyperlink that launches an empty email message to a specific email address when clicked.
	Named Anchor	Places a named anchor at the insertion point. Named anchors create hyperlinks within a file.
	Horizontal Rule	Adds a horizontal bar at the insertion point; used to separate different pieces of content.
	Table	Creates a table at the insertion point.
	Insert Div Tag	Adds a `<div>` tag, a common container tag used to store text and graphics. (Also in the Layout category.)
	Image	Places an image at the insertion point. (In the Images drop-down menu.)
	Image Placeholder	Inserts a placeholder for an image. (In the Images drop-down menu.)
	Rollover Image	Prompts you for two images: the regular image and the image that appears when the user puts the cursor over the image. (In the Images drop-down menu.)
	Fireworks HTML	Places HTML exported from Adobe Fireworks at the insertion point. (In the Images drop-down menu.)
	Navigation Bar	Inserts a set of button images to be used for navigating throughout the website. (In the Images drop-down menu.)

TABLE 2.1   Insert Panel Objects

Icon	Icon Name	Description
	Draw Rectangle Hotspot	Enables you to draw a rectangle over a specific region of an image and link it to a specific URL. (In the Images drop-down menu.)
	Draw Oval Hotspot	Enables you to draw an oval over a specific region of an image and link it to a specific URL. (In the Images drop-down menu.)
	Draw Polygon Hotspot	Enables you to draw a polygon over a specific region of an image and link it to a specific URL. (In the Images drop-down menu.)
	Flash (SWF)	Places an Adobe Flash movie at the insertion point. (In the Media drop-down menu.)
	FlashPaper	Inserts a Flash Paper document into the web page. (In the Media drop-down menu.)
	Flash Video (FLV)	Places and configures a Flash Video object at the insertion point. (In the Media drop-down menu.)
	Shockwave	Places a Shockwave movie (that is, an Adobe Director movie prepared for the Web) at the insertion point. (In the Media drop-down menu.)
	Applet	Places a Java applet at the insertion point. (In the Media drop-down menu.)
	param	Inserts a tag that enables you to enter parameters and their values to pass to an applet or an ActiveX control. (In the Media drop-down menu.)
	ActiveX	Places an ActiveX control at the insertion point. (In the Media drop-down menu.)
	Plugin	Places any file requiring a browser plug-in at the insertion point. (In the Media drop-down menu.)

TABLE 2.1   Insert Panel Objects

Icon	Icon Name	Description
	Date	Inserts the current date at the insertion point.
	Server-Side Include	Includes SSI code and simulates a server-side include at the insertion point.
	Comment	Inserts a comment at the insertion point.
	Meta	Inserts a meta tag into the head section of a web page. This object can insert a name type meta tag, aiding search engines, or an http-equiv type meta tag that can redirect the user to a different URL or give additional information about the web page, such as assigning parental control information to a page. (In the Head drop-down menu.)
	Keywords	Inserts a keywords meta tag into the head section, adding keywords to the web page to help search engines properly index it. (In the Head drop-down menu.)
	Description	Inserts a description meta tag into the head section, adding a description to the web page to help search engines properly index it. (In the Head drop-down menu.)
	Refresh	Inserts a refresh meta tag into the head section. This tag sets the number of seconds before the page automatically jumps to another web page or reloads itself. (In the Head drop-down menu.)
	Base	Inserts a base tag into the head section. This enables you to set a base URL or a base target window affecting all the paths on the web page. (In the Head drop-down menu.)

TABLE 2.1   Insert Panel Objects

Icon	Icon Name	Description
	Link	Inserts the address of an external file, usually a script or style sheet file. (In the Head drop-down menu.)
	Script	Inserts scripted code at the insertion point. (In the Script drop-down menu.)
	No Script	Inserts the `noscript` tag surrounding HTML code that is displayed by browsers that do not support scripts. (In the Script drop-down menu.)
	Make Template	Creates a Dreamweaver template from the current web page. (In the Templates drop-down menu.)
	Make Nested Template	Creates a nested Dreamweaver template from the current template. (In the Templates drop-down menu.)
	Editable Region	Adds an editable region to a template. (In the Templates drop-down menu.)
	Optional Region	Adds an optional region to a template; this region can be set to either show or hide. (In the Templates drop-down menu.)
	Repeating Region	Adds a repeating region to a template. (In the Templates drop-down menu.)
	Editable Optional Region	Adds an editable optional region to a template. (In the Templates drop-down menu.)
	Repeating Table	Adds a repeating table to a template and defines which cells can be edited. (In the Templates drop-down menu.)
	Tag Chooser	Enables you to choose a tag to insert from a hierarchical menu of all available tags.

TABLE 2.1   Insert Panel Objects

Icon	Icon Name	Description
Layout Category		
Standard	Standard mode	Turns on Dreamweaver's Standard mode, disabling the Expanded Tables mode.
Expanded	Expanded Tables mode	Turns on Dreamweaver's Expanded Tables mode, temporarily adding cell padding and borders to all tables.
	Insert Div Tag	Adds a <div> tag, a common container tag used to store text and graphics. (Also in the Common category.)
	Draw AP Div	Draws an AP Div container in a web page.
	Spry Menu Bar	A widget that creates a menu bar using the Spry framework. (Also in the Spry category.)
	Spry Tabbed Panels	A widget that creates a set of tabbed panels using the Spry framework. (Also in the Spry category.)
	Spry Accordion	A widget that creates a set of collapsible panels using the Spry framework. (Also in the Spry category.)
	Spry Collapsible Panel	A widget that creates a single collapsible panel using the Spry framework. (Also in the Spry category.)
	Table	Creates a table at the insertion point. (Also in the Common category.)
	Insert Row Above	Adds a row above the currently selected row of a table.
	Insert Row Below	Adds a row beneath the currently selected row of a table.
	Insert Column to the Left	Adds a column to the left of the currently selected column in a table.
	Insert Column to the Right	Adds a column to the right of a currently selected column in a table.

TABLE 2.1   Insert Panel Objects

Icon	Icon Name	Description
	IFrame	Inserts an inline frame that contains another HTML document.
	Left Frame	Creates a frame to the left of the current frame. (In the Frames drop-down menu.)
	Right Frame	Creates a frame to the right of the current frame. (In the Frames drop-down menu.)
	Top Frame	Creates a frame above the current frame. (In the Frames drop-down menu.)
	Bottom Frame	Creates a frame below the current frame. (In the Frames drop-down menu.)
	Bottom and Nested Left Frame	Creates a frame to the left of the current frame and then adds a frame below. (In the Frames drop-down menu.)
	Bottom and Nested Right Frame	Creates a frame to the right of the current frame and then adds a frame below. (In the Frames drop-down menu.)
	Left and Nested Bottom Frame	Creates a frame below the current frame and then adds a frame to the left. (In the Frames drop-down menu.)
	Right and Nested Bottom Frames	Creates a frame below the current frame and then adds a frame to the right. (In the Frames drop-down menu.)
	Top and Bottom Frame	Creates a frame below the current frame and then adds a frame above. (In the Frames drop-down menu.)
	Left and Nested Top Frames	Creates a frame above the current frame and then adds a frame to the left. (In the Frames drop-down menu.)
	Right and Nested Top Frame	Creates a frame above the current frame and then adds a frame to the right. (In the Frames drop-down menu.)

TABLE 2.1   Insert Panel Objects

Icon	Icon Name	Description
	Top and Nested Left Frames	Creates a frame to the left of the current frame and then adds a frame above. (In the Frames drop-down menu.)
	Top and Nested Right Frame	Creates a frame to the right of the current frame and then adds a frame above. (In the Frames drop-down menu.)
Forms Category		
	Form	Places a form at the insertion point.
	Text Field	Inserts a text field.
	Hidden Field	Inserts a hidden field.
	Textarea	Inserts a textarea, which is a multiline text field.
	Checkbox	Inserts a check box.
	Checkbox Group	Inserts a group of related check boxes.
	Radio Button	Inserts a radio button.
	Radio Group	Inserts a group of related radio buttons.
	List/Menu	Inserts a list or a drop-down menu.
	Jump Menu	Creates a jump menu that allows users to select a website from a menu and go to that site.
	Image Field	Inserts an image field, which enables an image to act as a button.
	File Field	Inserts a file field, which enables the user to upload a file.

TABLE 2.1   Insert Panel Objects

Icon	Icon Name	Description
	Button	Inserts a button.
	Label	Assigns a label to a form element, enabling browsers for people with visual impairments to access extra information about the form elements nested within the label.
	Fieldset	Groups related form fields to make the form accessible to browsers for people with visual impairments. Fieldset wraps around a group of form elements and appears to sighted people as a box drawn around the group, with the fieldset title at the top.
	Spry Validation Text Field	A text field that includes validation logic using the Spry framework. (Also in the Spry category.)
	Spry Validation Text Area	A text area that includes validation logic using the Spry framework. (Also in the Spry category.)
	Spry Validation Checkbox	A check box that includes validation logic using the Spry framework. (Also in the Spry category.)
	Spry Validation Select	A select object (called a list/menu in Dreamweaver) that includes validation logic using the Spry framework. (Also in the Spry category.)
	Spry Validation Password	A password field that includes validation logic using the Spry framework. (Also in the Spry category.)
	Spry Validation Confirm	A second password field whose value is compared to the Spry Validation password field to ensure that they match. (Also in the Spry category.)

TABLE 2.1   Insert Panel Objects

Icon	Icon Name	Description
	Spry Validation Radio Group	A group of radio buttons that include validation logic using the Spry framework. (Also in the Spry category.)

Spry Category

Icon	Icon Name	Description
	Spry Data Set	Defines an XML or HTML data source.
	Spry Region	Defines a container to receive data via the Spry framework.
	Spry Repeat	Defines a container to receive repeating data via the Spry framework.
	Spry Repeat List	Defines a list to receive repeating data via the Spry framework.
	Spry Validation Text Field	A text field that includes validation logic using the Spry framework. (Also in the Forms category.)
	Spry Validation Text Area	A text area that includes validation logic using the Spry framework. (Also in the Forms category.)
	Spry Validation Checkbox	A check box that includes validation logic using the Spry framework. (Also in the Forms category.)
	Spry Validation Select	A select object (called a list/menu in Dreamweaver) that includes validation logic using the Spry framework. (Also in the Forms category.)
	Spry Validation Password	A password field that includes validation logic using the Spry framework. (Also in the Forms category.)

TABLE 2.1   Insert Panel Objects

Icon	Icon Name	Description
	Spry Validation Confirm	A second password field whose value is compared to the Spry Validation password field to ensure that they match. (Also in the Forms category.)
	Spry Validation Radio Group	A group of radio buttons that include validation logic using the Spry framework. (Also in the Forms category.)
	Spry Menu Bar	A widget that creates a menu bar using the Spry framework. (Also in the Layout category.)
	Spry Tabbed Panels	A widget that creates a set of tabbed panels using the Spry framework. (Also in the Layout category.)
	Spry Accordion	A widget that creates a set of collapsible panels using the Spry framework. (Also in the Layout category.)
	Spry Collapsible Panel	A widget that creates a single collapsible panel using the Spry framework. (Also in the Layout category.)
	Spry Tooltop	Displays a helpful tip on mouseover using the Spry framework. (Also in the Forms category.)

InContext Editing Category

Icon	Icon Name	Description
	Create Repeating Region	Adds a repeating region to an InContext site template.
	Create Editable Region	Adds an editable region to an InContext site template.
	Manage Available CSS Classes	Allows you to administer which CSS styles will be available to an editor on an InContext-aware site.

TABLE 2.1   Insert Panel Objects

Icon	Icon Name	Description
Text Category		
B	Bold	Makes the selected text bold by using the b tag. This tag has been dropped from recent versions of HTML. The approved tag for bold text is the strong tag.
I	Italic	Makes the selected text italic by using the i tag. This tag has been dropped from recent versions of HTML. The approved tag for italic text is the emphasis tag.
S	Strong	Makes the selected text bold by using the approved strong tag.
em	Emphasis	Makes the selected text italic by using the approved emphasis tag.
¶	Paragraph	Makes the selected text into a paragraph.
["""]	Block Quote	Makes the selected text into a block quote, indented from the right and the left, by using the blockquote tag.
PRE	Preformatted Text	Makes the selected text preformatted (using the pre tag, displaying the text in a monospaced font and with the ability to enter spaces).
h1	Heading 1	Makes the selected text a heading size 1 (largest) by using the h1 tag.
h2	Heading 2	Makes the selected text a heading size 2 by using the h2 tag.
h3	Heading 3	Makes the selected text a heading size 3 by using the h3 tag.

TABLE 2.1   Insert Panel Objects

Icon	Icon Name	Description
ul	Unordered List	Makes the selected text into an unordered (bulleted) list.
ol	Ordered List	Makes the selected text into an ordered (numbered) list.
li	List Item	Makes the selected text into a **list item** (by using the li tag), a single item in an ordered or unordered list.
dl	Definition List	Creates a definition list. A **definition list** consists of definition terms and definition descriptions.
dt	Definition Term	Creates a definition term within a definition list.
dd	Definition Description	Creates a definition description within a definition list.
abbr.	Abbreviation	Wraps the abbr tag around text, adding a full-text definition to an abbreviation. This aids search engines in indexing a web page properly.
W3C	Acronym	Wraps the acronym tag around text, adding a full-text definition to an acronym. This aids search engines in indexing a web page properly.
BR↵	Line Break	Places a line break, the br tag, at the insertion point. (In the Characters drop-down menu.)
⤓	Non-Breaking Space	Inserts a special character ( ) that creates a space. The nonbreaking space character also prevents a line break from occurring between two words. (In the Characters drop-down menu.)

TABLE 2.1   Insert Panel Objects

Icon	Icon Name	Description
“	Left Quote	Inserts the special character for a left quote. (In the Characters drop-down menu.)
”	Right Quote	Inserts the special character for a right quote. (In the Characters drop-down menu.)
—	Em Dash	Inserts the special character for an em dash (—). (In the Characters drop-down menu.)
£	Pound	Inserts the special character for the pound currency symbol. (In the Characters drop-down menu.)
€	Euro	Inserts the special character for the Euro currency symbol. (In the Characters drop-down menu.)
¥	Yen	Inserts the special character for the yen currency symbol. (In the Characters drop-down menu.)
©	Copyright	Inserts the special character for the copyright symbol. (In the Characters drop-down menu.)
®	Registered Trademark	Inserts the special character for the registered trademark symbol. (In the Characters drop-down menu.)
™	Trademark	Inserts the special character for the trademark symbol. (In the Characters drop-down menu.)
	Other Characters	Opens a menu that displays many additional special characters. (In the Characters drop-down menu.)

NOTE

Viewing Live Code

For advanced developers, another view option—Live Code—can be clicked when Live View is enabled. This mode allows the developer to see the source code of the page as the Live View browser is interpreting it. It's not something you need in this book, but it's a handy tool to keep in mind as you begin adding more interactivity to your documents.

The Favorites category enables you to add objects that you use frequently to a single Insert panel category. You explore this functionality in Hour 24, "Customizing Dreamweaver," when you learn how to modify Dreamweaver to your own way of working. By the end of this book, you will have a better idea of the types of objects you want to place in the Favorites category to help you work more quickly in Dreamweaver. These are your personal favorites, the objects you use most often, collected in one handy Insert panel category.

The Document Window

By default, the Document window is maximized, and its title and filename appear under the menu bar/Application bar at the top of the screen. You explore saving a file, giving it a filename, and giving it a title in Hour 4, "Dealing with Words: Adding Text and Lists." The Document window is the part of the Dreamweaver interface you will be using most often in your work. The Document toolbar appears at the top of the Document window.

The Document Toolbar

The Document toolbar, shown in Figure 2.13, gives you quick access to important commands. The three buttons on the left of the Document toolbar enable you to toggle among Code view, Design view, and a Split view with both Code view and Design view visible. A new Live View option toggles the Design view into a read-only mode that presents your site as if it were being viewed in a real web browser. The Live View makes it possible to preview advanced effects (such as rollovers or other JavaScript behaviors) without launching a web browser. The Live View drop-down menu allows you to disable JavaScript and other plug-ins to see the effect on your design.

FIGURE 2.13
The Document toolbar contains commands you commonly apply to web pages when editing in Dreamweaver.

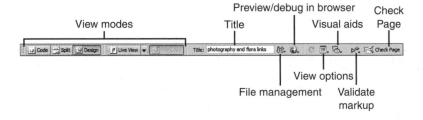

I probably use Design view 60% of the time and divide the other 40% of my Dreamweaver time between Code view and Split view—jumping into Live

View mode as needed to preview the page. The Split view showing both the Design view and the Code view is useful when you're learning HTML because it enables you to see the tags that Dreamweaver adds while you create a web page.

The Title text box in the Document toolbar is where you give a web page a title (the default title, Untitled Document, isn't very interesting!). This appears in the visitor's browser title bar when the visitor views the page. The web page title is saved in the browser's Favorites or Bookmarks list as the name of the web page, so it should be meaningful. The web page title is also important because it affects the ranking of your page in many search engines such as Google.

Six drop-down menus are on the Document toolbar:

▶ **File Management**—This menu lists commands such as those for getting files to and from a web server. You explore these commands in Hours 22 and 23, when you upload and manage a website.

▶ **Preview/Debug in the Browser**—This gives you quick access to the list of browsers you'll use to preview web pages.

▶ **View Options**—This menu changes, depending on whether you have selected Design or Code view. While in Design view, the menu displays commands such as those for viewing head content or the rulers. While in Code view, the menu contains commands that affect the way the code is displayed, such as Word Wrap and Line Numbers.

▶ **Visual Aids**—The Visual Aids menu is active only in Design mode. The menu gives you access to turn on and off all the visual aids that are also available in View, Visual Aids.

▶ **Validate Markup**—This checks to see that the code is properly written.

▶ **Check Page**—This menu enables you to check that your web page works correctly in various browsers.

The Document toolbar also contains the Refresh Design View button. This button refreshes the Design view when you are editing the code (in Code view or the Split view) so that you can instantly see the changes you make to the code. This button is active only when you are viewing the Document window in Code view or the Split view.

NOTE

Where's My Document Toolbar?

If the Document toolbar isn't visible, select View, Toolbars, Document.

The Status Bar

The Dreamweaver Document window has a status bar along its bottom. It contains the tag selector, the Window Size drop-down menu, the magnification and selection tools, download statistics, and character encodings, as shown in Figure 2.14. These convenient tools are just some of the nice touches that Dreamweaver CS4 offers to help you have a productive and fun experience designing for the Web.

FIGURE 2.14
The status bar contains tools that help you get information about a web page.

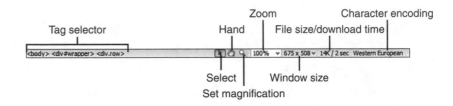

The tag selector in the lower-left corner of the Document window provides easy access to the HTML tags involved in any object on the screen. If, for example, the cursor is located in a table cell, the tag selector enables selection of any of the HTML tags which control that object. The currently selected tag is shown in bold in the tag selector. The tags to the left of the selected tag are the tags wrapped around the selected tag.

On the right side of the status bar, you find three icons that control how the cursor appears and functions in the Document window. By default, the Select tool (arrow cursor) is selected. You can also select the Hand tool, enabling you to drag the cursor to scroll across the web page in the Document window. The Zoom tool turns the cursor into a magnifying glass and enables you to zoom in on the web page. Next to the Zoomtool is the Set Magnification menu, from which you can select a certain magnification level from 6% to 6400%.

The Window Size drop-down menu helps you re-create a target screen resolution by resizing the Document window. You always want to make sure that your design looks good at a low (800×600) and high screen resolution. You can use the Window Size drop-down menu (see Figure 2.15) to quickly resize the Document window to view the approximate amount of screen real estate you have at a particular resolution. The Window Size drop-down menu works only when you do not have the Document window maximized.

TIP

The Tag Selector Is Your Friend

The tag selector will be important later, when you start using behaviors in Hour 18, "Adding Interactivity with Behaviors." You apply behaviors to specific tags, and sometimes the tags are difficult to select—especially the <body> tag, which contains the entire web page content. The tag selector makes it very easy to select the entire body of a web page by clicking the <body> tag.

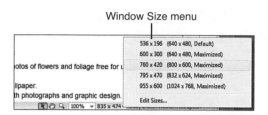

Window Size menu

FIGURE 2.15
The Window Size menu resizes the screen, approximating how the page will look at different screen resolutions.

Notice the sizes available in the Window Size menu:

- ▶ The dimensions listed on the right (in parentheses) represent the screen resolutions.

- ▶ The numbers listed on the left are the estimated browser window dimensions. They are smaller than the screen resolutions because the browser interface (buttons and menus, for instance) takes up space. For example, when the viewer's monitor is set to 640×480, the viewable area is only 536×196 pixels.

Because bandwidth might be an issue when you're developing for the Web, it's nice to know the estimated file size and download time of a web page. The estimated download time shown in the status bar is based on the modem setting in the Status Bar category in the Dreamweaver Preferences dialog box. The default modem setting is 128Kbps; you might want to change this setting to whatever the bandwidth speed is for the targeted viewer of your web page. (Most people in the United States browse the Web at a speed of at least 56Kbps or better; 128Kbps is the slowest speed of most DSL Internet connections.) Dreamweaver takes into account images and other assets contained in the web page when calculating the file size and download time.

Panels and Inspectors

You set properties of objects and add functionality to web pages through Dreamweaver's panels and inspectors. Most commands in Dreamweaver are available in several places, usually as menu commands, Insert panel commands, Document toolbar commands, and panel commands. Dreamweaver's panels are grouped into Tab groups beside the Document window.

You can open every panel from the Window menu, and by default Dreamweaver has all the important panels and the Property inspector open. If a panel or an inspector is open, its menu selection has a check mark

TIP

Define Special Window Sizes

Create your own custom settings for the Window Size menu by selecting the last choice in the Window Size pop-up menu, the Edit Sizes command. This command takes you to the Status Bar category in the Dreamweaver Preferences dialog box, where you can add your custom window size. For instance, do you want to create a web page that is readable on your wireless phone? My Apple iPhone has the capability to display 320×480 pixels, so I could create a custom size to create a web page for my phone.

TIP

Toggle All Panels On and Off

Pressing F4 on your keyboard triggers the Hide Panels/Show Panels command (Window, Hide Panels). This command is a great way to get more screen real estate temporarily in order to see the entire web page. When the panels are visible, F4 hides them; when they are hidden, F4 shows them. This toggle button is a quick way to hide and then show the Dreamweaver panels.

TIP

Save Your Workspace

You might have different panel configurations that are handy for different projects. Dreamweaver enables you to save individual configurations to use later by selecting Window, Workspace Layout, New Workspace, and then giving the configuration a name. For instance, you might have a configuration when a site requires creating Cascading Style Sheets (CSS) that has the CSS Styles panel, the AP Elements panel, and the Files panel visible. You could save that with the name *CSS Site*.

FIGURE 2.16
Expand and collapse Tab groups by double-licking their titles.

beside it in the Window menu. To close a panel or an inspector, deselect the command in the Window menu. The panel doesn't actually go away, but the group collapses so that you see only its title tab.

Panels and Tab Groups

You can expand or collapse a Tab group or an inspector by double-clicking a panel title in the group, or the Tab group's gray title bar, as shown in Figure 2.16. You can undock a panel or Tab group by dragging its title (or the gray title bar itself for a Tab group) from where it currently docks. To dock a panel or group, drag and drop it from its title to another Tab group or the Document window. When it docks, you see an outline around the group or panel. Because the Macintosh version of Dreamweaver has floating panels, you can move them wherever you want anytime!

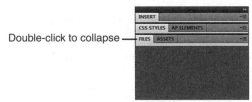

Double-click to collapse —

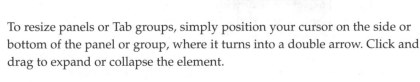

To resize panels or Tab groups, simply position your cursor on the side or bottom of the panel or group, where it turns into a double arrow. Click and drag to expand or collapse the element.

The Property Inspector

The Property inspector displays all the properties of the currently selected object. The Property inspector is like a chameleon that changes depending on the environment; it looks different and displays appropriate properties for whichever object is selected in the Document window. For example, when text is selected, the Property inspector presents text properties, as shown in Figure 2.18.

FIGURE 2.17
Panels can be collapsed to individual icons that take up much less space.

TIP

Advanced Panel Maintenance

You can completely close a Tab group, removing it from display on the screen, by selecting the Close Tab group command from the contextual menu that appears when you right-click the Tab group title bar.

You can also choose Collapse to Icons, which displays the panels in Tab groups as single icons, which, when clicked, open for quick access. This is shown in Figure 2.17.

FIGURE 2.18
The Property inspector displays text properties when text is selected.

In Figure 2.19, an image is selected, and the Property inspector presents image properties.

FIGURE 2.19
The Property inspector displays image properties when an image is selected.

Sometimes the Property window may have more information that it can show you beyond just the basics. If this is the case, you see a small down-pointing arrow in the lower-right corner of the Property inspector. You can expand the Property inspector by using the Expander icon so that you have access to every available property. You do this by simply clicking the arrow, which changes to an upward pointing arrow when the inspector is expanded. The Property inspector is expanded in Figure 2.19.

Sometimes you will notice an HTML and CSS button appear in the property inspector. These buttons toggle between attributes that you can apply to an object in HTML and those that require CSS. We make sure you know which should be selected as we work through the book!

Context Menus

You can access and modify object properties in multiple ways in Dreamweaver. I'm sure you'll find your favorite ways very quickly. Context menus are one of the choices available. These menus pop up when you right-click an object in the Document window. The contents of the menu are dependent on which object you clicked. For instance, Figure 2.20 shows the context menu that pops up when you right-click a table.

Getting Help

You select Help, Dreamweaver Help (or use the standard help shortcut key, F1) to launch the Dreamweaver help files. The left side of the help page contains the Contents and Index tabs. The right side of the page is where the help content files appear. The Next and Previous arrow buttons enable you to page through all the help topics.

NOTE

Keep the Property Inspector Expanded

I think it works best to always keep the Property inspector expanded so that you have access to all the properties displayed there. If you don't have Property inspector expanded, some properties might be hidden, and you need to see all the properties, especially while you are learning about Dreamweaver. If you need more space on the screen, either use the F4 command to hide all the panels (and then to show them again) or use the Expander arrow button in the upper-left corner of the Property inspector to close the entire panel.

TIP

Using Help to Learn About Dreamweaver

While you are getting familiar with Dreamweaver, you might want to use the Next and Previous arrow buttons to navigate through the topics. The topics are grouped, so you might get more information on your current topic on the next page. If you keep clicking either of these arrows, you will eventually go on to another topic. This is a good way to expand your knowledge on the topic you are currently researching.

The Contents tab displays the table of contents. The table of contents is organized in subject categories. Selecting one of the categories expands the list, with subtopics under that category. The Index button shows an alphabetical index of all topics in the help system. Use the Search box at the top of the help viewer to enter a topic for which you want to search.

One of the easiest ways to get help on your current task is to launch context-sensitive help. When you have an object selected (and you can see its properties in the Property inspector), click the Help icon in the Property inspector, shown in Figure 2.21, to go directly to information about that object.

FIGURE 2.21
Clicking the Property inspector Help icon takes you directly to information about the properties of the object currently selected. In this instance, you go directly to help information about tables.

Help

Summary

In this hour, you learned about the Dreamweaver Document window and other elements of the Dreamweaver user interface, such as the Insert panel, the menus, the status bar, and the panels. You explored expanding Tab groups. You saw the commands available in Dreamweaver's menus, Insert panel, and status bar. This hour introduced you to the Property inspector and showed you how to access Dreamweaver help.

Q&A

Q. How do I get as much room in the Document window as I possibly can?

A. You could collapse the groups and expand the document window manually, but there's a much easier way! Press F4 (the shortcut for the Hide Panels command in the Window menu). The F4 command works in most of Adobe's products to hide much of the user interface so that you see only your project. The F4 command also toggles the panels back on.

Q. There's something wrong with my Dreamweaver installation because it looks very different from the examples In your book. All the panels appear out of place, and I don't know how to move them. Help!

A. When Dreamweaver was sct up, someone changed the default workspace from Designer, which is used in this book. You can switch it back by selecting Window, Workspace Layout, Designer.

Workshop

Quiz

1. Which menu do you use to open a Dreamweaver panel that isn't currently visible in the Tab groups?

2. What icon in the status bar enables you to magnify web pages in the Document window?

3. Is Dreamweaver an HTML editor, an authoring tool, or a website management tool?

Quiz Answers

1. The Window menu enables you to turn on and off all the panels and inspectors. There is a check mark beside a command if the panel is currently visible.

2. The Zoom tool enables you to magnify web pages in the Document window.

3. Sorry, this is a trick question! Dreamweaver is all these things.

Exercises

1. Open the Dreamweaver Preferences dialog box from the Edit menu (the Dreamweaver menu for Mac users). Select the General category and examine each of the available settings. Experiment with changing any of these settings. Click the Help button and read about each of the settings. Don't change settings randomly, especially if you don't understand what the settings do.

2. Experiment with expanding and collapsing Tab groups. Resize the Tab groups. Explore some of the panel drop-down menus found in the upper-right corner of the panel. Use the F4 key (Hide Panels/Show Panels command) to toggle the options.

3. Launch the New Features tour (the link that says New Features) from the Welcome screen that appears when you open Dreamweaver CS4. You must be connected to the Internet to take this tour.

4. Click HTML under the Create New column in the middle of the Welcome screen. This creates a blank HTML document in the Document window.

HOUR 3
Setting Up a Website

Dreamweaver makes it very easy to open and edit single web pages—much like you would a word processing document. If you're planning to create multiple pages, however, the very first thing you should do is define a site. That's what you'll do this hour. Defining a site gives you a home base to work from. Without a site definition, Dreamweaver may run into difficulties linking or organizing your files.

You use Dreamweaver's Files panel to plan, create, and manage projects. Eventually you'll have lots of files: web pages (HTML, or hypertext markup language, files), image files, CSS (Cascading Style Sheets) files, and other types of files. It's important that you define your website to start off on the right foot.

Defining a New Website

This hour introduces creating a storage directory for your website and then telling Dreamweaver about it. This directory will be the home of your site, and you'll build a logical structure beneath it with directories to hold supporting files such as images, scripts, and style sheets (more about this in later hours). Many beginning web developers simply start making web pages, skipping the site definition step—this is not recommended. You'll make your web development life easier by completing this important step before any development takes place.

Every website has a root directory. The **root** of a website is the main directory that contains files and other directories. When you define a website, Dreamweaver considers that directory and all the files (or other directories) within it to be the entire universe of that particular website. If you attempt

WHAT YOU'LL LEARN IN THIS HOUR:

▶ How to define a website by using the Site Definition Wizard

▶ How to modify a website definition

▶ How to organize a website

TIP

Directories or Folders?

I (and many other people) use the terms *directory* and *folder* interchangeably. Both terms refer to a named container for files and other directories or folders. If you create a reference to a file in another directory, you must provide the name of the directory (also called a "path") that contains the file.

FIGURE 3.1
Select the Manage Sites menu to define a new site in Dreamweaver.

FIGURE 3.2
The Manage Sites dialog box lists all the websites you have defined and enables you to manage them.

to insert an image from outside that universe, Dreamweaver prompts you to save the file inside the website.

Dreamweaver needs you to define your website so that it knows how to find files. For instance, if an image is located in an `images` directory within the site, Dreamweaver knows how to properly reference the image within a web page. If, however, the image is somewhere outside the defined site, Dreamweaver might not be able to reference it properly, and you might end up with bad links in your website. You learn more about how Dreamweaver links to files in Hour 5, "Adding Links: Hyperlinks, Anchors, and Mailto Links."

You have to define a new website for every project you create. Even when projects are related, you might decide to break them down into smaller sites so that the number of files isn't unwieldy in a single site. For instance, I create websites for a college within a major university. Rather than trying to create a single site for the entire college, I find it easier to break down the information into different sites by department. This creates more manageable chunks of information than lumping everything together. Regardless of the size of your site, you can have only a single site open in Dreamweaver at once.

To begin defining a website, open the Manage Sites dialog box by selecting Site, Manage Sites, as shown in Figure 3.1.

The Manage Sites dialog box, shown in Figure 3.2, is where you can create, edit, duplicate, remove, export, and import Dreamweaver site definitions. The title says it all: This is where you manage your websites! To begin defining a new site, click the New button in the Manage Sites dialog box and choose Site. The Site Definition dialog box appears.

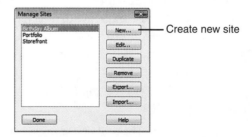

Create new site

The Site Definition dialog box is where you name your site and point Dreamweaver to where the files are stored on your computer. You can define a site even if you don't have any files; you simply define the site in an empty directory that is ready to hold all the web pages you create.

Using the Site Definition Wizard

The Site Definition dialog box, shown in Figure 3.3, has two tabs at the top: Basic and Advanced. You begin by using the settings on the Basic tab, so make sure that tab is selected. The Basic tab contains the Site Definition Wizard, which walks you through the site definition. Later this hour, you learn how to edit your site definition using the Advanced tab in the Site Definition dialog box.

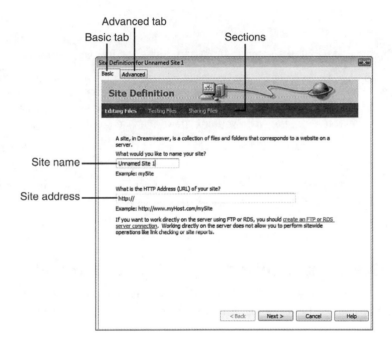

FIGURE 3.3
The Basic tab of the Site Definition dialog box walks you through setting up a site definition.

The Site Definition Wizard has three stages, shown as the section names at the top of the wizard:

- **Editing Files**—This section enables you to set up the local directory where you'll store the website. You tell the wizard whether your site uses server-side technologies. The sites and web pages in this book do not use these technologies, which connect web pages, servers, and often databases.

- **Testing Files**—This section is needed only for sites that use server-side technologies. We can skip over it!

TIP

Open Manage Sites from the Site Menu

You can open the Manage Sites dialog box from the Files panel or from the Site menu. Many of the commands available in the Site menu are repeated in the Files panel so that you can access the commands from either location.

▶ **Sharing Files**—This section enables you to tell Dreamweaver how you want to transfer files to a server or another central location to share. You explore this functionality in Hour 22, "Uploading, Sharing, and Managing Website Projects."

Filling In the Editing Files, Part 1, Section

Make sure that you have the Basic tab selected at the top of the Site Definition dialog box.

▼ TRY IT YOURSELF

Filling In the First Editing Files Site Setup Section

Fill in the Editing Files section of the wizard using the following steps:

1. In the Site Definition Wizard (refer to Figure 3.3), give your site a name. This name is used only inside Dreamweaver, so it can be anything you want. The site name should be meaningful—it should identify the purpose of the website when you drop down the Site menu to change sites.

   My Dreamweaver installation has about 30 to 40 sites defined at times, so clear names help me quickly find the site I want to edit.

2. If you know the final HTTP address of your site, you can enter it here on the first page of the wizard; it's also fine to leave this empty.

3. Click the Next button.

Filling In the Editing Files, Part 2, Section

The next page of the wizard, Editing Files, Part 2, enables you to specify whether you will be using server-side scripting to create dynamic web pages.

▼ TRY IT YOURSELF

Completing the Editing Files, Part 2 Site Setup Section

Fill in the Editing Files, Part 2, section of the wizard:

1. Your web pages in this book are regular HTML pages, so you should click the top radio button that says No, I Do Not Want to Use a Server Technology, as shown in Figure 3.4.

2. Click the Next button.

TIP

HTML and Dynamic Websites

Although we concentrate on HTML web pages, that doesn't mean they can't be interactive and dynamic experiences for the end user. You learn how to create pages with animation and how to change content later in the book.

Do not use a server technology for
the sites you create in this book.

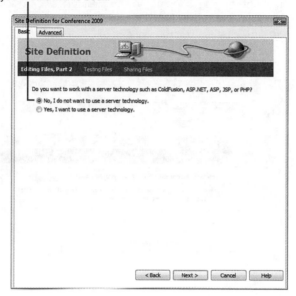

FIGURE 3.4
You indicate whether you will be using server-side scripting in your site.

Filling In the Editing Files, Part 3, Section

The next page, Editing Files, Part 3, helps you specify where the files in your
site are located. The site that you are creating here is your **development site**,
not the final site that other people will view over the Web. You have to
move the files in your development site to a server for people to view the
files over the Web (doing so is the subject of Hour 22). The website located
on a web server and available to the public is called the **live site**. I always
work on an up-to-date copy of a website that is located on my local hard
drive. You can store your development files in two places:

- ▶ On your local machine
- ▶ On a network drive

Fill in the Editing Files, Part 3, section like so:

1. Select the top radio button, Edit Local Copies on My Machine, Then Upload to Server When Ready (Recommended), to elect to store the development files on your local machine; this is where most web developers
   store their files. If you are working in a networked environment (at your
   office, for instance), you could use the Edit Directly on Server Using Local Network selection.

▼ TRY IT YOURSELF

Completing the Editing Files, Part 3 Site Setup Section

continued

FIGURE 3.5
You enter the directory that houses your development files.

2. As shown in Figure 3.5, the text box at the bottom of the dialog box asks you to enter the location of the site directory. Click the folder icon to the right of the text box to navigate to the directory where you will store your local site, the files you will work on in Dreamweaver. Either use an existing directory on your hard drive or create a new directory for your site.

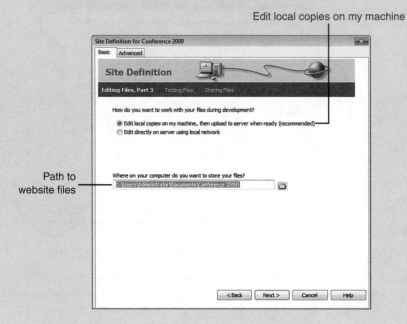

Edit local copies on my machine

Path to website files

3. Click the Next button.

CAUTION

Don't Develop on the Live Site

Never edit directly on the final live site during development. You do not want to make a mistake on the real site; always make sure that you are working on a copy of the site.

Filling In the Sharing Files Section

The next section in the Site Definition Wizard enables you to configure how you upload files to a server and share them with the world. You can also set up a central location where members of your team can share files. You learn how to configure remote servers and transfer files in Hour 22. Fill in the Sharing Files section in the following way:

1. Drop down the top menu and select None, as shown in Figure 3.6.

2. Click the Next button.

Reviewing the Summary

The last page of the wizard displays a summary of your site, as shown in Figure 3.7. You can come back to this wizard at any time to change your site

FIGURE 3.6
To set up the remote connection information later, simply select None.

definition by selecting the Edit Sites command from the Site menu (either the one in the Files panel or the one in the Document window). Click the Done button to finish defining your site to finish creating your site definition.

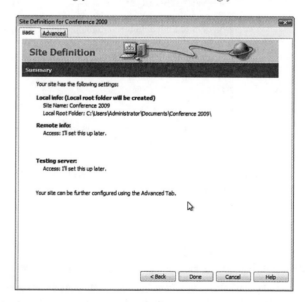

FIGURE 3.7
The Site Definition Wizard displays a summary of your site definition.

Building the Site Cache

After you click the Done button, Dreamweaver displays a message, telling you that it will now create the initial site cache. When you click OK, a

FIGURE 3.8
You might see a progress bar as
Dreamweaver creates a cache for
your site. This file speeds the updating of links when you move or
rename a file.

progress bar like the one in Figure 3.8 appears (and disappears very quickly
if you have nothing in your site). The initial site cache is created each time
you create a new site. The **site cache** stores information about the links in
your site so that they can be quickly updated if they change. Dreamweaver
continues to update the cache as you work.

Using the Files Panel

After you've defined your site, the site title you specified appears in the Site
drop-down menu at the top of the Files panel (shown in Figure 3.9). As you
create web pages and save them to your site, they appear in the Files panel.
You use the Files panel to open web pages to edit in Dreamweaver. Right
now you might not have any web pages in your site, but eventually you'll
want to use the Files panel to create folders to organize the many web pages
you've created.

FIGURE 3.9
The Files panel enables you to
change sites and open web pages.

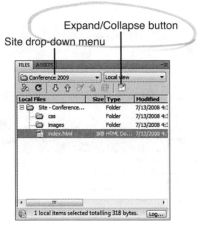

The Site drop-down menu is where you access the websites you have defined. If you work on multiple projects, you have multiple sites to choose
from. For instance, you might have your own personal website defined,
plus a site for your child's school or a site for a client whose website you are
creating.

There is no special procedure for importing an existing website into
Dreamweaver. If a copy of the existing website exists in a folder on your
hard drive, simply define a site in Dreamweaver which points to that folder.
That is all you need to do. All the files are available to edit in Dreamweaver,
and you can easily modify web pages and then save them. Open a web page
by double-clicking the filename listed in the Files panel.

So far you've used the collapsed version of the Files panel, but the next section introduces the expanded version of the Files panel.

Expanding the Files Panel

There is a larger version of the Files panel, available to use when you need to work with files in your site and need access to more site-oriented commands. To open the expanded Files panel, perform the following actions:

1. Click the Expand/Collapse button in the Files panel, shown earlier in Figure 3.9.

   The Expanded Files panel, shown in Figure 3.10, is a larger representation of the Files panel and has two panes: Local Files (on the right, by default) and Remote Site (on the left), which you set up in Hour 22. Because you have not yet defined a remote site, you should not have any files in the Remote Site pane at this point.

Remote files   Expand/Collapse button   Local files

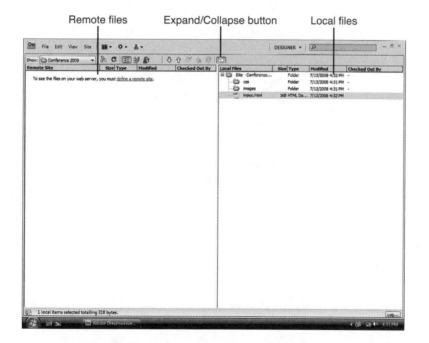

FIGURE 3.10
The Expanded Files panel has two panes: Local Files and Remote Site.

   When you click the Files Expand/Collapse button on the Macintosh, the Expanded Files panel opens in a new window. On Windows, it expands to fill the majority of the screen.

2. Click the Expand/Collapse button again to return to the smaller version of the Files panel.

Creating New Files in the Files Panel

You can create new files and new folders right in the Dreamweaver Files panel. Right-click in the Files panel to open the Files panel menu. This context menu, shown in Figure 3.11, has two commands of interest at the top: New File and New Folder. You use those commands to create files and folders (also called **directories**) in the Files panel.

FIGURE 3.11
The Files panel context menu contains commands to create new folders and files in a website.

Create new files and folders

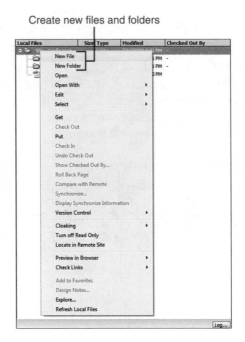

▼ TRY IT YOURSELF

Creating an Images Directory

The websites you create need directories for organization; probably every site will at least have an images directory for all the images in the site. To create an images directory, follow these steps:

1. Right-click in the Files panel.

   You need to be careful about what is selected when you select the New Folder command so that you do not nest the folder within another folder. To add a folder at the site root, select the top line in the Files panel, which begins with the word *Site*.

2. Select the New Folder command. An untitled folder is added to your site.

3. Name the new folder **images**.

4. Repeat steps 1 and 2 and create a folder called **css**.

Now try adding a new file to your site with these steps:

1. Right-click on the root folder and select the New File command.

2. A new untitled web page is created in the website. Name the web page index.html, which is one of the popular default page names for many servers.

Using the **default page name** enables users to find your page more easily by just entering a basic web page address without the specific page appended. Another common default page name is default.htm. Both the .htm and the .html file extensions are acceptable. The .htm file extension became popular because the older versions of Microsoft Windows could handle only three-character file extensions; this is no longer a limitation in newer versions of Windows. After you add the new folder and a new file, the site should look as shown in Figure 3.12.

Folder —
File —

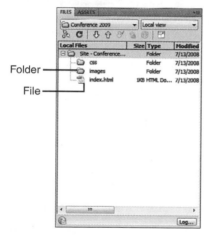

FIGURE 3.12
You can add files and folders in Dreamweaver's Files panel.

Editing a Site Definition

So far in this hour, you have used the wizard on the Basic tab in the Site Definition dialog box to define a website. Now let's explore the Advanced tab and use it to edit site settings.

To edit the site definition, follow these steps:

1. Open the Manage Sites dialog box again by selecting the Manage Sites command from the Site menu, or by choosing Manage Sites from the File panel's Site drop-down menu.

2. Select the site you just created from the list and then click the Edit button. The Site Definition dialog box opens again.

TRY IT YOURSELF

Editing the Site Definition

▼ TRY IT YOURSELF

**Editing the Site
Definition**

continued

FIGURE 3.13
The Advanced tab contains all the
site properties.

3. Click the Advanced tab at the top of the dialog box. As shown in Figure
   3.13, this is another view of the information you entered into the wizard.

Advanced tab   Default images folder

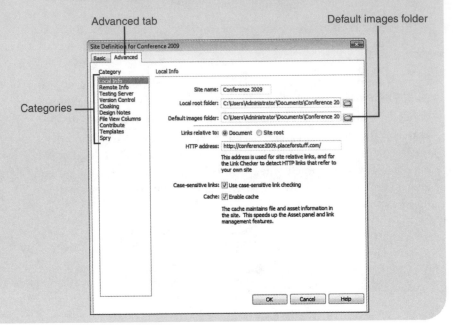

Categories

The left side of the Site Definition dialog box shows categories, and the right
side lists the selected category's properties. Select the Local Info category.
Don't some of these fields look familiar? That's because they are the same
fields you set up using the wizard.

▼ TRY IT YOURSELF

**Setting a Default
Images Folder**

Set up a default images folder in the Local Info category in this way:

1. Select the folder icon next to the Default Images Folder text box.

2. Navigate to the images folder you just created. Now Dreamweaver knows
   where you keep your images for the site.

3. Click the OK button to save your changes.

4. Click the Done button to close the Edit Sites dialog box.

TIP

Check Case Sensitivity

In the Advanced tab of the Site Definition dialog box is the Use Case-Sensitive
Link Checking check box. If you select this setting, Dreamweaver checks that the
links in your site use the same case (uppercase or lowercase) as the filenames.
This is very useful if you are eventually uploading your website to a case-
sensitive UNIX server.

You learn about other advanced options later in this book. In Hour 22, you set up the Remote Info category in order to upload your files to a remote website. In Hour 23, "Maintaining a Website," you explore the Cloaking and the Design Notes categories.

Considering Site Organization

There are many opinions about the proper way to organize a website. Some people like to compartmentalize all the files into directories and subdirectories. Some people like to have a very shallow structure, with many files in a single directory. As you get more experienced at web development, you'll find your ideal method of organization. It's nice to exchange ideas with other web developers or hobbyists so that you can learn from the successes and failures of others and they can learn from yours.

I have a Projects directory on my hard drive, represented in Figure 3.14. The Projects directory contains a directory for each project on which I'm working. Within each project directory is a Web directory. This is the directory where I keep all the development files for the site and the directory that I set as the root in Dreamweaver.

This directory structure enables me to put other files, such as correspondence, contracts, invoices, and spreadsheets, in the client's folder without making them part of the website. It's good practice to keep other files separate from those you plan to transfer to the Web. You might prefer to have one directory that contains all your websites. Do whatever works best for you.

Put some thought into how you'll organize the files in your website before you start a project. You probably want to create a separate images folder to hold your images, as shown in Figure 3.15. If you have other types of assets, such as sound or video, you might want to create separate folders for those too. I always create a scripts directory to hold external JavaScript files and external Cascading Style Sheets files; you explore these in the later hours of this book.

I try to logically break up sections of websites into separate directories. If your website has obvious divisions (departments, lessons, products, and so on), you can create directories to hold the web pages for each division. You'll be surprised at how even a small website becomes quickly unmanageable when all the files are dumped into one directory.

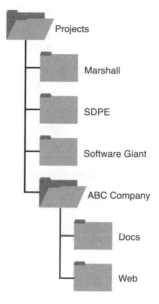

FIGURE 3.14
An example of a directory structure in which the website is housed in the **Web** directory.

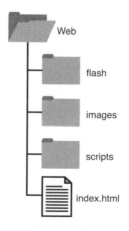

FIGURE 3.15
You can organize your website into images and other directories.

TIP

Plan Now, Benefit Later

It's a good idea to set up a common directory structure even if you aren't anticipating an extensive site. Websites have a way of growing over time. As developers come and go, a standardized structure helps ensure that all of the components of the site can be located and maintained.

Most websites use many image files. If you have different sections in your website, do you want to have separate images directories in each section? It might be a good way to organize your site. Then again, if images are used across multiple sections, it might make the images hard to find. Make sure that your organizational logic isn't going to break down as you add files to your site.

Luckily, if you do have to rearrange assets, Dreamweaver updates any links for you. When you move a file, Dreamweaver asks you whether you want to search and update links to that file. That's what the site cache is created for. However, it is still best to make wise design decisions at the beginning of a big project.

Summary

In this hour, you learned how to define a website and determine its root. You learned how to quickly add files and folders to a site. In addition, you learned how to use the Files panel and expand it into the Expanded Files panel. You also learned how to open a site and edit it using some of the advanced site definition features. And you explored ideas about how to organize a site.

Q&A

Q. How do I import a website into Dreamweaver?

A. There is no set procedure for importing a site. You simply define a site exactly as you did this hour, pointing to the root directory of the site you'd like to import. Dreamweaver presents all the files in the Files panel, enabling you to open and edit them. If the site you need to import is on a web server, you first need to read Hour 20, "Creating a Form and Collecting Data," and set up remote site settings pointing to the server.

Q. If I need to move files within my site, is it okay to do it within Dreamweaver?

A. If you need to do some housekeeping or rearranging, it's best to do it within Dreamweaver. Dreamweaver automatically updates links to files and warns you if deleting a file will affect other files within your site. Be sure to take care of these tasks within Dreamweaver and not elsewhere; otherwise, you might break links or other dependencies between files in the site.

Workshop

Quiz

1. Why do you need to define a website?

2. What is the purpose of the Files panel?

3. True or false: You must go through a conversion process to import an existing website into Dreamweaver.

Quiz Answers

1. You define a website so that Dreamweaver knows where the root of the site is and what your site management preferences are.

2. The Files panel can be used to create new files and folders, edit existing files, and access site management features.

3. False. No conversion process is necessary to import an existing website into Dreamweaver.

Exercises

1. Try defining a new website. Add some files and folders to the new site. Name one of the files `index.htm`.

2. Search for *Site Map* in Google (http://www.google.com) and look at the organization of other sites on the Web. The folders used to store web pages might or might not reflect the same structure outlined in the site map. Click some of the pages and look at the folder structure in the URLs.

3. Open up the Site Definition dialog box and explore the other categories in the Advanced tab (Design Notes or Cloaking, for instance). We cover the other categories in upcoming hours.

Dealing with Words: Adding Text and Lists

Content is king on the Web. Without compelling content, you won't get visitors, and without visitors, you won't have a site! In this hour, we start dealing with the most common type of content: text. You get started creating web pages with Dreamweaver by becoming familiar with adding text and setting text properties. You learn how Dreamweaver formats the appearance of text using Cascading Style Sheets (CSS). This hour introduces the role of CSS, and Hour 6, "Formatting Web Pages Using Cascading Style Sheets," gives more in-depth information on using CSS.

Creating a New Page

The New Document dialog box enables you to select the type of document you want to create. This dialog box is organized into several categories:

- ▶ Blank Page
- ▶ Blank Template
- ▶ Page from Template
- ▶ Page from Sample
- ▶ Other

Each category lists different types of documents and layouts you can create. You are going to start with a completely blank HTML document. In other hours, you explore selecting document types from other categories in the New Document dialog box.

WHAT YOU'LL LEARN IN THIS HOUR:

- ▶ How to create a new web page and set up properties for the whole page
- ▶ How to use the Property inspector to change text fonts and font sizes
- ▶ How Dreamweaver creates CSS styles and how to rename and apply styles
- ▶ How to align text and add unordered and ordered lists
- ▶ How to preview a web page in different browsers

▼ TRY IT YOURSELF

Creating a Blank HTML Page

To create a new blank HTML web page, do the following:

1. Select File, New.

2. Select the Blank Page category.

3. Select HTML from the Page Type column, as shown in Figure 4.1.

FIGURE 4.1
The New Document dialog box enables you to select the type of document you want to create.

Page type   Page layout

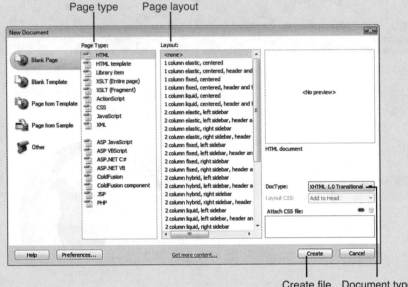

Create file   Document type

4. Select <none> from the Layout column.

5. Ensure that XHTML 1.0 Transitional is selected in the DocType drop-down menu.

6. Click the Create button.

A new document is created, and you can add text, images, and other objects to it.

The keyboard shortcut to open the New Document dialog box is Ctrl+N (Command+N on the Macintosh). You can also create a new page from Dreamweaver's Welcome page. (Remember the screen that is visible in the Document window when you first open Dreamweaver?) The middle column in the Welcome page is titled Create New, and you can select HTML from that column to quickly create a blank web page.

Saving a File

Even if you haven't added anything to a new page, it's always a good idea to save and name it right away. The insertion of images, movies, links, and other objects requires that you save the web page first. Remember to save the file in the directory you've previously defined as the site root as discussed in Hour 3, "Setting Up a Website."

NOTE

Name Your Files Properly to Avoid Problems

Spaces, punctuation, and special characters in file and directory names might cause problems. You can use underscores or dashes instead of spaces in names. All files should be named using a combination of letters, numbers, and underscores. Although it is possible to use spaces and other "special" characters in HTML filenames, this can lead to confusing links that aren't easy to type into a browser.

CAUTION

Servers Might Be Case-Sensitive

Filenames are case-sensitive on many web servers. Servers running the various flavors of the UNIX operating system enable you to create files named `mydog.gif`, `Mydog.gif`, and `MYDOG.gif` in the same directory because the capitalization differs. Microsoft operating systems, such as Windows, are not case-sensitive. So, if you are developing in Windows, your links might work perfectly and then cease to work when you upload them to a case-sensitive server!

NOTE

What Are Document Types and XHTML?

You might have noticed the Doc-Type (Document Type) drop-down menu in the New Document dialog box. By default, Dreamweaver creates an HTML type defined using the XHTML 1.0 Transitional document type, often called **doctype** because it is defined using the `doctype` tag. XHTML (Extensible Hypertext Markup Language) is the most recent version of HTML, combining HTML with the structure of XML (Extensible Markup Language). You explore document types more in Hour 7, "Looking Under the Hood: Exploring XHTML."

To save a web page, perform the following steps:

1. Select File, Save.

2. Navigate to the correct directory, either the root of the defined site or a subdirectory within the root of the defined site.

3. Enter a filename. Dreamweaver automatically adds an `.html` extension.

4. Click the Save button.

TRY IT YOURSELF ▼

Saving a Web Page

The `.htm` and `.html` file extensions are interchangeable. Traditionally, the `.html` extension has been more popular with developers working on the Mac or UNIX platforms because those operating systems have always supported longer file extensions. The `.htm` file extension reflected the older Windows version three-character file extension limit. Windows no longer has a character limit for file extensions, so using the universal `.html` extension is a good choice.

TIP

Spelling and Grammar Are Important!

I like to create text for web pages in a robust word processing application such as Microsoft Word so that I have the automatic spell check and grammar check. I can then copy and paste the text into a web page in Dreamweaver. You can, of course, use Dreamweaver's spell-checker, but there is no grammar-checker in Dreamweaver.

Adding Text to a Web Page

To enter text into the new web page you just created, you can simply type into the Document window. Type some text to serve as a heading at the top of the page, press the Enter key, and type a couple of sentences. This is the best way to add text to the web page if you are writing it as you create the page. If the text exists elsewhere, however, such as in a Microsoft Word document, an email, or another type of text file, you want to look at the next section on copying and pasting text into Dreamweaver.

Copying and Pasting Text from a File

Often you need to transfer text that exists as a word processing document into a web page. You can easily copy text from another application, such as Microsoft Word or even the spreadsheet application Microsoft Excel, and paste it into Dreamweaver. Dreamweaver can paste text two ways: with and without text formatting.

▼ TRY IT YOURSELF

Copying and Pasting Text from Another Program

To copy and paste text from a word processing program or another program, follow these steps:

1. Open a Word document (.doc) or another word processing document.

2. Select at least a couple of paragraphs.

3. Copy the text by selecting Edit, Copy or using the keyboard command (Ctrl+C for Windows or Command+C on the Mac).

4. Go to Dreamweaver and place the insertion point where you want to paste the text.

5. Select Edit, Paste or use the keyboard shortcut (Ctrl+V in Windows or Command+V on a Mac). The text is pasted into Dreamweaver, and it retains much of its formatting, including fonts, paragraphs, color, and other attributes.

CAUTION

Formatted Text and the Web

Even though you can copy and paste formatted text into Dreamweaver, this doesn't necessarily mean that all the formatting will transfer, nor does it mean that the text styles will look identical in a web browser. There are formatting and style constraints on the Web that just can't be accounted for in the copy and paste process.

Copying and Pasting Structural Formatting

I often want to reformat the text in the web page, so I usually paste into Dreamweaver without font formatting.

The following text details how to copy and paste text from a word processing program with only structural formatting (paragraphs, lists, tables) and no font formatting (bold, colored text, font sizes):

1. Open a Word document (.doc) or another word processing document.

2. Select at least a couple of paragraphs.

3. Copy the text by selecting Edit, Copy or using the keyboard command (Ctrl+C for Windows or Command+C on the Mac).

4. Go to Dreamweaver and place the insertion point where you want to paste the text.

5. Select Edit, Paste Special.

6. Select Text with Structure (Paragraphs, Lists, Tables, Etc.), as shown in Figure 4.2.

FIGURE 4.2
The Paste Special dialog box enables you to choose exactly what formatting properties get pasted along with your text into Dreamweaver.

If you have a preferred way to paste text from other applications, you can set that preference as Dreamweaver's default. You can then simply use the Paste command or the keyboard shortcut (Ctrl+V for Windows or Command+V on the Mac), as I prefer, to paste in your preferred way. Of course, you can always bring up the Paste Special command when you need to paste in a unique way. Change the default Paste command in Dreamweaver Preferences' (Edit, Preferences) Copy/Paste category, as shown in Figure 4.3. If you use Microsoft Word, be sure that you also check the Clean Up Word Paragraph Spacing option so that you don't get extra spaces between your paragraphs. This is a nice feature that saves you from cleaning up the extra spaces by hand.

FIGURE 4.3
The Copy/Paste preferences enable you to change the default formatting that Dreamweaver uses
when it pastes content from other
applications.

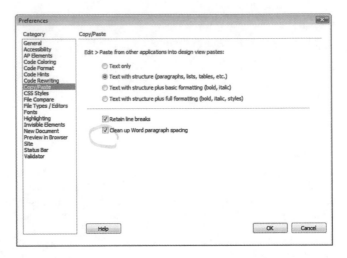

Applying Text Formatting

The Property inspector is the panel directly under the Document window.
You use this panel extensively to set properties of objects on a web page.
You can toggle the display of the Property inspector by choosing Window,
Properties. One way to format text in Dreamweaver is by using HTML formatting. HTML formatting consists of special tags that are added to stylize
the text in a document. To use HTML formatting, click the HTML button in
the Properties Panel, then select the Format drop-down menu in the Property inspector. There are four basic formatting options:

- **None**—This option removes any formatting styles currently applied
  to the selection.

- **Paragraph**—This option applies paragraph tags (<p></p>) to the selection. This adds two carriage returns after the selection.

- **Heading 1 through Heading 6**—These options apply heading tags to
  the selection. Heading 1 is the largest heading and Heading 6 is the
  smallest. Applying a heading tag makes everything on the line that
  heading size.

- **Preformatted**—This option displays text in a fixed-width, or mono-
  spaced, font (on most systems, 10-point Courier). The text resembles
  typewriter text. You probably won't use this format option too often.

Select the top line heading in your web page and apply Heading 1 formatting, as shown in Figure 4.4. While you are creating web pages, you use the different heading and paragraph formats all the time. These formatting options wrap the text you've selected with HTML tags. The Heading 1 format, for instance, adds the <h1> tag before the selection and the closing tag </h1> after the selection.

Text formats

Property inspector

FIGURE 4.4
The Format drop-down menu in the Property inspector applies heading, paragraph, and preformatted formatting to text.

Understanding Paragraph and Break Tags

It's important to understand the difference between the paragraph (<p>) and break (<br>) tags. Paragraph tags surround a block of text, placing two carriage returns after the block. You create a new paragraph by pressing the Enter or Return key. Think of paragraph tags as creating a container for the block of text. This container is a square box that contains text. In Hour 6, you understand how to modify this container with CSS.

The break tag is less commonly used, and inserts a single carriage return into text. You can insert a break into a web page by using the keyboard shortcut Shift+Enter or by selecting the Line Break object from the Characters drop-down menu in the Text category of the Insert panel. The break tag does not create a container as the paragraph format does. This tag is best used for creating a new line within a paragraph such as when formatting an address on different lines.

Pressing Shift+Enter to insert a line break and pressing Enter to create a paragraph look visually identical on a web page. However, because you haven't created a paragraph container when you press Shift+Enter, any formatting applies to the entire container. This distinction becomes more important as you begin formatting portions of web pages in different ways.

Setting Page Properties

You can set global page properties, such as the default font and font size for all the text on the page. You should always add a page title to a web page. Both global page properties and the page title can be added in the Page Properties dialog box. To get started, select Modify, Page Properties to open this dialog box.

The Page Properties dialog box, shown in Figure 4.5, has six property categories listed in the left column: Appearance (CSS), Appearance (HTML), Links (CSS), Headings (CSS), Title/Encoding, and Tracing Image. Next you learn about the property settings in the Appearance (CSS and HTML), Headings, and Title/Encoding categories; the Links category settings is covered in Hour 5, "Adding Links: Hyperlinks, Anchors, and Mailto Links." You simply click one of the categories to modify its property settings.

FIGURE 4.5
The Page Properties dialog box en-ables you to set properties for the entire web page.

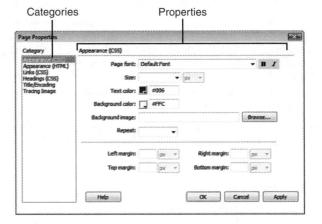

Setting Global Page Appearance

You use the settings in the Appearance category of the Page Properties dialog box to set the text font, size, and color, along with several other settings, for the entire web page. For instance, the text on a web page is black by default. You can change the default text color on the web page by changing this setting in Page Properties.

You might notice, however, that there are *two* Appearance categories in Page Properties window—Appearance (HTML) and Appearance (CSS)—and both have almost the same exact settings!

The Appearance (HTML) settings are provided for legacy purposes—these options use HTML to control the appearance. The Appearance (CSS) settings, on the other hand, use Cascading Style Sheets to set the appearance. Cascading Style Sheets are the modern way of applying visual styling to web pages and should be used whenever possible.

Setting the Global Page Font and Font Size

Select the Appearance (CSS) category in the Page Properties dialog box by clicking the category name on the left side of the dialog box. You can select the default page font for the entire page along with the default text size and color. These settings may be overridden by any local text setting, such as the settings you apply later this hour.

To set the page font properties, follow these steps:

1. In the Page Properties dialog box, select the font family you want from the Page Font drop-down menu.

2. You can also set the default text to be bold, italic, or both. I don't suggest selecting either!

3. Select the font size in the Size drop-down menu. If you select a numeric font size, you also have to select a unit type, such as points or pixels.

4. Click the Apply button at the bottom of the Page Properties dialog box to view the font changes you've made so far. You might have to adjust the position of the Page Properties dialog box so that it isn't blocking your view. The Apply button enables you to view your changes without closing the Page Properties dialog box.

TIP

Use Ems Instead of Points

Many web designers standardize on using relative measurement units such as ems or percent for font measurement. **Ems** are a measurement based on the height of the capital letter "M"; 1em is equal to the height of M in the default font size. **Points** are used for designing type for print but are often unpredictable for displaying text on a computer screen. The great thing about using a relative measurement like ems is that you are respecting your user's font-size choices. If they have set the browser font size to a higher setting, if they have problems seeing, for instance, then your font measurements will be relative to those choices. If you set the font size to 1.25ems for a heading, the text will be a quarter size bigger than the default font that the user has set.

Setting the Global Text Color

In a number of areas in Dreamweaver, you can change the color of an object or text. In HTML and CSS files, colors are specified by using a hexadecimal numbering system, but if you don't know the hexadecimal translation of the color you'd like to use, you can use Dreamweaver's color picker. You access the Dreamweaver color picker by clicking on the color picker box, shown in Figure 4.6. Dreamweaver's color palette appears.

FIGURE 4.6
Select the color picker to open Dreamweaver's color palette.

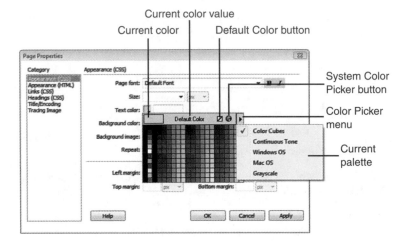

You can experiment with picking a color by using the color picker in a number of ways:

▶ Pick one of the available color swatches by clicking it with the eyedropper.

▶ By default, the Color Cubes palette displays. You can select one of the five other panels: Color Cubes, Continuous Tone, Windows OS, Mac OS, and Grayscale.

▶ Use the eyedropper to pick up any color onscreen by simply clicking the eyedropper on it. You can pick up any color on the computer screen, not just colors in Dreamweaver. Try selecting a color from one of the icons in the Insert panel. You need to arrange Dreamweaver so that you can see other Windows and click the eyedropper on the colors.

▶ Click the System Color Picker button to create a custom color as shown in Figure 4.7. This opens the system color picker, where you can either pick one of the basic colors or click anywhere in the color spectrum to mix your own color. Click the Add to Custom Colors button and then click the OK button to use the color.

You can also type the color information directly into the color text box in the Property inspector:

Windows System Color Picker

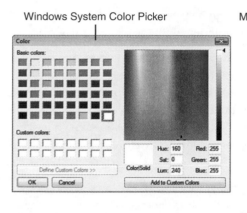

Macintosh System Color Picker

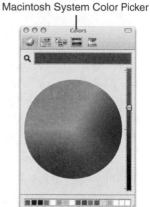

FIGURE 4.7
The system color picker enables
you to mix your own custom colors
on either a Windows (left) or Macintosh OS X (right) computer.

▶ Colors are represented in HTML by three hexadecimal numbers preceded by the pound (#) sign. For instance, the hexadecimal RGB (red,
green, blue) value for a light blue hue is represented as #0099FF,
where the value for R is 00, the value for G is 99, and the value for B is
FF. If you know the hexadecimal value for a color, you can simply
type it in. CS4 also understands the color shortcuts (removing repeated values) so #0099FF could also be entered as #09F.

▶ Browsers also support a wide range of color names in addition to
hexadecimal values. For instance, you could type in **red** instead of
#FF0000.

To clear the current color without picking another color, click the Default
Color button in the color picker.

Setting the Background Color and Background Image of a Web Page

You can set the background color of an entire page in the Appearance (CSS)
category of the Page Properties dialog box. For example, if you'd like to set
the web page background color to white, you can enter the hexadecimal
color code (#FFFFFF) into the Background Color text box, type **white** into
the box, or use the color picker. Of course, you can pick any color that you
want as the background color, but make sure that the combination of the
background color and the text color doesn't make your web page difficult to
read. If you apply a dark background color, you should use a light text color
for contrast so that the viewer can easily read the text.

You can also set a background image for a web page. For the web page
background to look nice, you should find or create an image especially designed as a web page background. You can find these specially designed

TIP

Utilities to Identify Color Values

For Windows users to easily
identify the hexadecimal value of
a color on the screen, download
ColorCop, a freeware program
available at http://prall.net/col-
orcop/. I use this utility all the
time! On Mac OS 10.5 (Leopard), you can select DigitalColor
Meter from the Utilities
folder in Applications to identify
RGB values on the screen as
hexadecimal values.

CAUTION

Eight to Ten Percent of People Are Colorblind!

You should check that your color
combination is visible to the
many people who are colorblind.
Use the Colorblind Web Page Filter at http://colorfilter.wickline.
org/ to check your design. The filter returns a version of your web
page displayed as it would look
to someone who is colorblind.

background images on the Web or in image galleries that you purchase. A background image should never interfere with the readability of a page.

To add a background image, click the Browse button and navigate to an image file saved on your hard drive. The image has to be saved in the GIF, JPEG, or PNG format. (You learn more about image formats in Hour 8, "Displaying Images.") Click the OK button. You might receive a message from Dreamweaver that a `file://` path will be used until you save your document. Just click OK; Dreamweaver automatically corrects that path after you save the web page.

When an image is smaller than the browser window, you can choose whether it repeats horizontally, vertically, or both. Use the Repeat drop-down menu to choose whether the image won't repeat at all (No Repeat), will repeat in horizontal and vertical directions (Repeat), or will repeat horizontally or vertically (Repeat-x and Repeat-y, respectively).

Setting the Page Margins

Margins set the amount of space between the contents of the web page and the edges of the browser window. You set the margins for a page in the Page Properties Appearance (CSS) dialog box. The default setting for page margins varies from browser to browser, so it's impossible to predict the amount of whitespace that will be visible around the border of your web page design. You might want to change the margins if you notice that there are gaps at the top and on the left side of your web pages.

You can change the page margins by entering values into the margin boxes, as shown in Figure 4.8. There are four page margin settings: Left Margin, Top Margin, Right Margin, and Bottom Margin. Many web designers set the Left and Top Margin settings to 0 pixels so that the design is snug to the upper-left corner of the browser window.

FIGURE 4.8
Set the page margins, the space between your web page design and the edge of the browser window, in the Page Properties Appearance category.

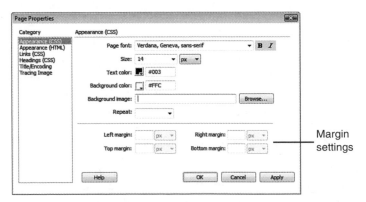

Setting Global Heading Properties

You create a heading by selecting one of the heading formats, Heading 1 through Heading 6, in the Format drop-down menu in Dreamweaver's HTML Property inspector. In the Headings (CSS) category of the Page Properties dialog box, you can set global properties for these headings, as shown in Figure 4.9. You can select a Heading Font for all six heading sizes. You can also set a unique font size and color for each size.

Heading category

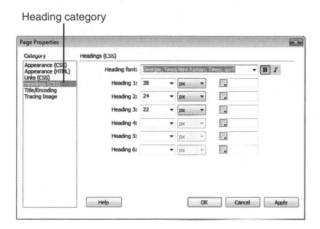

FIGURE 4.9
Set the font, font size, and color for headings in the Headings category of the Page Properties dialog box.

To set how Heading 1 will appear, follow these steps:

1. Select Modify, Page Properties if you don't already have the Page Properties dialog box open. You should already have some text set to Heading 1 on the page.

2. Select a default font for all the headings by selecting one of the fonts beside the Heading font setting. You can also click the Bold or Italic button if you'd like.

3. Enter a large font size beside Heading 1. A good size to try is 36 pixels. You can also change the color by clicking on the color picker in the Heading 1 settings.

4. Click the Apply button (refer to Figure 4.9) to apply your changes without closing the Page Properties dialog box.

TRY IT YOURSELF ▼

Setting a Heading Style

CAUTION

Heading Sizes

Remember that headings become smaller as the heading number increases. So, Heading 1 is logically meant to be larger than Heading 2. You can override these sizes, but it isn't a good idea to do so.

Adding a Page Title

The Title/Encoding category of the Page Properties dialog box enables you to set the document title of your web page along with the document and encoding types. The title of your web page is important because it appears in the title bar of the browser when someone views the page. This same title is saved to a user's browser Bookmarks or Favorites list when the address of your site is saved; therefore, you should make it meaningful and memorable.

TIP

Search Engines Want Your Page Title

It's important to give your web page a meaningful title, especially if you want people to be able to find your page by using the major search engines. Although search engines use many factors to find and rate web pages, the page title is often an important factor. You can find Keith Robinson's excellent discussion on writing better web page titles at http://www.7nights.com/dkrprod/gwt_seven.php.

▼ TRY IT YOURSELF

Adding a Title to a Document

To add a title to a document, follow these steps:

1. Select Modify, Page Properties if you don't already have the Page Properties dialog box open.

2. Select the Title/Encoding category.

3. Type a descriptive title in the Title box at the top of the Page Properties dialog box.

4. Click the OK button to save the settings. The current page title also appears in the Title text box in the Document toolbar shown in Figure 4.10. You can always add the title in this text box instead of opening the Page Properties dialog box. By default, all pages are titled "Untitled Document" before a title is added.

FIGURE 4.10
The document title can be entered in the Page Properties or in the Title text field.

Title/Encoding category   Document title field

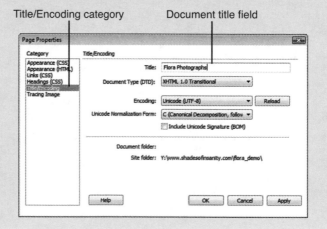

The Title/Encoding category houses the Document Type setting, which you first encountered earlier this hour when you created a new HTML file. By default, Dreamweaver applies the XHTML 1.0 Transitional document type, which is a good choice because XHTML is the most current standard and the transitional version of XHTML provides a good balance of older HTML functionality and new XML structure. Dreamweaver automatically adds a tag at the top of each web page to describe the document type for the browser. This tag tells the browser the flavor of HTML that your web page is written in and helps the browser interpret the page.

There are various alphabets in the world, and using the Encoding command is how you tell a web browser which one you are using for your web page. By default, Dreamweaver lists the Unicode (UTF-8) encoding type that has become the standard for computer code creation in all languages. Creating pages using Unicode encoding ensures that your web pages will be standards-based and viewable all over the world.

Introducing Cascading Style Sheets

As I mentioned earlier, you were creating CSS styles while you were modifying settings in the Page Properties dialog box. Dreamweaver automatically adds CSS to your web page, and the styles created are visible in the CSS Styles panel (Window, CSS Styles), as shown in Figure 4.11. To view the styles in a web page, make sure that the All button is selected at the top of the CSS Styles panel and expand the list of styles by clicking the Expand/Collapse (+) button next to <style>.

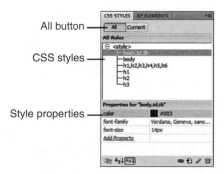

FIGURE 4.11
The CSS Styles panel displays a list of styles created by Dreamweaver when you set properties in the Page Properties dialog box.

The styles created by the Dreamweaver Page Properties dialog box are **redefined** tag styles. These styles add formatting properties and alter the default appearance of various tags. For instance, when you change the

NOTE

Goodbye, `<font>` Tag

Note that older browsers—pre-1997 browsers older than Internet Explorer 4 or Netscape Navigator 4—don't support CSS. The older method of formatting text is to use the `<font>` tag. This tag has been deprecated by the World Wide Web Consortium (W3C), the Web standards organization. **Deprecated** means that the W3C is removing it from the approved tag list and eventually it might not be supported by browsers. Dreamweaver CS4 does not insert any `<font>` tags into your code. If you have existing web pages in your website that use this tag, you should plan to update them by replacing the `<font>` tags with CSS.

background color of the page, Dreamweaver redefines the `<body>` tag, which is the tag that contains everything on the web page. These styles are defined in the web page you are working in, but in Hour 6, you learn how to place these styles in an external style sheet that can be shared by multiple web pages.

Changing Text Attributes in the Property Inspector

In the first part of this hour, you learned about the global page settings that affect text. In the next section, you explore setting properties of sections of text on the page using Dreamweaver's Property inspector. The Property inspector enables you to change the font, font size, and color for sections of text using either HTML or CSS—by clicking the HTML or CSS buttons at the left of the panel. Again, CSS is the modern standard for styling pages, so that's what we'll focus on.

When referring to the two modes of the Property inspector, I call them simply CSS or HTML modes. Just click the appropriate button to switch to the correct mode.

Selecting a Text Font

To apply a specific font, select some text and then click the CSS button in the Property inspector. Next, select the Font drop-down menu in the Property inspector, as shown in Figure 4.12.

FIGURE 4.12
The Font drop-down menu has several font groups from which to choose.

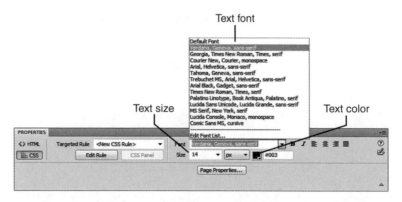

The fonts in the Font drop-down menu are defined in groups. Specifying a group instead of an individual font increases the odds that your viewers will have at least one of the fonts in the group. The browser attempts to display text with the first font listed, but if that font isn't available, the browser continues through the list. Dreamweaver has predefined groups to choose from, and you can create your own groups.

After choosing your font, Dreamweaver opens a New CSS Rule dialog. We get into this window in depth in Hour 6, but, for now, just enter a unique name for your style in the Selector Name field and then click OK, as shown in Figure 4.13.

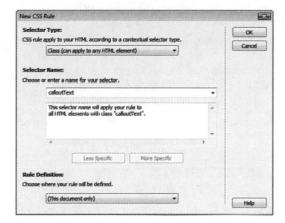

FIGURE 4.13
Choose a selector name for your style.

CAUTION

Choose Your Fonts Wisely

Remember, just because you can see the font and it looks great on your machine doesn't mean that everyone has that font. If a font isn't available, the browser uses the default font—usually Times New Roman—instead. The fonts in the predefined font combinations in Dreamweaver are commonly available fonts in popular operating systems.

The selector name is a unique identifier that refers to a CSS style. By changing a font setting, you're creating a new CSS style for your document, and you must provide a name. You can reuse a style that you've already created by choosing the selector name from the Targeted Rule pop-up menu in the CSS mode of the Property inspector or the "Class" popup menu in the HTML mode.

Changing Text Size

As with the font settings, you change text size by selecting one of the size settings in the Property inspector Size drop-down menu shown in Figure 4.14, or by typing a number in the text box. If you select one of the numbers at the top of the list, the Units drop-down menu becomes active so that you can select the unit type. Point and pixel are the most common unit types. You can also select one of the relative sizes (xx-small, medium, large, and so on). These text size settings enable the text to appear relative to the size settings that the user configures in his browser. This is particularly helpful for users who have vision impairment, but it makes it difficult for you to strictly control how your web page appears to the user.

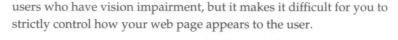

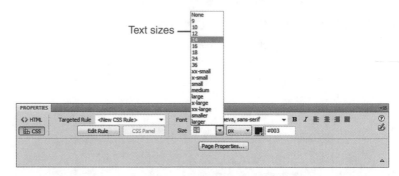

As with choosing a font, if you haven't defined any other styles, you are asked to create a new CSS selector name for the font size. If you've already set a style (and it is selected in the Targeted Rule menu), the size attribute is added onto your existing CSS selector—creating a compound style.

Selecting a Text Color

You change the text color by either selecting a color using the color picker or by entering a hexadecimal color value, such as #0000FF for blue, into the Text Color text box.

Once again, the same CSS process is enforced. If the color is the only attribute you're setting, Dreamweaver forces you to define a new CSS Selector name. If another style has already been defined and is selected in the Targeted Rule menu, the color becomes an additional attribute of that style.

Viewing and Changing CSS Styles

As you create new styles, you may want to review them to see what effects they apply, and what their names are, and maybe even change a selector name to better match its use in your document. To do this, we can open the CSS Styles panel, by choosing Window, CSS Styles.

Click the All button to show all the defined styles in the active document. Styles are represented by the name you provided, preceded by a "." (period). To see what effects the style applies to your page, highlight the style name, and then view the properties at the bottom of the CSS Style panel, as shown in Figure 4.15.

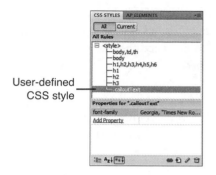

User-defined
CSS style

FIGURE 4.15
The name of the CSS style that
Dreamweaver created is displayed
in the CSS Style drop-down menu.

To delete an existing style (if, for example, you've defined a given style under more than one name):

TRY IT YOURSELF ▼

Deleting an Existing Style

1. Select the style in the CSS Styles panel.

2. Right-click on the style name.

3. Choose delete.

To edit the name of a style to make it more meaningful, do the following:

TRY IT YOURSELF ▼

Editing a Style Name

1. Double-click the style name in the CSS Styles panel.

2. Give the style a name that describes the function of the style in the page.

3. Click OK.

You should never re-create the same formatting by creating additional, identical CSS styles. Instead, you should reapply an existing CSS style.

Follow these steps to apply a CSS style:

TRY IT YOURSELF ▼

Applying a CSS Style

1. Select the appropriate text on the web page.

2. With the CSS button highlighted in the Property inspector, select a style from the Apply portion of the Targeted Rule drop-down menu in the Property inspector.

3. Repeat this process until you have styled all the text you'd like restyled.

You learn how to edit the style definition in Hour 6.

NOTE

CSS Styles in HTML Mode

If you happen to be in the HTML mode of the Property inspector, you can still apply CSS styles by selecting your text, then choosing the style name from the Class drop-down menu in the inspector.

You might have noticed that not all the styles listed in your CSS Styles panel appear in the Targeted Rule or Class drop-down menus in Dreamweaver's Property inspector. For instance, the h1 style and the body, td, and th styles don't appear. That's because you apply these redefined tag styles by simply applying the HTML tag to text. In the case of the h1 style, you simply select Heading 1 from the Property inspector's Format drop-down menu in HTML mode. The styles you defined begin with a period, and are known steps to apply a CSS style: as **class selectors**, a special type of style that you apply individually to selections of text.

Aligning Text

You can align text to the left, center, or right just as you can in a word processing program. You can also justify the text so that the left and right margins are evenly set down the page.

▼ TRY IT YOURSELF

Creating an Unordered List

To align some text in the center of the page, follow these steps:

1. Select the text.

2. Click the Align Center icon (see Figure 4.16) in the Property inspector (CSS mode). These icons are very similar to icons in popular word processing programs.

FIGURE 4.16
The alignment icons in the Property inspector look and act like the alignment commands in word processing software.

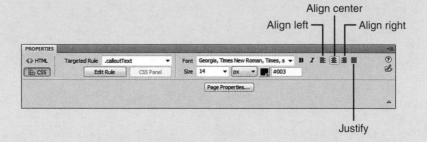

3. Enter a new CSS selector name, if you're prompted. If you're not, the alignment will be added to the currently selected CSS selector.

Alternatively, with the text selected, select Format, Align, Center. The Text menu also contains all the text formatting commands used in this hour.

Creating Lists and Indenting Text

By using Dreamweaver, you can create bulleted lists, called **unordered lists** in HTML, and numbered lists, called **ordered lists** in HTML.

The Unordered List and Ordered List buttons appear in the Property inspector (HTML mode) when you select text.

TRY IT YOURSELF ▼

Creating Lists and Indenting Text

Create an unordered list by following these steps:

1. Type three items for the list, pressing the Enter (or Return) key after each item so that each item is on its own line.

2. Drag the cursor over all three items to select them.

3. Click the Unordered List button in the Property inspector (HTML mode), as shown in Figure 4.17.

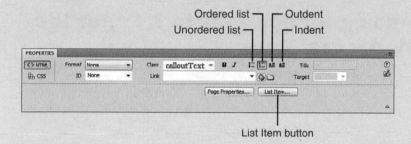

List Item button

FIGURE 4.17
The Property inspector has buttons to create ordered and unordered lists. You can click the Indent and Outdent buttons to nest lists and to indent and outdent text.

TRY IT YOURSELF ▼

Creating Nested Lists

A bullet precedes each line in an unordered list. Now let's see how we can add a second list within that list:

1. Place the insertion point after the last item.

2. Press the Enter key to make a new line. The new line should be preceded by a bullet.

3. Type three items, as you did in the previous list.

4. Drag the cursor over these new items and click the Indent button in the Property inspector.

Now the second list nests within the third item of the first list. You can tell because it is indented and preceded by a different style of bullet. Use the Outdent button to place the nested list back in line with the main list.

TIP

Customize Your Bullets and Numbers

You can change the bullet or number style by clicking the List Item button in the Property inspector (refer to Figure 4.17) when your cursor is located within the list. Oddly, the List Item button does not appear if you select the entire list. Pick the bullet style (either bullet or square) for an unordered list or pick a number style for an ordered list. You can also start the number count at a number other than 1 by entering the initial number in the Start Count box.

To turn the nested unordered list into an ordered list, select the three items in the nested list again and click the Ordered List button in the Property inspector. To bring the nested list back in line with the main list, click the Outdent button.

With regular text, you use the Indent and Outdent buttons to modify the margins of a block of text. In HTML there is no easy way to tab or indent text, so Dreamweaver uses the `<blockquote>` tag to indent. This tag actually indents both the left and the right sides of the text, so it might look strange if you indent multiple times.

Adding a Separator to a Page: The Horizontal Rule

A graphical item that has been around since the Stone Age of the Web (about 15 years ago!) is the horizontal rule. That little divider line is still useful. A horizontal rule is a shaded line that divides a web page into sections. Note that you can't place anything else on the same line with a horizontal rule.

Add a horizontal rule to your web page by selecting the Horizontal Rule object from the Common category of the Insert panel. If you're a menu kind of person, you can do this by selecting Insert, HTML, Horizontal Rule. In Figure 4.18, the Property inspector presents the properties of a horizontal rule. You can set width and height values in either pixels or percentages of the screen. You can also set the alignment and turn shading on and off.

FIGURE 4.18
Horizontal rule properties appear in the Property inspector when you select the rule.

Many objects in HTML have width and height values either in absolute pixel values or as a percentage of the size of the container they are in. If a horizontal rule in the body of a web page is set to a percentage value and the user changes the size of the browser window, the horizontal rule resizes to the new window size. If the horizontal rule is set to an absolute pixel size, it does not resize, and the user sees horizontal scrollbars if the horizontal rule is wider than the screen.

Previewing in a Browser

Even though Dreamweaver is a WYSIWYG (what you see is what you get) tool, you need to see how your page really looks in particular browsers. You should save your work before you preview it in a browser. Saving your work lets Dreamweaver correctly set the paths to linked files, such as images. Dreamweaver prompts you to save the web page before it launches the page in a browser.

Adobe says you can define up to 20 browsers for previewing. Good luck finding 20 browsers! I generally have the following browsers installed for testing: Mozilla Firefox, Microsoft Internet Explorer, Safari, and Opera on my Windows machine and Safari, Firefox, Camino, and sometimes Opera on my Mac. You must have these programs installed on your computer before you can use them to preview your web pages. All the browsers mentioned have free versions and are available for download over the Internet.

To set up a browser, follow these steps:

1. Select the File, Preview in Browser, Edit Browser List command. Dreamweaver's Preferences dialog box opens to the Preview in Browser category. Dreamweaver might have already located browser(s) and entered them here during the installation process, so the list might not be empty.

2. Click the plus button to add a browser, as shown in Figure 4.19.

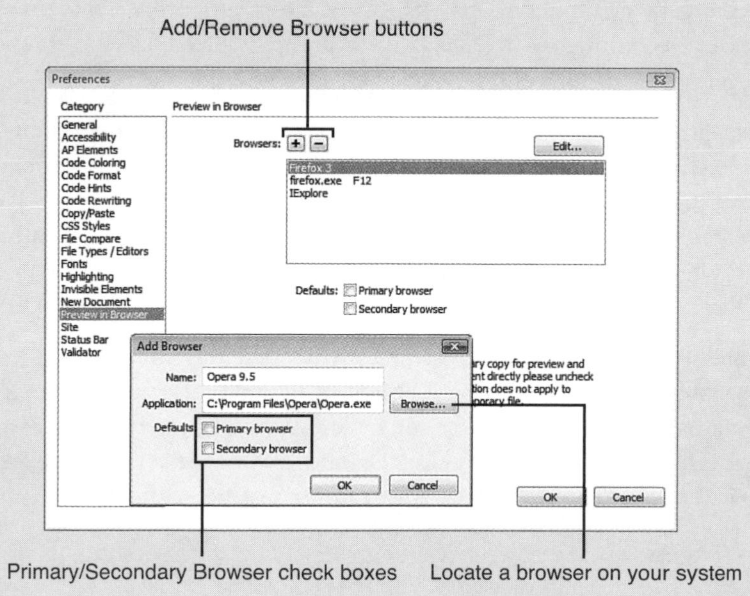

Add/Remove Browser buttons

Primary/Secondary Browser check boxes   Locate a browser on your system

TIP

Firefox, the Universal Browser

My favorite browser, which I use on a daily basis, is Firefox. You can download it at http://www.firefox.com. Firefox provides a standards-based, cross-platform browsing experience. Web developers love designing for Firefox because its behavior is entirely predictable regardless of whether it is running on Windows or the Mac.

TRY IT YOURSELF ▼

Setting Up a Browser for Previewing

FIGURE 4.19
Set the browsers you will use to preview your web pages in the Preview in Browser category in the Preferences dialog box.

▼ TRY IT YOURSELF

Setting Up a Browser for Previewing

continued

3. Leave the Name text box empty for now; Dreamweaver automatically picks up the name of the browser.

4. Click the Browse button next to the Application text box and navigate to the browser program. For computers running Windows, the default installation location for most browsers is in the `Program Files` directory. For the Mac, look in your `Applications` folder.

5. Click either the Primary Browser check box or the Secondary Browser check box. This determines which keyboard shortcut you use to launch the browser. The keyboard shortcut for one primary browser is F12, and the shortcut for one secondary browser is Ctrl+F12.

6. Repeat steps 2–5 until all browsers have been added.

7. Make sure that the Preview Using Temporary Files option is not selected. Click the OK button when you are done.

Below the browser list is a single check box option that controls whether you directly view your web page in the browser or whether you want Dreamweaver to create a temporary file to display in the browser. When the box is checked, you won't need to save your web page before previewing in a browser because Dreamweaver creates a temporary file for you to display in the browser. If you uncheck this box, you have to save your web page before previewing it in the browser. I prefer to uncheck this box and know that I'm viewing the actual web page instead of a temporary file. Even after you've saved your page in Dreamweaver and previewed it in the browser, you can still undo changes that you made before saving the page.

Select File, Preview in Browser or select Preview/Debug in Browser on the Document toolbar to view the current web page. Select the browser you want to use from the menu. If the browser is already open, you might have to switch to the application to see your page. If the browser isn't already open, Dreamweaver opens it and loads the requested page so that you can preview it.

Dreamweaver actually checks each page you open in Dreamweaver for potential browser errors. The Check Browser Compatibility menu on the Document toolbar displays whether you have any browser check errors in the target browsers selected. By default, Dreamweaver checks your page for errors in the following browsers:

▶ Firefox

▶ Internet Explorer

- ▶ Netscape

- ▶ Opera

- ▶ Safari

Modify the browsers and versions in the Target Browsers dialog box, shown in Figure 4.20, by selecting Check Browser Compatibility, Settings.

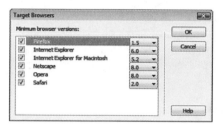

FIGURE 4.20
Select which browser definitions Dreamweaver uses to automatically check for errors.

Summary

Congratulations! You've created your first web page in Dreamweaver and learned a lot about formatting the page and text on the page. Many of the tasks described in this hour will become habitual to you with every web page you create, and you will be able to quickly move through the steps you've practiced here.

In this hour, you learned how to enter and import text into a web page. You set text properties, including headings, fonts, lists, and alignment. You were introduced to CSS, the language of presentation on the Web. You used a horizontal rule to separate the page into sections, and previewed your work in a browser.

Q&A

Q. Where can I learn more about CSS styles? They seem important.

A. CSS styles are important, and they are part of the movement in web development toward separating content (the words and images on the web page) from the presentation (font size, colors, and positioning). This separation is important because it is becoming more and more common to deliver content to various devices, such as PDAs (personal digital assistants), and to people with disabilities, such as impaired sight.

You learn much more about CSS styles in Hour 6.

Q. I indented a line of text by clicking the Indent button. I wanted it to act as a tab acts in my word processing program, but it seems to indent both the beginning and the end of the line. What's going on?

A. There is no easy way in HTML to tab as you do in your word processing program. The Indent button applies the < `<blockquote>` tag to the text. This tag, as you noticed, actually indents both the left and the right of the text. The block quote tag was originally designed for quotes in research-type documents. One way to indent text is to place your text in a table. You learn about tables in Hour 12, "Displaying Data in Tables." Another way to indent text is to use CSS-Positioning techniques that you learn about in Hour 13, "Using CSS for Positioning."

Workshop

Quiz

1. What button in the Property inspector do you select to nest a list?

2. By default, which heading size is largest on the screen: Heading 1 or Heading 6?

3. Why is Firefox a popular browser for web developers?

Quiz Answers

1. The Indent button nests one list within another.

2. Heading 1 is the largest size and Heading 6 is the smallest.

3. Firefox presents web pages virtually identically on Mac and Windows platforms and does an excellent job adhering to web standards.

Exercises

1. Try changing the alignment, shading, and size of a horizontal rule. Use a pixel size value and then use a percentage size value. Test each of your experiments by previewing the page in a web browser.

2. Experiment with creating lists. Create an ordered list, an unordered list, a definition list (see the Text tab of the Insert panel), and some nested lists. As you do this, look at the tag selector in the status bar and see which HTML tags are used. What do you think the `<li>` tag is for?

3. Select one of the color boxes in the Page Properties dialog box and set up a custom color. Use the eyedropper to pick a color from anywhere onscreen. You can even pick a color from another application you have open.

Adding Links: Hyperlinks, Anchors, and Mailto Links

Clicking a **hyperlink** allows the viewer to jump to another web page, jump to another section of the current web page, or launch an email message. A website is made up of a group of web pages, and hyperlinks enable viewers to navigate from page to page. Hyperlinks, in the simplest form, are the familiar underlined and colored (usually blue) text that you click. You can also make an image a hyperlink.

Hyperlinks help make the Web a powerful source of information. If you've surfed the Web at all, I'm sure you've clicked many, many hyperlinks. But hyperlinks can also make the Web confusing. Sometimes it is difficult to remember the exact path you took to find information, and that can make it difficult to get back to the information when you want to see it again.

A web address is called a **uniform resource locator (URL)**. You can link many types of files over the Web, but a browser displays only a few file types. A browser can display the supported image formats, HTML, player applications (such as Flash), and a few other specialized types of files. If a link leads to a file that the browser can't display (a .zip file, for example), the browser usually asks you whether you'd like to save the file to your hard drive.

Exploring Relative and Absolute Paths

Whenever you create a hyperlink to another web page in a web page, you have to enter a path to the file. You must also enter a path when you add an image to a web page. Dreamweaver helps make sure that these paths are

WHAT YOU'LL LEARN IN THIS HOUR:

▶ When to use relative and absolute paths

▶ How to create a hyperlink to another page within a website and a hyperlink to a page outside a website

▶ How to create hyperlinks within a page

▶ How to add a link that opens a preaddressed email message

correct, but it's important that you understand the difference between the three types of paths:

> ▶ An **absolute path** (also called a **full path**) is the full URL to a web page. The path points to the exact same file regardless of where the path is referenced from. This type of path always begins with the transfer protocol (HTTP, FTP, File, and so on).

> ▶ A **document-relative path** points to the location of a file in relationship to the page being viewed. The path points to the file relative to the file location of the file that contains the reference.

> ▶ A **site root–relative path** points to the location of a file in relationship to the root of the site. This type of path always begins with a forward slash (/).

You explore each of these types of paths in order to understand how to correctly reference files in hyperlinks.

Understanding Absolute Paths

An absolute path is a like a house address. If I gave the address of my house to someone who lives in another town, I would say, "I live at 123 Spruce, Columbus, Ohio 43210, USA." This is all the information that anyone would need to get to my exact location or to send me a letter (this isn't my real address, so if you really want to send me a letter, send it in care of the publisher!).

The link to Flora Photographs shown in Figure 5.1 is an absolute path. It contains the entire path to a file on the Internet. Because you have no control over this site, linking to it means that you need to check to see that the link remains valid. If the site moves in the future, you have to update the link.

A URL consists of up to five sections, as shown in Figure 5.2 and listed here:

> ▶ **Protocol**—The first part of the URL is the protocol. It is http for web pages to indicate Hypertext Transfer Protocol (HTTP). Sometimes you might want to link to a file on a File Transfer Protocol (FTP) server (another method of communicating over the Internet to move files to and from a server), using ftp instead of http as the protocol in the URL.

> ▶ **Domain Name**—The second part of the address is the domain name. This is the web server where the web page is located; for example, in

Link text

FIGURE 5.1
Entering an absolute path links to a specific web page.

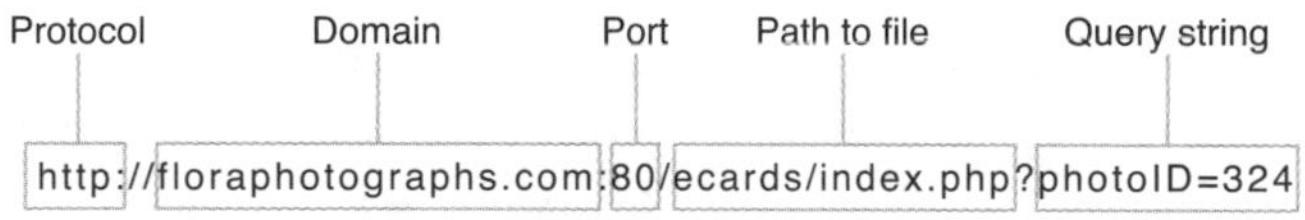

Absolute path

Protocol   Domain   Port   Path to file   Query string

`http://floraphotographs.com:80/ecards/index.php?photoID=324`

FIGURE 5.2
A URL consists of multiple sections. Every URL must contain a protocol, a domain name, and the complete path to a file.

Figure 5.2, the domain name is floraphotographs.com. A colon and two forward slashes (://) separate the protocol and the domain name.

▶ **Port**—An optional third part of a URL is the port. The default port for a web server is port 80. When you enter http as the protocol, port 80 is implied and doesn't usually need to be included. You might need to enter port information when entering addresses to specialized web applications that listen on a port other than port 80.

▶ **Path and filename**—The fourth part of the address is the path and filename. The path includes all directories and the filename. Most web pages end in .htm or .html. Other common file endings are .cgi for Common Gateway Interface; .asp for Active Server Pages; .jsp for JavaServer Pages; .aspx for ASP.NET files; .php for PHP pages; and .cfm for ColdFusion Markup Language.

> ▶ **Query string**—The filenames might be followed by an optional fifth part of a URL: a query string. A query string is added to a URL to send data to a script for processing. We explore query strings in Hour 21, "Sending and Reacting to Form Data."

You might see a URL that does not have a filename referenced at the end, such as http://www.adobe.com/devnet/mx/dreamweaver/. No specific file is referenced in this URL, but only the final directory is included (/dreamweaver/ in this case). This type of address works because the web server looks for a default page in the directory. Most web servers have a default page name that doesn't need to be explicitly entered at the end of the URL. Usually the default page name is index.html, index.htm, default.htm, default.html, or welcome.htm. On some servers, any of these names work. This functionality can be configured in web server software.

Default pages in the root of a site are often referred to as **home pages**. To create a home page for a website, ask your webmaster or web hosting service for the default page name for your web server. If you don't have a default page on your website and a visitor doesn't enter a filename at the end of the URL, that person might see all the contents of your directories instead of a web page. Or the user might get an error message!

Most browsers don't require that you enter the protocol into the browser's address box to go to a web page. The browsers assume that you want to use the HTTP protocol to access a web page. However, if you are surfing to an FTP file, you have to enter **ftp** as the protocol at the beginning of the URL. Even though browsers assume HTTP, you still need to preface absolute links entered into Dreamweaver with http://.

TIP

Browsing Directories

You can set whether browsing of directories and files is enabled on most web servers. If you use a hosting service and you cannot turn off directory browsing, make sure that you have a default web page in each directory. You don't want people to be able to browse around the file structure of your website.

Understanding Document-Relative Paths

Remember the house-address analogy I used in my absolute path discussion earlier? If I gave directions to my house to someone who knows my mom, I might tell them, "I live next door to my mom and always will." (I love my mom but I do not actually live next door to her!) The directions in this case are relative to my mom's location and assume that if my mom moves, I will move, too, so as to continue living next door to her. This is analogous to a document-relative path.

Within your own website, you usually use document-relative paths so that you can move your site anywhere and your links still work. While developing in Dreamweaver, you create a website on your local hard drive but eventually move the site to a web server. Document-relative paths work the same in both locations.

It's important to use document-relative paths instead of absolute paths in your website. If you have an absolute path to a file on your local drive, the link looks like the following:

```
file:///C¦/My Documents/first_page.html
```

This file, `first_page.html`, is on the C: drive in a directory called `My Documents`. If the creator of this web page previews this page in his browser, it works fine for him. So what's the problem? The reason it works fine for him is that he has the page available on his hard drive. But other people don't have access to his hard drive and will not be able to access the page.

Document-relative paths don't require a complete URL. The path to the linked file is expressed relative to the current document. You use this type of path when inserting images into a web page. You also use a document-relative path when creating a hyperlink to a web page within your website. Luckily, Dreamweaver saves the correct document-relative path after you save a web page.

The following are some examples of document-relative paths:

> ▶ When linking to a file that is in the same directory as your current file, you enter only the filename as the path. For instance, if the file `trees.html` in Figure 5.3 has a link to `flowers.html`, the path would simply be the filename because both files are in the same directory.

NOTE

Links Work with Other Files, Too

You don't have to limit your links to web pages. You can link to movies, word processing files (`.doc` files, for instance), PDF files, and audio files. The URLs work the same regardless of the content. Of course, the browser you use has to recognize the content type to display it properly. You learn more about the players necessary to play audio files and how to view PDF documents in Hour 10, "Adding Flash and Other Multimedia to a Web Page."

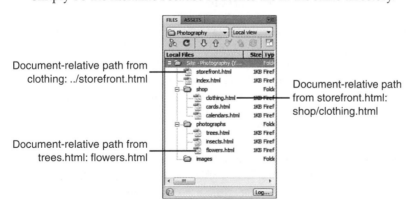

Document-relative path from clothing: ../storefront.html

Document-relative path from storefront.html: shop/clothing.html

Document-relative path from trees.html: flowers.html

FIGURE 5.3
Document-relative paths depend on the relative position of the files in the directory structure.

> ▶ To link to a file in a directory nested within the current file's directory, you enter the directory name and the filename as a path. For instance, if the `storefront.html` file in Figure 5.3 has a link to the

clothing.html file in the shop directory, the path is
shop/clothing.html.

▶ When linking to a file in a directory above the current directory
(called the **parent directory**), you enter ../ plus the filename as a
path. The ../ means go up to the next parent directory. For instance,
if the clothing.html file in Figure 5.3 has a link to the
storefront.html file in the site root, the path is
../storefront.html.

If you add links before first saving your web page, Dreamweaver inserts
them as absolute links; you might receive an error message warning you of
this when you add a link. It does this because it cannot calculate a relative
link until the file has been saved. After saving the file, Dreamweaver can
tell where your document is relative to all linked files and changes the links
to document-relative addresses. Accidentally using absolute paths is an
easy mistake to make. Dreamweaver looks out for you, however, and
attempts to correct these problems for you.

Understanding Site Root–Relative Paths

There is a third type of path, called **site root–relative**. Sticking with the
house analogy (and I might be stretching the boundaries of this analogy), a
site root–relative link is like two people living in the same city. As long as
they live in the same city, they can give directions to each house via a fa-
mous landmark in the middle of the city. Creating site root–relative links is
similar because each link references the site root.

In a site root–relative link, the path is relative to the root of the entire website. The **root** of the website is defined as the top level of a website, usually
where the site's main home page is located. Site root–relative linking is
used when many different sections of the website need to access a common
group of files, such as a corporate logo or common button images.

Site root–relative paths are not the best choice for beginning web development workers. The main difficulty occurs when you preview pages: You
might have references to site root–relative links that aren't available on
your local hard drive. In that case, you won't be able to preview your work
properly in a browser without loading it onto the server.

Adding a Hyperlink Within a Website

In this section, you create several new web pages and save them to your website. You can use these pages to practice linking by using document-relative paths.

TIP

Click Here...

It's generally bad form to explicitly reference a hyperlink by saying, "Click *here* to see our statistics." It's better to incorporate a hyperlink into a natural sentence, such as, "The *Q4 2009 statistics* show that sales increased by 32%." This hyperlink would open another web page showing the detail of the Q4 statistics. Ideally, hyperlinks seamlessly blend into the text of your documents.

Do the following to create a simple multipage structured website:

1. Create a new website that holds your files. Make sure that the site is selected. You will be creating "home," "products," "links," and "contact us" pages.

2. Select File, New to open the New Document dialog box.

3. Choose Blank Page, HTML, Layout <none>, as shown in Figure 5.4. We're interested only in creating links, so blank pages work just fine for this example.

Linking a Multipage Website

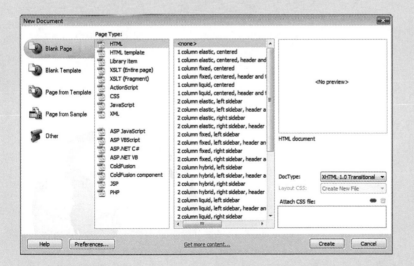

FIGURE 5.4
Create a new blank page for your links.

4. Select XHTML 1.0 Transitional from the DocType drop-down list.

▼ TRY IT YOURSELF

Linking a Multipage Website

continued

5. Click the Create button.

6. Immediately save and name the page `index.html`. This is the home page for the site.

7. Repeat steps 1–6 and create the following pages:

> ▶ `products.html`

> ▶ `contactus.html`

> ▶ `links.html`

Now you add hyperlinks so that you can navigate among the Products, Links, and Contact Us pages, as well as return to the Home page.

TRY IT YOURSELF   ▼

Adding Hyperlinks

To add hyperlinks, follow these steps:

1. Open the home page (`index.html`).

2. Enter the text you need for navigation, styling it as you please. A popular way to separate navigation elements is with a vertical pipe: Products | Links | Contact Us.

3. Select the text *Products* by either dragging your cursor over the letters or simply clicking within the text.

4. Select the Browse icon (which looks like a folder) next to the Link drop-down menu in the Property inspector (HTML mode). Select the filename `products.html`.

5. In the Select File dialog box, make sure that the Relative To drop-down menu at the bottom shows Document, making the link document-relative, as shown in Figure 5.5.

6. Click OK. Dreamweaver enters a relative address into the Link drop-down menu, as shown in Figure 5.6.

7. Repeat steps 1–6, linking each of the links to the other pages (`links.html` and `contactus.html`).

8. Your home page is now linked to the other pages in your site. You must now establish the links from the other content pages to the home page.

9. Open each of the linked pages (`links.html`, `contactus.html`, and `products.html`) and create breadcrumb text (see the following Note to learn about breadcrumbs) at the top of the page that resembles "Home > Products" (in `products.html`) and "Home > Contact Us" (in `contactus.html`) and so on.

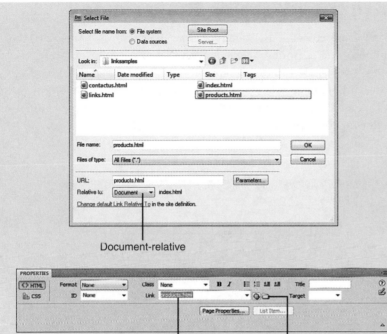

Document-relative

FIGURE 5.5
In the Dreamweaver Document window, select text that you want to become a hyperlink.

Document-relative link   Browse icon

FIGURE 5.6
When linking to a relative file within the same website, Dreamweaver enters the path to the file in the Property inspector's Link box.

10. Finally, revisit each of the pages (`products.html`, `contactus.html`, `links.html`), select the label Home, and use the linking tool to link back to the home page (`index.html`).

Each hyperlink appears as an underlined blue hyperlink in the Dreamweaver Document window. Preview the web page in the browser and click a link. You should jump to another page! When you click the HOME link, you should return to the home page.

NOTE

Breadcrumbs

Breadcrumbs are a navigation technique commonly used in web design. The term refers to a trail of links displayed horizontally across the top of the web page. The rightmost link displays the page that you are currently viewing, whereas the links to the left display the pages you used to get there. For instance, HOME > ABOUT US > JOBS shows a web page listing jobs that is in the About Us section of a website. The term *breadcrumbs* refers to the technique used by Hansel and Gretel to return home by leaving a trail of breadcrumbs to follow.

Setting Link Color Preferences

You set the link colors in the Page Properties dialog box just as you set the default text color in Hour 4, "Dealing with Words: Adding Text and Lists." Open the Page Properties dialog box (Modify, Page Properties) and select the Links (CSS) category, as shown in Figure 5.7. You set the link font and font size for all the links on the page at the top of the dialog box. You can set the following four options here:

Link colors

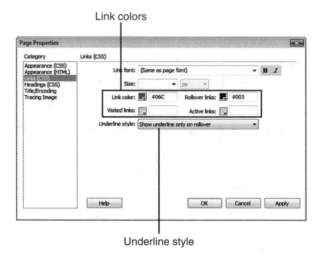

Underline style

- ▶ **Link Color**—The default color of all the links on the page.

- ▶ **Visited Links**—The color of a link after it has been visited by the browser.

- ▶ **Rollover Links**—The color of a link when the cursor is over the link.

- ▶ **Active Links**—The color of the link when the user is actively clicking the link (while the mouse button is down).

Use the color picker to add a link color, visited link color, rollover link color, and active link color. When you apply the changes to your web page, you should see all your links in the link color. When the viewer's browser has visited one of your links, the link appears in the visited link color. The viewer sees the active link color while the mouse is actively clicking the link. The link colors are defined for the entire page, so all your links will be the color you specify.

Dreamweaver sets the link colors by using CSS styles. You can also turn off the hyperlink underline by setting the Underline style. There are four choices: Always Underline, Never Underline, Show Underline Only on Rollover, and Hide Underline on Rollover. After you click the OK button, Dreamweaver saves the CSS describing how the links appear on the web page in the code of the page.

Organizing a Long Page by Using Named Anchors

Have you ever visited a web page on which you clicked a link and it took you to another part of the same web page? For instance, frequently asked questions (FAQs) often have hyperlinks at the top of the page listing the questions; when you click one of the hyperlinks, you jump farther down the page to the question's answer. That type of web page is created with **named anchors**. You use named anchors because sometimes it's less confusing to jump within the same web page than to jump to another web page.

To create a long page with named anchors, first add a named anchor to the location on the page where the user jumps. Then create a hyperlink that links to the named anchor. You can start creating a named anchor with a page that has multiple sections, such as the one shown in Figure 5.8.

TIP

The Hyperlink Underline

Many usability experts advise against removing the underline because it makes links on the page more difficult to identify. That said, this practice is becoming more acceptable and can look very nice when properly applied.

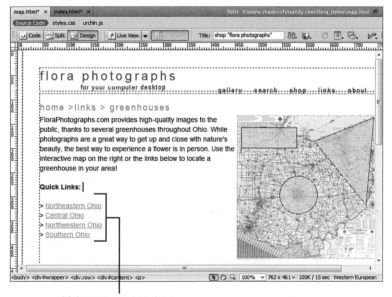

Links to named anchors

FIGURE 5.8
A website can have multiple sections, with a menu at the top of the page linking to the sections.

To create a page for this example, follow these steps:

1. Create a new blank web page by selecting File, New, Blank Page, HTML, <none>. Add several headings that are links to other parts of the page at the top of the page. Save your page.

2. Create sections relating to the headings at the top of the page. You can simply enter dummy text. You can use the "Greeking Machine" at http:/ /www.duckisland.com/greekmachine.asp to quickly generate nonsensical content.

3. Place the insertion point at the beginning of one of the sections. This is the area of the page to which users jump when they click the link to the named anchor.

4. Select Insert, Named Anchor or select Named Anchor in the Common category of the Insert panel. The Named Anchor dialog box, shown in Figure 5.9, appears.

FIGURE 5.9
After you select the Named Anchor command, give the anchor a name.

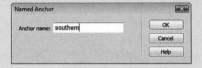

5. Name the anchor and then click OK.

6. Repeat steps 1–5, creating a named anchor and then creating a link to that anchor, until the web page is complete.

Understanding Invisible Elements

You might have received a message stating that you will not see a named anchor because it is invisible. Or you might have a small yellow symbol, which is an invisible element, appear in the Document window at the location where you inserted the named anchor; it is the visual representation of a named anchor.

Some objects that you insert into a web page aren't designed to be viewable. Because Dreamweaver is a WYSIWYG (what you see is what you get) design tool, Adobe had to design a way for you to view objects that are invisible on the web page. So how can you see invisible objects, such as named anchors and forms, on the page? You choose View, Invisible Elements.

You can also turn on or off invisible elements using the Visual Aids dropdown menu in the Document toolbar, shown in Figure 5.10. When the Invisible Elements feature is enabled, Dreamweaver displays the invisible elements such as the markers that represent named anchors (they look like little anchors on a gold shield). You can select the markers and view or edit the properties for the objects that they represent in the Property inspector.

Invisible element

Visual Aids menu

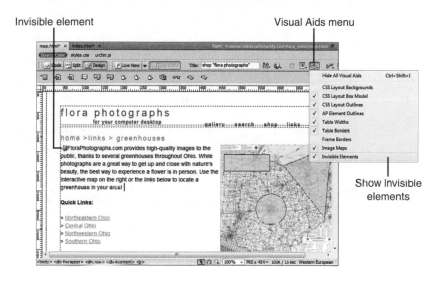

Show Invisible elements

FIGURE 5.10
You can turn invisible elements on and off using the Visual Aids drop-down menu.

Linking to a Named Anchor

You've created a named anchor, but that really isn't very useful unless you link something to it. Add a text link at the top of the page. It might not be obvious that your web page is jumping to the named anchor location unless you have enough content to scroll in the browser, so add some extra text or simply some blank space so that you can see the jumping effect when you test your page in the browser. To link to the new named anchor, follow these steps:

1. Select the text that links to the named anchor.

2. Enter the name of the named anchor, preceded by a pound sign (for example, **#schedules**) in the Link box, as shown in Figure 5.11.

You can also link to a named anchor in another file. To do so, you simply append the name of the named anchor to the filename, as demonstrated in the following line:

```
http://www.floraphotographs.com/gallery.html#flowers
```

FIGURE 5.11
You enter the name of a named anchor, preceded by a pound sign, to
create a link to it.

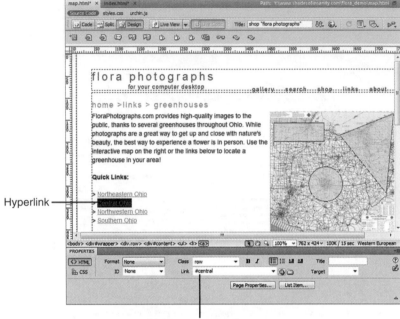

Link to named anchor

Using the Point-to-File Icon

There's a little cross-hair icon that you might have noticed on the Property
inspector: the Point-to-File icon. This tool enables you to create links visually. You can drag the Point-to-File icon, shown in Figure 5.12, to a named
anchor or a file located in the Files panel.

When the Point-to-File icon is dragged over a named anchor, the name of
the anchor appears in the Link box of the Property inspector. To select the
named anchor, simply release the mouse button while the Point-to-File icon
is over the named anchor. Using this icon is a nice way to link to objects or
files without having to know or type in the filenames. You can also use the
Point-to-File icon to link to files listed in your Files panel by dragging the
icon over to the panel and highlighting a particular file.

Adding a Mailto Link

It's nice to put a link in a web page to allow a viewer to send email. This
type of link is called a **mailto link**. The Dreamweaver Email Link object
helps you implement a mailto link. The user must have an email application set up to work with the browser for these links to work.

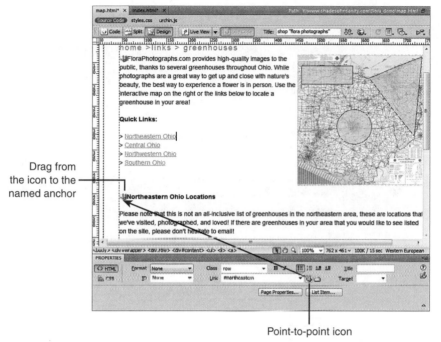

Drag from the icon to the named anchor

Point-to-point icon

To create a mailto link, select some text to be the link. Click the Email Link object (in the Common panel of the Insert panel), and the Email Link dialog box appears (see Figure 5.13). Enter the email address and click OK. The text looks like a hyperlink, but instead of linking to another page, it opens a preaddressed email message.

FIGURE 5.13
Use Dreamweaver's Email Link object to insert an email link.

Spammers troll the Internet for mailto links. If you use mailto links in your web pages, expect to get a lot of **spam**, or junk email, sent to the email address used in the mailto links.

An effective way to cut back on the spam is to use an email link obfuscator, such as the ASCII Email Obfuscator (http://digitalcolony.com/lab/maskemail/maskemailascii.aspx). These tools generate mailto links that work in your browser, but are very difficult for spammers to harvest. All you do is provide the email information you want to obfuscate, and the tool generates a piece of HTML code that you can paste into your page, as shown in Figure 5.14.

FIGURE 5.14
Cut down on spam by making your email links difficult to harvest.

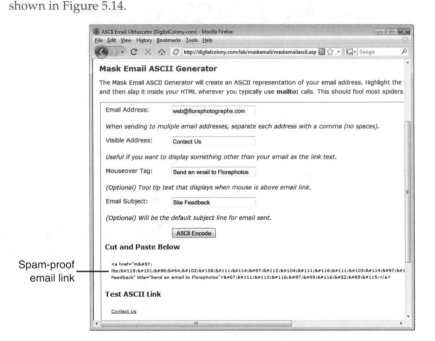

Spam-proof email link

Also available are several extensions, for example the Mail Spam Blocker object, that can hide an email address in mailto links from spammers. Hour 24, "Customizing Dreamweaver," describes how to download Dreamweaver extensions from the Adobe Exchange.

Summary

In this hour, you learned the difference between absolute, document-relative, and site root–relative paths. You created links to external websites and relative links to pages within a website. You learned how to insert a named anchor and then link to it, and you created a mailto link to allow a viewer to launch an email message directly from a web page.

Q&A

Q. The named anchor that I want to link to is low enough on the page that I can't see it onscreen. How can I use the Point-to-File tool to reach it?

A. If you drag the Point-to-File tool to either the top or the bottom of the Document window, the window scrolls. Hold the tool near the edge of the window until it has scrolled to the point where the named anchor is visible on the screen. Alternatively, first select the text that will be the hyperlink and then scroll down the page (carefully so as not to click on the window anywhere and deselect the text). When you see the named anchor, grab the Point-to-File icon and drag the tool to the anchor.

Q. I found a page on another site that I want to link to, but the URL is long. Do I have to retype it in Dreamweaver?

A. The easiest way to enter a lengthy URL is to copy the URL from the browser's address text box (by pressing Ctrl+C in Windows or Command+C on the Mac). You can then paste the URL into Dreamweaver's Link drop-down menu.

Q. Is there any way to add a subject line into an email link?

A. Yes! In the Dreamweaver Email Link dialog box, add a question mark immediately after the email address (no space) and then type `subject=` and the subject that you want to appear. You can also add some text for the body of the email message by typing `&body=`. You can also simply edit the link in the Property inspector's Link drop-down menu. The link looks like this:

```
mailto:jray@jraymail.com?subject=Sams Teach Yourself Adobe
Dreamweaver in 24 Hours&body=I'm interested in discussing this book.
```

Workshop

Quiz

1. How can you view a named anchor if it isn't currently visible onscreen?

2. What is the difference between a document-relative path and a site root–relative path?

3. When does a web page viewer see the active link color?

Quiz Answers

1. Select View, Visual Aids, Invisible Elements to see invisible element items.

2. A site root–relative path begins with a forward slash, whereas a document-relative path does not.

3. A web page viewer sees the active link color while actively clicking a hyperlink.

Exercises

1. Surf the Web for 10–15 minutes with your new awareness of the different types of links. When you place the cursor over a link, you can usually see the address of the link in the status bar of the browser. Look for links to named anchors, too.

2. Create a favorite links page, including links to all your favorite websites. You can either use the URL of the link as the text that displays or create a hyperlink out of a descriptive word or phrase. Hint: The major browsers have methods of exporting all your bookmarks or favorites. These methods can give you a huge head start on this exercise.

3. Create a frequently asked questions web page about a topic you understand well. List the questions at the top of the page as an unordered list. Repeat the question and add the answer at the bottom of the page, and then add a named anchor. Make the questions at the top of the page link to the appropriate named anchor below.

Formatting Web Pages Using Cascading Style Sheets

The Cascading Style Sheets (CSS) standard enables you to apply a visual property or group of visual properties to an object by applying a **style** to that object. You define and apply styles in Dreamweaver's CSS Styles panel or in the Page Properties dialog box, or by making settings (such as a font choice) in the CSS portion of the Inspector panel, as you did in Hour 4, "Dealing with Words: Adding Text and Lists." When thinking about styles, you probably think of creating and applying styles to text, which certainly is possible. However, you can use styles for positioning objects, creating borders, and lots more.

Modern web standards require the separation of the *presentation* of a web page (the way the page is displayed visually) from the *content* (the words and images that make up the page). Dreamweaver creates CSS styles to control the presentation of the HTML content. Separating the content from the presentation paves the way to supporting various operating systems, browsers, and devices; this also enables screen readers to easily navigate through web pages for people who are visually impaired.

One of the benefits of using styles is the capability to simultaneously update multiple objects that have the style applied to them. If you create a style for all the paragraph text on the page, say a style defined as Arial 14-pixel text, you can later change the style's font to Times Roman, and all the paragraph text instantly appears in the new font. You don't have to search through your entire page for updates but can simply make a change in one spot.

CSS is defined by the World Wide Web Consortium's (W3C) CSS specification (get more information at http://www.w3.org/Style/CSS). Your viewers must have a modern browser version to view styles and, luckily, most users of the Web do. Current browser statistics say that almost 98% of

WHAT YOU'LL LEARN IN THIS HOUR:

▶ How to create each of the four style types: classes, IDs, redefined HTML tags, and compound styles

▶ How to apply styles to elements in a web page

▶ How to create an external style sheet for an entire website

▶ How styles deal with conflicting and inherited properties

browsers are modern versions—that is, versions later than 4.0 (check out http://www.w3schools.com/browsers/browsers_stats.asp).

Dreamweaver displays a preview of how styles look in the browser. There are four types of CSS **rules**, also called CSS **styles**, and during this hour you learn how to create styles that use all four types. This hour covers the basics of CSS styles, how to use the CSS Styles panel, how to create styles that apply to text, and where to go for help. A subset of CSS deals with creating web page layouts, called **CSS-Positioning**, or **CSS-P**. Hour 13, "Using CSS for Positioning," shows you how to lay out your web pages. Then Hour 14, "Creating CSS for Mobile Devices and Printing," goes into more detail about using CSS to deliver content in various formats.

Styling Text with CSS

In Hour 4, we explored modifying text and introduced you to CSS styles that are created automatically by Dreamweaver when you modify text attributes in Dreamweaver's CSS Property inspector. The best way to create text styles for a website is to actually plan and think about what types of presentation are commonly used in the website. After planning these styles, you can implement them and apply them to the web pages in your site. Using the Property inspector isn't the best or most professional way to style text because it redefines similar styles over and over. There is no reason to have a dozen different heading styles if one or two well-thought-out styles suffice.

The CSS Styles panel lists styles that have been defined and are ready to be applied to objects on your web page. You use this panel extensively when creating new styles in Dreamweaver. This is where you find the buttons used to create new styles and where the style attributes of the styles display.

Figure 6.1 shows the CSS Styles panel in its primary mode. When you click the All button, the CSS Styles panel displays a list of all the styles available. Selecting one of the styles in the list at the top of the panel displays that style's attributes in the bottom of the panel.

When the Current button is clicked, as shown in Figure 6.2, the CSS Styles panel displays the attributes applied to whatever is currently selected in Dreamweaver's Document window. This view of the CSS Styles panel lists properties specific to one element instead of listing all the styles available in the web page.

TIP

Applying Styles in the Property Inspector

Any style that you define in the CSS Styles panel can be applied to a selection directly from the Class drop-down menu in the HTML Property inspector view, or the Targeted Rule drop-down menu within the CSS section of the Property inspector. Use the CSS Styles panel for defining, and the Property inspector for applying.

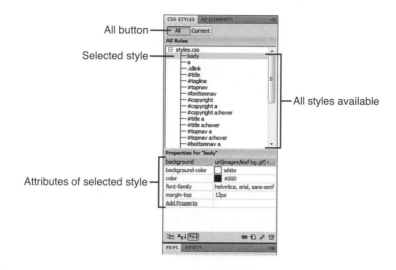

All button

Selected style

All styles available

Attributes of selected style

FIGURE 6.1
The CSS Styles panel is the command center for creating and viewing the attributes of styles.

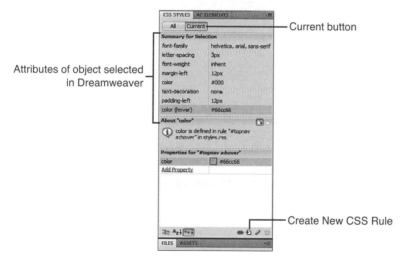

Current button

Attributes of object selected in Dreamweaver

Create New CSS Rule

FIGURE 6.2
The CSS Styles panel displays the properties applied to the currently selected object on the screen when the Current button is clicked.

Dreamweaver creates the CSS for you and displays it in the CSS Styles panel (and, of course, writes it in the code; but we get to more of that in Hour 7, "Looking Under the Hood: Exploring XHTML"). It's helpful to know a little bit about how the code behind CSS works. You saw a list of attributes in Figure 6.1, but what do they mean? A few definitions and an example should help you understand.

CSS styles are made up of **rules**. A rule contains two parts: a **selector** and a **declaration**. Here is an example:

```
h1 {font-size: 200%;}
```

TIP

The Art of Creating CSS

Creating CSS is often more an art than a science. How do you decide which type of selector is best for which type of content? What measurement units are best to use? A lot of these decisions depend on the website and what you are trying to accomplish. But experience and looking at the abundant examples available on the Web will help you make good decisions.

In this sample CSS rule, the selector is h1. This rule modifies the h1 (heading 1) tag and is a type of selector called an **element selector** that you explore in more depth later in this hour. The **declaration** is the part of the rule contained in curly brackets ({ }). The declaration in this rule sets the font-size property to 200%. This is the way all the attributes that you saw displayed in the CSS Styles panel are defined.

There are four basic types of selectors used to define CSS styles:

▶ **Class**—A type of selector, beginning with a period (.), which can be applied to any element in a web page via the class attribute. For instance, the class named .green would modify these elements: <p class="green"> and <hr class="green">.

▶ **Tag**—A redefined HTML tag, technically called a "type" selector.

▶ **ID**—A type of selector, beginning with a pound sign (#), that you apply by giving an element an id attribute with the same name as the id selector. For instance, the id selector named #mushroom would modify this element: <div id="mushroom">. An id selector can be applied only once per web page.

▶ **Compound**—A selector that uses a combination of the other selector types to choose content. For example, if you had a table with an ID of myTable and you wanted to style the rows within that table, you might use a compound ID and tag selector like this: #myTable tr.

You can create each of the four types of selectors with Dreamweaver. When you click the New CSS Rule button (shown in Figure 6.2) in the CSS Styles panel, it opens the New CSS Rule dialog box, shown in Figure 6.3. Before defining the properties of a new style, you have to assign it one of these types.

In the New CSS Rule dialog box, you use the Selector Type drop-down menu to choose one of the four types of selectors.

The rest of this hour introduces you to creating class, tag, and compound selectors. You explore creating id selectors in Hour 13 when you learn about using CSS for page layout.

Selector types

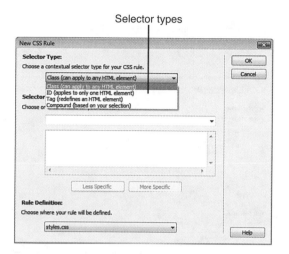

FIGURE 6.3
You select which of the three types of styles you are defining in the New CSS Rule dialog box.

Creating a Class Selector

The easiest type of selector to understand and to create is the class selector. You create a class and then you can apply it to elements in the web page. When creating the class, you can define properties such as the font, font size, and font color.

To create a class that modifies font attributes, follow these steps:

1. Click the New CSS Rule button from the CSS Styles panel (shown in Figure 6.2).

2. The New CSS Rule dialog box appears. Select the Class (Can Apply to Any HTML Element) option from the selector type drop-down menu.

3. Enter a name for the style in the Selector Name field. A class name must begin with a period. Dreamweaver enters the period for you if you forget to enter it.

4. Select This Document Only from the drop-down menu in the Rule Definition section, as shown in Figure 6.4. This places the style definition in the web page instead of in an external style sheet. We discuss external style sheets later this hour.

5. The CSS Rule Definition dialog box appears, as shown in Figure 6.5. The box opens with the Type category selected. In the Type category, select a font and font size from the appropriate drop-down menus. In addition, select a font color by using the color picker.

6. Click OK to save the style.

TRY IT YOURSELF ▼

Creating a Class Selector

CAUTION

Naming Classes

Don't use spaces or punctuation in style names (except for the period at the beginning!), and don't begin a style name with a number.

▼ TRY IT YOURSELF

Creating a Class Selector

continued

FIGURE 6.4
Begin defining a CSS style by selecting the type of style, giving it a
name, and indicating where it will
be stored.

FIGURE 6.5
The CSS Rule Definition dialog box
is where you set up the attributes
of a style.

TIP

Don't Blink

You might notice that Blink is
one of the attributes you can
define using CSS. Use it once to
have fun and get it out of your
system, throw away that web
page, and then never use it
again. Everyone finds blinking
text annoying and it's not
professional.

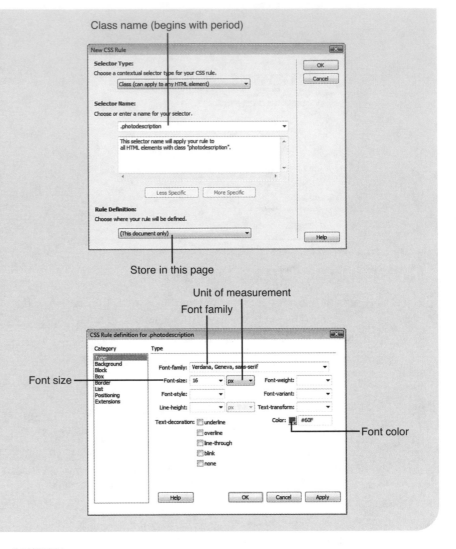

CAUTION

Class Selector Should Be Your Last Choice

Because the class selector is easy to create, understand, and apply, it tends to
be overused. Make sure you can't use an id or tag selector first before you create a class. For instance, don't create a class to make text blue and then apply it
to all your paragraphs. Instead, redefine the paragraph tag to have blue text using a tag selector or redefine the body tag so that all text on the page is blue.

The CSS Styles panel lists the new class (make sure that the All button is
clicked at the top of the CSS Styles panel). The top portion of the panel

shows the class selector you just created and the bottom displays its attributes. There are three different attribute display settings, shown in Figure 6.6. I prefer the Set Properties View, as displayed in the figure, because it shows only the properties contained in the style instead of every possible property.

Category view
List view
Set Properties view

FIGURE 6.6
You can set the way the properties are displayed in the lower half of the CSS Styles panel.

CAUTION

Apply Styles to the Correct Tag

Some style attributes work only when applied to certain tags. For instance, a style called bigcell with the cell padding values set in the Box category of the CSS Rule Definition dialog box does not have any effect on text because padding is not an attribute of text. Applying this style to an appropriate object, such as a table cell, does have an effect.

Applying a Class Selector

You select a block of text to apply your style to by dragging the cursor across it. You can also select other objects on the web page and apply the style. All the text in the object then appears as defined by the style. Apply the class to an object by first selecting the object and then selecting the class from the Class drop-down menu in the HTML Property inspector, as shown in Figure 6.7. Notice that the style names display in their respective fonts and font styles in the Style drop-down menu. Note that if you happen to be in the CSS section of the Property inspector, you can apply the style using the Targeted Rule drop-down menu instead.

Class selector

FIGURE 6.7
Select an object and then apply a class by using the Style drop-down menu in the HTML Property inspector or the Targeted Rule drop-down menu in the CSS portion of the Property inspector.

Removing a Class Selector

If you accidentally apply a style to an object, you can easily remove it. If you simply selected a few words instead of an entire block of text, Dreamweaver added a new tag around the text. Tags wrapped around the text are necessary because Dreamweaver needs to apply the class attribute to a tag. Instead of selecting the text by dragging the cursor over it, it's better to use

Dreamweaver's tag selector, shown in Figure 6.8. When you select the tag with the tag selector, Dreamweaver is smart enough to remove not only the class selector but also the extra tag that is now unnecessary.

FIGURE 6.8
The tag selector enables you to easily select and remove a class selector.

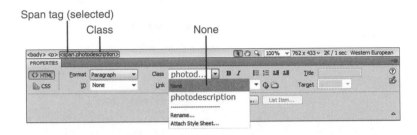

Span tag (selected)
Class   None

▼ TRY IT YOURSELF

Removing a Class Selector

To remove a style from text, do the following:

1. Select the object that has the unwanted style applied to it. Using the tag selector is highly recommended.

2. Select None from the Class drop-down menu in the HTML Property inspector, or select Remove Class from the CSS mode of the Property inspector.

Exploring Style Settings

The CSS Rule Definition dialog box has eight categories with numerous settings you can use to define a style. As you are defining a style, select the panels to gain access to the settings for each category. Any settings you do not need to set should be left alone. The following categories are available:

▶ **Type**—This category defines type attributes, such as font and font size. These style settings can be applied to text or to objects that contain text.

▶ **Background**—This category defines background attributes, such as color and image. These style settings can be applied to objects, such as layers and tables, where you can set a background.

▶ **Block**—This category defines type attributes for paragraphs.

▶ **Box**—This category defines attributes, such as margin size, which are applied to box objects, such as layers and tables.

▶ **Border**—This category defines attributes that are applied to objects that have borders, such as layers and tables.

▶ **List**—This category defines list attributes, such as bullet type.

▶ **Positioning**—This category defines layer attributes, such as visibility and z-index. See Hour 17, "Using Dynamic HTML and AP Divs," for an explanation of layers and layer attributes.

▶ **Extensions**—This category defines miscellaneous attributes that are either future enhancements or for Internet Explorer only.

Table 6.1 lists the style settings available in the various categories of the CSS Rule Definition dialog box.

TABLE 6.1   Style Settings in the CSS Rule Definition Dialog Box

Setting	Description
Type Category	
Font-family	Sets the font family.
Font-size	Sets the font size and unit of measurement.
Font-style	Specifies the font as normal, italic, or oblique.
Line-height	Sets the height of the line of text and the unit of measurement. This setting is traditionally called **leading**. It is added before the line.
Text-decoration	Adds an underline, an overline, or a line through the text. You can set the text decoration to blink, or remove the decoration by choosing None (to remove the underline on hyperlinks, for instance).
Font-weight	Adds an amount of boldface to text. Regular bold is equal to 700 and normal, nonbold text is equal to 400. Many browsers display only 400, 700, and 900.
Font-variant	Sets the small-caps variant on text. This displays with all the lowercase letters as uppercase letters but slightly smaller than the actual uppercase letters.

TABLE 6.1   Style Settings in the CSS Rule Definition Dialog Box

Setting	Description
Text-transform	Applies transformations to the text, such as capitalizing the first letter of each word or setting all the text to lowercase or uppercase.
Color	Sets the text color.
Background Category	
Background color	Sets a background color for an element. You can use this attribute to set the background color for the body (the entire web page), a table, a paragraph, or any element on the web page.
Background image	Sets a background image for an object.
Background repeat	Controls how the background image repeats. No Repeat displays the image only once; Repeat tiles the image horizontally and vertically; Repeat x tiles the image only horizontally; and Repeat y tiles the image only vertically.
Background attachment	Sets whether the background image scrolls with the content or is fixed in its original position.
Background position (X)	Specifies the initial horizontal position of the background image.
Background position (Y)	Specifies the initial vertical position of the background image.
Block Category	
Word-spacing	Controls the space around words. Negative values reduce the space between words, whereas positive values increase the space.
Letter-spacing	Adds space between letters. Negative values reduce the space between letters, whereas positive values increase the space.

TABLE 6.1   Style Settings in the CSS Rule Definition Dialog Box

Setting	Description
Vertical-align	Sets the alignment of the object relative to objects around it (these are the same alignment settings discussed in Hour 8, "Displaying Images").
Text-align	Aligns text within a container such as a paragraph, a table cell, or the entire web page. Choices are Left, Right, Center, and Justify.
Text-indent	Sets how far the first line is indented. Negative values create an outdent.
White-space	Sets how whitespace appears in an object; by default, whitespace is disregarded when HTML is displayed. Normal disregards whitespace, Pre displays all the whitespace, and Nowrap sets the text to wrap only when a break tag ( ) is encountered.
Display	Sets how and whether an element displays. The None setting, for instance, hides the item on the page; the Block setting displays the element with a line break before and after; and the Inline setting displays the element with no line breaks. The None setting is useful when you're creating dynamic style sheets—for instance, creating a style sheet for a printable web page that sets buttons and unnecessary interface elements to None so that they are not printed. You learn more about this subject in Hour 14.
Box Category	
Width	Sets the width of an element.
Height	Sets the height of an element.
Float	Sets whether the element floats beside other elements and whether it floats to the left or the right of the other element.

TABLE 6.1   Style Settings in the CSS Rule Definition Dialog Box

Setting	Description
Clear	Clears floating so that an element does not float around another element.
Padding	Sets the amount of space between the element and its border (or margin).
Margin	Sets the amount of space between the border of an element and other elements.
Border Category	
Style	Sets the style appearance of the borders. The choices are Dotted, Dashed, Solid, Double, Groove, Ridge, Inset, Outset, and None (for no border). If the browser doesn't support one of the styles, it displays as solid.
Width	Sets the border thickness. You can set the widths of the top, right, bottom, and left borders separately.
Color	Sets the border color. You can set the colors of the top, right, bottom, and left borders separately.
List Category	
List style type	Sets the appearance of the lists. The choices are Disc, Circle, Square, Decimal, Lower Roman, Upper Roman, Lower Alpha, Upper Alpha, and None.
List style image	Sets a custom image for bullets.
List style position	Sets whether the list content wraps to the indent (Outside) or to the margin (Inside).
Positioning Category	
Position	Sets how an element is positioned relative to the page. The choices are Relative (at the coordinates relative to its position on the page), Absolute (at the exact coordinates), and Static (at its place in the document flow).

TABLE 6.1   Style Settings in the CSS Rule Definition Dialog Box

Setting	Description
Width	Sets the width of a container.
Height	Sets the height of a container.
Visibility	Sets the container's visibility. The choices are Inherit, Visible, and Hidden. You learn more about the attributes in this category in Hour 17.
Z-Index	Sets the container's **z-index** (that is, its stacking order).
Overflow	Sets what happens when the container's contents exceed its size. The choices are Visible, Hidden, Scroll, and Auto.
Placement	Sets the left, top, width, and height attributes for a container. These settings enable a container to be placed at an exact pixel position on the web page. The pixel position can sometimes vary a bit from browser to browser.
Clip	Sets the top, bottom, left, and right clipping attributes for a container. Clipping defines how much of an element is visible.
Extensions Category	
Page-break-before	Forces a page break during printing, before the object. Be careful with this property; use it only when you absolutely must control where the page breaks for printing.
Page-break-after	Forces a page break during printing, after the object.
Cursor	Changes the cursor when it is placed over the object. This attribute is supported only in modern browsers and can confuse users, so use it only when it is necessary.

TABLE 6.1   Style Settings in the CSS Rule Definition Dialog Box

Setting	Description
Filter	Applies special effects, including page transitions, opacity, and blurs, to objects. The filters included with Dreamweaver are supported only in Internet Explorer 4.0 and later. See http://msdn.microsoft.com/en-us/library/ms532853.aspx for more information. You can hand-code filters for other browsers (check out http://www.mandarindesign.com/opacity.html).

Creating a Tag Selector

You can redefine HTML tags by creating tag selectors using CSS. You apply these styles by simply applying HTML tags as you normally would. By default, text formatted with the <h3> tag appears slightly larger than normal, in a bold font that is left-justified with one or two blank lines above and below. After you redefine the <h3> tag, any text with that tag applied to it immediately appears with the new CSS formatting.

▼ TRY IT YOURSELF

Redefining an HTML Tag

To create some text, make it a Heading 3, and modify its appearance with CSS:

1. Type some text in the Dreamweaver Document window.

2. Apply Heading 3 to the text by selecting Heading 3 from the Format drop-down menu in the Property inspector.

3. Create a new style by clicking the New CSS Rule button in the CSS Styles panel. The New CSS Rule dialog box appears.

4. Select Tag (Redefines an HTML Element) from the Selector Type drop-down menu, then select h3 from the Selector Name drop-down menu in the dialog box that appears, as shown in Figure 6.9.

5. Select This Document Only from the drop-down menu in the Rule Definition section, then click OK.

6. The CSS definition window appears.

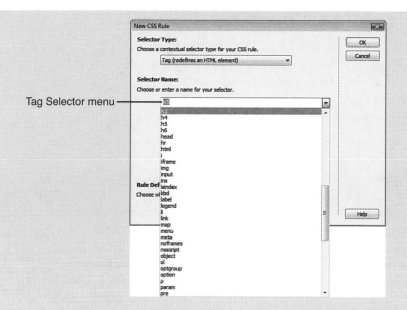

Tag Selector menu ⟶

FIGURE 6.9
The tag selector drop-down menu contains a list of all the HTML tags you can change by using CSS styles.

TIP

Select the Tag Before Creating a Style for It

When you select the tag in the Dreamweaver Document window before you click the New CSS Rule button, the tag drop-down menu automatically displays the tag so that you don't have to search for it in the list.

7. Select the Block category.

8. Select Center from the Text-align drop-down menu, as shown in Figure 6.10, and click the OK button.

9. Click OK and the h3 text in your web page should jump to center alignment.

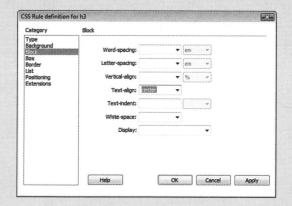

FIGURE 6.10
The Block category properties apply to blocks of text. You can change the default alignment of a text block in the Text-align drop-down menu.

Creating Compound Selectors

The final type of selector we look at in this hour is a compound selector. A compound selector isn't really a different type of selector, it is actually a combination of the different types of selectors we've already seen. A compound selector combines class, tag, and ID selectors to focus on specific elements more closely.

For example, assume that you have defined a class mySpecialTable to set your fonts and font styles perfectly for *some* tables in your site. You realize that you want the fonts used in the <th> headers in those tables to also have a certain styling, and you *don't* want that style applied to other tables. You can't redefine the <th> tag, because it applies to everything. Assigning a special new class to all of your mySpecialTable <th> elements is possible, but time-consuming and difficult to maintain. Wouldn't it be great if you could just target the <th> elements within your mySpecialTable class and nothing else? You can, with a compound selector! A compound selector of .mySpecialTable th applies a style to the <th> tags within an element that has the mySpecialTable style applied.

▼ TRY IT YOURSELF

Creating a Compound Selector

To create a compound selector, you can either start from scratch (if you know the selector elements you want to combine) or select an object within your document to inherit all the selectors currently applied to it. Let's see how this works:

1. If possible, select an object within a document—preferably an object that already has styles applied.

2. Create a new style by clicking the New CSS Rule button in the CSS Styles panel. The New CSS Rule dialog box appears.

3. Select Compound (Based on Your Selection) from the Selector Type drop-down menu.

4. If you have selected an object, you see the CSS selectors currently applied to that element, as shown in Figure 6.11. You can use these styles as your compound selector (meaning it selects only elements with these same styles), or you can modify them.

5. Use the Less Specific and More Specific buttons in the New CSS Rule dialog box to remove or add selector information to your compound selector to widen or narrow its focus, respectively. You can manually edit the selector as well.

6. Click OK to finish creating the compound selector and begin defining your new style.

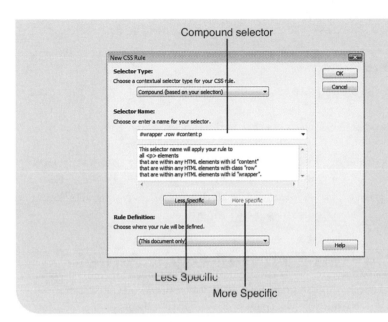

Editing Styles

Nobody's perfect! After you create a style, you might need to edit it. Oftentimes while I am working on a design, I modify styles many times before they are exactly the way I want them. Fortunately, it's easy to edit styles in Dreamweaver using the same CSS Rule Definition dialog box where you created the style.

To edit a CSS style, follow these steps:

1. Select one of the styles displayed in the CSS Styles panel.

2. Click the Edit Style button, shown in Figure 6.12, to reopen the CSS Rule Definition dialog box.

TRY IT YOURSELF ▼

Editing a Style

FIGURE 6.12
You can easily edit CSS styles by using the Edit Style button in the CSS Styles panel.

▼ TRY IT YOURSELF

Editing a Style
continued

3. Edit the style by selecting style categories and modifying properties.

4. Click the Apply button to see the modifications you've made displayed in the Document window.

5. When you are satisfied, click OK to save your changes.

You can also edit CSS style properties in the Properties pane in the bottom half of the CSS Styles panel. Simply click any of the properties in any of the three views (Category, List, or Add Property) to modify or add the property to the style definition. I think it is easier to edit a style using the Edit Style button. As you become more familiar with the properties available by using CSS, you might want to use these new property views to edit CSS styles.

Creating an External Style Sheet

Adding styles to a single web page is nice, but wouldn't it be great to apply the same styles to multiple web pages? External style sheets enable you to do this. Instead of defining styles in a single web page, you define all the styles in one text file and link that file to every web page. When you update a style in an external style sheet, the changes apply to every page which links to that style sheet.

Exporting Existing CSS Styles

When you've created some CSS styles in a web page, Dreamweaver makes it easy to move them to an external style sheet. You can move the existing styles to an external style sheet with the .css file extension and then easily link that sheet to the web page.

▼ TRY IT YOURSELF

Moving and Linking CSS Styles

Perform the following procedure to move and link CSS styles:

1. Select the styles to move in the CSS Styles panel, using Shift-click to select multiple styles.

2. Right-click the styles in the CSS Styles panel and select the Move CSS Rules command, as shown in Figure 6.13.

3. Select the radio button next to A New Style Sheet. Click OK.

4. Name the new external CSS file and click the Save button. Dreamweaver automatically moves the selected styles into this external file and links it to the current web page.

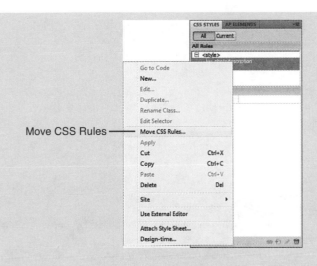

Move CSS Rules

FIGURE 6.13
Select the Move CSS Rules command to export styles to an external style sheet.

TIP

Where to Store the CSS?

Many web developers store external style sheets in a directory called CSS or Scripts.

5. Move additional styles by repeating steps 1 and 2, but selecting the existing external style sheet instead of creating another new one.

6. When all the styles in the CSS Styles panel are listed under the external style sheet, you can delete the embedded style sheet, the <style> heading. Select <style> and click the Delete button shown in Figure 6.14.

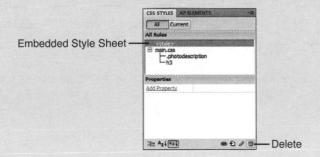

Embedded Style Sheet

Delete

FIGURE 6.14
Use the Delete button to remove the unnecessary embedded style sheet code.

Creating an External Style Sheet from Scratch

You might want to start with an external style sheet before you create any CSS styles. This is the way I usually work. Of course, you can have as many style sheets as you need, and I usually have at least two or three per website, each serving a different purpose. For instance, I usually have one external style sheet I name styles.css that holds all the page layout styles. (You learn more about using CSS for page layout in Hour 13.) I might also have an external style sheet named nav.css that has all the navigational styles affecting links and buttons. If the website is large, I might have different style sheets that are specific to unique parts of the site.

Creating and Linking a New External Style Sheet

To create and link to an external style sheet, follow these steps:

1. Select File, New, Blank Page, CSS.

2. Click the Create button.

3. Select File, Save and save the CSS file. You can name it `styles.css` and preferably save it in the directory in your website that holds CSS or script files (typically `css`).

4. Close the new CSS file and return to the web page that links to the new CSS file.

5. Click the Attach Style Sheet button in the CSS Style panel, shown in Figure 6.15.

FIGURE 6.15
The Attach Style Sheet button enables you to link a web page to an external style sheet.

Attach Style Sheet

6. Click the Browse button and select the new external style sheet.

7. Select the radio button next to Link.

8. Click the OK button.

TIP

Defining Styles in a New External Style Sheet

When you create a new style (using whatever means you want), one of the options in the Rule Definition drop-down menu is to define the rule in a new style sheet. This is a quick way to immediately create a new external style sheet when you go to create your first rule.

Saving CSS Styles in an External Style Sheet

After you create an external style sheet, you want to add any new CSS styles you create to the external style sheet instead of the web page. To add additional styles to the external style sheet, select the name of the external style sheet from the Rule Definition drop-down menu when you define a new style, as shown in Figure 6.16. As you create CSS styles, pay attention to where you save them. Of course, you can always use the Move CSS Rules command that you used earlier this hour if you need to move a style to a different location.

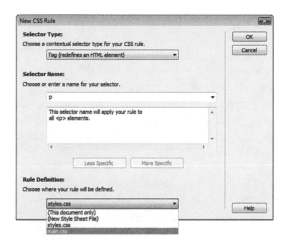

FIGURE 6.16
Select an external style sheet from the Rule Definition drop-down menu to create a new style in the external style sheet.

CSS and the Property Inspector

As I mentioned earlier, the CSS Styles panel is the best way to create and manipulate styles. It pulls all of your style controls together in one-easy-to-use interface. That said, many people prefer to work with the side panels hidden, and only the document and property inspector visible.

If this is your preferred way of working, never fear—CS4 gives you a quick and easy way to define a new style for selected content. To do this, just make sure that the CSS button is highlighted in the Property inspector. Then, when you find yourself in a position where you want to define a new style for a selection, choose New CSS Rule from the Targeted Rule pop-up menu, as shown in Figure 6.17.

Create New CSS Rule

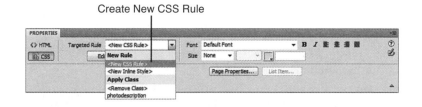

FIGURE 6.17
Create a new rule, straight from the Property inspector.

Now, click the Edit Rule button. This launches the CSS style editor that you know and love. After the style definition is complete, it is automatically applied to your selection in the document.

You can also use the Targeted Rule pop-up menu to select other CSS styles and apply them directly in your document.

Understanding the Cascade

The topic of this hour is *Cascading* Style Sheets, not just *Style Sheets*. *Cascading* refers to which styles and attributes take precedence over other styles. For instance, if you define paragraph text as the color blue by redefining the paragraph tag and then add a class selector to one of those paragraphs that defines the text as red, what color will the text appear in the browser? The rules of the cascade are what controls style precedence.

The CSS standard defines a complicated hierarchy of style precedence dependent on the style's proximity to the object it's applied to, the type of style, and when the style loads. You can simply remember a couple of rough rules of thumb to help you predict style precedence:

► The closer the style definition is to the object, the more dominant it is. Therefore, style properties defined in a web page override a conflicting style defined in an external style sheet.

► The type of selector matters. In order of most dominant to least dominant, the selector hierarchy is id selector, class selector, and tag selector. Properties contained in a redefined HTML tag will lose to conflicting properties defined in a class or id selector.

► A defined style is dominant over an inherited style.

The last rule of thumb in the list refers to *inheritance*, which is another element of the cascade. You'll understand more about nesting HTML tags after you've read Hour 7. Web pages consist of elements nested within other elements. For instance, everything in the page nests within the body tag. So if you redefine the body tag to have a certain background color, do all the tags (such as paragraphs, tables, and images) inherit that background color? CSS wouldn't be very useful if that happens.

TIP

Learning More About CSS

CSS is a complex topic that is very difficult for even seasoned web developers to grasp. As you work with the CSS tools, remember that Dreamweaver includes a CSS Reference (Window, Results, Reference) and a direct link to Adobe's CSS Forums (Help, CSS Advisor).

Some properties are inherited, though. When you use the Page Properties command (Modify, Page Properties) to modify the font and color of the text, those properties are inherited by all the text on the page. Dreamweaver enables you to view the cascade of properties applied to a selected element using the CSS Styles panel. Figure 6.18 shows the CSS Styles panel with the Show Cascade of Rules for Selected Tag button selected. In this example, some Heading 3 text is being edited on the page, and it inherits all the body attributes listed in Figure 6.16. The CSS Styles panel shown in Figure 6.19 shows that the Heading 3 text does not inherit the background image property from the body tag; notice that it is crossed out.

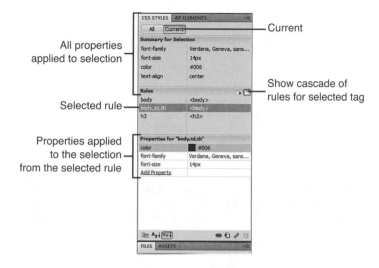

All properties applied to selection

Current

Show cascade of rules for selected tag

Selected rule

Properties applied to the selection from the selected rule

FIGURE 6.18
The CSS Styles panel can also display the cascade of styles applied to a certain element on the web page.

Selected rule

Property not inherited from body tag selector

FIGURE 6.19
Properties not inherited by the current element selected in the web page are shown with a line through them.

Summary

In this hour, you learned about CSS rule definition, properties, and how to create and apply classes and redefined HTML tags. You learned how to define CSS styles and how to edit them to make changes. You saw how Dreamweaver can store styles internally, in the same web page. And you made an external style sheet that allows the same styles to be used throughout an entire website.

Q&A

Q. Can I link more than one style sheet to a web page?

A. Yes. You can link as many style sheets to a web page as you'd like.

Q. How can I remove the underline from hyperlinks by using CSS styles?

A. Some people might advise against doing that, but if you feel your design demands it, it's your call. To remove the underline from hyperlinks, redefine the <a> (anchor) tag in the CSS Rule Definition dialog box. Set Decoration (in the Type category) to None. All the hyperlinks on the page are no longer underlined. You might want to define a:hover (select it from the Selector Name drop-down menu in the New CSS Rule dialog box) with an underline so that users can easily find the links when the cursor is placed over them.

Q. I know it's important to separate presentation from content, so how can I load a unique style sheet depending on the user's browser to optimize the user's experience of my web page?

A. In Hour 24, "Customizing Dreamweaver," you learn about **extensions** to Dreamweaver, files you can download and install into Dreamweaver to extend its capabilities. There are a couple of extensions on the Dreamweaver Exchange, Adobe's repository for extensions (http://www.adobe.com/exchange), which add code to your page that loads different style sheets, depending on the user's browser and version. You can download one of these extensions, install it into Dreamweaver, and then use the extension to accomplish your goal of using different style sheets depending on the user's browser.

Workshop

Quiz

1. What are the types of CSS style selectors?

2. What should you create in order to use the same styles for all the web pages in a website?

3. If you redefine the <h3> tag as red in an external style sheet and then redefine the <h3> tag as blue in the web page, what color will h3 text be in that page?

Quiz Answers

1. The types of CSS style selectors are classes, HTML tags, ID, and compound.

2. You need to create an external style sheet and link it to each page in your website.

3. The text will be blue because the internal style, the one defined in the page, is closer to the actual code and is dominant.

Exercises

1. Create a page as well as a class style that modifies text. Try applying this style to text in the page, table cells, layers, and other objects in the page. Save the style internally (choose the This Document Only setting) and then move the styles to an external style sheet. Practice adding additional styles to the external style sheet.

2. Create different definitions for the four hyperlink selectors: `a:active`, `a:hover`, `a:link`, and `a:visited`. You can find these selectors under the Selector Name drop-down menu when you select Compound from the New CSS Rule Selector Type menu. Create a unique style for each selector. Write down the four colors you used, and then figure out when each appears by previewing a link on the page with the style definitions in the browser.

Looking Under the Hood: Exploring XHTML

Even though Dreamweaver handles HTML (Hypertext Markup Language) behind the scenes, you might occasionally want to look at the code. Dreamweaver also makes the transition easier for those stoic HTML hand-coders who are making a move to a visual HTML development tool such as Dreamweaver. You won't be sorry! I'm a very competent HTML hand-coder, but I can get my work done much quicker by using Dreamweaver.

Dreamweaver offers several ways to access HTML code. During this hour, you explore the HTML-editing capabilities of Dreamweaver. You'll use Dreamweaver's capability to clean up the code produced when saving a Word document as HTML. You'll explore the numerous reference "books" available within Dreamweaver to look up tags and tag attributes. If you don't already know HTML, you'll find that viewing HTML while Dreamweaver creates it for you is a great way to learn.

By default, Dreamweaver creates a type of HTML called **XHTML**. This stands for *Extensible HTML*, which is a slightly stricter form of HTML based on XML. The code you see in Dreamweaver and in this book is XHTML, but I (and most other people) usually just call it HTML. In HTML, the code can have mistakes in it and still work, whereas XHTML has very specific rules that must be followed in order to work in all browsers:

- **XHTML elements (tags) must be lowercase**—Tags must be written in lowercase (`<p>Paragraph here</p>`) and not uppercase (`<P>Paragraph here</P>`).

- **XHTML elements must always be closed**—In HTML, some tags have a closing tag, such as `<p>` and `</p>`, while others you can use by themselves, like the break tag `<br>`. In XHTML, all tags must be closed, so the break tag is written as, `<br />` and is considered "self-closing."

WHAT YOU'LL LEARN IN THIS HOUR:

- ► How to structure the code in a web page

- ► How to use the Quick Tag Editor

- ► How to view and edit HTML code

- ► How to clean the HTML that Microsoft Word creates

- ► Which code reference books are available in Dreamweaver

▶ **XHTML elements must be properly nested**—In HTML, the browser renders the following code: `<strong><em>Bold and italic text</strong></em>`. But this code is not properly nested and XHTML requires it to look like this: `<strong><em>Bold and italic text</em></strong>`.

Exploring Code View

TIP

Large Monitor? Split Vertically?

If you have a large monitor, you may want to view your code beside your design view. You can switch to a vertically split view by choosing View, Split Vertically.

TIP

Toggle the Panels Off

You can toggle all the panels on and off by pressing the F4 key (or Window, Hide Panels). Pressing F4 again toggles the panels back on (or select Window, Show Panels). This is especially useful for Mac users whose floating panel version of Dreamweaver might cause the panels to block the view of the web page design or code.

The Dreamweaver Document window enables you to view a web page in either Design view or Code view. You can see the Design and Code views at the same time by clicking the Split Code View button in the Document toolbar (or choose View, Code and Design). When you do this, it's easy to pop back and forth between the views with just the click of a button. You'll probably do the majority of your web page development in Design view while occasionally looking at Code or Split Code view to tweak the code or troubleshoot a problem.

Create a new HTML page in Dreamweaver. Then click the Code View button in the toolbar to view the page's HTML code, as shown in Figure 7.1. The first line in the code is the **document type declaration**, which uses the `doctype` tag. In Hour 4, "Dealing with Words: Adding Text and Lists," you selected the document type in the Page Properties (Modify, Page Properties) dialog box. The document type declaration announces which version of HTML the page uses. Dreamweaver adds this line automatically, so you shouldn't have to worry about it. After the document type declaration, HTML tags enclose the entire web page.

By default, Dreamweaver creates web pages by adding XHTML tags. When you select an object from Dreamweaver's Insert panel, Dreamweaver inserts the appropriate tag or tags into your web pages. Tags have properties called **attributes** that Dreamweaver uses to fine-tune the way the object displays on the page. For instance, an image tag (`<img>`) has the `src` (source) attribute, which sets the files that the image tag displays. Most image tags also have height and width attributes that tell the browser the size of the image. These are just a few of the many attributes of an image tag. Here is an example of an image tag with standard attributes:

```
<img src="market.jpg" height="156" width="124"/>
```

FIGURE 7.1
Code view displays the basic code
of a new web page, including the
document type declaration, head,
and body.

Exploring the Head and Body of a Web Page

There are two main sections to a web page: the head and the body. You'll
see these sections in the code. Head tags surround the head, and body tags
surround the body. All the content visible in a web page is in the body. The
head of the document contains code that supports the web page. In the
head of the document, Dreamweaver automatically adds the `<title>` tag
because the document title is part of the head.

Right under the title, Dreamweaver inserts a meta tag, like this:

```
<meta http-equiv="Content-Type" content="text/html; charset=utf-8" />
```

This meta tag specifies the character set that the browser should use to display the page. The preceding example shows the Unicode (UTF-8) encoding that safely represents all character sets. This encoding setting should
work well for all languages, but you can set a different default character in
the New Document category of Preferences (select Edit, Preferences), as
shown in Figure 7.2. You can also set the default file extension in this Preferences category.

Dreamweaver places other content into the head of the page as you create
it. The head is where most JavaScript, CSS (Cascading Style Sheets) definitions, and other code resides. While in Design mode, if you'd like to see a
visual representation of the head content, select View, Head Content. You

FIGURE 7.2
You set the default character set and the default file extension in the New Document category of the Dreamweaver Preferences dialog box.

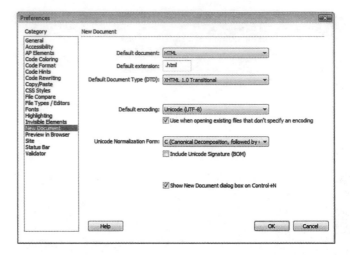

then see icons at the top of the Document window representing the elements in the head. When you click one of the icons, its properties appear in the Property inspector, as shown in Figure 7.3.

FIGURE 7.3
The elements in the head are represented by icons when you view the head content.

Head elements (title)

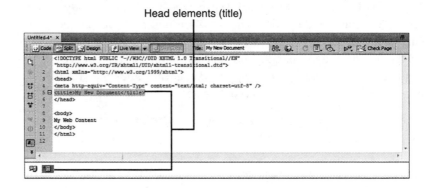

You display both Design view and Code view by clicking the middle button, the Split Code View button. While in Split Code view, place your cursor over the divider between the Design and Code views to modify the window sizes. Type some text into the Design view pane. The text is inserted into the body of the document. If you select an object in the Document window, the code for that object is highlighted in Code view. This is a quick way to get to the code of a selected object. If your web page is large, there might be a lot of HTML to go through, and it might not be easy to find the code for which you are looking. Try displaying only Design view. Highlight a single word that you typed. When you select Code view, the word is highlighted.

If you make changes to the code in Split Code view, Dreamweaver doesn't display the changes in the design portion of the window until you click the Refresh button in the Property inspector or click into the Design view.

Being able to see the changes made in code or design reflected in the corresponding view is a terrific time-saving feature of Dreamweaver, and an excellent way to learn more about the underlying HTML of complex web documents.

If you haven't yet tried editing HTML by hand, now is your chance to try! Follow these steps to test the Split Code view:

1. Create a new, empty HTML document.

2. Click the Split button to enter the Split Code view.

3. Look for the <body> tag in the document. Immediately after this tag is where you can start entering page content.

4. Type a few lines of text; then click the Refresh button (the circular arrow) in the document toolbar, or click directly in the design portion of the Document window.

5. Notice that the content you entered in the Code view is now accurately reflected in the Design view.

6. Repeat the process, but in reverse—editing the content in the Design view, then viewing the changes in the Code view.

7. Apply styles in the Design view and watch as the corresponding tags are shown in code.

Discovering Code View Options

When you are in Code view, the View Options menu, shown in Figure 7.4, enables you to change the way the code displays. These commands are also available from View, Code View Options.

The following options are available in the View Options menu:

▶ **Word Wrap**—Wraps the lines of code so that you can view it all without scrolling horizontally. This setting does not change the code; it simply displays it differently.

TIP

Coding by Hand? Use Live View!

If you find yourself frequently coding by hand in Split Code view, you may want to toggle on the Live View option in the Document window. This alters the design portion of your view so that it is a more accurate rendering of what a browser would show. Note that you won't be able to make any changes to the Design view until you toggle Live View back off.

FIGURE 7.4
The View Options menu enables
you to configure how code displays.

▶ **Line Numbers**—Displays line numbers in the left margin. This is helpful when you're troubleshooting errors or discussing code with colleagues.

▶ **Hidden Characters**—Shows paragraph and space characters in the code.

▶ **Highlight Invalid Code**—Turns on highlighting of invalid code that Dreamweaver doesn't understand.

▶ **Syntax Coloring**—Colors the code so that elements are easier to discern. You set the colors in the Code Coloring category of the Dreamweaver Preferences dialog box.

▶ **Auto Indent**—Adds an automatic indent so that your code is more readable. The indentation size is based on the settings in the Code Format category of the Preferences dialog box.

▶ **Syntax Error Alerts in Info Bar**—When a JavaScript error is encountered, this option displays an alert bar at the top of the Document window with the line that caused the error.

Discovering the Coding Toolbar

The Coding toolbar, shown in Figure 7.5, is visible only in the Code and Split Code views. The buttons in this toolbar run down the left side of the Document window. These buttons give you control over collapsing, expanding, and selecting the code within selected tags, along with highlighting invalid code, adding comments, indenting, applying formatting, and other commands.

TIP

Find and Fix Hand-Coding Mistakes!

If you select View Options, Highlight Invalid Code, Dreamweaver highlights all invalid tags in bright yellow in both the Code inspector and the Document window. When you select a highlighted tag, the Property inspector calls the tag invalid. It might give a reason why the tag is invalid and offer some direction on how to deal with it.

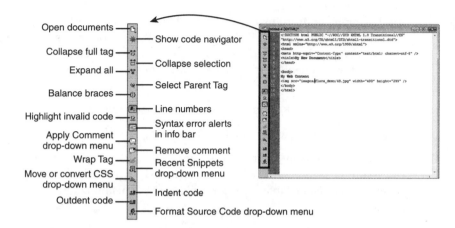

Open documents

Collapse full tag

Expand all

Balance braces

Highlight invalid code

Apply Comment
drop-down menu

Wrap Tag

Move or convert CSS
drop-down menu

Outdent code

Show code navigator

Collapse selection

Select Parent Tag

Line numbers

Syntax error alerts
in info bar

Remove comment

Recent Snippets
drop-down menu

Indent code

Format Source Code drop-down menu

FIGURE 7.5
The Coding toolbar is visible on the
left side of the Document window in
Code view.

The following options are available in the Coding toolbar:

▶ **Open Documents**—Lists all the documents currently open in
Dreamweaver.

▶ **Show Code Navigator** Allows you to quickly jump to a file linked
from your code (such as another web page or JavaScript file in your
site).

▶ **Collapse Full Tag**—Collapses all the code within the selected tag, displaying it as a single line with a small expand button to the left of it.

▶ **Collapse Selection**—Collapses all the selected code into a single line
with a small expand button to the left of it.

▶ **Expand All**—Expands all the currently collapsed code.

▶ **Select Parent Tag**—Selects the code within the parent tag of the currently selected tag. Continuing to click this button continues to move
up the tag hierarchy.

▶ **Balance Braces**—Checks your code to make sure that all tags, brackets, braces, and parentheses are balanced with two corresponding
characters.

▶ **Line Numbers**—Displays line numbers in the left margin.

▶ **Highlight Invalid Code**—Turns on highlighting of invalid code that
Dreamweaver doesn't understand.

▶ **Syntax Error Alerts in Info Bar**— Displays syntax errors (improperly
used code) in a status bar above the source code editing area.

▶ **Apply Comment drop-down menu**—Enables you to add various types of comments, such as HTML, CSS, or JavaScript comments, to the code. This is useful when you're troubleshooting problems in the code; simply comment out some code to see whether it is causing the problems.

▶ **Remove Comment**—Removes comments from the code.

▶ **Wrap Tag**—Wraps a tag around the selected tag.

▶ **Recent Snippets drop-down menu**—Gives you a list of code snippets you've used recently, along with a quick way to launch the Snippets panel. You learn more about snippets in Hour 24, "Customizing Dreamweaver."

▶ **Move or Convert CSS drop-down menu**—Enables you to convert **inline styles** (CSS styles defined in individual tags) to a CSS rule defined in the head of the document. There is also a command enabling you to move CSS rules to an external style sheet.

▶ **Indent Code**—Shifts the selected code to the right.

▶ **Outdent Code**—Shifts the selected code to the left.

▶ **Format Source Code drop-down menu**—Enables you to apply source formatting, which you learn more about later this hour.

Using the Code Inspector

If you have a dual monitor setup, you'll prefer to see the code in a separate window so that you can keep both Code and Design views open. You can use the Code inspector instead of Code view to accomplish this task. You launch the Code inspector by selecting Window, Code Inspector. The Code inspector is virtually identical to the Code view, but it launches in a separate window that you can drag to your other monitor if you are fortunate enough to work with dual monitors.

Using the Code Navigator

The Code Navigator is a useful, albeit strangely implemented, new feature of Dreamweaver CS4. As you work with your documents, you may notice a "ships wheel" icon appear as you hover your cursor over code or other linked elements. Clicking the icon opens the Code Navigator, shown in Figure 7.6.

The Code Navigator itself is just a small window that shows a link to another resource in your site, such as a JavaScript file. Clicking the link opens

Code navigator

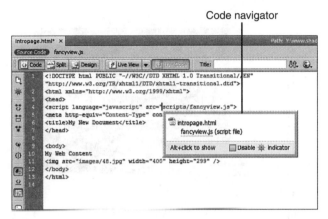

FIGURE 7.6
The wheel icon indicates that you can click to open the Code Navigator.

the file for editing. You can quickly invoke the Code Navigator using the Coding toolbar, or by simply Alt-clicking a linked file in Windows, or Command+Option-clicking on the Mac. If you find yourself needing to jump between linked files for quick edits, the Code Navigator is an indispensable tool.

Viewing and Editing HTML Tags by Using the Quick Tag Editor

Using Dreamweaver's Quick Tag Editor in Design view is often the quickest and easiest way to look at a single HTML tag and edit it. Remember, you can always tell which tag you have selected by looking at the tag selector at the bottom of the Document window. You can access the Quick Tag Editor in several ways:

▶ Click the Quick Tag Editor icon on the Property inspector, as shown in Figure 7.7.

▶ Select Modify, Quick Tag Editor.

TIP

Finding Your Linked Files

The Code Navigator is a useful means of finding your linked files, but you can also quickly open and edit JavaScript or other files by clicking the filenames that appear at the top of your content window. These filename "buttons" automatically appear in your document as you add links to other files in your site.

Quick Tag Editor icon

Quick Tag Editor

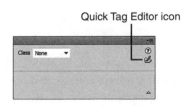
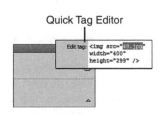

FIGURE 7.7
Click the Quick Tag Editor icon to view and edit the tag of the currently selected object.

▶ Right-click a tag in the tag selector and select the Quick Tag Editor command, as shown in Figure 7.8.

FIGURE 7.8
You can launch the Quick Tag Editor
directly from the tag selector.

Tag selector

When you click the Quick Tag Editor icon in the Property inspector, the tag pops up beside the Quick Tag Editor icon. When you open the Quick Tag Editor from the Modify menu, the tag pops up directly above the object in the Document window, and when you open it from the tag selector, it appears directly above the tag.

The Quick Tag Editor has three modes:

▶ **Edit Tag**—This mode enables you to edit the existing contents of a tag.

▶ **Wrap Tag**—This mode wraps another HTML tag around the selected tag.

▶ **Insert HTML**—This mode enables you to insert HTML in the web page.

When the Quick Tag Editor opens, you can toggle among the three modes by pressing Ctrl+T (Command+T on the Macintosh). The following sections explore each of the three modes.

Using the Edit Tag Mode

The Quick Tag Editor's Edit Tag mode enables you to edit the HTML of an existing tag and the tag's contents. To add attributes of the selected tag, place the insertion point at the end of the tag contents in the Quick Tag

Editor and add a space. The Tag drop-down menu appears, as shown in Figure 7.9, with attributes appropriate for the tag. You select an attribute from the list and then type in the value.

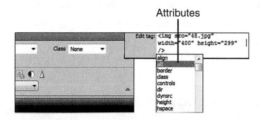

FIGURE 7.9
The Tag drop-down menu presents attributes appropriate for the current tag. It appears automatically after the delay that is set in the Preferences dialog box.

Using the Wrap Tag Mode

The Quick Tag Editor's Wrap Tag mode, shown in Figure 7.10, enables you to wrap HTML around the current selection. For instance, when you have text selected, you can wrap a hyperlink (`<a href></a>`) or text formatting (`<h1></h1>`) around the text. First select the tag you'd like to wrap by choosing it from a list. Dreamweaver adds the opening tag before the selection and the closing tag after the selection. You can also add attributes to the new tag.

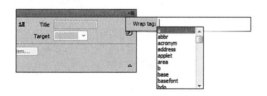

FIGURE 7.10
Wrap Tag mode wraps an HTML tag around the current selection.

Using the Insert HTML Mode

The Quick Tag Editor's Insert HTML mode, shown in Figure 7.11, shows a pair of empty tag angle brackets with the insertion point between them. You can enter text into the brackets, select from the Tag drop-down menu, or do both. Dreamweaver adds the closing tag automatically. The Quick Tag Editor starts in this mode when you do not have an object selected.

FIGURE 7.11
The Insert HTML mode in the Quick Tag Editor presents empty tag brackets. You can enter a tag name and attributes or select from the Tag drop-down menu.

Setting Code Preferences

You can set a number of preferences for viewing and maintaining code. The four categories in Dreamweaver preferences that apply to code—Code Coloring, Code Format, Code Hints, and Code Rewriting—help control the way Dreamweaver creates and displays the code in your web pages. If you are used to hand-coding your pages a certain way, don't complain about the way Dreamweaver formats it—change it!

Setting Code Color Preferences

Code view colors code according to the settings in the Dreamweaver Preferences dialog box. You must have syntax coloring turned on in the View Options menu to see colored code. Select the Code Coloring category in the Preferences dialog box. You select which type of code you'd like to edit here. Also, this category enables you to set the background color for Code view. Either enter a color in hexadecimal format or use the color picker to select a color.

Select the document type from the list and click the Edit Coloring Scheme button. The left side of the dialog box enables you to select a tag and then individually set a color for it on the right. To change a tag color, select a type of tag (HTML image tags are selected in Figure 7.12), and select a new text color or background color. You can also make the text bold, italic, or underlined.

FIGURE 7.12
You set the tag colors displayed in Code view in the Dreamweaver Preferences dialog box.

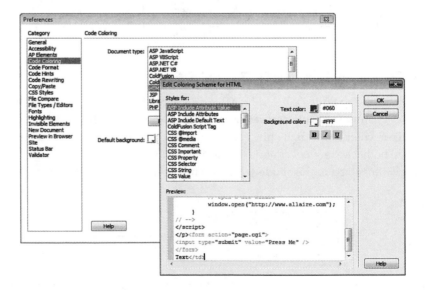

Setting Code Format Preferences

In the Code Format category of the Dreamweaver Preferences dialog box, shown in Figure 7.13, you set how Dreamweaver creates code. Dreamweaver indents code to make it easier to read. You can change the size of the indent in the Preferences dialog box. You can also select whether Dreamweaver should indent the code for tables and frames.

If automatic wrapping is selected, Dreamweaver wraps a line that exceeds the column width entered in the After field in the Code Format category. Some lines might end up a little longer than that number because Dreamweaver does not wrap lines that affect the appearance of the web page. You can also set the type of line break that Dreamweaver uses. This can affect the way your code looks in different operating systems.

Because the World Wide Web Consortium (W3C) standards specify lower case tags, it's a good idea to always use lowercase tags and attributes. (W3C is the group that develops web standards. Find out more at http://www. w3c.org.) By default, Dreamweaver uses lowercase for tags (the Default Tag Case setting) and attributes (the Default Attribute Case setting). In limited cases, you might want to override the case for tags or attributes. For instance, if you do not want Dreamweaver to change the tag or attribute case in an existing document, check the Override Case of Tags check box and the Override Case of Attributes check box, and Dreamweaver leaves the tag or attribute case as it exists.

TIP

Apply Dreamweaver Formatting to Any Page

The Code Format category options apply only to new documents created in Dreamweaver. However, you can select Commands, Apply Source Formatting to apply the same formatting to an existing web page. This is an easy way to tidy up the code in a web page when it gets messy.

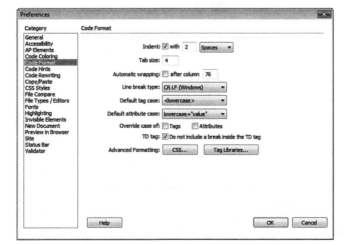

FIGURE 7.13
The Code Format category of the Dreamweaver Preferences dialog box enables you to set indentation, wrapping, and tag case.

Another setting is whether Dreamweaver should include a line break inside of TD (table data) tags. In some browsers, this can cause display problems, so leaving the setting Do Not Include a Break Inside the TD Tag is recommended.

The two final settings are advanced formatting rules for CSS and the HTML tag libraries. You can explore these options for controlling how Cascading Style Sheet code is generated and indented, as well as control the formatting for each individual tag within the HTML language! I recommend that you leave these settings as is, but if you want total control, this is where you'll find it.

Setting Code Hints Preferences

As you saw in the Quick Tag Editor examples earlier this hour, Dreamweaver drops down the **tag menu**, displaying tag attributes for you to pick from. This is called a **code hint** in Dreamweaver. You can set which code hints Dreamweaver displays in the Code Hints category of the Preferences dialog box, as shown in Figure 7.14. The Close Tags options determine when Dreamweaver automatically closes a tag for you—helping to ensure that you're creating correct code.

FIGURE 7.14
The Code Hints category enables you to set what Dreamweaver helps you with while you are coding.

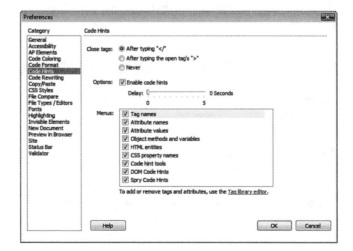

You can also set the time delay for Code Hints by dragging the Delay slider bar. Finally, you can go through the Menus list and deselect items you don't want Dreamweaver to provide hints for, such as tag names and attribute names.

Setting Code Rewriting Preferences

The code rewriting preferences, shown in Figure 7.15, set what changes Dreamweaver makes when it opens a web page. Dreamweaver automatically fixes certain code problems, but only if you want it to. If you turn off the Rewrite Code options in the Code Rewriting category, Dreamweaver still displays invalid code that you can fix yourself if you need to.

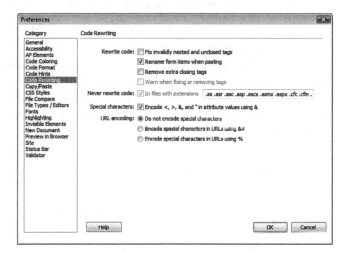

FIGURE 7.15
The Code Rewriting category of the Dreamweaver Preferences dialog box enables you to set the changes that Dreamweaver makes when it opens a web page.

Checking the Fix Invalidly Nested and Unclosed Tags check box tells Dreamweaver to rewrite tags that are invalidly nested. For instance, if you check this check box, Dreamweaver rewrites hello as hello (which is the correct way to write it). Dreamweaver also inserts missing closing tags, quotation marks, and closing angle brackets when this setting is checked. When you select the Remove Extra Closing Tags check box, Dreamweaver removes any stray closing tags left in the web page.

Cleaning Up HTML Created with Microsoft Word

It's very convenient while working in Word to save a document as a web page. Word does a great job of creating a web page that looks very similar to the Word document, and you can open and edit the web page in Word. The problem is that Word maintains a lot of extra code in the web page.

If you do not need to edit the web page in Word again and you'd like to put it on the Web, you can use Dreamweaver to clean up the extra code.

To save a Word document as a web page, select File, Save as Web Page. Word prompts you to name the document and adds the .htm file extension. The resulting page has a lot of extra code; Dreamweaver knows which code is extraneous and can delete it. It's fun to take note of the number of lines of code in the file before you run the Clean Up Word HTML command.

When you save a Word document as a web page, make sure that you close it before you work on it in Dreamweaver. Dreamweaver is not able to open and convert an HTML document that is open in Word. Apply the Clean Up Word HTML command to a web page that was created in Word and that you have opened in the Document window. To do this, select Commands, Clean Up Word HTML. This launches the Clean Up Word HTML dialog box, shown in Figure 7.16.

FIGURE 7.16
When you import a Word HTML document or select Clean Up Word HTML, the Clean Up Word HTML dialog box appears.

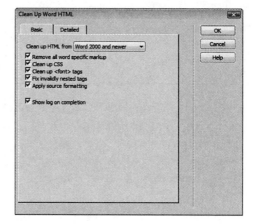

Dreamweaver should automatically detect which version of Word created the HTML file from tags that Word adds to the file. You can also choose the version manually by using the Clean Up HTML From drop-down menu in the Clean Up Word HTML dialog box. The Clean Up Word HTML dialog box has two tabs: Basic and Detailed. The Basic tab has the following options:

> ▶ **Remove All Word Specific Markup**—Removes all the unnecessary Extensible Markup Language (XML), meta tags, and link tags from the head section; it also removes all Word XML markup, all

conditional tags, all empty paragraphs, and all margins. You can select each of these options individually by using the settings on the Detailed tab.

▶ **Clean Up CSS**—Removes the extra CSS styles from the document. The styles removed are inline CSS styles, style attributes that begin with mso, non-CSS style declarations, CSS styles in table rows and cells, and unused styles. You can select these options individually by using the Detailed tab.

▶ **Clean Up <font> Tags**—Removes <font> tags.

▶ **Fix Invalidly Nested Tags**—Fixes the tags, particularly font markup tags that are in incorrect places.

▶ **Apply Source Formatting**—Applies the code formatting options that are set in the Code Format category in the Preferences dialog box.

▶ **Show Log on Completion**—Displays a dialog box with a summary of the changes that Dreamweaver made to the web page.

You can probably just accept the default options in the Basic tab of the Clean Up Word HTML dialog box and then click OK. Dreamweaver then cleans up the web page. Your selected options will appear the next time you select the Clean Up Word HTML command. Now your file is optimized for display on the Web. Make sure that you look in Code view and see how many lines of code were removed from the original.

Exploring References

Many useful references are built right into Dreamweaver and are accessible to you via the Reference panel, shown in Figure 7.17. Choose Window, References to display the Reference panel under the Property inspector. The Book drop-down menu enables you to choose from numerous reference books. Of special interest to you might be the O'Reilly CSS, HTML, and JavaScript references. Who needs to buy the book when these references are included in Dreamweaver? There's also UsableNet's Accessibility reference, which helps explain how to create websites that are accessible to people who have accessibility issues, such as visual impairment.

To use the references, you select tags, styles, or other objects from the drop-down menus and then read about the objects in the lower part of the panel.

FIGURE 7.17
The Reference panel provides access to several reference books, including books on CSS, HTML, and JavaScript.

Reference books

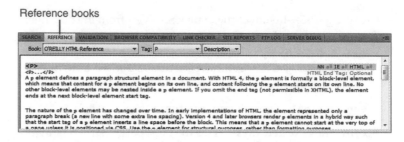

Notice that information on browser compatibility is located in the upper-right corner of the panel. When not using this panel, you might want to collapse it by double-clicking the panel title, or close it by right-clicking the panel or tab group title bar and choosing Close Tab Group.

Validating Your Code

Now that you have the tools to write HTML by hand, it's important that you also have the tools you need to write *valid* HTML code! Although Dreamweaver does what it can to help you as you go, it can't detect all problems as you code. To check your code for validity, you can use the Validate menu at the top of the Document window, as shown in Figure 7.18.

FIGURE 7.18
Choose to validate your current document or your entire site.

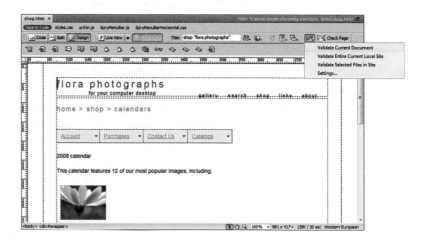

Dreamweaver takes a few seconds to scan your document, then displays a validation report that lists all the errors it has found, as demonstrated in Figure 7.19.

Validation result

FIGURE 7.19
Review the results of the code vali-dation process.

Step through the errors in the report; double-clicking a line opens and high-lights the problem in Code view.

Summary

In this hour, you learned how to use the Quick Tag Editor and Code view. You learned how to set preferences for HTML tag colors, formatting, and rewriting. You also learned how to use the Clean Up Word HTML com-mand. And you were introduced to the robust reference books that come with Dreamweaver and are available to help answer your questions about topics such as HTML, CSS, and JavaScript.

Q&A

Q. Which should I learn first, Dreamweaver or HTML?

A. It's helpful to know HTML when you are developing web pages. I think the best way to learn HTML is to first learn to use a web-editing pro-gram, such as Dreamweaver. Continue to view the code as you work and use the Reference panel (by selecting Window, Reference) to look up tags or attributes that you are curious about. If you still need grounding in HTML after that, get a good HTML reference book or take a class. A good book about HTML and XHTML is *Sams Teach Yourself HTML and CSS in 24 Hours*, 7th Edition (0-672-32841-0), by Dick Oliver and Michael Morrison.

Q. Can I add tag attributes that don't appear in the Tag drop-down menu? I saw a tag attribute listed on a website that isn't listed in Dreamweaver for that tag.

TIP

Working with Legacy Files?

The doctype tag specifies which version of HTML a document uses—and if it isn't set right, Dreamweaver might not be able to validate the file correctly. If you have to work with a number of legacy files that don't include a doctype, you can choose which default doctype Dreamweaver uses for its valida-tion using the Validator category of the applications preferences.

A. Yes. Use the Tag Library Editor by selecting Edit, Tag Libraries. This editor controls the attributes that appear in the Tag drop-down menu. Dreamweaver does not list every attribute that is available, so there might be one or two that you want to add.

Q. If I hand-code, how do I know which tags go in the head of the document and which go in the body?

A. It takes experience to understand where tags go in the HTML document, but luckily Dreamweaver puts the tags into the correct place for you. A rule of thumb is that everything you see on the web page belongs in the body of the document. And the supporting elements such as CSS, JavaScript, meta tags, and the title tag are all stored in the head of the HTML document.

Workshop

Quiz

1. How do you toggle through the three Quick Tag Editor modes?

2. What are the three ways to view a web page in Dreamweaver?

3. How do you preview a page without launching a web browser?

4. Does Dreamweaver automatically format the HTML that you type into Code view?

Quiz Answers

1. You toggle through the Quick Tag Editor's three modes by pressing Ctrl+T in Windows or Command+T on a Macintosh.

2. You can view a web page in Code view, Split Code view, or Design view in Dreamweaver.

3. Using the Live View renders your page in the same way as a web browser.

4. Dreamweaver can't indent your code for you, but you can format it by using the Apply Source Formatting command on any web page.

Exercises

1. Experiment with using the Quick Tag Editor modes. Pay attention to how the Property inspector reflects selecting attributes in the Quick Tag Editor. You can select many of the same attributes by using the Property inspector's radio buttons, text boxes, and check boxes.

2. Examine the HTML of a web page in Code view. First select an object in the Document window and then open Code view. Do you see the HTML for the selected object?

3. Create a new HTML page in Dreamweaver, open Code view, and briefly examine the general structure of the web page—head and body tags nested within HTML tags. Select and delete all the code and then re-create this general structure. What are the common tags that go into the head section of the page? Enter them. Notice that Dreamweaver enters closing tags for you if you've enabled that option in the Preferences dialog box. Press the spacebar after the tag name within any of the tags. What attributes are available for that tag? What happens when you select an attribute?

Displaying Images

The World Wide Web originally began as a text-based medium and the first browser displayed only text. Don't remember that? That is because the Web didn't become popular until it became visual. The key to making web pages visual, interesting, and attractive is including images. Access to digital images (with digital cameras, for instance) and fast Internet connections continues to increase, and this enables you to put more and better images into your web pages. However, an emphasis remains on optimizing image file sizes to make them as small as possible so that viewers are spending their time viewing your page, not waiting for it to download.

You can use images to create user interface elements such as buttons, borders, banners, titles, and backgrounds. Other images describe content: images of products, people, processes, and even pets. Images draw our attention and arouse our senses; they are an important element in websites. Images offer a powerful way to send a message. One drawing or photograph can communicate a huge amount of information.

Adding an Image to a Page

Images are separate files that appear within a web page. Because Dreamweaver is a WYSIWYG (what you see is what you get) program, it enables you to see web page images in the Dreamweaver Document window. Images are not actually part of the HTML; they remain separate files that the browser inserts when you view the web page.

WHAT YOU'LL LEARN IN THIS HOUR:

▶ How to insert an image into a web page and change its properties

▶ Which image formats can be used in a web page

▶ How to optimize images

▶ How to define an image map

▶ How to create a rollover image

Inserting an Image into a Web Page

FIGURE 8.1
The insertion point signals the placement of the image in the document.

To insert an image into a web page, follow these steps:

1. Place the cursor where you want to insert the image. You will see the insertion point blinking, as shown in Figure 8.1.

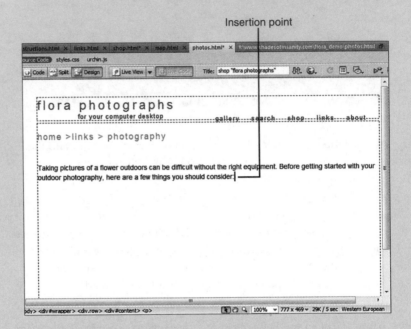

2. Select the Image element from the Images menu of the Insert panel (or select Insert, Image).

3. The Select Image Source dialog box appears.

   If you don't have any image files within the site you've defined in Dreamweaver, you can select a web image file from anywhere on your local drive and Dreamweaver prompts you to copy it into your site. A U.S. government site, such as NASA (http://www.nasa.gov/multimedia/downloads), is a good source of images and movies with which to practice.

4. Select an image file (see Figure 8.2), a file that ends with `.gif`, `.jpg`, or `.png`. A thumbnail image is visible on the right side of the dialog box if you enable the Preview Images check box.

   Notice the file size, the dimensions of the image, and the download time located under the thumbnail (by default, the download time is calculated at 128Kbps, but this can be changed in the Status Bar category of the Dreamweaver Preferences dialog box).

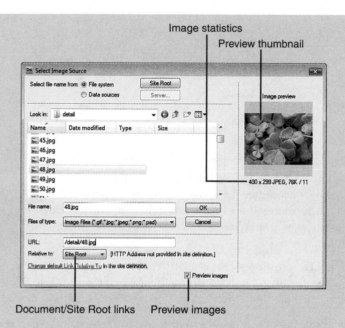

Image statistics

Preview thumbnail

Document/Site Root links   Preview images

FIGURE 8.2
The Select Image Source dialog
box enables you to preview an image before you select it.

NOTE

Would You Like to Copy the File?

If you select an image from outside your currently selected website, Dreamweaver asks whether you would like to copy the image to the current site. If you've added a default images folder in your site definition, Dreamweaver automatically copies the image into that directory if you agree. Otherwise, Dreamweaver asks you where you'd like to copy the image. This is an easy way to add images to your site.

5. Make sure that the link to the image is document-relative by selecting Document from the Relative To drop-down menu.

6. Click OK when you locate the correct image.

   If the Image Tag Accessibility Attributes dialog box appears, read ahead to learn how to fill in the attributes in this box and to find out more about accessibility.

Adding Alternative Text

Believe it or not, some people who might surf to your web pages are still using text-only browsers, such as Lynx. Others are stuck behind a very slow modem or Internet connection and have images turned off in their browsers. Other visitors are visually impaired and have text-to-speech (TTS) browsers that read the contents of web pages. For all these viewers, you should add alternative text to your images.

Accessibility is the technology of enabling people with disabilities to access content. People who are visually impaired—blind, for instance—obviously cannot see an image on a web page. Dreamweaver has several accessibility features turned on by default, including the Image Tag Accessibility Attributes dialog box, as shown in Figure 8.3, which popped up when you inserted the image earlier. This dialog box enables you to add two different types of accessibility information:

▶ **Alternate Text**—This is the description that a screen reader reads when it encounters the image reference. This should be fewer than 50 characters long. If the image is purely aesthetic (a border image, for instance), you should select <empty> from the Alternate Text drop-down menu.

▶ **Long Description**—This is a URL link to a web page describing the image. Use the Long Description field when the text describing the image is more than the 50 characters available for alternate text.

You can also enter or remove alternative text, sometimes called **alt text**, in the Alt drop-down menu in the Property inspector, as shown in Figure 8.4. Make the text descriptive of the image it represents. Don't enter something such as "London." A better choice would be "London's parliament building with a black taxi whizzing by." In some browsers, the alt text also pops up like a ToolTip when the viewer puts the cursor over an image. If the viewer has opted to turn images off in the browser, only the alt text displays, and the user can then decide whether to download the images associated with the web page.

FIGURE 8.4
Alt text is useful for viewers who don't have images in their browsers or are visually impaired.

No Alt text specified

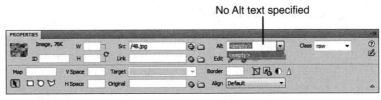

TIP

Missing Alt Text Reporting

You can run a Missing Alt Text report by selecting Site, Reports. This report shows you all the images that are missing alt text.

TTS browsers used by people who are visually impaired read the alt text description of an image to the user. When an image does not have the Alt attribute set, a TTS browser says the word *image*; listening to the browser say *image* over and over isn't very enjoyable! Some images on a web page are purely ornamental and do not add information to the page—a divider line, for instance. Select <empty> from the Alt drop-down menu (refer to Figure 8.4) in the Property inspector to add alt text with no content; this makes TTS browsers skip the image.

You can turn accessibility options on and off in Dreamweaver Preferences (Edit, Preferences). Select the Accessibility category and check the check boxes beside Form Objects, Frames, Media, and/or Images to have Dreamweaver automatically open a dialog box asking for the appropriate accessibility settings for each type of web page object. These settings force you to be conscious of the extra attributes required for screen readers.

Exploring Image Attributes

After you insert an image in a web page, the image is visible within Dreamweaver's document window, as shown in Figure 8.5. When you select the image, the Property inspector displays the image's properties. The Src (source) box displays the path to the image file. Notice that Dreamweaver automatically fills in the dimensions (width and height) of the image. Having the dimensions helps the browser by reserving the space for the image in the web page; if you don't reserve this space, the page content appears to move as the images load into it. The default unit of measure for width and height is pixels.

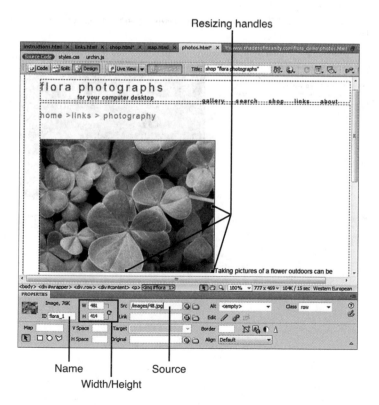

Resizing handles

Name

Width/Height

Source

> **NOTE**
>
> **Image Name Is Important for Rollover Images**
>
> Adding a name for an image becomes more important later this hour, when you explore rollover images. Each rollover image must have a unique name that you add in the Property inspector. The JavaScript that facilitates the rollover requires that each image have a name.

FIGURE 8.5
The Property inspector shows the image's width, height, and other properties.

Aligning an Image with Text

The Align drop-down menu in the Property inspector controls how objects that are located beside an image align with it. Align is very different from the text alignment settings you used in Hour 4, "Dealing with Words: Adding Text and Lists." You use the image alignment settings to align an image in the center, to the left, or to the right of whatever's next to the image. You use the Align drop-down menu to affect how *other* objects align with an image.

Change the Align setting of the image so that all the text appears to the left, beside the image. To do this, select Right from the Align drop-down menu in the Property inspector. Why select Right? The image is on the right, as shown in Figure 8.6. Remember that the Align options apply to the image, but affect other elements within its vicinity. Table 8.1 describes the alignment choices.

FIGURE 8.6
You can change how an image aligns with adjacent objects in the Align drop-down menu.

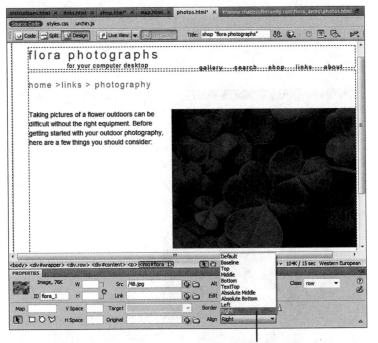

Alignment with other objects

TABLE 8.1   Image Alignment Options in the Property Inspector

Align Option	Description
Default	Normally the same as the Baseline option, but might depend on the browser.
Baseline	Aligns the bottom of the image with the bottom of the element.
Top	Aligns the image with the highest element. Additional lines of text wrap under the image.
Middle	Aligns the baseline of the text with the middle of the image. Additional lines of text wrap under the image.
Bottom	Aligns the baseline of the text at the bottom of the image.
TextTop	Aligns the image with the highest text (not the highest element, as with the Top option). Additional lines of text wrap under the image.
Absolute Middle	Aligns the middle of the image with the middle of the text beside it.
Absolute Bottom	Aligns the bottom of the highest element with the bottom of the image.
Left	Aligns the image to the left of other elements.
Right	Aligns the image to the right of other elements.

To increase the distance between the image and other page elements, adjust the V Space and H Space settings. *V* stands for vertical and *H* stands for horizontal. To add space to the right and left of an image, enter a value into the H Space text box, as shown in Figure 8.7. Changing the V Space setting means adding vertical space to both the top and the bottom of the image.

FIGURE 8.7
Put a value in the H Space text box
to increase the space to the right
and the left of the image. Put a
value in the V Space text box to increase the space above and below
the image.

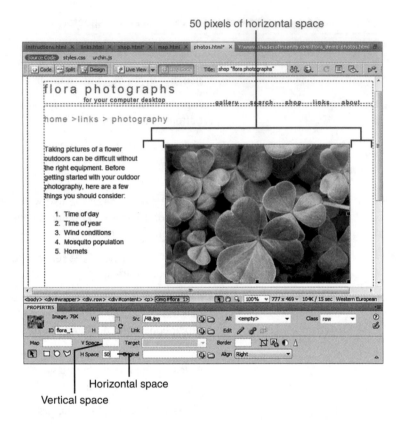

Exploring Image Flavors: GIF, JPEG, and PNG

All browsers support the two standard image formats, GIF (pronounced either "gif" or "jif") and JPEG (pronounced "j-peg"). There is also a newer
format, the Portable Networking Graphics (PNG—pronounced "ping") format. Here's a little more information about these three formats:

▶ **GIF**—This format is best for images that have blocks of continuous
color, usually drawings.

▶ **JPEG**—This format is best for photographic images and images that
do not have blocks of continuous color—for example, images that
contain color gradients.

▶ **PNG**—This format is a replacement for the GIF format. It supports alpha channels that are useful for transparency as well as the color quality of JPEGs. Although PNG is not as popular as the other two formats, its popularity is growing. This is the Adobe Fireworks native file format. If you have to be compatible with all the browser versions, including old browsers, avoid using PNGs.

The File Types/Editors category of the Preferences dialog box allows you to associate file extensions with different external programs, as shown in Figure 8.8. For example, you can associate the .gif, .jpg, and .png file extensions with Adobe Fireworks or Photoshop. When you select an image in Dreamweaver, you can click the Edit button to open the image file in Fireworks. You make your edits and save the file. To associate an editor with a file extension, select a file extension in the File Types/Editors category, click the plus button, and browse to the image editor program.

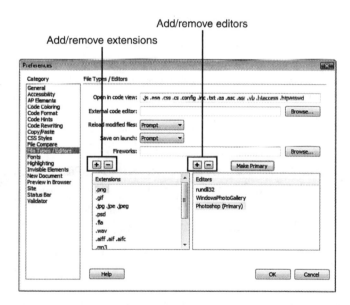

Add/remove extensions

Add/remove editors

FIGURE 8.8
The File Types/Editors category in the Dreamweaver Preferences dialog box configures other applications to edit linked files.

Editing Images Within Dreamweaver

Although you probably want to become somewhat familiar with a graphics tool to create and optimize images to put in your websites, Dreamweaver has a few basic image-editing capabilities to explore. Dreamweaver has the following image-editing tools built in:

▶ **Edit**—Opens the selected image in Fireworks for editing (of course, you must have Adobe Fireworks or another image-editing program defined in the Preferences dialog box for this command to work).

▶ **Edit Image Settings**—Opens Dreamweaver's Image Preview dialog box, where you can optimize and resave an image, modifying its properties so that it downloads more quickly.

▶ **Crop**—Lets you trim off unwanted portions of the image and saves the smaller file. This command works within Dreamweaver, enabling you to save the cropped image.

▶ **Resample**—This command becomes active after you've resized an image in Dreamweaver. It optimizes an image by adding or removing pixels in the image.

▶ **Brightness and Contrast**—Changes the brightness and contrast of an image to correct an image that is too bright or too dark.

▶ **Sharpen**—Sharpens a blurry image.

You can access all these image-editing commands from the Property inspector when you have an image selected, as shown in Figure 8.9. Make sure that you have a backup copy of any images you modify because Dreamweaver changes the actual image file.

> **CAUTION**
>
> **If You Accidentally Resize Images**
>
> If you accidentally resize an image in Dreamweaver, it's easy to return to the actual dimensions of the image. When you modify the image's dimensions, a small Refresh icon appears next to the width and height boxes in the Property inspector. Click this button to correct the image dimensions.

FIGURE 8.9
Dreamweaver has image-editing commands that enable you to jump out to an image-editing program or edit an image directly in Dreamweaver.

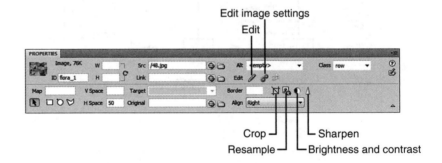

Optimizing Images for Use in a Web Page

Have you ever received an emailed photo that was so big you could hardly view it on your computer monitor? That's because the file was at a very high resolution (also known as dots per inch—dpi—or pixels per inch). Dreamweaver is able to optimize images so that they appear at a good size for a web page. You use the Dreamweaver Optimize feature to make sure that an image is the correct size and resolution.

Digital cameras are often set to take pictures at a high resolution. Although a higher resolution gives excellent results for printing, these files are much too large to display on a computer screen. Most photos that you scan or take with a digital camera have a resolution of 150 or 300 pixels per inch, but your monitor resolution is usually either 72 or 96 pixels per inch (the Mac and PC have different screen resolutions). You have to sample a photo down to the standard 72 or 96 pixels per inch before you use it in a web page.

You can get a photo from your digital camera, from a collection of clip art, or from a free source such as NASA (http://www.nasa.gov/multimedia/downloads). Most of the images you find on the Web have already been optimized, so you might want to look for a non-optimized file, using what is called a **source file** or **high-resolution file**. You need to optimize images to make sure that they aren't larger than they need to be because larger images mean longer downloads.

TIP

Keep Your Original Images, and Use Photoshop Smart Objects!

I usually create a directory called image_originals and make sure that I keep the original, unoptimized version of all images there. The image that displays in the web page is an optimized version of the original. That way I can always return to the original version if I need to make changes to the size or to how I've cropped the web page version of the image.

If you're a Photoshop user, you'll want to make use of Photoshop Smart Objects, which enable you to embed Photoshop files into your design, along with custom cropping and sizing information. You learn more about Photoshop Smart Objects in Hour 9, "Complementing Dreamweaver with Other Applications."

TIP

Optimization Wizards

Image-optimization software programs can help you decide which image format is the most efficient to use for a particular image. These programs also help you reduce the number of colors in an image and improve other factors that reduce file size and download time. Both Adobe Fireworks and ImageReady (comes with Photoshop) have wizard interfaces that walk you through optimizing an image.

To optimize an image in Dreamweaver, do the following:

1. Insert a non-optimized image into Dreamweaver (Insert, Image).

2. With the image selected in the Document window, click the Edit Image Settings button in the Property inspector.

3. The Image Preview dialog box opens, displaying a preview of the selected image on the right, as shown in Figure 8.10.

4. First make the image smaller by selecting the File tab. You can either scale the image file size down (never up!) or enter pixel values for a width (W) or height (H). Make sure that you enable the Constrain check box, as shown in Figure 8.11, so that the width and height automatically change proportionally to each other; you don't want to distort the image.

TRY IT YOURSELF ▼

Optimizing an Image in Dreamweaver

▼ TRY IT YOURSELF

Optimizing an Image in Dreamweaver

continued

FIGURE 8.10
The Image Preview dialog box displays a preview of the image along with information about the file's format and its download time.

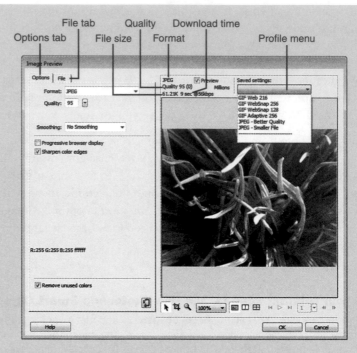

FIGURE 8.11
The File tab enables you to make changes to the size of the image.

TIP

Focus on Detail

While optimizing images, it's good practice to display the portion of the image that has the most detail in the preview. You can drag the image with your cursor until a portion of the image with a lot of detail is visible. This makes it easier to tell if you are optimizing while still keeping your image sharp and looking good.

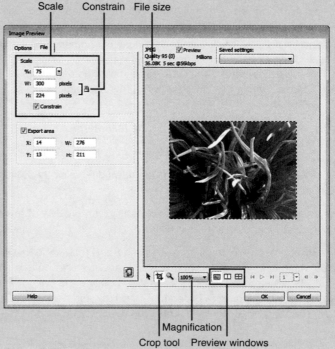

5. Next you should crop the image if necessary. This also shrinks the file size. Select the crop tool and reduce the magnification until the image edges are visible. Drag the edges inward to crop the image. Click the Pointer icon to finish cropping.

6. Select the Options tab and click the Four Preview Windows button. Now there are four different preview windows. Click one of the previews on the right to change its options on the left.

7. The Image Preview dialog box displays four versions of the image. I've set each of the previews to various JPEG quality settings: 80, 60, 40, and 20. The quality setting of 20 is unacceptable, whereas the others will probably be fine. For this image I would pick the preview with the 60 quality setting, shown in Figure 8.12.

TIP

Setting JPEG Quality

Depending on your original image, a JPEG quality setting somewhere between 50 and 80 usually works best. You need to examine the preview image while optimizing, paying attention to both the foreground and the background. Check that there aren't any areas of the image that are extremely **pixelated**, where the square pixels are visible to the user, making the image appear blocky and no longer realistic.

After you optimize a JPEG, you don't want to optimize it again. If you need to make a change to an image saved as a JPEG, open the original source file and reoptimize. If you are still working on the image in the graphics program and you haven't yet saved it, select File, Revert to return to the original, non-optimized version of the image.

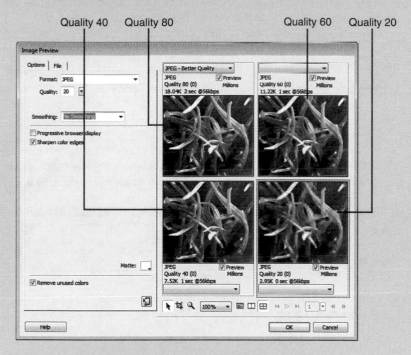

Quality 40   Quality 80   Quality 60   Quality 20

FIGURE 8.12
A display of four versions of JPEG quality enables you to balance image quality and file size.

8. When you are satisfied that your image is optimized, make sure that you have the correct version selected and click OK.

Your image is now optimized and incorporated into the web page!

Creating a Linked Image

The Link property appears in the Property inspector when you have text or an image selected. Linked images are common on the Web. When the user clicks a linked image, the browser loads the linked web page. With an image selected, you can add a hyperlink in the following ways:

▶ Type a URL into the Link box in the Property inspector.

▶ Browse for the linked page by selecting the Browse icon beside the Link box.

▶ Use the Point-to-File icon to link to a file. The Point-to-File icon enables you simply to drag the cursor over a file in the Files panel to create a link. You explored this tool in Hour 5, "Adding Links: Hyperlinks, Anchors, and Mailto Links."

▼ TRY IT YOURSELF

Creating a Linked Image

To create a linked image, follow these steps:

1. Select an image on your web page and make sure that the Property inspector is open.

2. Enter a URL in the Link box under the Src box.

3. All linked images have a blue border by default, just as a hyperlink is underlined with blue. Remove the border around the image by entering 0 in the Border text box in the Property inspector, as shown in Figure 8.13.

FIGURE 8.13
You set hyperlinks in the Link box in the Property inspector.

4. Preview the web page in a browser. When you click the image that has the hyperlink, your browser should go to the hyperlinked page.

Creating an Image Map

An **image map** is an image that has regions, called **hotspots**, defined as hyperlinks. When a viewer clicks a hotspot, it acts just like any other hyperlink. Instead of adding one hyperlink to an entire image, you can define a number of hotspots on different portions of an image. You can even create hotspots in different shapes.

Image maps are useful for presenting graphical menus that the viewer can click to select regions of a single image. For instance, you could create an image out of a picture of Europe and draw hotspots around the different countries. When viewers click a country's hotspot, they could jump to a web page with information about that country.

NOTE

An Image Map Doesn't Have to Be a Map

Although creating an image map out of an image of a physical map is useful, it's not the only application of image maps. You can also create an image map from a single image containing text that links to the major sections of the website. Or you could create an image map from an image with four quadrants, describing four steps in a process. Each quadrant could link to detailed information about that step in the process. There are many applications for image maps.

To create an image map, follow these steps:

1. Insert an image into a web page. The image must be selected for the image map tools to appear in the Property Inspector.

2. Give the map a name in the Map text box, as shown in Figure 8.14. The name has to be different from other map names in the page.

You set all the image properties for an image map just as you would an ordinary image. You can set the vertical space, horizontal space, alt text, border, and alignment.

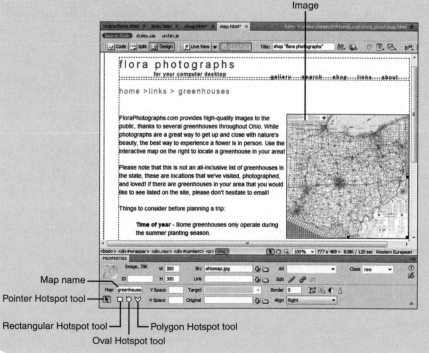

Map name
Pointer Hotspot tool
Rectangular Hotspot tool
Oval Hotspot tool
Polygon Hotspot tool

TRY IT YOURSELF ▼

Creating an Image Map

FIGURE 8.14
Give the image map a name and use the hotspot tools to draw hotspots within it.

TIP

Copying and Pasting Image Maps

If you copy and paste the image map into the same or another web page, all the image map properties come along, too.

Adding a Hotspot to an Image Map

When you select an image, you see four image map tools in the lower corner of the expanded Property inspector. These four tools define image map hotspots. The arrow is the Pointer Hotspot tool, which selects or moves the hotspots. There are three image map hotspot tools: One tool draws rectangles, one draws circles, and one draws polygons.

▼ TRY IT YOURSELF

Creating a Hotspot in an Image Map

To create a hotspot in an image map, follow these steps:

1. Select one of the hotspot tools.

2. Click and drag the crosshair cursor to make a rectangle or oval hotspot that is the dimensions of the hotspot you want to create. When using the Polygon Hotspot tool, continue to click the cursor to outline the hotspot and then click the Point Hotspot tool to finish.

3. With a newly drawn hotspot selected, type a URL in the Link box, as shown in Figure 8.15, or click the Browse icon to browse to a local web page. You can also link a hotspot to a named anchor by entering a pound sign followed by the anchor name.

4. Enter alternative text for the hotspot in the Alt text box.

FIGURE 8.15
Enter a URL to link a hotspot with another web page or a named anchor within the current page.

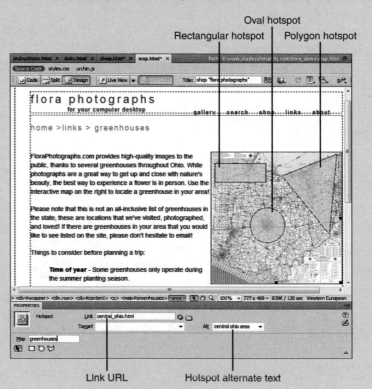

To move or adjust the size of the hotspot, you must first select the Pointer Hotspot tool. You can't use the other hotspot tools to adjust the hotspot or you will end up creating another hotspot. Click the hotspot with the Pointer Hotspot tool and either move the hotspot to another location or re-size the hotspot by using the resizing handles.

In the web page HTML, two sets of x and y coordinates define the hotspot (rectangular in this example). The upper-left corner of the rectangle is the first two coordinates in the code, and the lower-right corner of the rectangle is the last two coordinates. The coordinates are in pixels, and they are relative to the image, not to the web page. The HTML code for a rectangular area looks like this:

```
<area shape="rect" coords="127,143,251,291"
href="northwestern_ohio.html">
```

In this example, the upper-left corner of the rectangle is 127 pixels from the left of the image and 143 pixels from the top of the image, and the bottom-right corner of the rectangle is 251 pixels from the left of the image and 291 pixels from the top. It's nice to have a visual representation in Dreamweaver and not have to figure this out yourself, isn't it?

Three values define a circle: the circle's radius and the x and y coordinate values that define the circle's center. The HTML code defining a circular area looks like this:

```
<area shape="circle" coords="138,186,77" href="central_ohio.html">
```

A hotspot polygon is defined by as many x and y coordinates as you need, each representing one of the corner points. The HTML code for a sample polygon hotspot looks like this:

```
<area shape="poly"
coords=_"85,14,32,33,29,116,130,99,137,130,140,70,156,66,198,84"
href="northeastern_ohio.html">
```

Eight points define the polygon in this HTML, so there are eight pairs of x and y coordinates.

Aligning Hotspots

Dreamweaver has built-in alignment tools you can use to align the hotspots in an image map. First, you need to select the hotspots you want to align. To select multiple hotspots in an image map, hold down Shift as you click hotspots to add them to the selection. You can tell when hotspots are se-lected because you can see the resizing handles.

CAUTION

It's a Circle, Not an Oval

The Oval Hotspot tool always creates a perfect circle. I'm not sure why it's called the Oval Hotspot tool instead of the Cir-cle Hotspot tool! You can under-stand why you can have only a circle and not an oval when you see how Dreamweaver defines the circular hotspot coordinates.

Sometimes it is difficult to finely align hotspots with your mouse. You can use the arrow keys to move a hotspot or multiple hotspots one pixel at a time. The Arrange submenu under the Modify menu contains commands to align hotspots, as shown in Figure 8.16. You can align multiple hotspots on the left, right, top, or bottom. You can make multiple hotspots the same height by using the Make Same Height command, or the same width by using the Make Same Width command. To use these commands, select the hotspots you want to align or resize by shift-clicking or control-clicking to choose multiples, then pick your menu option.

FIGURE 8.16
The Modify menu's Arrange submenu has commands for aligning hotspots.

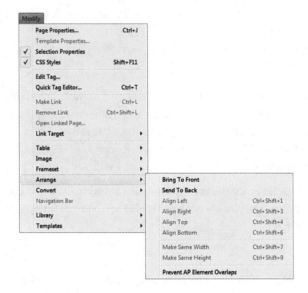

TIP

Which Hotspot Is Hot?

Hotspots can overlap each other. Whichever hotspot is on top (usually the one created first) will be the link triggered when the user clicks on the overlapping area. You might want to create overlapping hotspots on purpose as part of the design of an image map. For instance, you might use a circular hotspot over part of a rectangular hotspot. Alternatively, the overlapping might simply be a consequence of the limited shapes you have available to define the hotspots.

It's difficult to tell which hotspot is on top of another hotspot. If you've recently created the image map, you know which hotspot was created first and is therefore on top. You can manipulate the stacking order of the hotspots by selecting Modify, Arrange, Bring to Front or Send to Back. If a hotspot overlaps another and needs to be on top, select the Bring to Front command.

Creating Rollover Images

Our final image trick for today is creating a **rollover image**. A rollover image is one that swaps to another image when the viewer's cursor is over it. Rollovers add some dynamic action to an otherwise static image.

You need two image files with exactly the same dimensions in order to create a rollover image.

Dreamweaver makes it easy to implement rollover images by using the Rollover Image object. To create a rollover image, follow these steps:

1. Open an existing web page and place the insertion point where you want the rollover image to appear.

2. Select Rollover Image from the Images menu in the Insert panel or select Insert, Image Objects, Rollover Image. The Insert Rollover Image dialog box appears.

3. Type a name for the image in the Image Name text field.

4. Select both the original image file and the rollover image file by clicking the Browse buttons next to those options and selecting the image files.

5. Check the Preload Rollover Image check box if you'd like the rollover image downloaded into the viewer's browser cache. With a preloaded image, there is less chance that viewers will have to wait for the rollover image to download when they move the cursor over the image.

6. Add a link to the rollover Image by clicking the Browse button next to When Clicked, Go to URL, or type in the external URL or named anchor.

7. The Insert Rollover Image dialog box should look as shown in Figure 8.17. Click the OK button.

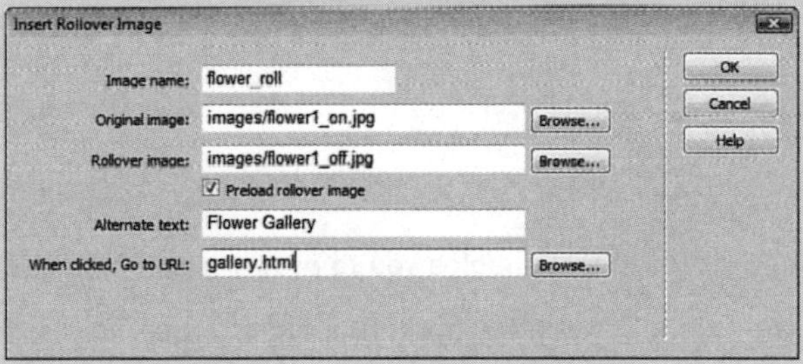

TRY IT YOURSELF ▼

Creating a Rollover Image

TIP

JavaScript and Rollover Images

Dreamweaver uses JavaScript, a popular web scripting language, to make a rollover image work. You don't have to add any code because Dreamweaver does it for you. Don't, however, delete the JavaScript that Dreamweaver puts into the head of the document. If you do, the rollover image no longer works.

FIGURE 8.17
A rollover image swaps one image for another when the viewer's cursor is over the image. You need to enter both image paths into the Insert Rollover Image dialog box.

Insert Rollover Image		
Image name:	flower_roll	OK
Original image:	images/flower1_on.jpg Browse...	Cancel
Rollover image:	images/flower1_off.jpg Browse...	Help
	☑ Preload rollover image	
Alternate text:	Flower Gallery	
When clicked, Go to URL:	gallery.html Browse...	

8. Save the page and preview it in the browser (File, Preview in Browser) to check the functionality of the rollover image.

Summary

In this hour, you learned how to insert an image into a web page and how to set a link, vertical and horizontal space, and alt text. You have learned how to change the size of an image border and edit the image by using an external editor. You have learned how to align an image in relationship to other elements beside it. You learned how to optimize an image to make it download quickly over the Internet. You have also learned how to create image maps and insert rollover images.

Q&A

Q. I have a lot of images from my digital camera that I'd like to display on a web page and share with other people. Can Dreamweaver help me with this?

A. Use Dreamweaver's Web Photo Album (Command, Create Web Photo Album) if you also have Fireworks installed. This command automatically optimizes all the images in a folder and displays them on a web page.

Q. What should I do if accidentally stretch an image?

A. It's easy to restore the original dimensions of an image by selecting the image and clicking the Refresh button that appears next to the width and height text fields in the Property inspector after you've resized an image.

Q. Every time I use the Polygon Hotspot tool, I make a mess of it. I get extra points in the wrong section of the image map. What am I doing wrong?

A. When you use the Polygon Hotspot tool to create a hotspot, remember to click, click, click around the edges of the hotspot border. After you have defined the border, do not click the image again. Instead, immediately select the Pointer Hotspot tool or double-click on the hotspot to signal Dreamweaver that you are finished creating the polygon hotspot.

Workshop

Quiz

1. Which image map tool enables you to draw irregular shapes?

2. What are the three widely supported image formats for web pages?

3. If you want an image on the left and text beside it on the right, what Align value would you give the image?

Quiz Answers

1. The Polygon Hotspot tool enables you to draw irregular shapes.

2. The three widely supported image formats for web pages are GIF, JPEG, and PNG.

3. You give the image the Align value Left.

Exercises

1. Insert an image into a new page. Resize it by using the resizing handles. Click the Refresh button. Resize the image by holding down Shift while dragging the corner resizing handle. Click the Refresh button. Change the width and height dimensions by entering different values into the W and H boxes in the Property inspector.

2. Add alt text to an image. Open your browser, select the browser preferences or Internet options, and turn off viewing of images. The command for this might be called Show Pictures or Automatically Load Images. Return to Dreamweaver and preview the web page in that browser so that you can see how the alt text looks.

3. Insert an image into a web page and experiment with Dreamweaver's image-editing tools. Try using sharpen, cropping, and brightness/contrast. Then resize the image and try image resampling. Does Dreamweaver actually change the original files? Be careful not to make any permanent changes to your files.

4. Try creating rollover images within a sample page. In general, rollover images should be small (such as images used for navigation), since two images are used to create the effect. To test this functionality, I recommend selecting an image, scaling it to a reasonable (100–200px) size, and then using image-editing software to create a black-and-white or hue-shifted version to represent the rollover "on" state.

Complementing Dreamweaver with Other Applications

In this hour, you explore some of the applications that complement your work in Dreamweaver. Several of the applications you explore are often bundled with Dreamweaver, and you might already have them installed. The other programs are part of Microsoft Office and are in common use, so you probably either have them or have some equivalent application.

Web pages use many types of media. Almost all web pages, for instance, at least contain images. We look at Adobe Photoshop, a very popular image creation program from Adobe, the company that makes Dreamweaver. You can use Photoshop to both create and optimize the images you use in your web pages.

You might also want to import tables of text from Microsoft Excel. This is very easy to do in Dreamweaver. You can store and manipulate your data in Excel but format it for the Web in Dreamweaver. I prefer doing this instead of using Excel's Save for the Web feature because it gives me more control over the look of the page in addition to creating more streamlined HTML.

Acquainting Yourself with Photoshop

Many people who purchase Dreamweaver buy it in a software bundle that includes Photoshop, so you'll create the examples in this hour using Photoshop. This hour simply touches on some of the important elements and describes a few image manipulation techniques. There is much more to learn about Photoshop than is possible in this hour.

Photoshop is an image optimization and creation tool that is an excellent addition to your web development toolbox. You have to create and

WHAT YOU'LL LEARN IN THIS HOUR:

- ▶ How to modify images in Photoshop
- ▶ How to import a Photoshop Smart Object into Dreamweaver
- ▶ How to create an image with text and shapes
- ▶ How to slice an image into smaller pieces
- ▶ How to import Excel data into a Dreamweaver table

optimize the images that you use in your websites, and Photoshop enables you to quickly create images that have cool effects such as bevels, glows, and drop shadows. If you do not have Photoshop, you can download a trial version at http://www.adobe.com/downloads.

The next portion of the hour demonstrates how to create and optimize images with Photoshop, but many of the techniques described here are achievable in other image-editing programs as well. Although the command names might differ in other image-editing programs, such as Adobe Fireworks, the techniques are similar. I used Photoshop for the examples because it is such a popular program and many, many web developers already have it.

The Photoshop Document window, shown in Figure 9.1, contains a Tools panel on the left, the Options bar at the top, and Tab groups on the right. You can open an existing image in Photoshop or create a new one from scratch.

FIGURE 9.1
Photoshop's integrated interface is similar to Dreamweaver's interface.

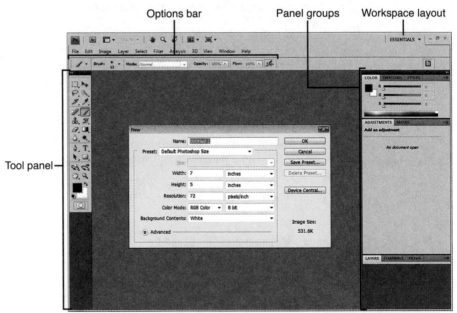

Modifying Images for Use in a Web Page

First we explore a few Photoshop features that are commonly used on web page images. To practice using these features, open an image, preferably a photograph, in Photoshop. You can get a photo from your digital camera,

from a collection of clip art, or from a free source such as NASA (http:/
/www.nasa.gov/multimedia/downloads). Here are a few of the common
edits I make to images for use in web pages:

- ▶ Rotate an image clockwise or counterclockwise

- ▶ Crop an image

- ▶ Change the size (that is, the number of pixels) of an image

- ▶ Feather an image's edges to blend with the background

- ▶ Revert to the original image

Rotating, Cropping, and Changing the Size of an Image

We try all of these modifications and then revert to the original image at
the end.

TRY IT YOURSELF ▼

Practicing Basic Photoshop Image Manipulation

To rotate, crop, and change the size of an image in Photoshop, do the
following:

1. With Photoshop open, open your selected image file (File, Open).

2. To rotate an image select Image, Image Rotation, as shown in Figure
   9.2, and then select the appropriate rotate command. These are the
   available commands:

   180°—Rotates the image a half turn.

   90° CW—Rotates the image a quarter turn to the right (clockwise).

   90° CCW—Rotates the image a quarter turn to the left
   (counterclockwise).

   Arbitrary—Enables you to enter the exact number of degrees of rotation
   and indicate whether it is clockwise or counterclockwise.

   Flip Canvas Horizontal—Flips the image horizontally (left to right).

   Flip Canvas Vertical—Flips the image vertically (top to bottom).

3. To crop an image, select the Crop tool and drag a crop marquee around
   the portion of the image you want to keep. Adjust the outline by moving
   the drag handles. Notice that the portion that will be cropped appears
   grayed out.

4. To complete the crop, double-click inside the crop marquee, shown in
   Figure 9.3.

▼ TRY IT YOURSELF

Practicing Basic Photoshop Image Manipulation

continued

FIGURE 9.2
You can rotate or flip the canvas of an image.

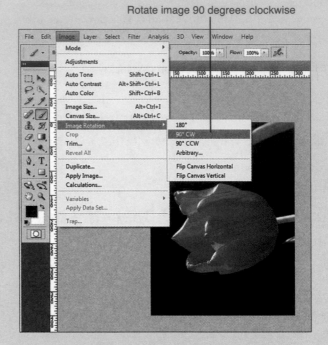

Rotate image 90 degrees clockwise

FIGURE 9.3
Use the Crop tool to drag a marquee and double-click the marquee to execute the crop.

Crop tool

Marquee

5. To modify the image size, select Image, Image Size to open the Image Size dialog box. This dialog enables you to change the resolution and size of the image.

6. Enable the Constrain Proportions check box and then examine the pixel dimensions of the image.

7. Change the Resolution setting to 96 pixels per inch. This is a typical pixel density for modern desktop computers.

8. Changing the resolution also changes the width and height shown at the top of the Image Size dialog box, shown in Figure 9.4. Make any further edits to the width and height. Notice that changing one value also changes the other value because enabling the Constrain Proportions check box maintains the image proportions.

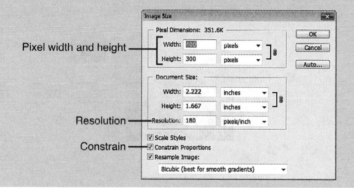

FIGURE 9.4
The Image Size dialog box enables you to change the size and resolution of an image.

The three image functions that you just completed are very common operations on image files. All image programs have commands to accomplish these same tasks. Photoshop can accomplish, of course, hundreds of other more complex image-manipulation tasks.

Purchase a good Photoshop book to delve more deeply into the program.

Feathering the Edges of an Image

Another task that web developers commonly want to accomplish is to feather an image. This enables the image to have a softer edge that fades gently into the background color. Of course, you must use the same background color in your image file as you used as the background color on your web page.

TIP

Be Smart with Smart Objects!

If you may use an image repeatedly with different croppings, you don't need to use the Photoshop tools or create multiple files. The Dreamweaver CS4 Photoshop Smart Objects (discussed later in this hour) enable you to use the same Photoshop file in different ways within a website.

The tools we're looking at in this section are for prepping your image to get it into a final form before you start using it in Dreamweaver.

▼ TRY IT YOURSELF

Blending an Image with the Background Using Feathering

To feather an image, do the following:

1. Open a new image or use the photo you used in the preceding exercise.

2. Set the background color to be the same color as the background color on the web page. Click Set Background Color in the Tools panel.

3. The Color Picker dialog box opens, as shown in Figure 9.5. Enter the appropriate background color in the hexadecimal box. This will be the same background color as in your web page. Click OK. You won't see any change in the image at this point.

FIGURE 9.5
Select the background color that bleeds through around the edges when you create a feather effect.

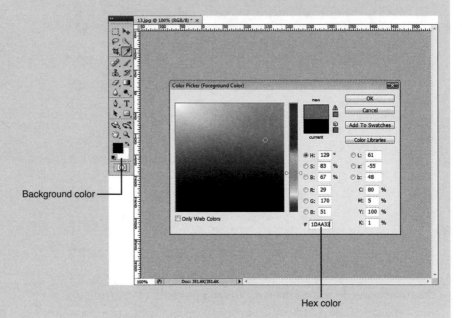

Background color

Hex color

4. Select the entire image with Select, All.

5. Feather the edges of the image by selecting Select, Modify, Feather.

6. Enter 20 pixels as the feather radius and click OK.

7. You need to invert the selection so that you can delete the outer edge of the image and let the background show through. Select the Inverse command from the Select menu.

8. Press the Delete key. You now have a feathered border, showing the background color, all around your image.

Now the image is ready to blend into the background of a web page!

Undoing Changes, Backing Up, and Reverting

When working in Photoshop, you inevitably create edits or changes that you have to undo. There are three ways to undo your changes:

- ▶ The **Undo** command (Edit, Undo) reverses the most recent command. You cannot undo multiple commands. After you use the Undo command, it becomes the Redo command.

- ▶ To undo multiple commands, use the **Step Backward** command (Edit, Step Backward). This command steps backward through all the history steps you've completed on the image. You can use the **Step Forward** command (Edit, Step Forward) if you accidentally undo a step and you want to reinstate it. You can also bring up the History window by choosing Window, History and use it just like the Dreamweaver CS4 History.

- ▶ To start fresh by removing all the changes you've made to an image, use the **Revert** command (File, Revert). This opens a fresh copy of the file without any of the changes you made.

It's important to remember to always save your modified image files under a separate filename. You should always keep your original image source files in case you have to modify the files in the future.

Creating an Image

In Photoshop, you can create a new image from scratch, such as a button graphic you can use in your website. First you create a new image, and then you add some color and text. Next you apply an effect to make it look interesting. Let's walk through the process, from start to finish, of creating a graphical button in Photoshop.

To try this, follow these steps:

1. Select File, New. The New dialog box appears.

2. Enter the specifications of the image in the New dialog box:

    Enter **Next** as the name of the image.

    Set the width to 70 pixels.

    Set the height to 26 pixels.

    Select 72 pixels/inch as the resolution.

TRY IT YOURSELF ▼

Creating a New Image in Photoshop

▼ TRY IT YOURSELF

Creating a New Image in Photoshop

continued

Set the Background Contents field to Background Color, as shown in Figure 9.6.

3. Click OK.

4. To change the background color, select Background Color in the Tools panel (see Figure 9.5) and then pick a color in the color picker.

5. Select View, Fit on Screen to make the new image larger so that it is easier to work with.

FIGURE 9.6
You set the width, height, and resolution in the New dialog box. You also set the background color here.

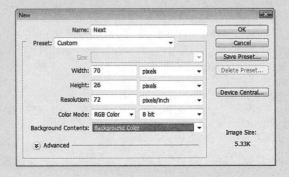

Adding Text to an Image

You can add text to any image in Photoshop. The Text tool in Photoshop enables you to place editable text into the Document window. You should enable guides so that you can judge whether you have the text centered in the button. You can use any font on your system, and you can apply antialiasing and other text effects. **Antialiasing** is a process of blending the edges of text with its background so that the letters look smoother.

▼ TRY IT YOURSELF

Aligning and Adding Text to an Image

Add and align a text label as shown here:

1. First, modify the default units of measurement in Photoshop so that you can work in pixels (instead of inches). Select Edit, Preferences, Units & Rulers. Select pixels from the Rulers drop-down menu. Click OK.

2. Use the magnifying glass to zoom in on the button-to-be.

3. Enable the rulers by selecting View, Rulers. You need the rulers to be visible because you add guides to an image by clicking and dragging from the ruler. **Guides** are useful for lining up text and other elements within an image.

4. Click within the left ruler and drag a vertical guide to the middle of the image. Make sure that your cursor is over the image when you finish dragging the guide. Drag a horizontal guide down from the top ruler to the middle of the image. You can open the Info panel (Window, Info) to help precisely place the guides at 13 pixels horizontally and 35 pixels vertically. The guides should look as shown in Figure 9.7.

Rulers   Info panel

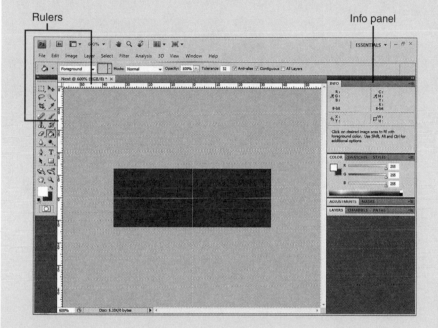

FIGURE 9.7
You can add guides to an image so that you know where the middle of the image is.

5. Select the Text tool from the Tools panel (the button shows the letter T). Don't click within the Document window quite yet. First you need to set up how the text will look.

6. In the Options bar, select a font, make the font size 14, and choose white for the color (unless white won't be visible on your canvas color).

7. Click on the canvas and enter some text for a button title (enter **Next** for a Next button). Leave enough room on the right side for a small arrow.

8. Pick up and position the text object using the Selection tool, the dark arrow button in the upper-left corner of the toolbar, shown in Figure 9.8. After you select the text object, you can use the arrow keys on your keyboard to fine-tune the object's positioning. The button should look something like the one in Figure 9.8.

NOTE

Remove or Hide the Guides

To remove the guides, simply drag them off the screen or choose View, Clear Guides. To leave the guides in place but hide them, select View, Show, Guides the guides again, simply toggle the same command, selecting View, Guides, Show Guides to replace the check mark next to the command.

▼ TRY IT YOURSELF

Aligning and Adding Text to an Image

continued

FIGURE 9.8
Create a text object and set its font, font size, and font color.

Text object

Text tool
Pen tool
Selection tool

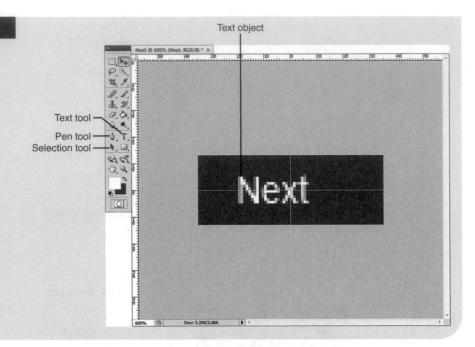

Adding a Shape to an Image

Photoshop has tools for drawing any type of shape you might want. Now you create a triangle shape that looks like an arrow to the right of the text on your button. After you create the triangle, you can modify the stroke (that is, the outline) and the fill.

▼ TRY IT YOURSELF

Using the Photoshop Drawing Tools

To create a triangle, follow these steps:

1. Select the Pen tool from the Tools panel. The cursor becomes an ink pen. The Pen tool adds points to create a shape. You create three points for a triangle.

2. Click to create one point in the triangle. Hold down the Shift key while you click to create a second triangle point. This forces the creation of a straight line. Click one more time to create the second side of the triangle, and then click the original point to close the shape.

3. The final line might not be perfectly straight, but you can adjust it. There are two arrow tools in Photoshop: the Path Selection tool and the Direct Selection tool (shown in Figure 9.9). You can use the Direct Selection tool (the white arrow tool) to select a single point in your triangle. Use this tool to select any of the points, and then press the arrow keys on

your keyboard to fine-tune the position of the points so that the triangle is even. Use the Path Selection tool to select the entire triangle and adjust its position.

FIGURE 9.9
Use the Path Selection and Direct Selection tools to select the triangle path.

4. Make sure that the triangle object you just created is selected (in case you clicked your cursor somewhere else after step 3). When the triangle is selected, you should see the three points. If the triangle is not selected, select the Path Selection tool from the Tools panel and click the triangle to select it.

5. Save your file as a Photoshop file (File, Save). This is the source file, but you still have to export the image to use in your web page.

TIP

Check the Final Size

You might want to reduce the magnification to 100% so that you can see what your button will look like at its final size. Make sure that the text is readable. If you want to make the font size larger, select the text object and adjust the font settings. Quickly jump to the actual size by double-clicking the Zoom tool in the Tools panel.

TIP

You Can Cloak Your Photoshop Files

You can save your original Photoshop source files to your website without cluttering it. Dreamweaver has a cloaking feature that you learn about in Hour 23, "Maintaining a Website," that enables you to easily store source files on your hard drive without uploading them to your remote site.

CAUTION

Antialiasing and Different Background Colors

When you antialias text, the graphics program blends the edges into the current background color. That's how the edges look smooth. But this means that you must display the image on the same background color or you will see pixels of the original background color around the text—an effect known as **ghosting**.

Adding a Filter to a Rollover Image

Now that you have a button, let's go one step further by creating a rollover version of the button. Remember that the trick to creating a rollover image is that the two images involved must be exactly the same size. You continue using the same button file you just created.

▼ TRY IT YOURSELF

Creating an Image Copy

To begin creating a rollover image, first follow these steps to create a copy of the original button:

1. Open the button file in Photoshop if it isn't already open. Select View, Fit on Screen.

2. Save a new copy of the button file named `Next_on` (or something else appropriate) to represent the ON button state.

3. Select the text tool and click and drag to highlight the "Next" label in the button.

4. The text attributes appear in the Options bar. Change the text color to a different, highlight color (try #FFFF00, a bright yellow color). Remember which color you use because you use it again in a few minutes to make the arrow glow.

Photoshop enables you to add a number of interesting filters to images to make them stand out. Even better, they are very easy to remove if they don't turn out quite the way you like. Each time you add an effect to an object, Photoshop lists it under the object in the Layers panel, with an eye beside it. You simply uncheck the eye to turn off the effect for an object.

▼ TRY IT YOURSELF

Adding an Image Filter

To add an effect to your image, follow these steps:

1. Open the Layers panel if it isn't already visible (Window, Layers).

2. Select the layer with the triangle; it is probably named Shape 1. Simply click it in the Layers panel.

3. Click the Effects (fx) button to drop down the Effects menu, as shown in Figure 9.10.

4. From the Effects menu, select Outer Glow. The Layer Style dialog box appears, as shown in Figure 9.11.

5. Using the color picker, select the same color you applied to the text in the preceding section. If you need to edit the effect, simply double-click it in the list.

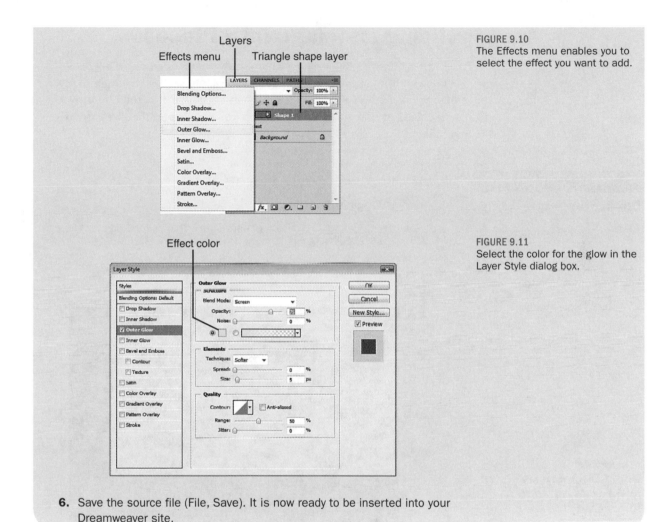

FIGURE 9.10
The Effects menu enables you to select the effect you want to add.

FIGURE 9.11
Select the color for the glow in the Layer Style dialog box.

6. Save the source file (File, Save). It is now ready to be inserted into your Dreamweaver site.

With Photoshop effects, you can add bevels, glows, and blurs to images, and you can emboss images, too. You probably want to experiment with the different filters. You can usually change the colors involved, too. For instance, you can make an object glow in yellow from its center or glow from the bottom of the image as if it were on fire. Photoshop effects enable you to get professional image results without having to know all the high-end tricks of the image trade.

Slicing an Image into Pieces

Photoshop enables you to slice an image into smaller pieces. Slicing facilitates creating a page layout by cutting images into pieces that easily fit into the implementation of your page design in Dreamweaver. You can draw slice objects over an image in Photoshop and then export the slices as individual graphics files.

To create a sliced image, follow these steps:

1. Open an image in Photoshop.

2. Select the Slice tool from the Tools panel and draw a rectangle on top of the image, as shown in Figure 9.12.

FIGURE 9.12
Draw slices over an image to create individual image files that an HTML table holds together.

Slice tool   Slice

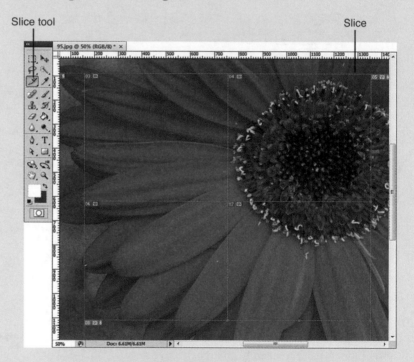

TIP

Using Slices to Optimize and Focus on What's Important

You can also use slices to both optimize and highlight a portion of an image. Create a single slice over the portion of an image that you want to be very clear because you want to highlight that portion. Create slices over the remainder of the image that can be highly optimized, lowering the JPEG quality to less than 50, for instance.

3. Slice the entire image by repeating step 2.

4. Select File, Save for Web & Devices.

5. Set the optimization settings and click Save. Photoshop saves each slice as a separate file.

Slice Only When Necessary!

Using slices is one of the best ways to optimize loading of very large images, but it is also a very inaccessible way of presenting an image within a web page. It clutters the page with complex table tags and can't be understood by screen readers. If you can avoid slicing, do so!

Adding Photoshop Images to Dreamweaver with Smart Objects

Starting in Dreamweaver CS4, Adobe has made our lives as web developers and designers easier than ever before. Dreamweaver now recognizes and works with Photoshop files directly within your page using "Smart Objects." A Smart Object enables you to make changes to an image in Photoshop and see the results reflected in Dreamweaver—even if the Dreamweaver image is cropped or sized differently from the Photoshop original! Best of all, this feature is extremely easy to use.

Whenever you have the option of choosing an image to insert into Photoshop, you can now choose a Photoshop (.PSD) file in addition to the traditional staple of .jpg, .gif, and .png files.

Dreamweaver creates the optimized version of the image and links it in the web page. When you select the image, the Property inspector shows that the image is a "PS Image," or Photoshop Image. The PS button takes you back into Photoshop to edit the original image.

To insert a Smart Object, follow these steps:

1. Start to insert an image into a document using any of the techniques you learned in Hour 8, "Displaying Images."

2. When prompted to choose a file, select a Photoshop file. Dreamweaver prompts you to crop, scale, and optimize the file, as shown in Figure 9.13.

3. After you set the optimization (file type, size, number of colors, and so on) that you prefer for the optimized version of the image, click OK.

4. Save the optimized version of the file.

5. Enter the alt text (alternative text) if prompted and click OK.

TRY IT YOURSELF

Inserting a Photoshop Smart Object in Dreamweaver

Inserting a Photoshop Smart Object in Dreamweaver

continued

FIGURE 9.13
Crop and optimize the image using the same tools you first used in Hour 8.

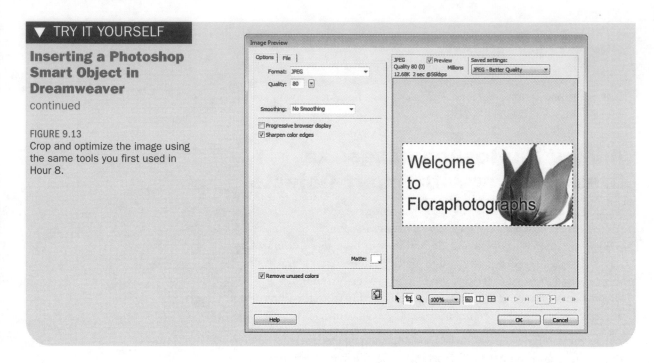

What's more, you'll notice that the image itself has a circular arrow on it, as shown in Figure 9.14.

FIGURE 9.14
Smart Objects are denoted by a circular arrow in the upper-left corner.

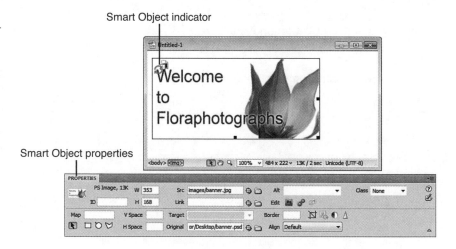

This arrow shows that the image is a Smart Object. When the arrow is entirely green, it means that your Smart Object is synced with your Photoshop document. If you make any modifications to your Photoshop file, the arrow becomes split—green and red. This indicates that changes have been made and the file must be resynced with the original. To do this, right-click the image and choose Update from Original. Your Smart Object immediately inherits the changes you made to the original Photoshop file!

The amazing thing about Smart Objects is that they maintain their cropping and other settings as you change the Photoshop document that serves as the source. This means that you can have a single Photoshop file serving as the source for a banner image, a main graphic, and a footer graphic—all with different croppings and sizings in Dreamweaver.

Importing Table Data from Excel

If you already have data in a spreadsheet or database, why retype it or paste it into Dreamweaver? You can import data exported from spreadsheet or database applications into Dreamweaver by using the Import Tabular Data command. Most spreadsheets and database applications can export data into a text file that Dreamweaver can import. You have to know which delimiter character is used in the data file before you can successfully import data into Dreamweaver.

To import table data to Dreamweaver, follow these steps:

1. Place the insertion point in the Document window where you want the table located.

2. Select the Tabular Data object from the Data category of the Insert panel or select Insert, Table Objects, Import Tabular Data. The Import Tabular Data dialog box appears, as shown in Figure 9.15.

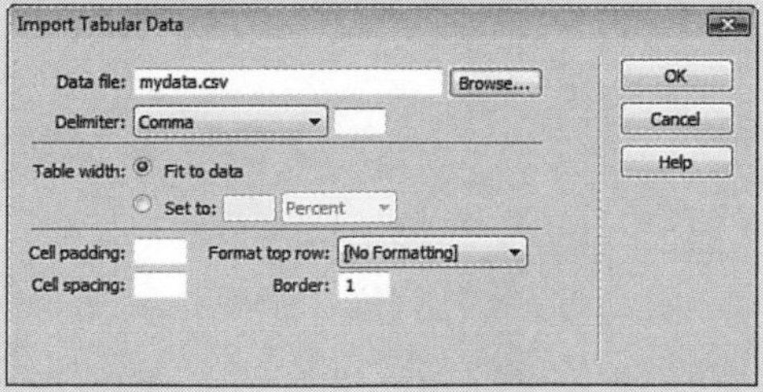

TIP

Exported Files from Excel

Microsoft Excel, a commonly used spreadsheet application, imports and exports files with the file extension .csv as comma-delimited files and those with the file extension .prn as space-delimited files.

TRY IT YOURSELF ▼

Importing Data into Dreamweaver

FIGURE 9.15
The Import Tabular Data dialog box enables you to import data files directly into a Dreamweaver table.

TIP

Create a Delimited Data File

Create your own data file to work with by opening a text editor, such as Notepad, and entering some data. Type some data, press the Tab key, type some more data, and then press the Enter (or Return) key; you just created a single record. Create multiple records by repeating this process on subsequent lines in the text file. Save your file and import it into Dreamweaver as a tab-delimited data file. Be sure to save your data file as plain text with the .txt file extension.

3. Click the Browse button to browse to the table data file to import it into Dreamweaver.

4. Dreamweaver attempts to automatically select the delimiter, but you can select the field delimiter manually from the Delimiter drop-down menu. If the delimiter isn't one of the four common delimiters listed, select Other from the Delimiter drop-down menu and enter the delimiter.

5. Using the Table Width radio buttons, select whether the new table should fit to the data or be a certain pixel or percentage value.

6. Enter values in the Cell Padding and Cell Spacing text boxes, if necessary. Remember, you can always change these values by editing the table later.

7. Find out whether the data file has column headings that appear as header cells in your HTML table, and select a value for the format of the first (header) row from the Format Top Row drop-down menu.

8. Enter a value for the table border size.

9. Click OK to import the table data.

Exploring Adobe Bridge

The final integration tool that we look at in this hour is Adobe Bridge. Bridge, as its name implies, attempts to "bridge" all the Adobe applications—in fact, you'll find a Browse in Bridge option under the File menu in all the CS4 applications, as shown in Figure 9.16.

FIGURE 9.16
The CS4 applications tie into Bridge to browse your resources.

Browse in Bridge ——

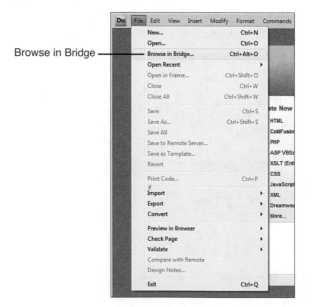

Bridge acts as the hub for your digital media assets. It can track the locations of the files that you're using and creating in the CS4 suite, as well as files created outside of CS4 that are supplemental to your projects. Think of Bridge as the ultimate media file browser for your system, which just happens to also include the following:

▶ An integrated browser for accessing online resources

▶ A photo downloader for your camera

▶ An advanced file tagger and search engine

▶ A control center for Adobe's Version Cue file-sharing system.

To launch Bridge, just choose Browse In Bridge from the File menu in any CS4 application.

The Bridge Interface

Bridge, as shown in Figure 9.17, looks strikingly similar to the other applications in the CS4 suite.

FIGURE 9.17
Bridge inherits the same look and feel as the other CS4 applications.

Along the top of the Bridge window is the toolbar, with simple icons and menus for navigating through your file system, similar to what you'd see in the Finder or Windows Explorer.

Along the sides are additional panels for quickly jumping to your favorite locations, navigating the folder structure on your computer, specifying filter criteria for image search, and viewing/previewing any information about files that you have currently selected.

In the center of the Bridge workspace is the primary content area, called the Content panel. When you select a folder from the Favorites or Folders panel, this area refreshes to show thumbnails of all the files within a selected folder. Alternatively, if you perform a search, the Content panel shows the search results.

At the bottom of the Bridge window is the status bar. On the right side of the status bar, you'll notice a slider bar—this controls the size of thumbnails within the content area. For example, in Figure 9.17 the thumbnails were sized at the default setting, whereas in Figure 9.18 the slider has been changed to show significantly more detail.

FIGURE 9.18
Use the slider in the status bar to increase the size of the Bridge thumbnails.

Increase thumbnail size

Browsing Your Files

The easiest way to start using Bridge to browse and manage your files is by using the Folders panel, shown in Figure 9.19.

This panel displays a hierarchical list of the folders on your computer, as well as any network connections you have in place. Using the icon in front of each folder, you can expand and collapse your directory structure and dig as deeply into your system as you'd like.

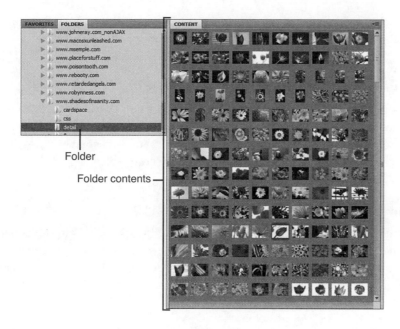

Folder

Folder contents

FIGURE 9.19
Use the Folders panel to navigate
through your files.

While you're working your way through the folders, you'll notice that the
main content area updates to show the contents of the folder that you currently have selected. You can use the icons in the content area to open files
(or navigate to other folders) by double-clicking the icons.

Using the Favorites Panel

Navigating to your most commonly used folders by using the Folders panel
(or Content panel) *works*, but is hardly efficient. To speed things up, you can
create shortcuts using the Favorites panel.

This panel lists several icons that provide quick access to different functions,
services, and locations. Items that appear below the divider line in the Favorites panel are specific folders or files that you access frequently. You can
add your own favorites simply by dragging any folder or file into the panel.
To delete a favorite, either drag it to your system trash or choose File, Remove from Favorites. You can also specify what does or does not appear in
the Favorites panel in the General panel in Bridge Preferences.

Viewing Files and Setting Metadata

As you click through your file locations in Bridge, you've probably noticed
that there are other things changing on your screen as well. These other

What Is "Metadata"?

Metadata is, simply, data about data. For example, when you take a picture, you have certain exposure settings on your camera. These settings can be used to help describe the picture. Similarly, a time-and-date stamp indicating when a picture was taken would also be considered metadata. For a song file the artist, song name, and album name could be stored as metadata.

Metadata isn't the "content" of a file itself, but is information that helps you identify or describe the file.

FIGURE 9.20
The metadata panel shows data about your...data.

Get a Closer Look

Clicking on an image in the Preview panel opens a very cool magnifying glass that you can position anywhere you'd like over the image to get an enlarged view.

panels provide previews of your files' contents, as well as a means of setting metadata for each file, and filtering your file view based on metadata.

The Preview Panel

In the upper-right corner is the Bridge Preview panel. As expected, this provides a preview of the content you are viewing. What might actually surprise you is that the Preview panel does more than just display pictures, it can also provide playback of audio and video files!

The Metadata Panel

Directly below the Preview panel (in the default workspace) is the Metadata panel (shown in Figure 9.20). Here you can view all the information about your currently selected file, including camera settings, file sizes, resolutions, color space, and more things than we can possibly mention here.

Media metadata —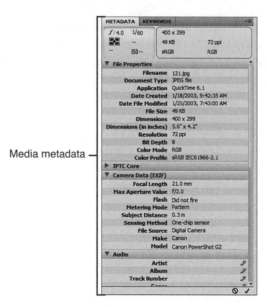

For some types of files, you'll notice that there is a pencil to the right of certain metadata field names. This means that the metadata is editable. To enter your own information, click the pencil and you can type into the field—it's as simple as that!

To save the changes, click the check mark in the lower-right corner of the panel, or click the circle with the line through it to cancel your modifications.

Filtering Based on Metadata

One of the nicest features of Bridge is the capability to filter the files you are viewing based on the metadata that has been set for a given file. By default, all files are shown when you view a folder. At the same time you're viewing a folder of files, the Filter panel (shown in Figure 9.21) is being populated with metadata information about the files.

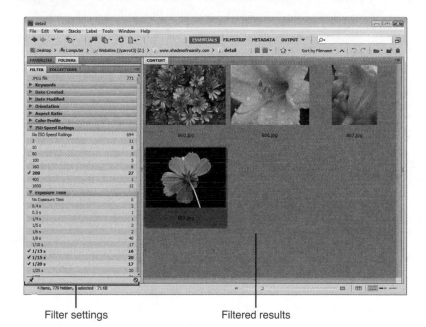

Filter settings   Filtered results

To limit your view to specific metadata attributes, scroll through the Filter panel and check or uncheck (just click) the items you want to use as filter criteria. As you activate or deactivate filter items, the Content view updates accordingly.

Note that in the top right of the Bridge window, is a drop-down "Sort by" menu that can be used to set how the files in the content area are sorted.

Further Exploration

Bridge has many other functions that are beyond the scope of this book. Thankfully, Bridge is easy to explore and can be a valuable tool for those seeking to organize their content resources. Here are a few things you might want to look for as you work with Bridge:

▶ **Bridge Home**—Found at the top of your favorites list, this is a great place to get information about the products in the CS4 suite. Bridge Home gives you direct access to training, conference information, and other resources.

▶ **Get Photos from Camera**—This can serve as your digital camera download application. To use this feature, simply plug in your camera, then choose Get Photos from Camera from the File menu. You are prompted for whether you want Bridge to start each time you plug in your camera (this can be reset in the Bridge General preferences).

▶ **Image Editing**—Perform basic image-editing functions directly from within Bridge, without using Photoshop or Dreamweaver.

▶ **Image Searches**—Create custom searches for images based on metadata, keywords, and other attributes. With a large image library, this can help you locate the right image for the job instantly.

Summary

This hour introduced you to Photoshop and showed you how to use it to create a new image. You learned how to add text and a shape, in addition to adding effects to the shape and slicing a single image into multiple images. You also explored Smart Objects and how they can be used to link Photoshop documents into Dreamweaver without the need for any image conversion. For those with data-heavy sites, we looked at how information can easily be imported from common data files into Dreamweaver. Finally, we scratched the surface of Adobe Bridge—Adobe's digital media management solution for the CS4 suite.

Q&A

Q. How can I tell which file format makes the smallest file?

A. That's what you use the optimization capabilities of Photoshop for. You don't have to know off the top of your head which format to use because you can experiment in Photoshop and find out which format creates the smallest file.

Q. Why would I want to import Excel files into a table instead of copying and pasting the data?

A. Importing the data from an Excel file into a table enables you to automatically set the table attributes. Often you have to import the data multiple times, each time the data changes in the spreadsheet. Later in this book, you learn to record a command (see Hour 24, "Customizing Dreamweaver") to create the table exactly as you want it every time with a single command.

Q. Why would I use Adobe Bridge rather than iPhoto or another tool to manage my images?

A. Adobe Bridge offers full integration with the CS4 suite and provides extensive support for metadata cataloging and searching.

Workshop

Quiz

1. How do you create a guide in Photoshop?

2. What are commonly used delimiters?

3. Edits made in Dreamweaver update the original Photoshop source files when you've imported from Photoshop. True or false?

Quiz Answers

1. Enable the rulers, click within one of them, and drag a guide into position.

2. Common delimiters are tabs and commas.

3. True. You don't need to make changes in two places!

Exercises

1. Try applying some of the various effects available in Photoshop to an image. What does Glow do? What's the difference between Drop Shadow and Inner Shadow? Try using the Bevel and Emboss effects. What do they do? Try changing the color by using the color picker.

2. Create a spreadsheet in Excel and save it first as a comma-delimited file and then a tab-delimited file. Import each into Dreamweaver.

3. Launch Adobe Bridge and use it to browse images or other files on your computer (even websites!).

Adding Flash and Other Multimedia to a Web Page

You aren't limited to displaying text and graphics in web pages. You can include movies, sounds, documents, and many other specialized types of content. Like images, these media are external files embedded in a web page. Unlike images, most multimedia files require some sort of an installed player in order to see or hear the content.

This hour introduces you to some of the issues and the techniques you can use to include multimedia files in your website. You have to be aware of bandwidth limitations, along with some of the differences among various browsers. You also have to understand how your viewers can download the players necessary to view the files you include in your web pages.

Exploring Multimedia and Bandwidth

Adding multimedia files, such as sounds, movies, and PDF (Portable Document Format) documents, grows more popular as modems become faster and people browse the Web with more bandwidth. Yes, that's right: Most multimedia files take up a lot of bandwidth. **Bandwidth** is the size of the Internet "pipe" you have when you connect to the Web. Increasingly more people are accessing the Internet using a **broadband** connection—DSL or a cable modem. If you are on a broadband connection, you have access to a higher Internet bandwidth than someone connecting with a 56Kbps modem.

Some formats, such as RealMedia, Flash Video, and Shockwave, get around the large bandwidth requirements of sound and video files by streaming content to the user. Streamed content begins to play after a short buffer period; the content continues to download in the background while previously buffered content plays. Ever-improving techniques compress most multimedia delivered over the Web.

WHAT YOU'LL LEARN IN THIS HOUR:

▶ How to add Flash and Shockwave movies to a web page

▶ How to add multimedia files, such as sounds, movies, and PDF documents, to a web page

▶ How to insert and configure a Java applet in a web page

Some of the traditional CD-based multimedia formats, such as WAV (audio), AVI (Windows movie), MOV (QuickTime movie), and AIFF (audio), are often too large to deliver over the Web. Some of these formats require the user to download the entire file before it plays. To deliver this type of sound and video content, you have to understand which technologies to choose; new compression and streaming tools appear all the time. The MP3 sound format is extremely popular because it can create very small files that still sound great.

Understanding Players

To play any multimedia file in a browser, the user must have a third-party program to play the file. These players are either plug-ins or ActiveX controls, and some install automatically with the browser or operating system software. A **plug-in** is a piece of additional software that adds new functionality to the browser. The user might need to restart the browser for the plug-in to work after installing it. Of course, you don't want to assume that a person viewing your web page has the same players installed that you have. You always want to give the viewer information about how to obtain the necessary player.

Browsers deal with multimedia files in two ways. Safari, Opera, and Mozilla Firefox extend their capabilities with plug-ins. Figure 10.1 shows a list of popular Firefox plug-ins available at http://addons.mozilla.org/firefox/plugins/. Each browser has a plug-ins folder where these programs are stored.

NOTE

ActiveX Installation Woes

Some users either have disabled their computers' capability to install ActiveX controls or are confused and possibly suspicious when a dialog box appears, telling them they will be downloading and installing something. In addition, some corporate networks block the installation of ActiveX controls. Make sure that you tell users what to expect if you include content that requires them to download and install something on their computers.

Microsoft Internet Explorer, on the other hand, uses its ActiveX technology to launch and run multimedia content. **ActiveX controls** are similar to plug-ins: They install on the user's machine and add the capability to play different file types. Many third-party browser extensions come as both plug-ins and ActiveX controls to accommodate all browser types. An ActiveX control usually installs itself in the background and does not require the user to restart the browser after installation. Figure 10.2 shows the ActiveX controls installed in my copy of Internet Explorer (use the Tools, Manage Add-Ons, Enable or Disable Add-ons command in Internet Explorer).

It's always good form to tell a viewer where to download a required player. You can place information in your web page that includes a link to download the player. Dreamweaver adds the `pluginspace` attribute to enable the browser to attempt a player download automatically.

FIGURE 10.1
A list of popular plug-ins is available for the Firefox browser.

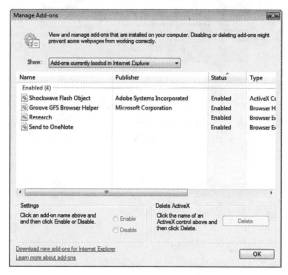

FIGURE 10.2
Internet Explorer displays a list of currently installed Active X controls.

Adding Flash Files

Adobe Flash has arguably become the standard for web animation. Adobe Director, originally created for CD-ROM–based interactive programs, also has a streaming web player (called Shockwave), but it is not as common as Flash. Flash is extremely fashionable for creating small, interactive, web-based animations. Flash is popular because of its **vector-based graphics**—a format that is small and scalable. Flash is easy to learn and is a fun tool to create in. Its scripting language, ActionScript, is based on the same standard as JavaScript, a popular scripting language for web pages.

Flash movies usually end with the .swf file extension, whereas Shockwave movies end with the .dcr file extension. You must have the appropriate players installed in your browser to view these movies; that is, you must have the Flash player to view Flash movies and the Shockwave player to view Director Shockwave movies. To insert a Flash movie into a web page, select the SWF object from the Media menu of the Insert panel (or Insert, Media, SWF). After you've chosen the Flash file, Dreamweaver may prompt you for accessibility attributes for the object—a title, as well as an access key (to select it), and its tab index (when it should be selected if you press the tab key within the page). This is demonstrated in Figure 10.3.

FIGURE 10.3
Set the accessibility attributes for the object.

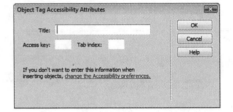

For most Flash files, you don't need to provide any of these values, because they have little impact on the accessibility of Flash. In fact, you can disable Dreamweaver from prompting for them within the Accessibility category of the preferences.

After the file has been added, you can select it to see the attributes in the property inspector. Figure 10.4 shows the Property inspector with a Flash movie selected.

The Property inspector displays the various settings for playing a Flash movie within a web page. There is a check box for Loop and another for Autoplay. Selecting Loop tells the Flash movie to play repeatedly; for the Flash movie to loop, it must have this functionality enabled. The Autoplay setting tells the Flash movie to play immediately when it is loaded. You can add vertical space (V Space text box) and horizontal space (H Space text box) to the Flash movie just as you can for an image.

TIP

Sample Flash Movie

Adobe provides a range of Flash samples you can use at http:/ /www.adobe.com/devnet/ flash/. You can download and use these files to test the Dreamweaver Flash functions on your own.

Flash content area

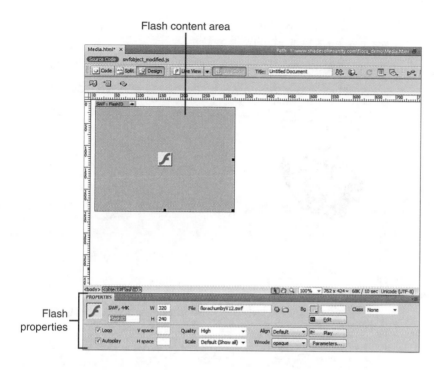

Flash properties

FIGURE 10.4
The Property inspector shows the
properties you can set for a Flash
movie. Some are standard properties, whereas others are specific to
Flash movies.

Previewing a Movie in the Dreamweaver Document Window

You can preview Flash movies and interact with them directly within
Dreamweaver. To preview a Flash movie in the Document window, click
the green Play button in the Property inspector. While the movie is playing,
the Play button turns into a red Stop button, as shown in Figure 10.5. Click
the Stop button to stop the movie.

Setting Alternative Content for Flash Media

At the upper left of every Flash object that you add to a page is a media
handle that includes the name of the object as well as a small "eye" icon.
This is shown in Figure 10.5. Normally, the eye is open, indicating that the
view is that of a browser which can play flash files.

If you click the eye, however, it closes and the Flash content is replaced with
alternative content that includes a message to the viewer stating that they
need to install Flash. You can edit this alternative content to suit your needs.

TIP

Flash Movie Quality Settings

I like to choose the Quality setting of Auto High; this balances
good appearance with fast loading, according to the user's connection speed. The other Quality
settings enable you to balance
appearance versus load time
manually.

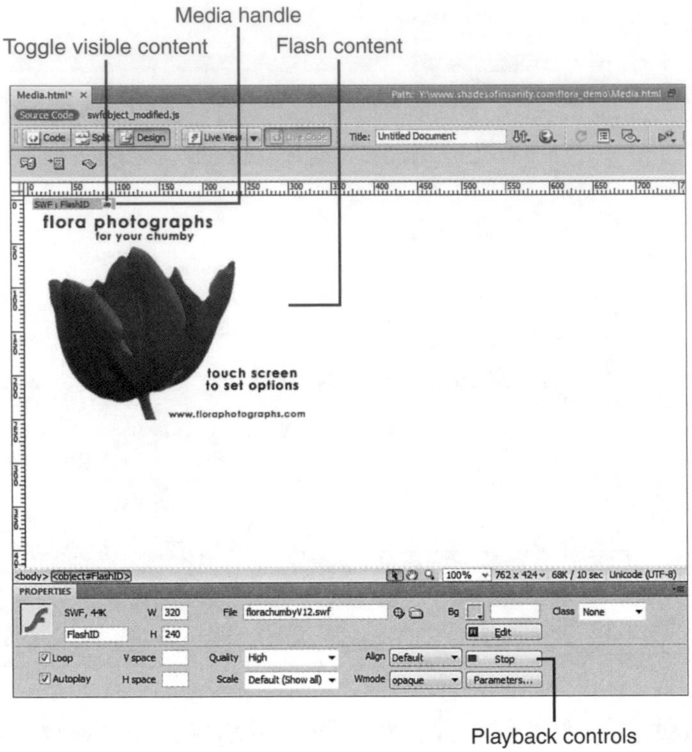

FIGURE 10.5
You can view a Flash or Shockwave movie, and other plug-in–based content, directly in the Document window.

Media handle

Toggle visible content   Flash content

Playback controls

TIP

Help! The Flash Movie Is the Wrong Size

If you accidentally resize a Flash movie, click the Reset Size button (the circular arrow between the W and H fields) to return the movie to its original size.

CAUTION

Objects Only!

Previous versions of Dreamweaver used an <embed> and an <object> tag to add Flash movies to a page in a way that was compatible with all browsers. In CS4, Dreamweaver uses the <object> tag only to improve its standards compliance.

If you find that a movie you've added to a page is not working in all browsers, you may want to revert to the original <object> and <embed> method of adding content. Visit http://www.alistapart.com/articles/flashsatay to see the "Twice-Cooked Method" of embedding Flash.

Adding a Link to a PDF File

So far in this hour, you've been embedding multimedia content into a web page. You can also link to content that appears by itself. You link to multimedia files just as you would link to another web page. If the multimedia file is within your defined website, you can use a document-relative URL. If the multimedia file is on another site, you must use an absolute URL (for example, http://www.irs.gov/pub/irs-pdf/fw9.pdf).

Adobe Reader is a freely distributed player that has become the standard for viewing formatted text files over the Web. PDF files enable the viewer to see a file exactly as you meant it to be seen—fonts, page layout, and graphics appear predictably. You create PDF files by using an application called Adobe Acrobat Distiller and view them with Reader. The Reader plug-in usually installs when you install the Reader application. Macintosh users can create PDFs using the Print function from any application and read them using the Mac OS X Preview application—no additional software is required.

To display a PDF file, you simply create a hyperlink with the URL to a PDF file. The file then opens within the browser if the Reader plug-in is present, as shown in Figure 10.6. If the plug-in isn't installed but Reader is, Reader runs as a standalone application and displays the PDF file. You can download Reader at http://www.adobe.com/products/acrobat/readstep2.html.

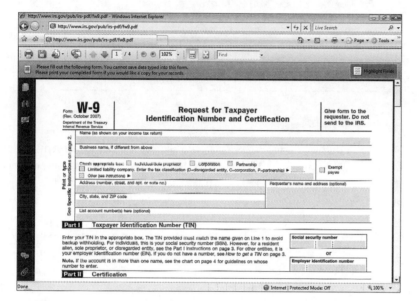

FIGURE 10.6
The PDF viewer, Reader, loads right in the browser window, displaying the PDF document.

Adding a Sound File to a Web Page

Adding a sound file to a web page can sometimes add to the experience, and it's a good way for you to become familiar with adding multimedia files. You select the Plugin object from the Media tab of the Insert panel (or select Insert, Media, Plugin) to insert a sound into a web page.

To insert a Plugin object, follow these steps:

1. Position the insertion point in the Dreamweaver Document window where you would like the sound control to appear when viewing the page in the browser.

2. Select the Plugin object from the Media tab of the Insert panel (or select Insert, Media, Plugin). The Select File dialog box appears.

3. Navigate to a directory that contains a sound file and select a file. Select All Files from the Files of Type drop-down menu. Then click the Select button.

4. Click OK to insert the Plugin object into the web page.

TRY IT YOURSELF ▼

Inserting a Plugin Object for Audio Playback

▼ TRY IT YOURSELF

**Inserting a Plugin
Object for Audio
Playback**

continued

Notice that the Property inspector for the Plugin object has some properties
that are similar to ones you have seen while working with images (see Figure
10.7). The Src box holds the filename and its location. There is an Align
drop-down menu, similar to the one for images, which affects how other objects align with the Plugin object. Other familiar properties are W (width), H
(height), V (vertical) Space, and H (horizontal) Space.

FIGURE 10.7
Some plug-in properties are similar to image properties, and some
are not.

Plug-in Playback

When you're delivering multimedia, what the user sees and hears much depends on which browser and plug-ins the user has. When the Plugin object
that we just discussed is used, the audio is played back through an existing
compatible plug-in on the computer. As you can probably guess, some plug-
ins and sound file formats are more popular than others. The popularity of
file formats is constantly evolving. As of this writing, QuickTime, Windows
Media Player, and the generic MP3 sound formats are popular and quite
common on the Web. MIDI files are common, too. Table 10.1 lists some of
the most popular sound file formats.

> **NOTE**
>
> **Learning More About
> Flash**
>
> Numerous websites about Flash
> have tutorials on using the pro-
> gram. Check out the Adobe web-
> site at http://www.adobe.com/
> products/flash/ to find out more
> about Flash file formats such as
> FlashPaper and Flash Video.
> Dreamweaver can insert all
> these file formats into web
> pages.

TABLE 10.1   Common Web Sound Formats

Sound Format	Streaming?	Description
RealMedia	Yes	Real-time streaming au-dio and video format.
Shockwave Audio	Yes	Real-time streaming au-dio format.
MP3 (MPEG 3)	Yes	Compact file size with ex-cellent sound quality. This open-standard sound format has be-come very popular.
Ogg Vorbis	Yes	Open, free, high-quality sound format.

TABLE 10.1 Common Web Sound Formats

Sound Format	Streaming?	Description
Liquid Audio	Yes	Small file sizes with excellent sound quality.
Beatnik	No	Sound format that combines MIDI and digital audio.
AIFF	No	A popular Macintosh sound format. Not ideal for longer sounds because of its large file size.
WAV	No	A popular Windows sound format. Not ideal for longer sounds because of its large file size.
u-Law (.au)	No	An initially popular web sound format from Sun Microsystems, but not very common today.
QuickTime	Yes	Apple's movie format, which can also play sounds. File sizes can be large.
MIDI	No	An open-standard sound format that uses defined MIDI sounds on the user's computer. Files are very compact.

What all of this means to you, the developer, is that if you use the sound embedding approach we've discussed so far, you're at the whim of the browser and plug-in for what the user's controls look like and how they act.

TIP

Flash Audio

I prefer to save audio files as Flash files simply because Flash is good at compressing audio (it uses the MP3 compression algorithms) and the Flash player is available to most viewers.

Resizing a Control

The default size of the Plugin object is 32×32 pixels. That's small. You can enter a width and a height in the Property inspector with the Plugin object selected. Predicting an appropriate size for a plug-in can be tricky because you can't predict which player application users will be displaying in their browser. If you have embedded a sound file into your web page, keep in mind that some viewers might use the QuickTime plug-in to play sounds in a web page, whereas others might use Windows Media Player or the Real-Media Player. The controls for these players are all different sizes.

First, preview the web page in the browser to see (and hear!) how the page is working. In Internet Explorer, you might get a security message like the one shown in Figure 10.8. The message directs the viewer to click the IE information bar to enable the plug-in. Microsoft added this safeguard to help keep people from playing unsafe content in the browser, and it makes our job as web developers a little more difficult.

FIGURE 10.8
Internet Explorer displays a message requiring viewers to click in the IE information bar.

Internet Explorer warning

Increasing the width and height of a plug-in can cause more controls to be visible. In Figure 10.9, for example, giving the plug-in a width of 300 pixels and a height of 40 pixels looks great in Internet Explorer. The height of 40 pixels in this case is necessary to display the Windows Media Player buttons. Depending on which player your browser has registered to play MP3 files, yours might or might not look the same. If a browser doesn't have a player configured to handle this type of file, it usually displays a button linking to a location to download an appropriate player.

FIGURE 10.9
The Windows Media Player in Internet Explorer with a width of 300 pixels and a height of 40 pixels displays all the audio controls.

Looping the Sound

Dreamweaver offers the flexibility to deal with advanced attributes of objects—even attributes that haven't been created yet—through the Parameters dialog box. Clicking the Parameters button in the Property inspector opens the Parameters dialog box. Parameters consist of two parts: a parameter name and a value.

Different plug-ins have different parameters available. Table 10.2 lists some common sound parameters. Many plug-ins have optional or required parameters you can set in the Parameters dialog box. The parameters available for sounds, such as `loop` and `autostart`, might or might not be available for other formats.

TABLE 10.2 Common Sound Parameters

Parameter	Values
loop	true, false, n (number of times playing)
autostart	true, false
hidden	true, false
volume	0–100
playcount	n (number of times playing—Internet Explorer only)

After you click the Parameters button, click the + button to add a parameter. Then do the following to make the sound loop:

1. Type **loop** as the parameter name. Tab or click in the Value column and type **true**. The default value is false, so if you want the sound to play only once, you do not need to enter the loop parameter.

2. Add the playcount parameter in addition to the loop parameter. The default for playcount is for the sound to play once. Enter the number of times you want the sound to play.

You can enter multiple parameters in the Parameters dialog box. Figure 10.10 shows the Parameters dialog box with parameters entered. You add the parameter name in the left column and then click or tab to the right column to add the parameter value. After you have finished adding parameters, click the OK button.

FIGURE 10.10
The Parameters dialog box can contain many parameters that affect the functionality of a plug-in.

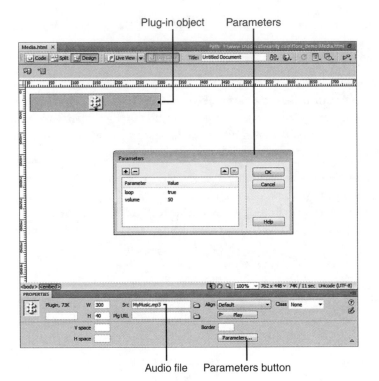
Plug-in object   Parameters

Audio file   Parameters button

To edit a parameter, again click the Parameter button in the Property inspector and then click in the parameter you want to change. To delete a parameter, click the - button. Use the arrow keys to rearrange the order of the parameters. Disregard the lightning bolt icons; they are involved in loading dynamic data into parameter fields when you are using server-side scripting.

Linking to an Audio File

So far, you have had the browsers display an **inline**, or **embedded** player, meaning that the player appears within the flow of your web page. However, if you create a hyperlink to a sound file, the user's browser launches the player controller in a separate window when the user selects the link. Figure 10.11 shows iTunes open in a separate window. Another computer configuration might launch the Windows Media Player, as shown in Figure 10.12.

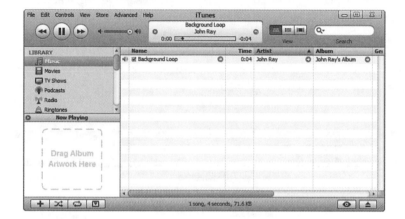

FIGURE 10.11
When the user clicks a link to an audio file, iTunes opens and plays the MP3.

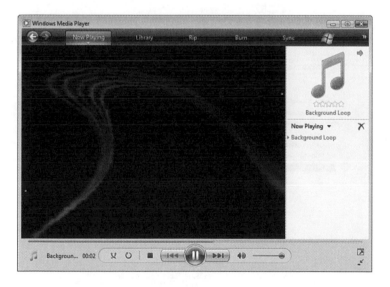

FIGURE 10.12
The Windows Media Player launches in a separate window to play an MP3 file on another person's computer.

Gaining Greater Control with an Embedded Player

You might be starting to get the sense that it is actually pretty difficult to determine exactly what the user experience is like when playing back audio files on a website. As long as you're depending on a built-in player, this is absolutely true. A different, more controllable approach is to use an embedded player. In this case, the player *and* the audio are loaded from your website and displayed in the browser, making the web page and the audio playback look identical on any system.

One popular player, JW FLV Media Player by Jeroen Wijering, features video, audio, and even image playback using Flash. By downloading this free player, you can easily embed almost any kind of media in your page by first embedding the Flash player, then setting parameters to point to your media files. In fact, the site offers a simple wizard that writes the embedded code for you, as shown in Figure 10.13.

FIGURE 10.13
Configure the JW FLV Media Player to meet your needs.

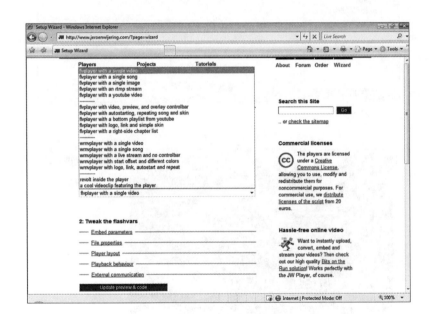

▼ TRY IT YOURSELF

Using the JW FLV Media Player to Embed Media on a Web Page

To embed media into your web page using the JW FLV Media Player, just follow these steps:

1. Download the JW FLV Media Player files at http://www.jeroenwijering.com/?item=JW_FLV_Media_Player.

2. Place the two files in the JW FLV Media Player archive (`player.swf` and `swfobject.js`) in a directory called `embed` inside your site directory.

3. Place the media file that you want to play back in a folder called media inside your site directory (for example, media/mysounds.mp3).

4. Visit http://www.jeroenwijering.com/?page=wizard in your web browser.

5. Choose flvplayer with a Single Song from the Select an Example Setup drop-down menu.

6. Under Tweak the flashvars, click File Properties.

7. Find the field called File and change it to your sound file's path (for example, media/mysounds.mp3).

8. Click Update Preview & Code.

9. You can now see a preview of how the player will appear on your web page along with code that you can copy and paste into your page code to show the media player, as shown in Figure 10.14.

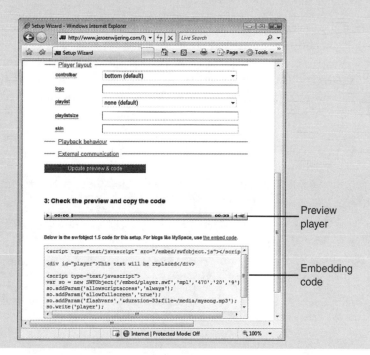

FIGURE 10.14
Preview the player and copy the necessary code, straight from the JW FLV Media Player website.

There are many parameters and customization options for JW FLV media player that you can take advantage of by using the simple configuration wizard we've seen here. I highly recommend using this approach to embedding media, because it ensures a consistent presentation across browsers and platforms.

Adding a Java Applet to a Web Page

Java is a programming language used to create self-contained programs called **applets**. Java applets run within the browser window just like the other multimedia objects you've been working within this hour. You can put a Java applet into your page, add parameters, and add some interesting multimedia to your web page.

To insert a Java applet into your web page, you must have all the appropriate files for the applet. The number and type of files might vary. You have to read the documentation for the applet you are using. The example here uses a classic snow applet, available from http://javaboutique.internet.com/snow_applet. Implementing the snow applet simply requires that you download the Java files (download and unzip `wintersnow_v1.zip`) and have an image file available as a background.

Any Java applet you intend to use in your web page should come with instructions on how to set it up. Be sure to read the instructions carefully and enter all the parameters correctly, or the applet might not work. If you do not set up the applet correctly, users simply see an empty gray box on the page. Dreamweaver creates the HTML code for you, but you must pay attention to the parameter values that you have to add to the Applet object.

To insert the RealSnow applet into a web page, follow these steps:

1. Create a new HTML file and save the file in the directory with the Java files. Copy an image file into this same directory. This is the image where the snow appears.

2. Select the Applet object from the Media tab of the Insert panel or select Insert, Media, Applet. This opens the Select File dialog box.

3. In the Select File dialog box, navigate to the directory where you saved the Wintersnow files from the Zip file.

4. Select `SnowApplet.class`.

5. Click OK to insert the applet into the web page.

6. Look up the width and height of the background image you'd like to use. In the Property inspector, enter this width and height for the size of the applet.

7. Enter the Background parameter required by the applet. Click the Parameters button in the Property inspector.

8. The snow applet requires a Background parameter that contains the name of the image file on which the snow appears. Add a parameter called **background** and enter the name of the image file you copied in step 1, as shown in Figure 10.15.

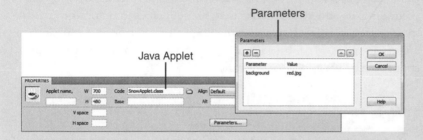

FIGURE 10.15
A Java applet requires parameters specific to the applet.

9. Save your web page and preview it in a web browser or in the Live View mode of Dreamweaver CS4 to make sure that it appears correctly. Figure 10.16 shows the snow applet in action.

FIGURE 10.16
The snow applet animates snow falling over the picture when viewed in Dreamweaver's Live View mode, or within a web browser.

Summary

In this hour, you learned how to add multimedia files, including Flash and Shockwave movies, to your web page. You added a URL that the browser can redirect viewers to if they do not have the appropriate player to view your files. You added parameters to multimedia files to change properties that weren't specifically shown in the Property inspector, and you inserted and configured a Flash-based media player. Finally, you downloaded and configured a Java applet for your site.

Q&A

Q. I placed a value in the Border text box in the Property inspector when I had the Plugin object selected, but no border appeared around the plug-in. Did I do something wrong?

A. Some plug-ins respond to the Border attribute and some don't. The plug-in that you tried to put a border around was not capable of adding a border.

Q. Why do I see only a gray box when I insert a Java applet into my page?

A. You haven't entered a required parameter or you have entered a parameter incorrectly. Go back into the Parameters dialog box and double-check that you have spelled everything correctly. If you misspell something or reference a file incorrectly, you won't receive an error message; your applet just appears as a gray box. In addition, make sure that you saved your web page so that the path to the Java applet is correct and relative to your web page.

Java applets can be problematic because the user might not have the correct version of Java installed. Check the documentation of the applet you are using in your web page and add a link that leads to the correct Java version so that the user can download it if necessary. Check the Sun website for download information: http://www.java.com/en/download.

Workshop

Quiz

1. What plug-in does a browser use to play back content?

2. Java and JavaScript are the same thing. True or false?

3. What are the two components of a parameter?

Quiz Answers

1. The browser uses the media player that is installed in the system and set as the default player for the chosen type of content. Unfortunately, this can vary dramatically among systems.

2. False. The two are unrelated. Java is a programming language and JavaScript is the language that Dreamweaver uses for behaviors, which you learn more about in Hour 18, "Adding Interactivity with Behaviors."

3. A parameter consists of a parameter name and a value.

Exercises

1. Insert a sound or movie file into a web page. Create a hyperlink to the same file. Explore how the embedded sound or movie works differently from the linked sound or movie.

2. Insert into a web page a hyperlink to a PDF file. The Internal Revenue Service (IRS) (http://www.irs.gov/formspubs) is a popular site for finding PDF files. Don't get me wrong—I'm not saying the IRS is popular, just its PDF files! (The IRS is the national tax agency for the United States, for those of you in other countries, and nobody likes paying taxes.) You can copy the URL to a file by right-clicking the link in the browser and then selecting either the Copy Shortcut command in Internet Explorer or the Save Link As command in Firefox. Paste the link into Dreamweaver's Property inspector as a hyperlink.

Managing Assets Using the Assets Panel

After you have designed your web page, you populate your page with content. The elements that make up your individual web pages are likely to come from various sources and be different types of objects. You might include Flash movies (SWF), images created in Fireworks, various colors, links, clip art, and photographs in your web pages.

You have to gather and organize these page elements before you start to create a web page. Unfortunately, with dozens of files on your hands, it's easy to misplace them or create duplicates. Thankfully, Dreamweaver's Assets Panel saves the day! After you copy the assets into the site, Dreamweaver's Assets panel enables you to organize the elements of a website to quickly access and reuse items. The Assets panel can help you become more efficient and better organized. Putting out a small effort to organize pays off especially well when you need to revisit a website for updates or want to use certain elements across different sites.

What Are Assets?

Web pages are not just made out of text and code. You use images, movies, colors, and URLs to present information in web pages. These web page elements are called **assets**.

The Assets panel organizes these elements, enabling you to quickly find an image or a color you want to use. You can preview assets in the Assets panel. You can also create a list of favorite assets—ones you use often. By default, the Assets panel nests behind the Files panel in the same tab group, as shown in Figure 11.1. You simply click the Assets tab to open the panel. If the Assets panel has been closed, you can open it again by selecting Window, Assets.

WHAT YOU'LL LEARN IN THIS HOUR:

- ▶ What assets are and how to manage them in your website
- ▶ How to create favorite assets and give them a nickname
- ▶ How to create and add assets to another website

Files tab   Assets tab

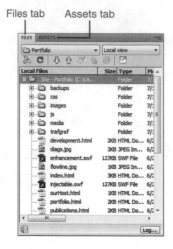

FIGURE 11.1
The Assets panel is nested behind the Files panel by default.

Managing Assets in the Assets Panel

Dreamweaver automatically catalogs the assets for an entire site. When you open the Assets panel, you can click one of the category buttons from along the left side of the panel to display a list of all the assets of that type in your site. The Assets panel includes the following categories:

- ▶ Images
- ▶ Colors
- ▶ URLs
- ▶ Flash Movies (SWF)
- ▶ Shockwave Movies
- ▶ Movies
- ▶ Scripts
- ▶ Templates
- ▶ Library

You can browse an asset category to preview the assets by clicking one of the asset category buttons shown in Figure 11.2. The Assets panel enables you to quickly add a selected asset to your current page. Later this hour, you learn how to set some assets as favorites so that you can find them even more quickly.

FIGURE 11.2
The Assets panel has buttons for the different categories along the left side and radio buttons at the top to select whether to view all the assets or just your favorites.

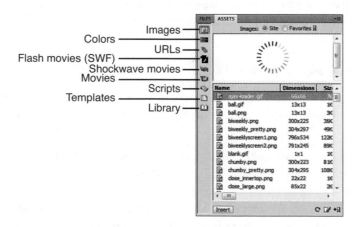

The Assets panel has different capabilities based on the asset category you've selected. For instance, when the Images category is selected, you can view a thumbnail of each image, but when you have the Colors category selected, the hexadecimal code for the color is displayed. Assets are specific to the current site you are working in.

The Library and Templates panels are part of the Assets panel. These panels have a special purpose and are covered in Hour 15, "Creating Library Items and Templates."

Listing Assets in a Site

When you open the Assets panel, Dreamweaver goes through the cache and automatically catalogs all the assets within your current site. It places the assets into the correct categories by examining the file extensions of the files in the website. The Assets panel lists only the assets that are in the currently selected site. When you change sites, a message box might appear briefly while the Assets panel is updating.

You can view all the assets in a category by selecting a category button along the left side of the Assets panel. Each of the categories, except the Library and Templates categories, has two radio buttons at the top of the panel, as shown in Figure 11.3, enabling you to select whether you want to see all the assets of that type within a site or see your favorites across all sites. You learn how to create a favorite asset in a few minutes.

View favorite assets

View all assets in site —

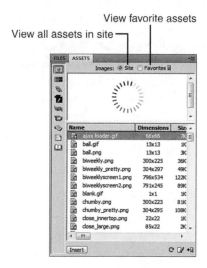

FIGURE 11.3
The Assets panel has buttons for the different categories along the left side and radio buttons at the top to select whether to view all the assets or just your favorites.

After you add an asset to your site, you might have to click the Refresh button to see it listed. You can refresh the list of assets anytime using the button in the lower-right corner of the Assets panel.

Previewing Assets

When you select a category in the Assets panel, the first asset in the list of that category is selected in the lower half of the panel, and a preview of that asset appears in the upper half. You can preview any asset by selecting it in the list, as shown in Figure 11.4.

FIGURE 11.4
A preview of the asset selected in the list appears in the upper half of the Assets panel.

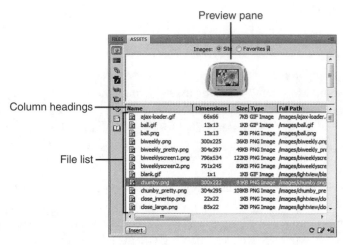

Preview pane

Column headings

File list

By default, Dreamweaver sorts the items listed in the Assets panel alphabetically. You can sort the items by any of the available column headings by clicking a column heading. For instance, if you want to sort your image assets by file size, you click the column heading Size.

Sometimes you might see an asset file in the Assets panel and wonder where that asset resides in the actual website structure. Highlight an item in the Assets panel and then right-click to bring up the context menu. Select the Locate in Site command and Dreamweaver opens the Files panel with the same file highlighted. This works only on assets that are individual files, such as movies or images; it does not work on assets that are elements of web pages, such as URLs or colors.

Exploring Image Assets

The Images category of the Assets panel displays all the images in your defined website (refer to Figure 11.2). Dreamweaver catalogs images in GIF, JPG, or PNG format. Dreamweaver displays a preview of the selected image in the top half of the Assets panel.

The Assets panel is very useful when you're trying to find an image in your website. Although the Files panel displays the filename, the Assets panel

TIP

Use the Arrow Key

When I'm looking for an image file in Dreamweaver, I open up the Assets panel and select the first image in the list. Then I simply press the down-arrow key while viewing the thumbnails, quickly scrolling through the image assets, until I find the image for which I'm looking.

NOTE

Does "Websafe" Matter?

An older color palette is the websafe palette, which contains the 216 colors that work on all browsers on both the Windows and Mac platforms when a computer is set to 256 colors. The Assets panel tells you whether the colors listed in the Colors category are within those 216 colors by marking them as Websafe or Non-Websafe in the Type column. You might have to widen the panel to view this column. Unless you are creating websites for very old computers, however, you shouldn't worry about whether your colors are websafe.

displays both the filename and a thumbnail of the image. It's often easier to quickly identify an image by what it looks like rather than its filename.

Exploring Color Assets

The Colors category of the Assets panel, as shown in Figure 11.5, displays all the colors used in the defined website. The Assets panel catalogs all the colors in the website and displays them in hexadecimal format. Dreamweaver displays a preview of the selected color, along with both its hexadecimal and RGB (red, green, blue) definition, in the top half of the Assets panel. Beside the color name, Dreamweaver indicates whether the color is part of the websafe palette.

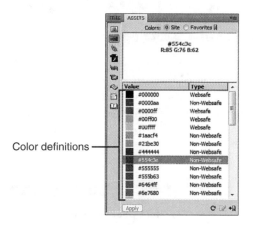

Color definitions

FIGURE 11.5
The Colors category shows the hexadecimal and RGB definition of the colors in the website.

You can select one of the colors in the Colors category of the Assets panel and drag and drop it onto text, a layer, a table, or another object that accepts color. Just as you created CSS styles in Hour 6, "Formatting Web Pages Using Cascading Style Sheets," this creates new CSS styles in the web page head. If you do this, you are automatically prompted for a new CSS selector name for the element you're styling.

Exploring Link Assets

The URLs category of the Assets panel holds all the hyperlinks contained in the currently defined website, as shown in Figure 11.6. This category lists all URLs in the site, including FTP, mailto, JavaScript, HTTP (Web), and HTTPS (secure Web). These are the absolute links in your website; the

CAUTION

Links Shouldn't Begin with file:///

You should not use URLs that begin with file:/// because those URLs do not work when you move your site anywhere other than on your computer. Find those locally referenced URLs in your site and change them by examining the URLs category of the Assets panel. Use Find and Replace (Edit, Find and Replace) to find the incorrect URLs.

document-relative links (links to other pages in the same site) are not listed in the URLs category.

Link asset

Exploring Movie Assets

The three movie asset categories are Flash Movies (SWF), Shockwave Movies, and Movies. The Movies category catalogs movie types other than Flash or Shockwave movies, such as QuickTime or MPEG movies. There is a Play/Stop button in the upper-right corner of the preview window (see Figure 11.7) that enables you to play the movie in the preview window.

Play/Stop button

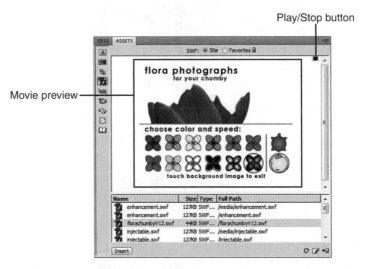

Movie preview

Exploring Script Assets

The Scripts category is where you see some of the scripts you create with Dreamweaver. (You learn more about scripts in Hour 18, "Adding Interactivity with Behaviors.") The Scripts category of the Assets panel catalogs all the external script files in your website, as shown in Figure 11.8. External script files end with the `.js` or `.vbs` extension. These script files contain JavaScript or VBScript functions that you can call from your web pages. The preview window shows the actual code in the script.

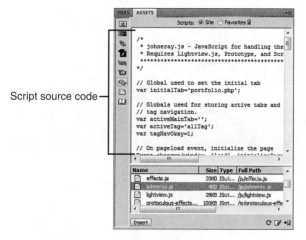

Script source code

FIGURE 11.8
The Scripts category of the Assets panel shows all the external script files.

To have access to the functions contained in an external script file, you reference the script in the head section of your web page. If you call a function contained in an external script, you have to link the external script file to your web page by dragging it from the Scripts category of the Assets panel into the Head Content (View, Head Content) section of the Dreamweaver Document window, as shown in Figure 11.9.

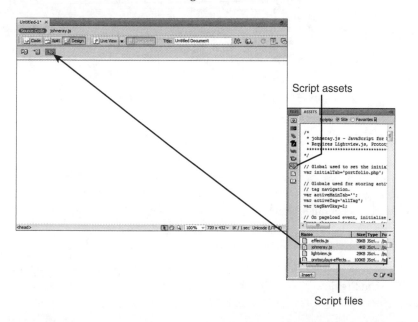

Script assets

Script files

FIGURE 11.9
Drag an external script from the Scripts category of the Assets panel into the Head Content section of a web page.

Adding Assets to a Web Page

Use the Assets panel to add assets to a web page.

To add an asset to your web page, follow these steps:

1. Select the category.

2. Find the asset you want to add by scrolling through the list for the name or viewing the preview in the Preview window.

3. Place the insertion point in your web page where you want the asset to be located.

4. Click the Insert button, shown in Figure 11.10, and Dreamweaver inserts the asset into your web page.

FIGURE 11.10
You insert an asset into a web page by clicking the Insert button.

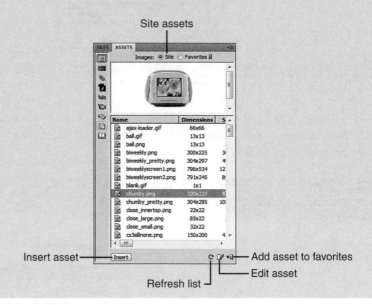

You can also use assets from the Assets panel to affect other objects on a web page. For instance, you can apply a color asset to some text on your web page as detailed here:

1. Select some text on the page.

2. Drag a color from the Assets panel by picking up the name in either the Preview window or the category list.

3. Drop the color on the selected text.

Instead of dragging and dropping, you can simply select the text and the color and then click the Apply button to apply the color to the text.

Adding a color to text creates a CSS style when it is added, and even prompts you for a new CSS selector name. After you've used a color on a page, don't keep dragging it from the Assets panel; this creates the same type of style repeatedly. CSS styles are meant to be reused!

TIP

Jump Assets Alphabetically

To quickly jump to a section in the Assets list, click within the Assets list and then type the first letter of the name of the item you are looking for. You jump to the first item that begins with that letter.

Creating Favorite Assets

You often use certain assets repeatedly in your websites. You can assign these assets to the favorites list so that they are easy to pick out of the Assets panel. The favorites list displays when you click the Favorites radio button at the top of the Assets panel.

To create a favorite asset, select the asset in the Assets panel and then click the Add to Favorites button (see Figure 11.10). When you click the Favorites radio button, the favorite assets that you just added should be listed, as shown in Figure 11.11. You can give a favorite a different name by clicking on the nickname and typing a name that is easy to remember.

NOTE

No Templates or Library Favorites

Favorites are not available for the Templates and Library categories of the Assets panel.

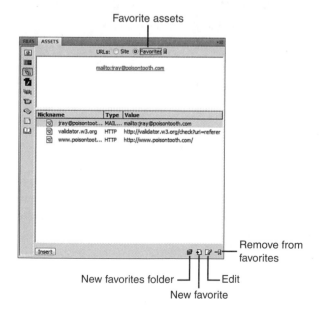

Favorite assets

New favorites folder —┘ └— Edit

New favorite

Remove from favorites

FIGURE 11.11
You can list only your favorite assets in a certain Assets panel category instead of all the assets in the site.

You can also add page objects as favorites in the Assets panel while you are working in Dreamweaver's Document window. Right-click on an image or color to bring up the context menu. Select the appropriate Add to Favorites command, as shown in Figure 11.12: Add to Image Favorites, Add to Color Favorites, or Add to Flash Favorites. This is a quick way to save a file to your favorites list in the Assets panel.

FIGURE 11.12
Add an image to the favorites in the Assets panel by selecting the Add to Image Favorites command in the context menu.

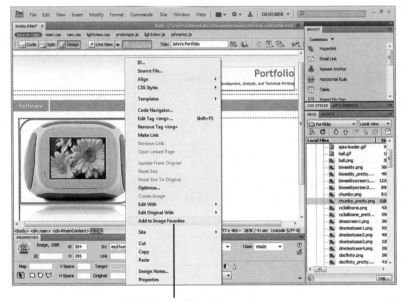

Add to Image Favorites

Another way to quickly add a favorite is to select it within your site assets, then click the Add to Favorites button in the lower-right corner of the Assets panel.

You can organize your favorites into groups by creating new folders within the favorites list. The New Favorites Folder button (refer to Figure 11.11) enables you to create a folder within the favorites list. After you create a folder, drag and drop items into the folder. Figure 11.13 shows favorite items organized into folders. Expand the folder to view the contents by clicking the + button next to the folder name. Collapse the folder view by clicking the - button next to the folder name.

Remove items from the favorites list by clicking the Remove from Favorites button. Doing so removes the item only from the favorites list; it is not

Image assets ⟶

Favorite assets

Favorites folder

FIGURE 11.13
Organize your favorite assets by creating folders in the favorites list.

deleted from the website. You can also delete an item from the list by right-clicking the item and selecting the Remove from Favorites command from the context menu.

Creating New Assets in the Assets Panel

You can use the Assets panel to help design your website. Dreamweaver enables you to create new assets in certain asset categories. You can add a new color, URL, template, or library item. Hour 15 describes how to create new library items and templates.

When you begin creating a website, you can organize your development effort with the help of the Assets panel. Organize your image assets into favorites so that commonly used images are easy to find. Define commonly used links and colors so that they can be quickly applied to web pages. When web designers work with graphic artists, the graphic artists sometimes provide a list of the colors and other specifications in the design they have created. You can use this list to add the colors to the Assets panel, assign them easy-to-recognize names ("header color," and so on), and then be ready to apply them when you start the project.

The Assets panel catalogs the assets that already exist in your site. When you are in the favorites list, you can also create new URLs and colors to use in your site. These new assets are then available, even though they haven't yet been used in your website.

▼ TRY IT YOURSELF

Creating a New Color or Link Asset

To create a new color or link asset, follow these steps:

1. Click the Favorites radio button at the top of the Assets panel. Select either the Colors category or the URLs category.

2. Click the New Color or New URL button at the bottom of the Assets panel. Either the color picker appears, as shown in Figure 11.14, or the Add URL dialog box appears, as shown in Figure 11.15.

FIGURE 11.14
Use the color picker to create a new color in the favorite colors list of the Assets panel.

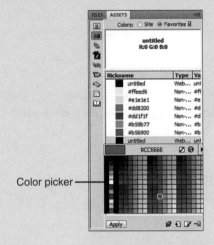

Color picker

FIGURE 11.15
Create a new favorite link in the URLs category of the Assets panel.

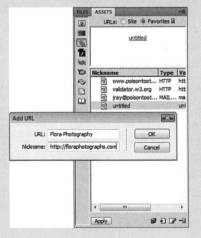

3. Pick a color from the color picker or fill in the URL and nickname in the Add URL dialog box.

When a new URL or color is added to your favorite assets, it is available from within any of your sites or pages.

Editing Assets

After you've added assets to your collection, you may eventually decide that you want to remove or edit one. To remove favorite assets, simply select them from your assets list, then press your Delete key. Keep in mind that site assets are generated automatically from the elements you use in your site, so you can remove them only by deleting the actual elements from your web page designs.

To edit an asset, select it in the list, then click the Edit button in the bottom of the Assets panel. Some elements, such as colors and URLs, can be edited directly in Dreamweaver. Complex objects, such as images and movies, launch an external editor for editing.

Copying Assets to Another Site

The Assets panel displays the assets of the current site. When you select a different site from the Site drop-down menu in the Files panel, the Assets panel displays the assets of the new site. Sometimes you might want to copy assets to a different website. You can copy a single asset, a group of assets, or a favorites group to another site.

To copy a single asset to another site, simply right-click the item name in the Assets panel and select the Copy to Site command. Select the site to which you want to copy the asset. Dreamweaver copies the exact folder structure and the file for an image or movie asset to the other site.

To copy a group of assets to another defined site, select multiple asset items by holding down the Shift key while clicking the item names in the Assets panel. Right-click the group and select the Copy to Site command from the context menu. Dreamweaver then copies all the assets to the other site. You can also copy a group of favorites to another site by following these steps.

CAUTION

Colors and Links Do Not Cascade!

Editing a color or URL in your assets does *not* change the instances of the asset that have already been used in your site, only assets you insert after the edit!

Summary

In this hour, you learned how to use assets from the Assets panel. You learned how to sort, add, and organize assets. You explored the various types of assets and learned how to create favorites. You also learned how to copy assets from site to site.

Q&A

Q. What is the best way to organize images?

A. Many web developers divide images into logical directory structures so that they can more easily find the images they want. The Assets panel can help you organize images so that you might not need to use various directories for organization. You might want to use a naming convention to help sort your images. For instance, all the images for section 1 of a website can begin with the number 1 (1_image1, 1_image2, and so on). After you've sorted the images, you can create favorites and folders to organize the favorites so that you can quickly find the images you need.

Q. I have some URLs that begin with `file:///` listed in the Assets panel. How can I find and fix these?

A. When you notice in the Assets panel that you have links beginning with `file:///`, you know you have a problem with your site. The way to identify the pages that contain these links is to run the Check Links report from the Site panel. Select each file that appears in the report as having a link that begins with `file:///` and change the URL to a document-relative address.

Workshop

Quiz

1. Which asset categories list the individual files referenced (or embedded) in a web page?

2. How can you organize favorite assets?

3. When you copy assets to another site, Dreamweaver creates exactly the same folder structure in the site to which it copies the assets. True or false?

Quiz Answers

1. The Images and Flash Movies (SWF), Shockwave Movies, Movies, and Scripts categories list the actual files referenced in web pages.

2. You create and name folders to organize your favorite assets to make them easier to find and use.

3. True. The assets are stored in exactly the same folder structure.

Exercises

1. Create some favorite assets and then create folders. Organize the favorites in the folders you created. Right-click an image in a web page and add it to the favorites list.

2. Practice copying image assets to another site. Open the site you copied the files to in the Files panel, and confirm that Dreamweaver created a new directory and copied the images to that directory.

Displaying Data in Tables

Not only do tables provide the capability to logically present data in columns and rows, but they also are used by developers for creating quick and easy visual layouts. This hour introduces you to creating tables.

Using tables can be a powerful way to organize and display data. You use tables in HTML just as you use them in a word processing application. Tables consist of rows, columns, and cells. Dreamweaver presents many ways to format tables the way you would like them to appear to your viewer.

In the past, tables have been heavily used for page layout—in fact, this was originally the only way to create complex page designs. Since the advent of CSS, however, using tables for layout has become a no-no. CSS is cleaner and provides a more flexible and accessible means of defining a page's look and feel. Hour 13, "Using CSS for Positioning," introduces you to using CSS for page layout. Using tables to lay out a new page is not suggested, but because you might have to make edits to existing pages that use layout tables, having a good understanding of table tools is important.

Creating a Table for Data

Let's begin exploring tables by adding a table that holds some data. Examples of this type of table are a phone list of people in your company or class at school, a list of wedding gifts and prices, and a recipe with amounts and ingredients. This type of table usually has a border around the cells, although it doesn't have to. If you've ever used Microsoft Excel to keep track of a list, you'll feel right at home with HTML tables.

WHAT YOU'LL LEARN IN THIS HOUR:

► How to create and format a table

► How to add and sort data in a table

► How to export data from a table

► How to align the contents of table cells

► How to nest a table within a table cell

Inserting a Table into Your Web Page

To insert a table into your web page, follow these steps:

1. Place the insertion point in your web page where you want to insert the table.

2. Select Insert, Table. The Table dialog box appears, as shown in Figure 12.1.

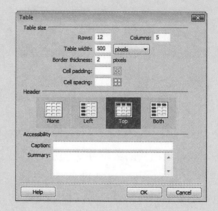

FIGURE 12.1
The Table dialog box enables you to set the initial values of the table. You can always edit these values in the Property inspector later.

3. Accept the default values or enter your own values into the Rows and Columns text boxes.

4. Set the width of the table (for example, 500 pixels) and the border size (for example, 2 pixels) in this dialog box. You learn about all these parameters, including the accessibility settings at the bottom of the dialog box, later in this hour.

5. When you finish setting values in this dialog box, click OK.

Tables (`<table>` and `</table>`) are made up of table rows (`<tr>` and `</tr>`) that contain either table cells (`<td>` and `</td>`) and `</th>`) for row or column headings. In HTML, tables are structured by their rows; you do not need to define columns, and no tag in HTML creates columns. In the rest of this hour, you modify the attributes of tables, table rows, and table cells.

When you select a table or when the insertion point is within a table, Dreamweaver displays the width of the table and the width of each column in the table header menu, which appears either above or below the table. The Table Selector menu, shown in Figure 12.2, is the green menu that is visible only in Dreamweaver and doesn't appear in the web browser. To turn off the display of the Table Selector menu in Dreamweaver, select

View, Visual Aids, Table Widths. You explore the Table Selector menu a bit more later this hour.

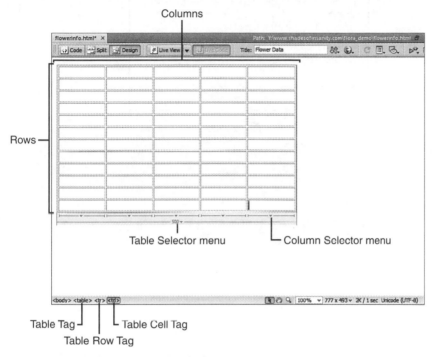

Columns

Rows

Table Selector menu

Column Selector menu

Table Tag

Table Row Tag

Table Cell Tag

FIGURE 12.2
Dreamweaver displays the Table Selector menu below a table.

Selecting Table Elements

You can select a table in a couple ways. I think the easiest way to select the table is to click the little arrow in the Table Selector menu, as shown in Figure 12.3. Choose the Select Table command from the Table Selector menu to select the table. You can also use the tag selector in Dreamweaver's status bar by clicking the table tag to select a table. Click inside one of the cells in your table. The status bar displays the tag hierarchy, including the table tag that you can click on to select the entire table.

To select a cell, simply click inside it. To select an entire row, position your cursor slightly to the left of the table row until the cursor turns into a solid black arrow. Click while the cursor is the solid black right-pointing arrow and the row turns red to select the row. Use the same procedure, positioning your cursor slightly above the column, to select an entire column, as shown in Figure 12.4. Or click the little arrow below the column to open the Column Selector menu, and then choose Select Column.

You can select a group of cells by dragging the cursor across them. Another way to select a group of cells is to first select one cell and then hold down

FIGURE 12.3
The Table Selector menu contains
commands, including the Select
Table command.

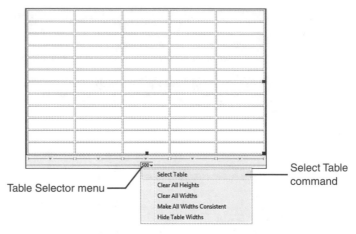

Select Table
command

Table Selector menu

FIGURE 12.4
The cursor, positioned slightly to
the left of a table row, turns into a
solid black arrow. Select an entire
row by clicking with this cursor.

Arrow cursor

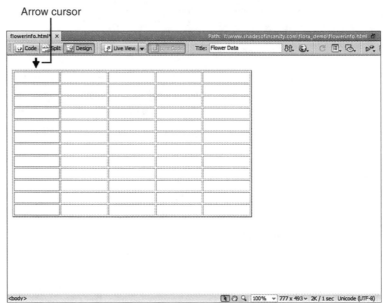

CAUTION

Drag Over Cells Carefully

When a table is empty, it's easy
to drag the cursor across the
group of cells you want to select.
Start dragging while your cursor
is inside the first cell. When the
cells contain assets, however,
it's too easy to accidentally
move objects from their cells
when you use this procedure.

the Shift key while you click another cell. All the cells between the two cells
are then selected. To select cells individually, hold down Ctrl while you
click (or Command+click on the Mac) a cell to add it to the selection.

If you find that you just can't quite get used to the methods we've already
covered for selecting a table, you may want to switch to Expanded Tables
mode by choosing View, Table Mode, Expanded Tables Mode. When in this
mode, your tables appear with very large borders, making them quite easy
to select. One word of caution: Although this doesn't alter the appearance
of the table in your browser, it means that Dreamweaver's Design mode

isn't showing an accurate representation of your page. You'll want to switch back to Standard mode after completing your table manipulations.

Regardless of how you select tables and table elements, the Property inspector shows different attributes depending on what is selected. There are two basic ways that the Property inspector appears while you're working with tables:

▸ When you select an entire table, the Property inspector looks as shown in Figure 12.5, displaying properties of the entire table.

Table properties   Rows   Width

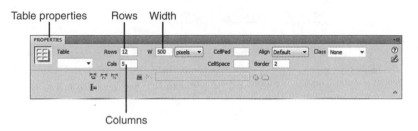

Columns

FIGURE 12.5
The Property inspector displays properties that apply to the entire table when you select the entire table.

▸ When you select an individual cell, entire row, or entire column, the Property inspector looks as shown in Figure 12.6, displaying properties that affect the selected cells.

Row, column, or
cell properties

FIGURE 12.6
The Property inspector displays properties of selected cells when you select an individual cell, entire row, or entire column.

Setting Cell Padding, Cell Spacing, and Header Options

Let's start over by adding a new table. Click the Table icon in the Common category of the Insert panel (or select Insert, Table). In the Table dialog box, set the number of rows and columns you'd like the table to have (you can always change this later). Set the table width to either a pixel or a percentage value. Set the border thickness also.

The next settings in the Table dialog box are for cell padding, cell spacing, and header (see Figure 12.7):

FIGURE 12.7
Set the cell padding, cell spacing, and header settings in the Table dialog box.

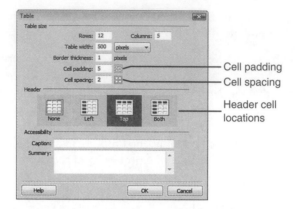

▶ **Cell padding**—This is where you set the amount of space between an object contained in a cell and the border of the cell. The cell padding sits between the contents of the cell and the inside cell border.

▶ **Cell spacing**—This is where you set the amount of space between table cells. The cell spacing sits between the outer cell borders of adjacent cells.

▶ **Header**—The header settings enable you to add a header row at the top of the table, along the left, or along both edges. By default, the text in header cells appears bold and centered.

The Table dialog box displays illustrations next to each of these settings, highlighting the area of the cell that the setting affects.

Making a Table Accessible to People with Disabilities

Users who are visually impaired and using text-to-speech synthesizer software to read your web page will have the most trouble reading large tables full of data. These users will greatly appreciate your small effort to design a table that is easier for people to navigate and extract data from. Dreamweaver has made this easy for you by placing the accessibility settings at the bottom of the Table dialog box.

You can add a caption for a table that appears in the browser and is visible to everyone. You should always add a summary for your table, as shown in Figure 12.8. Only text-to-speech browsers read the summary, and it helps the user evaluate whether to progress through the table data or skip the information.

TIP

Dreamweaver Keeps Your Table Settings

Did you notice that when you inserted another table, Dreamweaver kept the row and column settings you entered earlier? That makes it easy to create multiple tables that have similar settings.

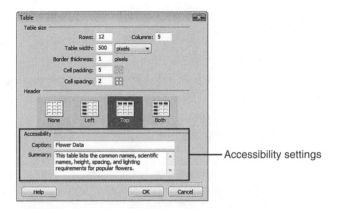

Accessibility settings

FIGURE 12.8
The Accessibility settings are important for people who have visual impairments.

After you've entered all the settings into the Table dialog box, click the OK button to create the table.

Modifying a Table and Adding Content

When you have your table structure determined, you can start adding text or images to the table. You can also fine-tune the structure as you work in Dreamweaver by using the Property inspector and selecting table cells or entire tables. Later in this hour, you use some of the built-in table color schemes available in Dreamweaver.

Adding and Sorting Data

To enter data, you click in a table cell, type, and then tab to the next cell. You can press Shift+Tab to move backward through the table cells. When you reach the rightmost cell in the bottom row, press Tab to create a new row. Add data to your table until you have enough data to make it interesting to sort.

Dreamweaver makes it easy to sort the data in your table by using Commands, Sort Table. To sort a table by using the Sort Table command, follow these steps:

1. Select the table and then select Commands, Sort Table. The Sort Table dialog box, shown in Figure 12.9, appears. It contains several drop-down menus to help you sort the table.

TIP

Layout Tables Are Not Accessibility Friendly

Accessibility is one of the main reasons it's not a good idea to use tables for layout. Although pages that use tables for layout look good visually, they are difficult to navigate for people using text-to-speech browsers—regardless of whether you completed the accessibility settings.

NOTE

Creating New Table Rows

When you press the Tab key to create a new table row, Dreamweaver gives the new row the attributes of the previous row. This might be what you want. But if you use the Tab key to create a new row from a header cell row, your row will be more header cells!

TRY IT YOURSELF ▼

Sorting a Table Using the Sort Table Command

▼ TRY IT YOURSELF

Sorting a Table Using the Sort Table Command

continued

2. Select the column to sort in the Sort By drop-down menu.

3. Select whether you want to sort the column alphabetically or numerically in the Order drop-down menu.

4. Select whether you want to sort in ascending or descending order in the drop-down list directly to the right of the Order drop-down menu.

5. Below this first set of sorting options, you can set up a secondary search, if necessary. If you do this, Dreamweaver first sorts by the primary column and then sorts by the secondary column.

6. If the first row of the table is a header row, leave the Sort Includes the First Row box unchecked. If you don't have header cells, you should include the first row in the sort.

7. If you'd like the header and footer rows of the table to be sorted, select Sort Header Rows or Sort Footer Rows, respectively.

8. The Keep All Row Colors the Same After the Sort Has Been Completed check box allows you to keep table row attributes with the row after the sort. If you have formatted your table in a certain way, you should check this box so that your formatting isn't lost.

9. Click OK to start the sort.

FIGURE 12.9
The Sort Table dialog box contains drop-down menus with sorting options.

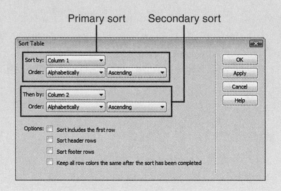

Figure 12.10 shows an example of a sorted table.

Adding and Removing Rows and Columns

To remove a row or column from a table, use the context menu that pops up when you right-click a table cell. Right-click a table cell and select the Table submenu; another menu appears, with a number of commands to add and

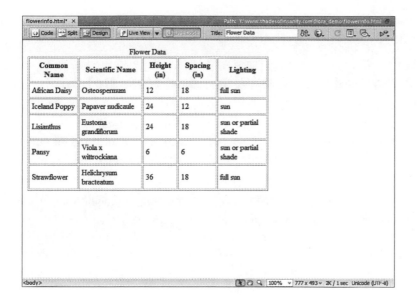

FIGURE 12.10
Data can be sorted alphabetically or numerically in either ascending or descending order by the Sort Table command.

remove rows, columns, or both, as shown in Figure 12.11. Select one of these commands to make a change to the table.

FIGURE 12.11
The context menu has a Table submenu that contains many commands to add, remove, or change the rows and columns of a table.

Use the icons in the Layout category of the Insert panel to add rows either above or below the current row or to add columns to the left or the right of the current column. You can also add or remove rows and columns by editing the table properties in the Property inspector. Adjust the number of

NOTE

Modifying the Number of Rows and Columns

When you use the Property inspector to adjust the number of rows and columns, Dreamweaver inserts a new column to the far right of the table. It inserts a new row at the bottom of the table. If you remove columns or rows in the Property inspector, Dreamweaver removes the columns from the right side and the rows from the bottom. You lose any data that is in the removed columns or rows.

rows and columns in the Property inspector with an entire table selected to add or remove groups of cells.

Changing Column Width and Row Height

You can change column width and row height by dragging the cell borders or by entering values in the Property inspector. If you prefer to eyeball the size, position the cursor over a cell border until the cursor turns into the double-line cursor. Drag the double-line cursor to change the column width or row height.

Use the W (width) and H (height) boxes in the Property inspector to give exact values to widths and heights. Values are expressed in either pixels or percentages. As with the horizontal rule you created in Hour 4, "Dealing with Words: Adding Text and Lists," a percentage value changes your table size as the size of the browser window changes, whereas a pixel value always displays the table at a constant size.

Resizing and Coloring Tables

Just as you can change the size of cells, rows, and columns, you can change the size of an entire table. With the entire table selected, drag the resizing handles to make the table a different size. If you have not given width and height values to cells, rows, and columns, the cells distribute themselves proportionally when the entire table size is changed. Or use the W and H boxes in the Property inspector, with the entire table selected, to give the table either pixel or percentage size values.

To clear all the width and height values from a table, select the Table Selector menu when the table is selected in the Document window. This menu contains commands to clear the cell heights and widths. It also contains commands to convert all the values to pixel or percentage values. These commands are handy if you set table attributes to pixel values and want to change them to percentage values and vice versa. Buttons for these commands are available in the lower half of the Property inspector when you select the table, as shown in Figure 12.12.

Merging and Splitting Table Cells

You might want some rows in your table to have fewer cells than other rows. For example, you might want the top row of a table to have a title centered over all the columns. How do you accomplish that?

Convert buttons

Clear buttons

FIGURE 12.12
When you select an entire table, the Property inspector has buttons available to clear the row height and the column width. There are also buttons to convert dimension values to pixels or percentages.

You can increase or decrease the column span and row span by either **splitting** or **merging** cells. To merge an entire row so that it appears as one cell, select the row and click the Merge button (see Figure 12.13) or right-click anywhere on the row and select the Merge Cells command from the Table submenu of the context menu. Now you can position the content of the entire row over all the columns.

Merge cells

Split cells

FIGURE 12.13
The Merge button appears in the Property inspector when you select an entire row. This button causes all the selected cells to appear as one cell.

Use the Split Cell command to add additional rows or columns to a cell. The Split button is beside the Merge button in the Property inspector. Click the Split button or right-click in the cell and select the Split Cell command from the Table submenu of the context menu, and the Split Cell dialog box appears. Enter the number of rows or columns you would like to split the cell into and click OK. Now a single cell splits into multiple cells.

Aligning Table Cell Contents

You can align the contents of a cell or a group of cells vertically—from top to bottom. The Vertical Alignment drop-down menu sets the vertical alignment for the contents of an individual cell or a group of cells. When setting the vertical alignment, you have the following options:

▶ **Default**—This is usually the same as middle alignment of the cell contents.

▶ **Top**—This aligns the cell contents at the top of the cell.

- ▶ **Middle**—This aligns the cell contents in the middle of the cell.
- ▶ **Bottom**—This aligns the cell contents at the bottom of the cell.
- ▶ **Baseline**—This is applied to multiple cells in a row, aligning the bottom of the objects across all cells. For instance, if you have very large text in the first cell and small text in the second cell, the bottom of each line of text aligns with baseline vertical alignment.

Align the contents of a cell or a group of cells horizontally—from left to right—with the Horizontal Alignment drop-down menu. When setting the horizontal alignment, you have the following options:

- ▶ **Default**—This is usually the same as Left for cell content and Center for header cell content.
- ▶ **Left**—This aligns the cell contents on the left of the cell.
- ▶ **Center**—This aligns the cell contents in the center of the cell.
- ▶ **Right**—This aligns the cell contents on the right of the cell.

Adding Color to a Table

You can add color to a table in several places:

- ▶ A background color for a table cell
- ▶ A background color for a table row
- ▶ A background color for a table column

Figure 12.14 shows where the color settings are located in the Property inspector. Cell properties always have priority over the same properties in the row or column. For instance, if you applied blue as the row background color and then applied red to an individual cell, the single cell would be red and all the other cells in the row would be blue. Set the background color in the Property inspector.

Exporting Data from a Table

You can export table data from an HTML table. You can then import the data into a spreadsheet, a database, or another application that has the capability to process delimited data—that is, data separated by a delimiter.

A **delimiter** is the character used between the individual data fields. Commonly used delimiters are tabs, spaces, commas, semicolons, and colons. When you are exporting a data file, you need to pick a delimiter that does not appear in the data.

Colored cells

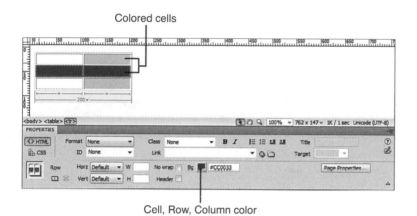

FIGURE 12.14
Adding colors in the Property inspector controls the background color attributes of table cells.

Cell, Row, Column color

To export table data from Dreamweaver, follow these steps:

1. Select a table or place your cursor in any cell of a table.

2. Select File, Export, Table. The Export Table dialog box appears, as shown in Figure 12.15.

TRY IT YOURSELF ▼

Exporting Table Data from Dreamweaver

FIGURE 12.15
Open the Export Table dialog box by selecting File, Export. You use this dialog box to export delimited data that can be imported by other applications.

3. Select the data delimiter from the Delimiter drop-down menu.

4. Select the line break style from the Line Breaks drop-down menu. The line break style is dependent on the operating system, so select the operating system that will be running when the data file is imported. For example, if you are sending the data file to someone who will be running a spreadsheet on a Macintosh computer, select Macintosh.

5. Click the Export button and save the file. Give the file a title. Usually comma-delimited files end with .csv and tab-delimited files end with .txt.

Get Data from Pages on the Web

Dreamweaver's Export Table command is useful to get information from any web page. You can save a web page with table data from anywhere on the Web by using the browser's Save As or Save Page As command and then open the web page in Dreamweaver. Select a table on the page and then export the data. This enables you to use the data in a spreadsheet application, such as Excel, or to import it into your own web page.

In Chapter 19, "Using AJAX Frameworks and Libraries," we look at how table data can be reused directly from a web page, without having to import anything!

Don't Use Too Many Nested Tables

It's fine to nest tables within tables within tables. But if you nest too much, the browser might display the tables slowly. Make sure that your design doesn't become too complicated.

Nesting a Table Within a Table

Placing a table within a table cell creates a **nested** table. The dimensions of the table cell limit the nested table's width and height. To nest a table, place the insertion point inside a table cell and insert a new table (Insert, Table).

Summary

In this hour, you learned how to add a table to a web page. You also learned how to add and remove table cells and rows and how to set the column width and row height of a table. You entered data into a table and then sorted that data by using the Sort Table command. You also learned how to export table data for an external application to use.

Q&A

Q. When I set a column width to a certain value, such as 50 pixels, why doesn't the column display at that value in the browser?

A. Have you set the width of the entire table to a value that is the sum of all the column values? If not, the table might be stretching the columns to make up for the extra width that the table has in its width attribute.

Some browsers do not make an empty table cell a given width. Web developers came up with the trick of stretching a 1-pixel GIF, called a **spacer image**, to the desired width to force a table cell to be the correct width. If you use a spacer image, it requires hardly any download time and viewers will not see it.

Q. Are pixel values or percentage values better to use with tables?

A. It depends. If you want your table always to appear the same size, use pixel values. However, if the browser window is narrower than the table, the viewer has to scroll horizontally to view the entire table. Horizontal scrolling is not desirable. If you use percentage values in your table, it's much harder to predict what the final table is going to look like in the viewer's browser. If you use tables with pixel values, you might need to mandate a certain screen resolution to view the table. Be aware that some people disapprove of this type of mandate on the Web.

Workshop

Quiz

1. What are the HTML tags, as displayed in the Dreamweaver tag selector, for a table, a table row, and a table cell? Extra credit: What's the tag for a table header?

2. If you apply a background color to an entire table and a background color to a cell, which color shows up in the cell?

3. What's the name of the character that separates cell data held in a data text file that you can import into Dreamweaver?

Quiz Answers

1. The tag for a table is `<table>`, the tag for a table row is `<tr>`, and the tag for a table cell is `<td>`. The tag for a table header is `<th>`.

2. The cell attributes take precedence over the table attributes, so the color you applied to the cell shows up.

3. The character that separates cell data held in a text file is a delimiter.

Exercises

1. Create a table with text in column 1 and numbers in column 2. Try both ascending and descending sorts on both the alphabetic (text) data in column 1 and the numeric data in column 2.

2. Create a table in Dreamweaver, enter some data, and export the table data by using the Table Export command. Remember where you saved the file and then open it with a text editor, such as Notepad. What does the file look like? Add another record in Notepad, making sure that you use the same delimiter, and then import that data back into Dreamweaver.

3. Insert a table and experiment with merging and splitting cells. Insert a nested table into one of the cells in Standard mode. Create a complex layout, such as a back statement or some other tabular design.

Using CSS for Positioning

In Hour 6, "Formatting Web Pages Using Cascading Style Sheets," you worked with CSS (Cascading Style Sheets) styles and applied them to text. This hour builds on that knowledge, enabling you to write CSS styles that create a page layout. **Page layout** refers to designing the way a page looks when viewed in a browser. When you lay out a page, you position text, menus, and other page elements in an efficient and attractive way.

This hour uses a subset of CSS called **CSS-P**, in which the *-P* is for *positioning*. Instead of dealing with fonts and background colors as with the CSS you created in Hour 6, CSS-P defines properties such as width, height, margins, padding, and borders. These properties are important when you're creating the structure of a web page.

Although table tags have traditionally been used as the "layout containers" for content in traditional websites, in CSS-P div tags serve the role of the containers. You apply the CSS to the div tag to define its width, height, margins, and so on. Dreamweaver makes it easy to insert a div tag and give it a style.

Understanding the CSS Box Model

To create a page layout, you have to start thinking of the elements in your web page as a collection of boxes. Each box has attributes you can modify using CSS. You can think of a single paragraph as a box, for instance, but it's more likely that you will want to wrap a div tag around a group of paragraphs and make that a section of your web page. The CSS box model describes the following box characteristics:

Choose a Screen Resolution for Your Design

Design for a specific screen resolution by first selecting a resolution from the Window Size drop-down menu in Dreamweaver's status bar. When creating complex and very precise layouts, you'll want to design for a common screen size, such as 1024×768.

▶ **Width and Height**—The width and height properties can be either a fixed number (for example, 300 pixels) or a relative number (for example, 45%). The width and height values affect the content area. The total width and height may be larger than these values because the padding, border, and margin values add into the total size of the box.

▶ **Margin**—The distance between one box and another box. This part of the box is always transparent.

▶ **Padding**—The distance between the content of the box and the border. This part of the box picks up the background color of the content.

▶ **Border**—The delineation between the padding and the margin. The border is invisible (0 pixels) by default. You can set the thickness, style, and color properties of a border.

Figure 13.1 shows the relative positioning of the various parts of a box. The content area is on the inside, surrounded by the padding. The border surrounds the padding. The margin is the transparent area outside of the border.

FIGURE 13.1
The CSS box model describes the properties of all containers.

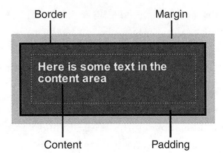

The size of a box reflects the sum of the width or height plus the size of the margin, padding, and border. For instance, if a box has a width of 200 pixels, a left and right padding value of 10 pixels, a left and right border value of 2 pixels, and a left and right margin value of 20 pixels, its total width would be 200 + 20 (both padding values) + 4 (both border values) + 40 (both margin values) = 264 pixels.

The preceding width example uses only fixed pixel values, but it's often useful to use relative measurement units such as ems (related to the size of the letter *m*) or percentages. For instance, you might want to set the left margin of a paragraph to a fixed pixel value so that it sits a specific distance away from a sidebar on the left. But you could set the top margin using ems so that the vertical spacing between paragraphs is proportional to the font size.

Exploring a CSS Page-Layout Example

Dreamweaver comes with numerous layout examples. The New Document dialog box enables you to create a new page layout, including the CSS. It also gives you the option of saving the CSS in an external style sheet. In the next few minutes, we explore a CSS page-layout example that creates a page with two columns, a header, and a footer. This is a common layout for web pages.

To create a CSS page layout, do the following:

1. Select File, New to open the New Document dialog box.

2. Select the Blank Page category, select HTML as the page type, and find the following layout: 2 Column Liquid, Left Sidebar, Header and Footer. You should see the layout preview to the right, as shown in Figure 13.2.

Preview

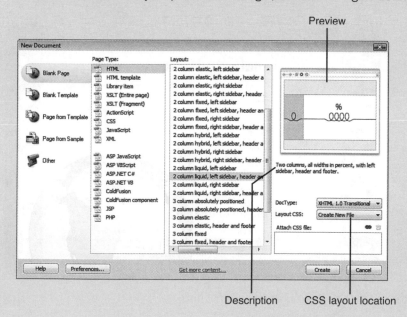

Description   CSS layout location

TRY IT YOURSELF ▼

Creating a CSS Page Layout

FIGURE 13.2
Dreamweaver's New Document dialog box enables you to select from many page-layout designs. The design preview is visible on the right side of the dialog box.

▼ TRY IT YOURSELF

Creating a CSS Page Layout

continued

3. Select XHTML 1.0 Transitional as the DocType.

4. Select Create New File from the Layout CSS drop-down menu.

5. Click the Create button.

6. You are prompted to save the CSS in an external file. Create a directory called `css` if you'd like and save the file as `layout.css`.

7. Save the new file as `layout.html`.

TIP

Comments in the Code

The sample page layouts that come with Dreamweaver have abundant comments written in both the HTML and the CSS. Simply select Code view and read the comments that Adobe has left to help you understand some of the ideas implemented in the code.

FIGURE 13.3
The page layout is made up of containers having different width, height, margin, padding, and border properties.

The design is a fluid (liquid) layout. The left sidebar and main content area maintain the same relative size to one another as you change the size of the window. (You can do this in Dreamweaver or preview the page in a browser.) The header and footer span the entire width of the sidebar and main content area. Note that the design is horizontally centered on the page.

Figure 13.3 shows the combination of containers (boxes) on the screen. Div tags define these containers. As you click around the screen, you can see the name of the divs in the tag selector; you can also see any parent divs that contain the currently selected div. Clicking the tags in the tag selector enables you to select the container on the screen.

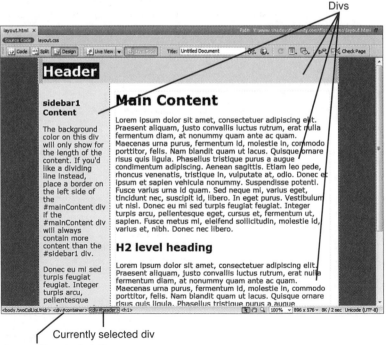

Divs

Currently selected div

Parent of currently selected div

Viewing the CSS Visually

Dreamweaver enables you to display your CSS page layout in a couple of different ways so that you can see the margins, padding, borders, and the relative positioning of all the CSS box model elements. Three CSS view options are available in the Document toolbar's Visual Aids menu (see Figure 13.4):

CSS Layout visual aids

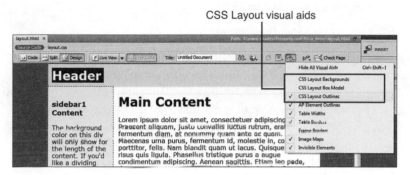

FIGURE 13.4
The Visual Aids menu contains commands enabling you to view the boxes in different ways. This helps you view and modify the page layout.

▶ **CSS Layout Backgrounds**—This visual aid displays each of the containers with a different background color in the content area. These colors, of course, are not displayed in the browser—only in Dreamweaver for design purposes. This view helps you clearly see the boxes.

▶ **CSS Layout Box Model**—This visual aid displays the padding and margins of a selected box. The padding displays using fine diagonal lines and the margins display using larger diagonal lines.

▶ **CSS Layout Outlines**—This visual aid displays a thin yellow outline around all boxes. When you roll your cursor over one of the outlines, it becomes red, meaning that you can click to select the box.

You'll practice inserting div tags in a few minutes, but let's continue exploring the sample layout page that Dreamweaver created for you. This page contains the following five divs:

▶ **header**—This is the div at the top of the page.

▶ **sidebar1**—This is the div along the left side of the page.

▶ **mainContent**—This is the div in the middle of the page.

▶ **footer**—This is the div at the bottom of the page.

▶ **container**—This is the div that contains all the other divs.

An id selector stored in the external style sheet defines each div. The following id selectors correspond to the five divs in the preceding list:

- ▶ `.twoColLiqLtHdr #header`

- ▶ `.twoColLiqLtHdr #sidebar1`

- ▶ `.twoColLiqLtHdr #mainContent`

- ▶ `.twoColLiqLtHdr #footer`

- ▶ `.twoColLiqLtHdr #container`

Each style begins with the class selector `.twoColLiqLtHdr`. A selector consisting of several different selectors is called a **compound selector**. For the properties of the selectors to be applied, the elements must match all the selectors. For instance, if a selector is defined as `p .pink`, it applies only to paragraphs that have the class `.pink` applied; other paragraphs are not affected by the style. The definitions for the five divs each have the `.twoColLiqLtHdr` at the beginning because that class defines the body tag that applies to everything on the web page.

As you select each of the CSS styles in the CSS Styles panel, you can see the style properties in the Properties section of the panel, as shown in Figure 13.5. As you examine each of the styles, you can see that the width, padding, border, and margin properties have been set, along with other properties such as background color and text alignment. You can edit these styles, modifying this layout to look the way you'd like it to look.

FIGURE 13.5
Each of the five divs is styled by an id selector.

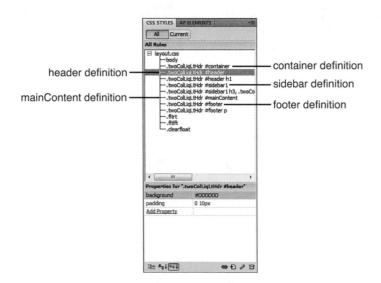

Understanding Float and Clear

Float and Clear are essential properties to use when creating page layouts. These properties enable you to control when elements sit next to each other and when they sit under other elements. The properties available for each are as listed here:

▶ **Float**—Selecting Left positions the element to the left, Right positions it to the right, and None removes the Float property.

▶ **Clear**—Selecting Left ensures that nothing sits to the left of the element, Right ensures that nothing sits to the right, Both ensures that nothing sits on either side of the element, and None removes the Clear property.

In the sample page-layout page you created, the sidebar floats to the left. Examine the selector `.twoColHybLtHdr #sidebar1` to see the Float property. The mainContent div appears to the right of the sidebar div because of the 26% left margin that pushes the content of the div to the right. The Clear property forces the footer div under the sidebar and mainContent divs. This is implemented in the page layout using a break tag with the `.clearfloat` class selector applied: `<br class="clearfloat">`. You have to look in the code to see the tag directly above the footer div.

Positioning a Div

Now it's your turn to create a page layout. You create a series of divs and CSS styles, positioning the divs into a page layout, and store the styles in an external style sheet.

Creating a CSS page layout is a repeating process of creating a CSS style, inserting a div tag or another container tag, applying the style, and then editing the style to make it work. You continue this process until your page layout is what you want. Generally there is a common page layout for multiple web pages. Sometimes websites will have one page layout for the home page and a second page layout for all the secondary web pages linked from the home page.

Inserting Divs

You begin creating a page layout at the top of a new, empty web page. The first div you create at the top is called banner.

Creating a New Page and External Style

First, create the page and define a CSS style as described here:

1. Create a new blank document by selecting File, New, Blank Page, HTML, <none>.

2. Save the file (File, Save) as my_layout.htm.

3. Click the New CSS Rule button in the CSS Styles panel to open the New CSS Rule dialog box.

4. Choose ID from the Selector Type drop-down menu. We look at what this means in a few minutes.

5. Enter the name **#banner** in the Selector Name text box.

6. Select (New Style Sheet File) from the Rule Definition drop-down menu.

7. Click OK.

8. Save the new style sheet as my_layout.css.

9. In the CSS Rule Definition dialog box, select the Background category. Give the style a background color.

10. Click OK to save the style.

Using id Selectors

Dreamweaver saves the #banner style and links the external style sheet to the web page. The form of the CSS name, #banner (with the pound symbol), indicates that #banner is an id selector. This means that there can be only *one* element on the page that uses this style (that is, we can have only one banner). The default CSS style selector is a "class," which can be applied to as many elements as you want.

Creating a Banner Div

Next you have to insert the div tag into the web page and apply the style by adding the id attribute to the tag:

1. Select Insert, Layout Objects, Div Tag. The Insert Div Tag dialog box opens.

2. Select At Insertion Point from the Insert drop-down menu.

3. Select Banner from the ID drop-down menu, as shown in Figure 13.6. This adds the id attribute to the div tag so that it looks like this: <div id="banner">.

4. Click OK. Dreamweaver inserts a div tag into the web page.

5. Select the placeholder text that Dreamweaver inserts into the div and apply Heading 1 from the Property inspector's Format drop-down menu (HTML mode).

ID attribute

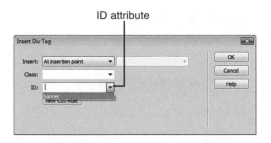

FIGURE 13.6
The Insert Div Tag dialog box enables you to define where the div
tag will be inserted. You can add a
class or id attribute to the tag.

Notice the tag selector with the new div selected: The div tag appears as
<div#banner>. Did you also notice that the div is sitting away from the web
page edges? That's because the web page has a default margin value.

To remove the default margins, you must redefine the body tag. Let's do that
next with the following steps:

TRY IT YOURSELF ▼

Changing Page Margins

1. Click the New CSS Rule button in the CSS Styles panel to open the New
   CSS Rule dialog box.

2. Choose Tag from the Selector Type drop-down menu.

3. Type **body** into the Selector Name field.

4. Select the external style sheet my_layout.css as the location to save
   this style.

5. Click OK.

6. Select the Box category.

7. With the Margin Same for All option selected, enter 0 (zero) into the Top
   Margin text box. The value is automatically entered for the Right, Bottom,
   and Left values as well, as shown in Figure 13.7.

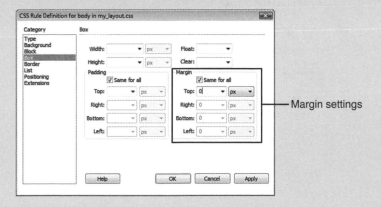

FIGURE 13.7
Modify the Margin attributes in the
Box category of the CSS Rule Defi-
nition dialog box.

8. Click OK to save the style.

Now the banner div hugs the left, top, and right margins of the web page.

NOTE

Use a Flattened Image for Tracing

I'm lucky enough to get to work with talented graphic designers when I work on most of my projects. They usually design the page layout in a graphics tool such as Fireworks or Photoshop. I can ask them to give me a **flattened** version of the file, meaning a single JPG with all the layers in the graphic merged into one. Then I can use this as a tracing image in Dreamweaver.

Using a Tracing Image

A **tracing image** is useful when you are creating a page design and you have an image showing all the completed page elements. You can use this image as a tracing image. Instead of estimating where the elements go on-screen, you can display a tracing image and lay the individual image and text elements over the tracing image perfectly. A tracing image makes it easy to align objects.

Load a tracing image into Dreamweaver in the Page Properties dialog box. The tracing image is visible only in Dreamweaver and is never visible in the browser. A tracing image covers any background color or background image, but the background color or background image is still visible in the browser.

▼ TRY IT YOURSELF

Using a Tracing Image

To load a tracing image into Dreamweaver, follow these steps:

1. Open the Page Properties dialog box (by selecting Modify, Page Properties).

2. Select the Tracing Image category.

3. Click the Browse button beside the Tracing Image box to select the image that is a tracing image. Browse to the tracing image file. It must be a GIF, JPEG, or PNG.

4. Drag the Transparency slider to set how opaque (solid) or transparent the tracing image will be, as shown in Figure 13.8.

FIGURE 13.8
You can load a tracing image into the Page Properties dialog box. Set the transparency with the slider.

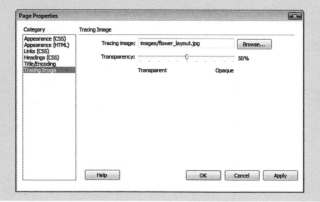

5. Click OK. Your tracing image appears in the background of the Document window, with the transparency setting you specified.

Creating Compound Selectors

A **compound selector** defines the properties of the rightmost selector in a list of selectors. For instance, the compound selector #banner h1 would apply only to h1 tags contained in an element with the id equal to banner.

A compound selector is useful when you'd like elements to appear with unique properties in individual circumstances. This is better than creating and applying a class selector.

To create a compound selector, do the following:

1. Click the New CSS Rule button in the CSS Styles panel to open the New CSS Rule dialog box.

2. Select Compound.

3. Enter **#banner h1** in the Selector Name field.

4. Select the external style sheet my_layout.css as the location to save this style.

5. Click OK.

6. Select the Box category.

7. Uncheck the Same for All check box for the Margin properties.

8. Enter **10** pixels into the Top Margin box and **20** pixels into the Left Margin box.

9. Click OK.

▾ TRY IT YOURSELF

Creating a Compound Selector

Floating Page Elements

Now you add another container that holds two columns below the banner div. You use a different technique from what was used in the sample page-layout page we examined at the beginning of the hour. This div holds two other divs that are left and right columns.

First, create a container div to hold the column divs. Before you create the new div, it's important that you don't have an existing div selected on the

TIP

Link Selector Styles

If you drop down the Selector Name menu instead of typing tags into the box, you see a list of the selectors. These are the same CSS styles you modified in the Page Properties dialog box in Hour 5, "Adding Links: Hyperlinks, Anchors, and Mailto Links," when you changed the link attributes.

web page because you might accidentally nest the new div. The easiest way to move the cursor off a div is to press the right-arrow key on your keyboard. You can also place your cursor after the div's closing tag by viewing the web page in Code view.

The following steps create a new div:

1. Select Insert, Layout Objects, Div Tag. The Insert Div Tag dialog box opens.

2. Select At Insertion Point from the Insert drop-down menu.

3. Enter the name **main** in the ID drop-down menu.

4. Click the New CSS Rule button, shown in Figure 13.9. This opens the New CSS Rule dialog box with the id selector name, #main, already entered.

FIGURE 13.9
You can launch the New CSS Rule dialog box directly from the Insert Div Tag dialog box.

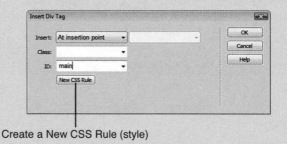

Create a New CSS Rule (style)

5. Select the external style sheet my_layout.css as the location to save this style.

6. Click OK.

7. Select the Background category and define a background color for this id selector.

8. Click OK to save the style properties.

9. Click OK in the Insert Div Tag dialog box. Dreamweaver inserts a div tag with id="main" into the web page.

Creating Columns

Now you have a container for the two columns. Next you insert two divs into this container. You have to make sure that this time the cursor is inside of the main div because you need to nest the two columns within this div.

First, add the left column like so:

Adding the Left and the Right Columns

1. Select Insert, Layout Objects, Div Tag. The Insert Div Tag dialog box opens.

2. Select At Insertion Point from the Insert drop-down menu.

3. Enter the name **leftcol** in the ID drop-down menu.

4. Click the New CSS button. This open the New CSS Rule dialog box with the id selector name, #leftcol, already entered.

5. Select the external style sheet my_layout.css as the location to save this style.

6. Click OK.

7. Select the Box category.

8. Set the Width to 45%.

9. Select Left from the Float drop-down menu, as shown in Figure 13.10.

Float

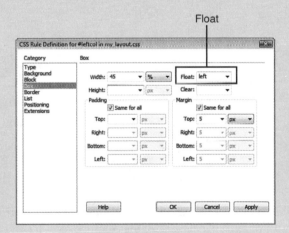

FIGURE 13.10
You set the float properties in the Box category of the CSS Rule Definition dialog box.

10. Set all the margins to 5 pixels (leave the Same for All check box selected).

11. Click OK to save the style properties.

12. Click OK in the Insert Div Tag dialog box. Dreamweaver inserts a div tag with id="leftcol" nested within the main div.

To create the right column, you can simply copy the style for the left column and modify it. Do the following to add the right column:

1. Right-click the #leftcol style in the CSS Styles panel.

2. Select the Duplicate command from the menu, as shown in Figure 13.11.

FIGURE 13.11
Instead of starting from scratch, you can duplicate a similar style, save it with a different name, and then modify it.

Duplicate existing style ———

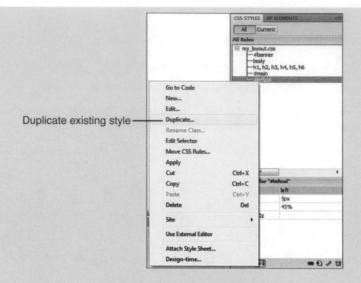

3. Enter the name **#rightcol** in the Duplicate CSS Rule dialog box, and save the style in the external style sheet my_layout.css.

4. Click OK.

5. Select #rightcol in the CSS Styles panel and click the Edit Style button.

6. Select the Box category and change the Float property to Right.

7. Position the cursor in the main div but not inside of the leftcol div.

8. Select Insert, Layout Objects, Div Tag. The Insert Div Tag dialog box opens.

9. Select Rightcol from the ID drop-down menu and click OK.

You have to enter placeholder text into the column to get a realistic look. Add a couple of paragraphs to each of the columns. When you preview the page in the browser, you'll notice that the background color of the main div isn't showing up behind the columns. That's because the main div is collapsing. Next you add an element to the page that clears the float and forces the div to not collapse.

Clearing the Float

You have to do a little hand-coding for this to work because there isn't an easy way to get Dreamweaver to add this code via Design view. First, you define a class selector that you can add to any element to clear any floating elements. Then you apply that class to a break tag.

To create a clearing class selector, do the following:

1. Click the New CSS Style button in the CSS Styles panel.

2. Choose Class as the Selector Type.

3. Enter the name as **clearfloat**, as shown in Figure 13.12, and save the style in the external style sheet my_layout.css.

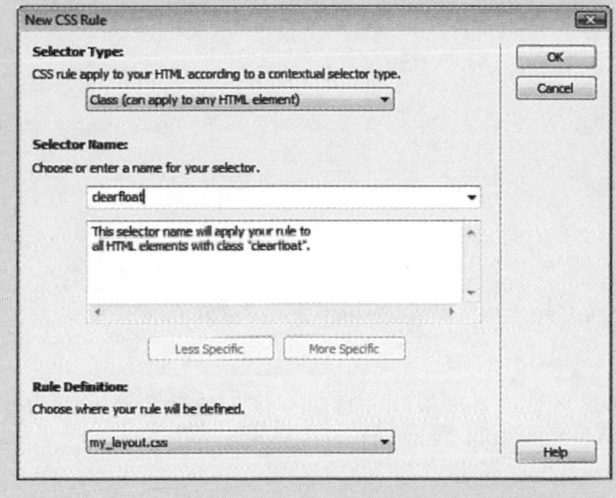

TRY IT YOURSELF ▼

Creating and Applying a Clearing Class Selector

FIGURE 13.12
Create a new class selector to clear the floating elements.

4. Click OK.

5. Select the Box category.

6. Select Both from the Clear menu.

7. Click OK to save the style definition.

To apply the clearing class selector:

1. In Code view, create a new blank line between the closing div tag (</div>) for div#rightcol and div#main. These will probably be the two closing div tags immediately before the closing body tag (</body>).

2. In the blank line, type the following: **<br class="clearfloat" />**. Notice that Dreamweaver helps you with your choices as you type.

3. Return to Design view.

Now when you preview the page in the browser, the main div should no longer collapse and you should be able to see the background color behind the columns.

CAUTION

Fluid...to an Extent

Fluid designs have become popular because they make the best use of screen space by expanding as needed. Fluid designs, however, can sometimes lead to web pages that stretch out of control. On 24-inch monitors, a browser window can be almost two feet wide! Trying to read a line of text across two feet can be difficult. As a result of growing monitor sizes, fluid designers have had to reevaluate their design goals and create pages that limit their maximum size.

Centering Your Design on the Page

Sometimes you might want a fluid (also known as **liquid**) design that completely fills the browser no matter what the screen resolution. Often, though, that makes it hard to create a nice design. Many web pages are designed with fluid elements in the middle of the page (such as setting the columns to 45%) but with a fixed value for the total width of the design.

In the next few minutes, you wrap a container around all the divs in your current page, holding the design to a specific width. Then you center the design horizontally on the web page.

▼ TRY IT YOURSELF

Centering Page Content with a Div

Follow these steps to wrap a container around the entire page and center the design:

1. The easiest way to select all the content on the page is to click <body> in Dreamweaver's tag selector.

2. Select Insert, Layout Objects, Div Tag. The Insert Div Tag dialog box opens.

3. Dreamweaver understands that you already have something selected in the Design window because Wrap Around Selection is already selected in the Insert drop-down menu. You'll want to wrap this div around all the other divs in the page.

4. Enter the name **all** into the ID drop-down menu.

5. Click the New CSS Rule button.

6. The name #all should be automatically entered into the Selector Name text box. Save the style in the external style sheet my_layout.css.

7. Click OK.

8. Select the Box category.

9. Set the Width to 500 pixels.

10. Uncheck the Margin Same for All check box.

11. Select both the Left and Right Margin drop-down menus and select Auto, as shown in Figure 13.13.

12. Click OK to save the style definition.

13. Click OK to insert the div.

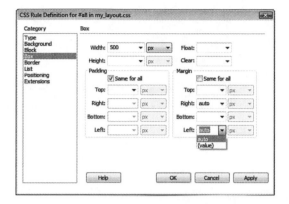

FIGURE 13.13
Setting the left and right margins to Auto centers the design horizontally on the page.

Now the design is fixed-width and centered on the web page. This is a simple technique to create a horizontally centered design. Most of the websites you design will have some elements that have a fixed width and other elements that have widths relative to the element they are contained within.

Fine-Tuning Your Design

When creating a page layout, I find it's easier to begin adding divs and content from the upper-left corner of the web page. Then I work down and to the right, adding divs, content, and nesting divs.

There are several tools in Dreamweaver that can help you create a page layout. First, the Grid tool (View, Grid, Show Grid) displays evenly spaced horizontal and vertical lines. You can change the grid spacing by choosing View, Grid, Grid Settings. Similarly, turning on Guides (View, Guides, Show Guides) displays lines on the screen that you can use to guide your design. For instance, select View, Guides, 1024×768, Maximized to add guides outlining the page design space that you would have available for a web page displayed at that screen resolution.

You can also create your own guides. First, turn on the rulers by selecting View, Rulers, Show. Notice that you can also set the measurement units to pixels, inches, and centimeters under View, Rulers. I usually work in pixels.

To add a new guide on the screen, click within the ruler and drag a guide into the Document window. As you are dragging, the cursor displays the current pixel location so that you can precisely position the guide, as shown in Figure 13.14. You add a horizontal guide by dragging one from

TIP

Remember to Test Your Design Carefully

Page layout can be tricky so it's important that you test your page-layout design in many different browsers under different conditions. For instance, be sure to make your browser window larger and smaller to see what happens to the design at different screen resolutions or if the visitor doesn't have the browser maximized. You also may want to modify the default browser font size to see what that does to your design.

the horizontal ruler and add a vertical guide by dragging one from the vertical ruler.

FIGURE 13.14
Drag a custom guide from the ruler
and position it in the Document
window.

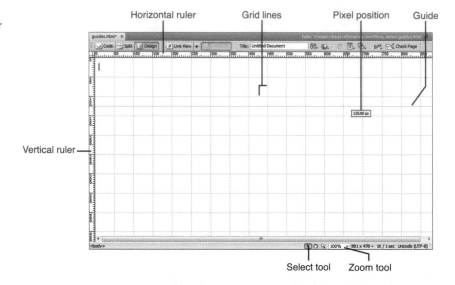

It's easy to accidentally move a guide while working in Dreamweaver, so you should lock your guides after you've set them (View, Guides, Lock Guides). You can always unlock them by choosing this command again later. Sometimes the guides get in the way of viewing the page design, so you can turn the guides off without actually removing them by selecting View, Guides, Show Guides and removing the check mark by the command in the Guides submenu.

The Zoom tool is also helpful while you're designing a page layout in Dreamweaver. This tool is in the status bar of the Dreamweaver Document window, next to the Select tool and the Hand tool. Select the Zoom tool, shown in Figure 13.14, and click on the Document window to zoom in on the design to fine-tune positioning. After you've zoomed in, choose the Select tool to select objects such as table cells or images. To quickly return to 100%, simply double-click the Zoom tool.

CAUTION

Don't Zoom Accidentally

It's good to get into the habit of clicking on the Select tool immediately after finishing using the Zoom tool. Otherwise, you waste a lot of time accidentally zooming.

Summary

In this hour, you learned about the CSS box model and about using div tags styled with id selectors to create a CSS page layout. You explored one of the sample page layouts that Dreamweaver provides. You explored the Float and Clear properties to create floated columns. You centered a design horizontally on the page and learned how to use Dreamweaver's tool to fine-tune the design.

Q&A

Q. I'm in charge of a bunch of web pages that were designed using tables. Should I redo all of them?

A. Most websites go through design revisions every few years (some much more often). I would wait for one of these revision cycles and make the structure change at that point. It's a lot of work to re-create the page structure on an existing site. You should take a lot of time to plan that type of update.

Q. Are there any differences in the way browsers display CSS?

A. Unfortunately, yes. If you look in the code of the sample page we created in this hour, you'll notice in one of the Adobe sample page layouts that Adobe has entered some code at the top of the page to fix some potential browser errors. You can also see comments in the CSS.

Adobe has recently added a CSS Advisor area to its website. A link to the CSS Advisor can be found in the Dreamweaver Developer Center CSS area at http://www.adobe.com/devnet/dreamweaver/css.html. The CSS Advisor enables developers to exchange information and provides tips on what CSS works in various browser versions.

Q. Why should I use div tags for page layout instead of span tags?

A. Span tags are meant to wrap around small items, such as a few words within a paragraph, to apply a style. Div tags are meant to create containers for page layout. You could use the tags interchangeably, but that wouldn't be the appropriate use for the tags.

Workshop

Quiz

1. How many times can you apply an id selector to a web page?

2. How would you write the selector for a compound selector to style a paragraph (`<p>`) that is contained in a div with the `id="smile"`?

3. What is the difference between margins and padding?

Quiz Answers

1. Just once. You can have only one element per page with a certain id name applied, so only that element will have the corresponding id selector applied.

2. It would be either div#smile p or #smile p.

3. The padding is between the content and the border, whereas the margins are between the border and other elements on the page. In addition, the padding picks up the background color of the content, whereas the margins are always clear.

Exercises

1. Review and test the different layouts provided within Dreamweaver. Try combining portions of one layout into another. The included templates can be easily modified to create almost any layout you want without extensive CSS coding.

2. Explore inserting divs using the Insert Div Tag command. Insert a div and add content within the div. Add some content to another part of the page and wrap a div tag around that content using the Insert Div Tag command.

Creating CSS for Mobile Devices and Printing

In Hour 6, "Formatting Web Pages Using Cascading Style Sheets," you learned about CSS (Cascading Style Sheets) fundamentals and applying CSS to text. In Hour 13, "Using CSS for Positioning," you learned about CSS layout. In this hour, you explore using CSS for delivery to devices other than a computer screen. The other devices will most likely be either printers or mobile devices such as PDAs or mobile phones. But the techniques presented can be used to deliver unique web page layouts to projection devices, televisions, and even devices designed for people who are hearing or vision impaired.

You've explored attaching an external CSS style sheet to a web page, but you might not have realized that you can attach multiple style sheets to the same web page. You could create one style sheet for the screen, one style sheet for printing, and maybe another style sheet for a small-screen device like a mobile phone. Each of the style sheets can tailor the elements on the screen to the way the web page is delivered.

In this hour, you explore techniques for adding CSS for delivery to different devices. This is a complicated topic, so this is only an introduction. You'll be able to get started applying these techniques to your websites right away.

Understanding the CSS Media Attribute

Up to this point, you've created CSS generically without specifying the delivery medium. Actually, we've assumed that the delivery medium is a

WHAT YOU'LL LEARN IN THIS HOUR:

▶ How to add multiple external style sheets to a web page

▶ How to design a style sheet specifically for printing

▶ How to hide elements on the page

▶ How to troubleshoot problems with conflicting styles

▶ How to preview a page designed for handheld devices in Adobe Device Central

computer screen. And the majority of those using the Web are probably looking at your content on a computer screen.

But how many of you have looked up a website on your Internet-enabled PDA or smartphone or mobile phone? I have, many times, and sometimes the pages I encounter are difficult to read on my device. Even if you haven't browsed the Web on your phone or PDA, you've most likely printed a web page. Often you end up with a lot of information that isn't necessary: buttons, links, and other content that is obviously not necessary in a paper version of the information.

Remember that when you link to an external style sheet, Dreamweaver puts a reference to that style sheet in the head of the web page. The HTML looks like this:

```
<link href="../css/tours07.css" rel="stylesheet" type="text/css" />
```

To tell a browser to use the style sheet when displaying the web page in a specific medium, such as printing or the computer screen, Dreamweaver adds the media attribute to the link tag so that it looks like this:

```
<link href="../css/tours07.css" rel="stylesheet" type="text/css"
media="screen" />
```

The media attribute can contain the following:

- ▶ **All**—Applies CSS to all media types.

- ▶ **Screen**—Applies CSS to content displayed on a computer screen.

- ▶ **Aural**—Controls the speed, tone, pitch, and other attributes of synthesized text delivered via a TTS browser. So far, this media type is not commonly recognized.

- ▶ **Braille**—Controls a Braille-tactile device used by those with visual impairments.

- ▶ **Embossed**—Formats the web page content for Braille printers.

- ▶ **Handheld**—Formats the web page content for handheld devices such as PDAs and mobile phones.

- ▶ **Print**—Formats the web page content for printers.

- ▶ **Projection**—Formats the web page content for full-screen projection or kiosk delivery without the browser toolbars.

- ▶ **TTY**—Formats the web page content for TTY (teletype) devices commonly used as a telecommunications device for the deaf (TDD).

NOTE

Alternative Ways to Reference Media Types

In this hour, we are going to cover a single way to reference different media types using CSS: using external style sheets. However, there are multiple methods of using CSS to target different media types. I think using an external style sheet is easier to troubleshoot and maintain, so we're using that technique here.

▶ **TV**—Formats the web page content for delivery to a television.

In this hour, we explore the most commonly used (and most widely recognized) media types: Screen, Print, and Handheld. You specify the media type when you link to an external style sheet. The Attach External Style Sheet dialog box, shown in Figure 14.1, displays the list of media types in the Media drop-down menu. When you select a media type, Dreamweaver automatically adds the media attribute to the linked style sheet.

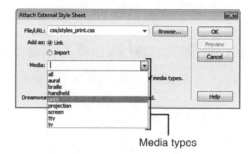

FIGURE 14.1
You set the media type attribute when linking to an external style sheet.

Previewing Style Rendering in Dreamweaver

One of the difficulties of designing for different devices is that you are viewing your work on a computer screen and it's difficult to tell what the page is going to look like on other devices. Dreamweaver enables you to view how the styles for a particular media type look. The Style Rendering submenu of the View menu enables you to select which media type's CSS is displayed in the Dreamweaver Document window.

You can also add a Style Rendering Toolbar to the Dreamweaver interface by choosing View, Toolbars, Style Rendering, as shown in Figure 14.2.

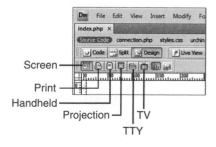

FIGURE 14.2
Use the Style Rendering Toolbar to preview a media type.

Dreamweaver controls only how the web page looks within Dreamweaver. All the styles will apply when you view the web page in a browser. These commands are extremely useful while you're designing in Dreamweaver because they enable you to apply only the CSS that you are currently working with. For instance, while you are developing a style sheet for print, you can choose to display the Print media type in Dreamweaver so that you see how the page will look when it is printed. You won't see the screen style sheet in Dreamweaver until you change the way the page renders.

I usually design a web page for the screen and then redesign it for other devices. That's what we are going to explore next!

Adding an Alternative Style Sheet

In the next few minutes, you see how to create a style sheet that specifically styles a web page for printing. The easiest way to begin is to copy the existing style sheet designed for the screen.

To create a copy of an existing style sheet, do the following:

1. Open an existing website—something from Hour 13 would be a perfect choice. Make sure that the Files panel is visible.

2. Select the CSS file in the Files panel.

3. Right-click the file and choose Edit, Duplicate from the context menu, as shown in Figure 14.3.

4. Edit the name of the copied CSS file. Because the new file is for printing, you could add _print to the name—flora_print.css, for example.

Now you have two external style sheets: the original file and a copy of that file. Next you link to the external style sheet, setting the media type.

Setting the External Style Sheet Media Type

We assume that when you originally linked to the external style sheet, you didn't specify a media type for the style sheet. If you don't specify a media type, the browser applies the styles to everything. This has the same effect as the All media type listed earlier.

We could easily go into the code to add the media attribute to the external style sheet, but instead we're going to use another easy technique. You first unlink the external style sheet from the page and then relink it, adding the media attribute.

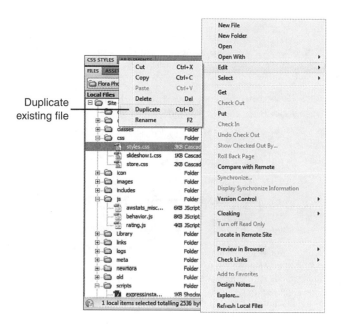

FIGURE 14.3
Quickly duplicate the CSS file from the Files panel.

Duplicate existing file

To unlink the style sheet and relink it, follow these steps:

1. Select the name of the external style in the CSS Styles panel.

2. Click the Delete button, as shown in Figure 14.4, in the CSS Styles panel. This deletes the reference to the external style sheet but doesn't delete the actual file.

Unlinking and Relinking a Style Sheet

Attach Style Sheet

Delete

FIGURE 14.4
When you delete the external style sheet, you delete the reference to it but don't delete the file.

▼ TRY IT YOURSELF

Unlinking and Relinking a Style Sheet

continued

3. Reattach the style sheet by clicking the Attach Style Sheet button.

4. Select the file and be sure to select the radio button beside Link.

5. Select Screen from the Media drop-down menu.

6. Click OK. The external style sheet again links to the web page. Notice that the media type appears beside the style sheet name in the CSS Styles panel, as shown in Figure 14.5.

FIGURE 14.5
The media type appears beside the name of the external style sheet in the CSS Styles panel.

Media type

Link to a Second External Style Sheet

There are two ways to start designing an external style sheet specifically for printing:

▶ Create a new external style sheet by creating a new style and electing to save the new style in a new style sheet, as shown in Figure 14.6.

▶ Save a copy of the existing style sheet for the screen.

As we've mentioned, it's often easier to start with a copy of the existing style sheet because then you don't have to start from scratch and redefine everything. You can simply link the copy of the style sheet to the same web page and begin to edit the style sheet for printing.

TIP

Comments in CSS

You can enter a comment in CSS files by surrounding the comment text like this: /* This is a comment */. This is useful for describing the purpose of a particular file.

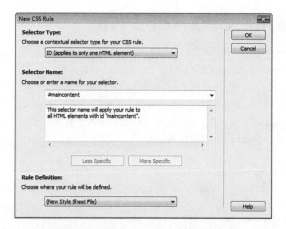

FIGURE 14.6
You can create a new external style sheet by simply defining a new CSS style.

Follow these steps to link the copy of the style sheet:

1. Click the Attach Style Sheet button in the CSS Styles panel.

2. Select the file and be sure to select the radio button beside Link.

3. Select Print from the Media drop-down menu.

4. Click OK. The external style sheet links to the web page.

5. If you have a number of styles listed in the external style sheet, you might not be able to see both style sheets listed in the CSS Styles panel. Click the Collapse button below the external style sheet name.

Notice that the Print media type appears beside the newly linked style sheet name in the CSS Styles panel, as shown in Figure 14.7.

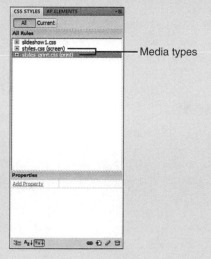

— Media types

FIGURE 14.7
The media type appears beside each filename in the CSS Styles panel.

Designing CSS for Print

To edit the style sheet for print, you have to make sure that Dreamweaver is displaying the design controlled by the Print style sheet. Select View, Style Rendering, Print Media Type. Because you haven't edited the Print style sheet, the page should still look the same, but that soon changes as you begin making edits. When designing CSS for print, pay attention to these commonly used web page sections:

▶ **Navigation**—You can't navigate on a piece of paper, so navigation isn't necessary in a printed web page. Navigation includes buttons and breadcrumbs.

▶ **Hyperlinks**—Again, these navigational objects are not necessary in a printed document. You can modify the CSS for print so that hyperlinks blend into the other text.

▶ **Search**—You can't search a piece of paper with this utility, so it should be removed.

▶ **Interactions**—Zooming, resizing, scrolling, or any other types of interactions should be removed from a printed version of the web page.

▶ **Feedback and Email Contact**—Because the viewer cannot contact you or give you feedback by clicking a link when reading a printed page, you should add information making it easy to call you if necessary.

▶ **Fonts and Font Sizes**—In Hour 6, we explored using proportional font size measurement units, such as percentage and ems, for the screen. But the point measurement unit was designed for print and works very predictably. Also, it's popular to use sans-serif fonts designed for the screen, such as Verdana or Tahoma, in web pages. Serif fonts such as Times New Roman are actually easier to read in print.

Hiding Elements

When you are delivering the same content to multiple devices (the screen and a printer in this example), how can you hide parts of the page? CSS has the display property that can have multiple values, but the one we are interested in is `display:none`. Applying this property to an element in a web page makes it disappear!

Figure 14.8 shows a web page in Dreamweaver's document that contains multiple elements that I listed earlier as elements to pay attention to. There are links, breadcrumbs, hyperlinks, and a linked map image. If someone is interested in printing the content of the page, they won't need these elements, because they're solely useful for web visitors.

Breadcrumbs   Hyperlinks

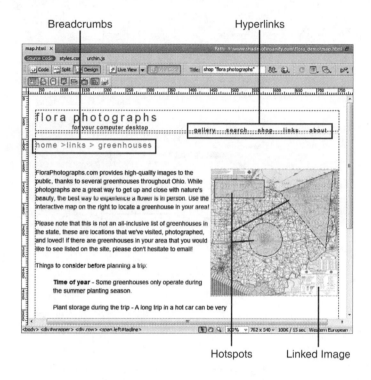

Hotspots   Linked Image

FIGURE 14.8
You have to identify items on the page that might need modification for the printed version of the web page.

The first step in creating a print design for the web page is to use the display property to turn off these elements in the printed version.

TRY IT YOURSELF ▼

Hiding an Element Through CSS

To turn off an element in the web page, do the following:

1. Select the element in Dreamweaver's Document window and look in the tag selector to identify the selector applied to it. This is the style you need to edit in the style sheet.

2. Select the style you identified in step 1. Make sure that you are working in the style sheet that is for print.

3. Click the Edit Style button in the CSS Styles panel.

4. Select the Block category.

5. Select None from the Display drop-down menu, as shown in Figure 14.9.

▼ TRY IT YOURSELF

Hiding an Element Through CSS

continued

6. Click OK to save the change.

7. Repeat steps 1 through 6 for each element that you want to hide in the printed web page.

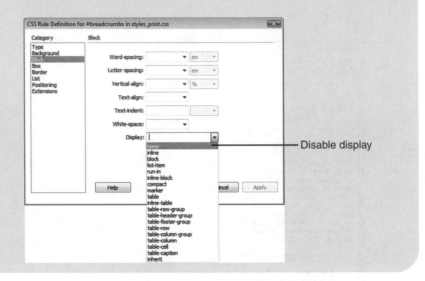

FIGURE 14.9
The display property can be set in the Block category of the CSS Rule Definition dialog box.

— Disable display

TIP

Cleaning Up

Some of the elements you hide using the display property might have other styles defined in the external style sheet that are no longer necessary. For instance, if you hide the ID selector #cart, then #cart a:hover and #cart p are no longer necessary. You can delete these unnecessary styles from the print version of the style sheet. Be careful to delete them from the correct file!

If you selected View, Style Rendering, Print Media Type, the elements should disappear from Dreamweaver's Document window. If you switch to the screen view (View, Style Rendering, Screen Media Type), the elements reappear. When you view the page in the browser, you see the styles in the Screen style sheet.

▼ TRY IT YOURSELF

Creating a New Style to Hide Unprintable Elements

If some of the elements you'd like to hide do not have an id or class selector already applied, you can quickly create one and apply it using this procedure:

1. Click the New CSS Rule button in the CSS Styles panel.

2. Using the Contextual Selector Type drop-down, choose Class to create a new class or ID to create a new ID selector.

3. Give the style selector a name.

4. Select the Print style sheet from the Rule Definition drop-down menu.

5. Click OK.

6. Select the Block category.

7. Select None from the Display drop-down menu.

8. Click OK.

9. Select the element in Dreamweaver's Document window and identify the tag in the tag selector.

10. Right-click on the tag in the tag selector and select either the Set Class or the Set ID command.

11. Select the new style you created to apply to the element on the page, as shown in Figure 14.10.

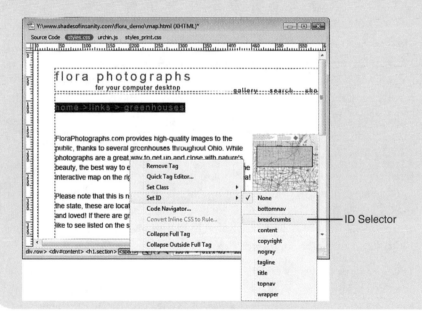

FIGURE 14.10
Set the style using the menu that drops down from the tag selector.

Modifying the Default Font

Next we explore changing the default font on the page to a serif font that is set to 12 points. This makes the text easier to read when printed. You need to edit the style that redefines the body tag.

To modify the default page font, do the following:

1. Using the CSS Styles panel, choose the Print style sheet, and identify and select the style that redefines the body. If defined using Dreamweaver's Page Properties command, the style looks like this: `body, td, th`.

2. Click the Edit Style button.

3. Select the Type category.

4. Select Times New Roman, Times, Serif from the Font drop-down menu.

5. Enter 12 points as the size.

6. Click OK.

When you save the style, the font for the text on the page should change. If the size does not change, other styles might be affecting the text. It's useful to be able to tell where the style conflict is coming from.

Identifying Style Conflicts

You can use the CSS Styles panel to identify which styles are applied to the currently selected element in Dreamweaver's Document window. We've mostly used the CSS Styles panel in All mode with the All button selected. The Current mode, with the Current button selected, is useful for troubleshooting and identifying why elements on the screen do not look the way you'd like them to.

Even though we set the text to 12-point Times New Roman, it's not appearing that size. To begin troubleshooting, highlight the text and then within the CSS Styles panel click the Current button. Immediately you can see, within the Summary section, as shown in Figure 14.11, that the font size is set to 80%, not the 12 points we're expecting.

The Summary shows us which styles are being applied to the selection. Start by clicking through the different lines in the Summary and looking at the properties. In this example (Figure 14.11), we can see that the `body`, `td`, `th` selector is trying to set a font, but it is crossed out. To find out why, we just place our cursors over the crossed-out line and Dreamweaver tells us that the font size is being overridden by the rule for p (the paragraph tag).

An even easier way to arrive at this conclusion is to just look through the summary for what seems amiss. When we notice the "80%" set for the font size, clicking that item in the summary quickly shows us that it is the p rule that is setting the size, as shown in Figure 14.12.

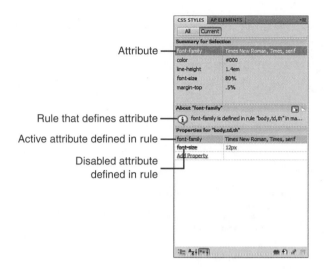

FIGURE 14.11
Different styles apply to the same element. You can investigate the properties in the CSS Styles panel.

Attribute

Rule that defines attribute

Active attribute defined in rule

Disabled attribute defined in rule

FIGURE 14.12
The properties can be identified and edited in the CSS Styles panel.

Active font size

Rule defining font size

When you've identified the problem elements in your document, select the property you want to change in the CSS Styles summary section, and then click the Edit button to jump to the CSS editor with that style selected.

Hiding Hyperlinks

Displaying hyperlinked text, colored and underlined, is unnecessary in a printed web page. It's easy to use CSS to modify links created using anchor (a) tags.

The following shows you how to make links blend into the text by redefining the a tag:

1. Click the New CSS Rule button in the CSS Styles panel.

2. Choose Tag as the selector type from the Contextual Selector Type drop-down menu.

3. Select a from the Tag drop-down menu.

4. Select the Print style sheet in the Rule Definition section, as shown in Figure 14.13.

FIGURE 14.13
Redefine the a tag and save it in the Print style sheet.

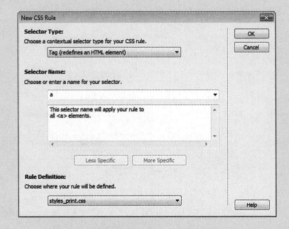

5. Click OK.

6. Set the text color to be the same as the default text color for the page.

7. Select the check box next to None as the Text-decoration property, as shown in Figure 14.14. This removes the underline from the hyperlinks.

FIGURE 14.14
Set the Text-decoration property to None to remove the underline from links.

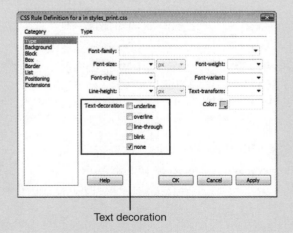

Text decoration

8. Click OK.

Now all the hyperlinks should blend into the text in the printed version of the web page.

Adding a Print-Only Message

So far we've discussed hiding elements in the web page that should appear on the screen but not the print version. But you can do the opposite as well. It's a nice touch to give a message on the printed version of the web page acknowledging that it's been designed for print. It's also a great idea to include a phone number, making contact away from the computer easy to achieve.

TRY IT YOURSELF ▼

Creating Printable-Only Content

Follow these steps to add a message to the printed version of the web page:

1. Select Insert, Layout Objects, Div Tag to add a new container to the web page.

2. Enter a name into the ID text box. A good name might be `printnotice`.

3. Enter some text into the div which explains that the page has been formatted for printing and provides a contact number, as shown in Figure 14.15.

FIGURE 14.15
Create a div and enter a message explaining that the page has been formatted for printing.

Print-only div

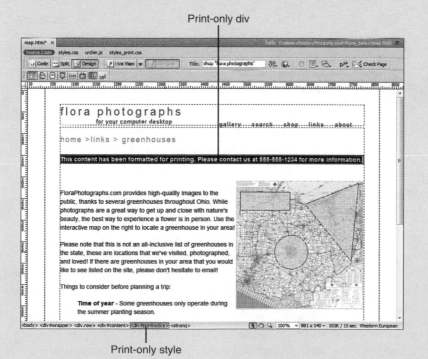

Print-only style

▼ TRY IT YOURSELF

**Creating Printable-
Only Content**

continued

4. Switch Dreamweaver to screen rendering by selecting View, Style Rendering, Screen Media Type. Note that the div also appears in this view.

5. Hide the `div#printnotice` in the screen style sheet. Click the New CSS Rule button in the CSS Styles panel.

6. Choose ID from the Contextual Selector Type pop-up menu.

7. Enter the div ID (`printnotice`) as the selector.

8. Make sure that you define this style in the external style sheet for the *screen*. Select the Screen style sheet from the Rule Definition drop-down menu.

9. Click OK.

10. Select the Block category.

11. Select None from the Display drop-down menu.

12. Click OK.

Now the print-only div is hidden in the screen view, but it is printed when the viewer chooses to print the web page.

CSS for Handheld Devices

Handheld devices come in many different shapes and sizes and are increasingly being used to surf the Internet. If you're a web developer, chances are, you're going to have handheld devices surfing your site sooner or later. The trouble with handhelds is that their capabilities vary greatly. Devices like the Apple iPhone provide full web browser capabilities (just like a desktop), whereas most other cellphones offer a far more limited view.

Thankfully, *most* typical handhelds can be dealt with easily using a *Handheld* style sheet. Let's review that process now.

Using the Handheld Style Sheet and Device Central

You can follow the same steps you used to create a style sheet for printing to create a style sheet for most handheld devices. You create a set of styles in an external style sheet and attach the sheet to a web page specifying the media type as **Handheld**. The browsers in handheld devices such as mobile phones and PDAs use this style sheet to display the web page content.

In the previous printing example, you used the style-rendering commands to preview how the web page looks with a specific set of styles applied. Because it's difficult to preview how pages will look on the small screen of a

handheld device, Adobe includes Adobe Device Central CS4 with
Dreamweaver. You use this application to preview how web pages will
look in a browser on various handheld devices.

To preview a web page in Device Central, do the following:

1. Open the page in Dreamweaver and use the "Preview in Browser" menu
   (the small globe) to choose "Preview in Device Central," as shown in
   Figure 14.16.

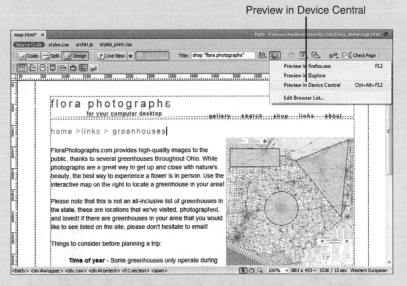

Preview in Device Central

TRY IT YOURSELF ▼

**Previewing a Page in
Device Central**

FIGURE 14.16
The Preview in Device Central command is located in the same menu
used to preview in browsers.

2. Device Central opens with the web page displayed.

3. Select the targeted device from a list of available devices on the left, as
   shown in Figure 14.17.

4. Return to Dreamweaver, make any necessary changes, and preview the
   page again. Use the scroll buttons to preview how scrolling vertically and
   horizontally looks.

Targeting the iPhone and Advanced Handhelds

Advanced handhelds (specifically the iPhone), don't play by the same rules
as other mobile browsers. These devices aim to put the Web in the palm of
your hand and do so by rendering web pages using the same Screen style
sheet as a normal desktop web browser, as shown in Figure 14.18. So how
can we make something that uses the Screen style sheet selector, but also
identifies the device as being a handheld?

FIGURE 14.17
Adobe Device Central includes numerous device definitions, or you
can create your own.

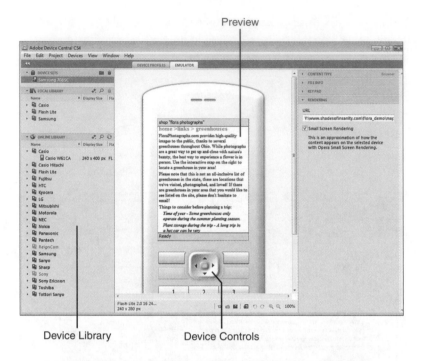

Preview

Device Library   Device Controls

FIGURE 14.18
The iPhone acts like a desktop
browser, using the Screen media
type.

The answer is by using a complex selector for the media. Instead of just
specifying "screen", we can set a media type of "only screen and (max-
device-width: 480px)". This selection loads a specific style sheet that is
visible only on devices with a screen resolution of 480px or less. The entire
rule, to be inserted in the <head> content of your web page, is this:

```
<!—[if !IE]>—>
<link media="only screen and (max-device-width: 480px)"
  rel="stylesheet" type="text/css" href="iphone.css"/>
<!—<![endif]—>
```

This includes a conditional statement (if !IE) that hides the code from Microsoft's IE browser, which may interpret it incorrectly. After inserting this code, you can create an iphone.css file that displays only on iPhone and iPhone-like devices.

So, what about all the other devices out there that you may want to target? Unfortunately, these can be a bit of a problem. The reason that developers flock to Apple's iPhone isn't just because it is a "cute" device; it's because it is a very strictly defined standard. Windows Mobile devices can come with different screen resolutions and very different capabilities. In other words, an iPhone is an iPhone is an iPhone—and that simply isn't true for other platforms.

If you want to target Windows Mobile devices, an elaborate and effective means of setting up a style sheet has been documented at this site: http://johannburkard.de/blog/www/mobile/Linking-CSS-for-handheld-devices-revisited.html. The caution that I leave you with, however, is that unless you're developing a very specific site for a very specific type of handheld, just knowing that something is Windows Mobile does not give you enough information to create complex and compelling layouts. Instead, I would recommend that you simply target this class of devices using the Handheld media type.

> **TIP**
>
> **An iPhone Expert**
>
> This code sample has been widely copied and repeated online. I believe that the original source (and an excellent place for more information) can be found at Tom Boutell's website: http://www.boutell.com/newfaq/creating/iphone.html.

Summary

In this hour, you learned how to use the media type to specify that certain styles apply to certain devices. You learned how to format a web page for a printing device, including how to hide elements and hyperlinks, and how to add a print-only message. You also explored previewing a web page designed for a handheld device in Adobe Device Central.

Q&A

Q. I've printed the page I created a style sheet for, and it's too wide for the printed page. Is there a way to control this?

A. You can wrap a container (div) around the page and set this to a standard printed page width. For instance, the standard paper width in the United States is 8 1/2 inches wide. Accounting for a 1-inch margin on each side, you can make the total width of the container 6 1/2 inches.

Q. Do I have to create a style sheet for the printing?

A. Although it's not necessary to create a style sheet for printing, it's a nice touch on a professional website. If people have a reason to print out the content on the web page, it's worth the effort to design a style sheet specifically for that purpose. If there is no reason to print the page, you might be wasting your time creating a special Print style sheet.

Workshop

Quiz

1. What is the value of the display property that creates a style that makes an element not appear on the web page?

2. What media type signals that a style sheet is specific for viewing a web page on the computer?

3. Why is it easier to target iPhone as a web development platform than it is to target other handheld devices?

Quiz Answers

1. Giving the display property the value of None makes an element not appear on the web page.

2. The Screen media type is specific for viewing a web page on the computer.

3. The iPhone has a full desktop-like browser, and, more important, it is well-defined as a platform. There are no variances in browser capabilities between iPhone devices.

Exercises

1. Create a traditional web page designed to be displayed using a browser. Create a new CSS style sheet to display that page on a mobile device. Use the Adobe Device Central to preview the redesigned page in a simulated handheld device.

2. Modify a traditional web page designed to be displayed using a browser to instead be printed. Create a Print CSS style sheet. Preview the web page in a browser and use the Print Preview command to view how the page will look when printed.

Creating Library Items and Templates

In this hour, you work with two features of Dreamweaver that enable you to create reusable items. First you explore **library items**, reusable chunks of code that you can insert into web pages. During the second half of the hour, you explore **templates**, which are whole web pages that include elements you can change and elements you can't change from page to page. Both library items and templates enable you to update all the instances in the website by simply updating the original library item or template.

Library items and templates help you maintain consistency in a website. They also allow you to share design elements with other web developers. When you are in the design phase of a website, you should be thinking about common elements across all the web pages in your site that would be appropriate to create as Dreamweaver library items. You should also be thinking about common structures that would lend themselves to templated pages.

Managing Library Items and Templates in the Assets Panel

When you are creating and applying library items, you open the Library category of the Assets panel, shown in Figure 15.1. To create and apply templates, open the Templates category of the Assets panel, also shown in Figure 15.1. The Library and Templates categories of the Assets panel show all the library items and templates that exist in the current website. Each website you create can have a different set of library items and templates.

The Library and Templates categories of the Assets panel are in halves. The bottom half of the Assets panel lists the names of the library items and tem-

WHAT YOU'LL LEARN IN THIS HOUR:

► How to create library items and templates

► How to add a library item to a web page

► How to edit and update library items and templates

► How to apply a template to a web page

► How to edit an original template and update linked web pages

► How Dreamweaver can work with Adobe content management systems

plates in the website, and the top half displays a preview of the library item or template you selected in the bottom half. The buttons at the bottom of the panel include the following:

▶ **Refresh**—You click this button to refresh the list in the Assets panel. This is useful for refreshing the list after you've added a new item.

▶ **New**—You click this button to create a new, blank library item or template.

▶ **Edit**—You click this button to open the library item or template in its own Dreamweaver Document window for editing.

▶ **Delete**—You click this button to remove the original library item or template from the library. This doesn't affect any instances of the library item or template (although the item no longer updates throughout the site).

There are also Insert and Apply buttons for the Library and Templates categories, respectively:

▶ **Insert**—You click this button to insert the currently selected library item at the location of the insertion point in the web page.

▶ **Apply**—You click this button to apply the currently selected template to the web page.

You use the Library and Templates categories of the Assets panel to manage your library items and templates.

FIGURE 15.1
The Library (left) and Templates (right) categories of the Assets panel display all the items in the current website.

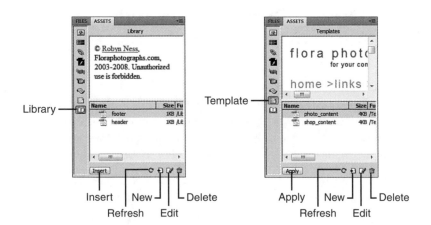

Creating a Library Item

When designing web pages, you can create library items from objects you use often. If you update the original library item, it updates everywhere throughout your site. This is very handy!

You can turn all sorts of objects into library items. For instance, a navigation bar or a set of links that is present in many of the pages in your website would be an excellent candidate for a library item. When you need to add a new button or link, it is simple to add the button or link to the original library item and then update your entire site automatically with the change.

You can create a library item, save it to the Library category of the Assets panel, and then apply it to any web page within your website. Anyone working on the same website can use the library item (after you have shared it, of course), and you can use library items created by others. You can include a library item in a web page multiple times. Library items can be created from any object contained in the body of the web page, such as forms, tables, text, Flash movies, divs, and images.

You have to define a website before Dreamweaver can insert a library item. Dreamweaver creates a directory called Library, where it stores all the library items, in the root of your website. When you insert a library item into your web page, Dreamweaver inserts into the page a copy of everything contained in the library item.

There are two ways to create library items:

- ▶ From an existing object or group of objects—After you decide to create a library item out of a group of objects on a web page, you select the objects and save them into the library.

- ▶ From scratch, as a new, empty library item—You can create a new library item, open it, and add objects to it just as if it were a regular web page.

NOTE

The Difference Between Library Items and Templates

Library items differ from Dreamweaver templates in that **library items** are portions of a page, whereas a **template** is the structure of an entire page. Libraries and templates are similar, though, because both can automatically update all the linked items and pages. A template contains the entire structure for a web page, including both the head and the body sections of the page. A library item is simply a chunk of code and not a complete page.

Creating a Library Item from Existing Content

You create a library item from an existing object or group of objects on your web page as shown here:

1. Select an object or a group of objects. Select multiple objects either by dragging your cursor over them or by holding down the Shift key and clicking objects to add to the selection.

TRY IT YOURSELF ▼

Using Existing Content in a New Library Item

▼ TRY IT YOURSELF

Using Existing Content in a New Library Item

continued

2. To add the selection to the library, drag and drop it to the bottom half of the Library category of the Assets panel. Alternatively, select Modify, Library, Add Object to Library.

3. Give the library item a meaningful name. The Name field is selected immediately after you create the library item; at any time, you can reselect the name with a long single-click on the Name field.

NOTE

Library Files

Dreamweaver creates an individual file for each library item. The file extension for a library item is .lbi. If you look in the Library directory of your website, you will see one .lbi file for each library item you have in your website.

When you select a library item in the Assets panel, you see the contents of the library item in the top half of the Library category of the panel, as shown in Figure 15.2. The contents might look different from how they will look in the web page because the Library category of the Assets panel is small and the objects wrap. In addition, because the library item is only a portion of a web page, it appears with no page background color or applied CSS (Cascading Style Sheets).

FIGURE 15.2
The Library category of the Assets panel displays a preview of a single library item in the top half and lists all the library items in the bottom half.

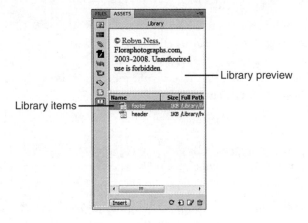

Creating a Library Item from Scratch
===========

▼ TRY IT YOURSELF

Creating and Editing a New Library Item

To create a library item from scratch, follow these steps:

1. Click the New Library Item button at the bottom of the Library category of the Assets panel. Dreamweaver creates a new, blank library item, as shown in Figure 15.3. A message telling you how to add content to the blank library item appears in the top half of the Library category of the Assets panel.

2. Give the library item a name. For example, create a copyright statement to go at the bottom of each of your web pages. The name Copyright would be a good choice.

3. Double-click the library item in the Library category of the Assets panel. Dreamweaver opens the library item in a separate Document window. You can tell that you have a library item open because Dreamweaver displays <<Library Item>> along with the name of the library item in the title bar, as shown in Figure 15.4.

4. Insert objects into the library item's Document window just as you would in any web page. Insert the copyright symbol (from the Text category of the Insert panel or by selecting Insert, HTML, Special Characters), a year, and a name.

5. Close the Document window and save the library item. The Library category of the Assets panel reflects your changes.

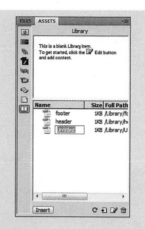

FIGURE 15.3
Create a new library item, open it, and add content.

FIGURE 15.4
To add content to a library item, open it in a separate Dreamweaver Document window. The window shows <<Library Item>> in the title bar.

Indicates you're editing a Library item

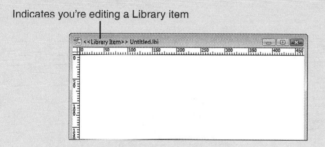

The Library category of the Assets panel has a pop-up menu containing useful commands, as shown in Figure 15.5. This same menu also pops up when you right-click a library item in the Library category of the Assets panel. Using the New Library Item command is another way to create a library item.

Adding a Library Item to a Page

After you have created a library item, you simply drag it from the list in the Library category of the Assets panel and drop it onto your web page, as shown in Figure 15.6. You can pick up the library item and move it to a different location in the Document window. You are not able to select individual objects contained in the inserted library item. When you click any of the objects, you select the entire library item; the group of objects in a library item is essentially one object in your web page.

FIGURE 15.5
The Library category of the Assets
panel pop-up menu has commands
to add, rename, open, and delete library items.

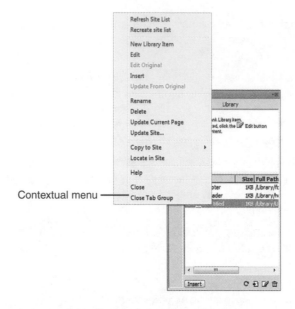

FIGURE 15.5
The Library category of the Assets
panel pop-up menu has commands
to add, rename, open, and delete library items.

Contextual menu

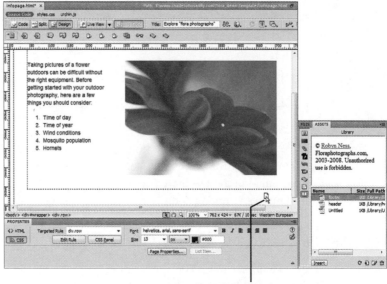

FIGURE 15.6
Drag a library item from the Library
category of the Assets panel and
drop it onto your web page.

Drag assets to the page

TIP

Sharing Library Items on the Server

Consider uploading the library to
your server so that others can
use the library items, too. When
collaborating with a group, you
can share a library so that everyone creates consistent web
pages using the same library
items.

When you insert a library item into a web page, you insert a copy of its content. You no longer need to have the original library item present. When
you upload your web page onto a remote website, you do not need to upload the Library directory. It is a good idea to keep the directory, though, in
case you want to make changes to library items throughout the website.

The Property inspector, as shown in Figure 15.7, displays the library item's attributes when you select that library item in the Document window. The Src box displays the name of the library item (which you cannot change here). The following three buttons in the Property inspector help you manage the library item:

▶ **Open**—This button opens the library item you want to edit.

▶ **Detach from Original**—This button breaks the link between this instance of a library item and the original item. If the original library item changes, the detached item does not update. If you detach a library item from its original, the individual objects contained in the item are editable.

▶ **Recreate**—This button overwrites the original library item with the currently selected instance of the library item. This is useful if you inadvertently lose or edit the original library item.

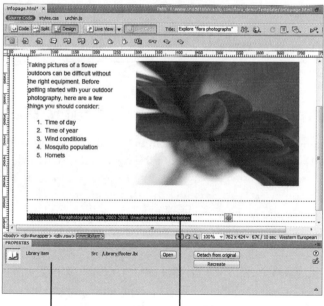

Library item properties   Instance of Library Item

FIGURE 15.7
The Property inspector contains buttons to manage a library item. You can detach the item from its original or overwrite the item as the original.

Dreamweaver applies a highlight to library items so they are easy to see in the Document window. The highlight appears only in Dreamweaver and not in the browser. In addition, the highlight appears only if Invisible Elements is selected (View, Visual Aids, Invisible Elements). You set the highlight color for both library items and template items in the Highlighting category in the Dreamweaver Preferences dialog box, as shown in Figure 15.8.

FIGURE 15.8
Set a highlight color for all library items in the Dreamweaver Preferences dialog box. The highlight appears only in Dreamweaver and not in the browser.

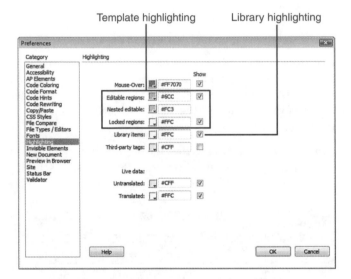

Template highlighting   Library highlighting

Making Changes to a Library Item

You edit a library item by opening the item to add or change objects in the Document window. Don't worry about the page background color when editing library items; the item appears on the background color of the page into which you insert it. After you've inserted your previously created library item into a page, open the library item to edit it. Apply different formatting to some of the objects in the item.

After you have finished editing, save the library item (File, Save). Dreamweaver asks whether you want to update all the documents in the website that contain the library item, as shown in Figure 15.9. Click Update to update all linked library items automatically.

When the update is complete, the Update Pages dialog box, shown in Figure 15.10, displays statistics on how many files Dreamweaver examined, how many it updated, and how many it could not update. Check the Show Log check box if you want to see these statistics. Click Close to close the

FIGURE 15.9
Click Update to begin updating all
the library items that link to the selected library item throughout your
entire website.

Update Pages dialog box. You can also use this dialog box to update all the
library items and templates on your entire site should you need to force an
update.

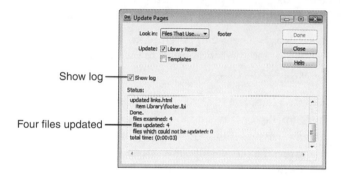

Show log

Four files updated

FIGURE 15.10
With Show Log checked, the Update
Pages dialog box shows how many
files Dreamweaver examined, how
many files it updated, and how
many it could not update.

You can manually update linked library items at any time. Right-click the
library item in the Library category of the Assets panel and select either the
Update Current Page command to update the current web page or the Update Site command to update the entire website. The Update Current Page
command acts immediately and no dialog box appears. When you issue the
Update Site command, the Update Pages dialog box appears. Click the Start
button to begin updating all the linked library items in the website. Alternatively, choose Update Pages from either the Library submenu or the Templates submenu under the Modify menu.

Creating a Template

You create templates to provide a foundation for consistent, controlled web
pages. **Templates** contain objects that you mark as editable; the rest of the
template locks. When you update an original template, the changes you
make to it update throughout your site.

You can create a template, save it to the Templates category of the Assets
panel, and then use it to create a new web page within a website. Anyone

CAUTION

Check Out Web Pages to Update

Dreamweaver might not update
web pages containing library
items if you do not have those
pages checked out. Pages you
don't have checked out are read-
only, meaning that you cannot
make changes to them.
Dreamweaver cannot update any
library items in files marked
read-only. Make sure that you
have all the appropriate files
checked out before you update a
library item.

NOTE

More Differences Between Templates and Library Items

A template differs from a library item in that a template is the structure (minus content) of an entire web page, not just a portion of one. In addition, templates can define certain regions as editable by the user, whereas library items placed in web pages are not editable at all.

TIP

Download Templates from the Web

Does the Templates category of the Assets panel look bare? Copy one or more of the sites available in the Templates directory from the Dreamweaver CD-ROM to your hard drive and set them up as a site in the Files panel. These templates are also available for download from the Adobe website at http://www.adobe.com/software/dreamweaver/download/templates.

working on the same website can use the template, and you can use templates created by others.

You have to define a website before Dreamweaver can insert a template. Dreamweaver creates a directory called Templates, where it stores the original template files, in the root of your website. Dreamweaver keeps the code of a template in a file in the Templates directory and inserts a copy of the code when you insert a template in a web page.

Just as with library items, there are two ways to create templates:

▸ **From an existing web page**—When you decide to create a template from of a web page, you can save the page as a template.

▸ **From scratch, as a new, empty template**—You can create a new template, open it, and then add objects to the template just as though it were a regular web page.

When you apply a template to a web page, you insert a copy of all the content that the template contains into the page. You no longer need to have the original template present for the web page to display. When you upload your web page to a remote website, it is not necessary to upload the Templates directory for the template-based pages to be visible. You should keep the directory in case you want to make changes to templates throughout your website.

Creating a Template from an Existing Web Page

▼ TRY IT YOURSELF

Creating a Template from an Existing Page

To create a template from an existing web page, follow these steps:

1. With an existing web page open, Select File, Save as Template.

2. The Save as Template dialog box appears, as shown in Figure 15.11. Enter a meaningful name for the template. Click the Save button to save the template to the Templates directory.

FIGURE 15.11
Give a new template a meaningful name in the Save as Template dialog box. This dialog box displays a list of existing templates in the current website.

3. A dialog box might appear, asking whether you'd like to update links. Click the Yes button to agree. This tells Dreamweaver to make sure that the document-relative links are correct when it saves the template to the `Templates` directory.

NOTE

Back Up Your Templates to the Server

Keeping the templates on the server ensures that you have a backup copy in case you accidentally change a template and need to restore the original. You learn more about moving your files to the server in Hour 22, "Uploading, Sharing, and Managing Website Projects."

TIP

Cloaking Affects Templates

Use Dreamweaver's Cloaking feature to prevent the `Templates` directory from synchronizing or uploading when you are transferring files. You enable and disable cloaking in the Site submenu (or advanced site definition) within the Files panel pop-up menu. To cloak Templates, right-click the `Templates` directory in the Files panel and select Cloaking, Cloak. The folder appears in the site with a red line through it.

NOTE

Template Files

Dreamweaver creates an individual file for each template. The file extension for templates is `.dwt`. In the `Templates` directory of your website, you see one `.dwt` file for each template you have in your website.

Creating a Template from Scratch

To create a new, empty template and then add objects to it, follow these steps:

TRY IT YOURSELF ▼

Creating a Template from Scratch

1. Click the New Template button at the bottom of the Templates category of the Assets panel. Dreamweaver creates a new, blank template. A message appears in the top half of the Templates category of the Assets panel, telling you how to add content to the blank template.

2. Give the template a name. For example, create a template for displaying your CD or book collection and call it CD or Book.

3. Double-click the template in the Templates category of the Assets panel. Dreamweaver opens the template in a separate Document window. You can tell that you have a template open because Dreamweaver displays <<Template>> along with the name of the template in the title bar.

4. Insert objects into the template's Document window just as you would with any web page.

5. Close the Document window and save the template. The Templates category of the Assets panel reflects your changes. Don't worry right now about the message you receive about your template not having any editable regions. You add some editable regions in a few minutes.

The Templates category of the Assets panel has a pop-up menu that contains useful commands. Different commands are available, depending on the current selection.

Making the Template Editable

TIP

Placeholder Images

Use a placeholder image in your template to represent an image that can change between pages. You add a placeholder image to the page by selecting Insert, Image Objects, Image Placeholder.

Before you apply a template to a web page, you must mark regions of the template as **Editable**. By default, Dreamweaver locks all the regions of the template. If you don't mark any regions as editable, you won't be able to modify the web page based on the template, and that isn't very useful! Mark a region as editable if you need to change, add, or update the content of this region in the pages you create based on this template.

You should leave locked all regions that do not need to be changed. If you need to make changes to a locked region, you can change the original template file and update all the web pages that link to that template. The commands for manipulating editable regions are located in the Templates submenu of the Common category in the Insert panel, or by choosing Insert, Template Objects, as shown in Figure 15.12.

FIGURE 15.12
The Template Objects submenu of Dreamweaver's Insert menu contains the commands needed to manipulate editable regions.

To make an existing region editable, follow these steps:

1. Open a template and select the region that needs to be editable.

2. Select Insert, Templates, Editable Region. The New Editable Region dialog box appears, as shown in Figure 15.13.

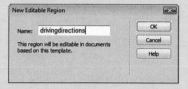

3. Give the region a meaningful name.

After you create an editable region, the name of the region appears at the bottom of the Templates submenu of the Modify menu while you are working on the template. Select one of the region names in the menu to highlight that region in the Document window. Dreamweaver automatically creates an editable region for the title of the document (called **Doctitle**) and an empty region in the head of the document that is available for JavaScript code.

Dreamweaver enables you to create editable regions on various objects in a template. For instance, you can make a div editable. You can then change any of its properties after you apply the template to a web page. Or you can leave the div locked and create an editable region within the div. Then you can't change the div properties when you've applied the template, but you can put content within the div.

Dreamweaver highlights editable regions only while you are editing the original template file so that they are easy to pick out in the Document window. Just the opposite is true in a web page with a template applied: Dreamweaver highlights the locked regions. The highlights are visible in Dreamweaver but not in the browser. To see the highlights, select View, Invisible Elements. Set the highlight color in the Highlighting category in the Dreamweaver Preferences dialog box.

Making a New Editable Region

You can create an optional editable region in a template. To do so, select Insert, Templates, Optional Region. Then name the new region in the New Optional Region dialog box that appears. An optional editable region enables the web page author to decide whether this region on the web page needs content. If the region isn't necessary, the author can turn it off. An editable region appears with a rectangle around it and a tab showing its name, as shown in Figure 15.14.

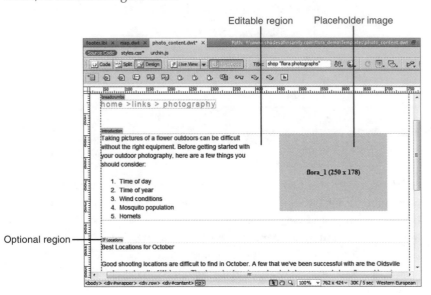

Making a New Optional Region

Inserting an optional region (Insert, Templates, Optional Region) enables an author using the template to turn the region on or off in the page. Optional regions are not automatically editable. You must either nest an editable region inside an optional region or add an optional editable region (Insert, Template, Editable Optional Region) in order to edit the content in a web page based on the template. The New Optional Region dialog box, shown in Figure 15.15, prompts you to name the optional region.

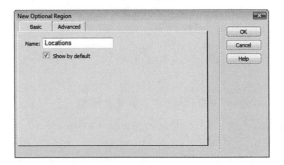

To lock a region that has previously been marked as editable, select Modify, Templates, Remove Template Markup while you have the region you'd like to remove selected. Don't do this after you've created web pages with the template because your web pages lose any content that you entered into the region when you update.

Creating a Web Page from a Template

Web pages based on templates allow you to edit content only in the editable regions. You can see these editable regions highlighted in the Document window (you must have Invisible Elements turned on in the View menu and Highlighting turned on in the Preferences dialog box). Dreamweaver blocks the rest of the web page from editing. Simply remove any placeholder text or images within the editable region and add the final content to create a new web page.

To create a new page from a template, do the following:

1. Select the New command (File, New) and choose the Page from Template icon, as shown in Figure 15.16.

Defined templates   Template preview

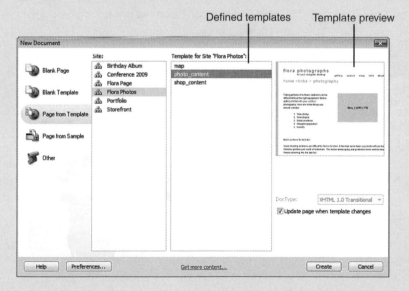

TRY IT YOURSELF ▼

Creating a New Page from a Template

FIGURE 15.16
Create a new web page from a template by choosing the Page from Template tab from the New Document dialog box.

2. Select the site on the left side of the dialog box and choose a template from the list in the middle of the dialog box. You can see a preview of the template on the right side of the dialog box.

▼ TRY IT YOURSELF

Creating a New Page from a Template

continued

3. Make sure that you enable the Update Page When Template Changes check box. This links the new page you are creating to the original template and updates the page if the template changes.

4. Click Create.

5. Modify the placeholder content in the editable areas. Notice that you cannot change any of the locked content.

6. To edit optional regions, select Modify, Template Properties to open the Template Properties dialog box, as shown in Figure 15.17, to either turn on or turn off the optional region.

FIGURE 15.17
Turn an optional region on or off in the Template Properties dialog box.

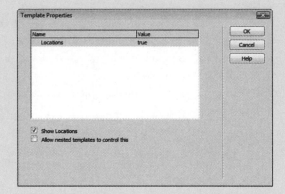

The Template Properties command is available only when you are working on a page based on a Dreamweaver template; it isn't available while you're actually editing a template file.

Making Changes to a Template and Updating Pages

You edit a template by opening it to add or change its contents. You can open the template from the Templates category of the Assets panel, or you can open it from the Files panel. Edits to locked objects apply to all the web pages that use the template. Edits to editable objects have no effect on web pages that use the template.

After you edit and save a template, Dreamweaver asks you whether you want to update files. Select the files you want to update in the Update Files dialog box and then click Update to automatically update the linked files. The Update Pages dialog box displays statistics on how many files Dreamweaver examined, updated, and could not update. Check the Show Log check box to see these statistics. Click the Close button to close the Update Pages dialog box.

You can also manually update files linked to templates. To do so, right-click the template in the Templates category of the Assets panel and select either the Update Current Page command (to update the current web page) or the Update Site command (to update the entire website). The Update Current Page command acts immediately and no dialog box appears. When you issue the Update Site command, the Update Pages dialog box appears. Click the Start button to update all the linked templates in the website.

Using CSS Styles with Library Items and Templates

When you create a CSS style, Dreamweaver inserts the style definition into the head of the HTML document. A library item does not have a head section because it's just a small piece of code. When you insert a library item that has CSS styles applied to it, the web page must already reference those styles. Usually the page links to an external style sheet.

You can use behaviors (you learn about them in Hour 18, "Adding Interactivity with Behaviors") and CSS styles in templates. You apply CSS styles and JavaScript to a web page based on the template. For you to be able to edit CSS styles and behaviors, the object to which they are applied must be editable. If it's editable, select an object that has a style or behavior and edit the style or behavior in the CSS Styles panel or the Behaviors panel.

Most web designers add links to external style sheets to their templates. That way the template content has access to all the styles in the external style sheet. They often place library items within templates, too. Even though Adobe designed Dreamweaver templates to update the web pages created from them, it's not a good idea to do this all the time. Placing visual formatting in external style sheets enables you to update the look of the site without changing the template.

Dreamweaver and Content Management

Dreamweaver provides a great way for web developers to create pages and deliver standards-based, structured websites. It is not, however, a tool that is necessarily appropriate to be used in making day-to-day website updates.

Much of today's web maintenance is distributed throughout an organization—from administrative assistants to directors. People in these positions may not have the technical knowledge or time to work with an editor like Dreamweaver, so they have been increasingly turning toward content management systems. A content management system enables you (the web developer) to create the structure and functionality of a site, while the maintainers are given a simple word processor–like interface for updating the site content. Content maintainers don't have access to any of the underlying site files, making it less likely for any serious mistakes to occur.

Contribute

So what does this have to do with Dreamweaver? As you saw earlier in the hour, the templates enable you to create locked and editable page regions. These templates can be used with an Adobe product called Contribute to create a simple type of content management system. Contribute works just like a web browser, allowing a maintainer to browse through a live Dreamweaver-created website. When they reach a page they want to edit, they click an Edit button and the editable portions of the page can be changed directly within the Contribute browser. There is no need to understand style sheets or URLs or other complexities of development—the combination of Dreamweaver/Contribute makes it simple to create a distributed web management environment with users of any skill level.

You can learn more about Contribute at http://www.adobe.com/products/contribute/.

FIGURE 15.18
Use the InContext Editing tools to add editable regions to pages.

InContext Editing

With Dreamweaver CS4, Adobe is introducing a new content management feature—InContext Editing, or ICE. ICE uses Adobe's servers along with your own web servers and web browser to build sites that are editable directly in popular browsers (Safari, Firefox, IE) without the need for additional software. Using the InContext Editing category of the Insert panel, shown in Figure 15.18, you can insert editable regions into a page, just as you would a template.

You'll also notice the Create Repeating Region tool and the Manage Available CSS Classes tool. The Repeating Region tool is mostly useful for dynamically generated sites, but the CSS Classes tool can be very helpful in controlling what an editor can change in a site. If you've linked CSS style sheets to your page, the CSS Classes tool displays a window enabling you to explicitly specify which style sheets someone editing the site can use, as shown in Figure 15.19. You might, for example, have one style sheet with layout information that shouldn't be touched, and another that contains all the text styles needed for the content.

FIGURE 15.19
Choose the styles that can be used in InContext Editing.

After you've built your site and included the appropriate ICE settings, you deploy it on your own server, just like any other site. To actually edit the site, however, you must first register the site with Adobe's InContext Editing service (http://incontextediting.adobe.com). Adobe's servers manage the process of making the actual changes to your files and control the different users who have access to the site.

Finally, after the site is deployed and registered, a user can simply press Ctrl+E on their keyboard to open a login window. After login, the site is displayed in your browser along with editing tools, as shown in Figure 15.20.

To learn more about Adobe's new InContext Editing service, visit http://incontextediting.adobe.com.

NOTE

ICE Templates

ICE settings can be made on a per-page basis. You can also, however, include ICE editable regions in templates for easily creating ICE-enabled websites.

Summary

In this hour, you learned how to create library items and templates, both from existing content and from scratch. You learned how to use the Library and Templates categories of the Assets panel to manage, open, and edit library items and templates. You also learned how Dreamweaver automatically updates all the linked library items and templates and how you can launch the process manually. In addition, you learned how to make regions of a template editable regions and optional regions. Finally, you looked at how Dreamweaver can interact with two content management options— Adobe Contribute and Adobe's InContext Editing service.

FIGURE 15.20
InContext Editing occurs right in
your browser window.

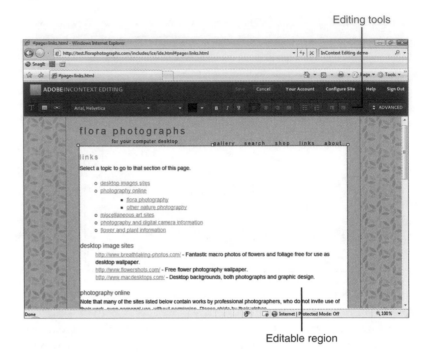

Editing tools

Editable region

Q&A

Q. How can I apply edits I made to library items in only some of the linked files?

A. I caution you to be careful if you are maintaining various pages, some containing the newest version of a library item, and some containing an old version. You *can* select only the pages you want to update. But, instead, why not open the library item, save it with a different name, apply your edits, and then replace it in the selected pages?

Q. What types of objects are appropriate to put in the library?

A. Here are some examples of objects you might want to put in the Dreamweaver library: a company logo, a group of layers that appear on each page as a background, a search box (small form), a frequently used button, a custom bullet image, and a placeholder for content that isn't finalized (you can detach it later). You will find plenty of uses for the library.

Q. Is there any way I can use templates without having locked and editable regions?

A. Yes. You can create a template with everything laid out perfectly, create a new page, and make sure you do *not* enable the Update Page When Template Changes check box. That way, you have a standard beginning point but have the freedom to do what you want with the page.

Q. Why would I use an optional or editable optional region?

A. An optional or editable optional region enables you to give people using the template the option to add or delete standard content with very little work. For instance, imagine that you have a template that presents the biographies of college professors. Some biographies have photos, but others do not. You can make the photo region optional so that people creating the web page can quickly turn off that region if it is unnecessary.

Workshop

Quiz

1. What is the file extension for library files? For template files?

2. Which regions, editable or locked, does Dreamweaver highlight when you are editing the original template file?

3. How do you turn an optional region on and off?

Quiz Answers

1. The file extension for library item files is .lbi. The file extension for template files is .dwt.

2. Dreamweaver highlights the editable regions when you are editing the original template file. It highlights the locked regions when you are in a web page based on a template.

3. In a web page based on a template that contains editable regions, select Modify, Template Properties, and turn on and off the properties in the list.

Exercises

1. Create a template and practice marking various objects as editable. Apply the template and see which objects can be marked as editable and which cannot. What properties can you edit?

2. Open a template you have already applied to a page, edit it, and practice updating the linked page. Open the page. Do you see the edits you made?

3. Create a library item and add it to a page. Experiment with reopening the library item, editing it, and then updating the page to which it's connected. Try adding a CSS style to the library item and then insert the item into a web page that has the style already defined.

Adding Navigation: Navigation and Menu Bars

Websites are repositories of information, and it's important to give visitors the correct tools to navigate to the information they need. You want to design your website's navigation to be clear and logical. It's always a good idea to create a mock-up of your proposed navigation structure and test it out with some customers or friends. You learn a lot by watching potential visitors try to find the gold buried within your website.

Understanding Navigation

Website navigation should be clear, well-thought-out, and intuitive. You should break the content in your website into logical groupings and give each grouping a name that represents it. In most websites, there are two types of navigation: primary and secondary. **Primary navigation** is usually located at the top or on the left side of the page and represents the main content groupings in the website. **Secondary navigation** includes the standard website links, such as contact information, privacy policy, an About Us section, and others.

The primary navigation is how visitors get to all the sections of the website. Developers usually design this navigation to blend into the interface, using the same graphics and colors as the design. It's important that the primary navigation be consistent on every page in the website because many visitors will arrive at a page in your site via a link from a search engine instead of navigating from your home page. You need to give these visitors an easy way to explore the other information on your site.

Websites designed for languages that read from left to right (the English language, for instance) have the primary navigation either at the top or on the left side of the page. That way people read this information first.

WHAT YOU'LL LEARN IN THIS HOUR:

▶ The importance of planning good navigation for a website

▶ How to add a navigation bar

▶ How to add a Spry menu bar

▶ How to modify links so that the web page opens in a new browser window

Languages that read from right to left (Hebrew or Arabic, for instance) might have the primary navigation on the right side of the page. Generally, the secondary navigation is at the bottom of the page or in a submenu of the primary navigation.

There are several common forms of website navigation (Figure 16.1 shows some examples):

▶ **Links**—Hyperlinks on the page, the most basic form of navigation.

▶ **Breadcrumbs**—A group of links showing the path to the current page. Usually breadcrumbs begin with the home page (listed on the left) and then list each of the sections navigated to get to the current page (listed on the right). An example: Home > Gallery > Summer Flowers.

▶ **Navigation bar**—A group of images (usually rollover images) that link to sections of a website.

▶ **Menu bar**—A list of navigational options in a horizontal or vertical format, much like the menu bar in your desktop applications.

▶ **Site map**—A list of all the content on your website and where it is located.

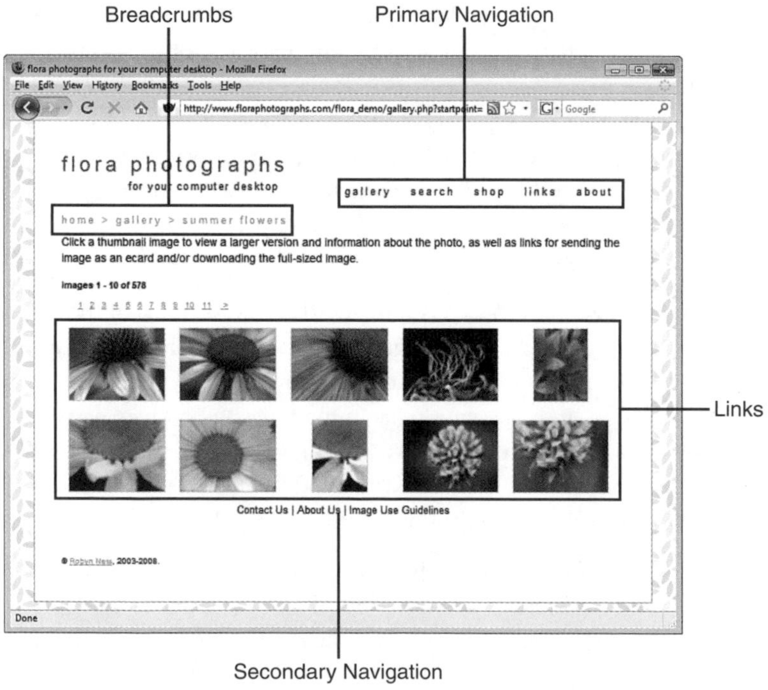

FIGURE 16.1
Various types of navigation can appear on a web page, including primary and secondary navigation.

You've already explored creating links, so you can easily create the preceding list's first two bullet items: links and breadcrumbs. The final bullet item, the site map, is also just a group of links to resources in the website. In this hour, you explore the navigation bar and menu bar.

Creating a Navigation Bar with Rollover Images and Links

In Hour 8, "Displaying Images," you learned how to use images as links and how to create rollover image effects from two separate image files. Frequently, web developers use several rollover images as their primary navigation elements.

You could create all these elements individually using the Rollover Image object, or you could take advantage of the Dreamweaver Insert Navigation Bar dialog box to create all the buttons at once.

As you may recall from Hour 8, developers can simulate graphical button functionality by swapping images as the mouse passes over or clicks on them.

Each image represents a **button state**. The default button state is up. The down state appears when the user clicks the mouse on the button; the down-state image usually modifies the up-state image so that it looks pressed down. The over state appears when users pass the mouse over the button. The navigation bar can also add an over-when-down state, which appears when the user rolls the mouse over the button when it is already in the down state. You must add an up-state image to a navigation bar, but all the other button states are optional.

TIP

Make Button States

In Hour 9, "Complementing Dreamweaver with Other Applications," you created a rollover image by placing slightly different-looking images in two frames. To create a down state for a button, simply add a third frame. Photoshop can then export the third graphic to use in a navigation bar. You can also create these button images in Fireworks.

NOTE

One Navigation Bar Per Customer

Dreamweaver restricts you to only one navigation bar per web page.

To create a navigation bar from an existing set of images, follow these steps:

1. Open a web page and place the insertion point where you'd like the navigation bar to appear.

2. Select Insert, Image Objects, Navigation Bar. The Insert Navigation Bar dialog box appears.

3. An initial, unnamed button element is visible. Change the element name to the name of your first button. (If you simply go to the next step, Dreamweaver automatically gives your button the same name as the name of the image file.)

TRY IT YOURSELF ▼

Creating a Navigation Bar

▼ TRY IT YOURSELF

**Creating a
Navigation Bar**

continued

4. Browse to load a button-up image, a button-over image, and a button-down image. You can also enter an over-while-down image, which is a rollover image for the down state of a button. All these images must be the same size.

5. Enter a hyperlink in the When Clicked, Go to URL box. Type in a URL or browse to a web page.

6. Check the Preload Images check box if you want the images to be automatically preloaded.

7. Add additional buttons by clicking the plus button and repeating steps 2–5. Rearrange the order of the buttons by using the arrow buttons at the top of the Insert Navigation Bar dialog box. To delete a button, click the minus button.

   If you accidentally close the Insert Navigation Bar dialog box, simply select Modify, Navigation Bar to reopen it and edit your settings.

8. At the bottom of the Insert Navigation Bar dialog box, choose to insert the navigation bar either horizontally or vertically into the web page. Select the Use Tables check box if you'd like to create the navigation bar in a table.

9. The Insert Navigation Bar dialog box should look as shown in Figure 16.2 after you have added several elements. When you finish adding buttons, click OK.

FIGURE 16.2
Each element in a navigation bar consists of multiple images linked to a URL. The navigation bar can have vertical or horizontal orientation.

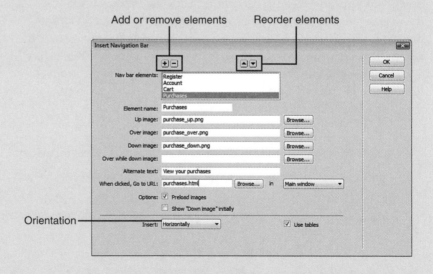

Add or remove elements   Reorder elements

Orientation

10. Save the page and preview it in the Live View or a web browser (File, Preview in Browser) to check the functionality of the navigation bar.

To test the buttons, save your file and preview it in a browser, as shown in Figure 16.3. If you've made a mistake, don't fret! You can edit the navigation bar by selecting the Navigation Bar object again.

Navigation bar

CAUTION

Make Button State Images the Same Size

Rollover and button images work best if the up, over, and down images are all the same size. Otherwise, the over and down images stretch to the size of the original up image and are distorted.

You can edit some of the elements in a Dreamweaver navigation bar, whereas you cannot edit others. When you open a navigation bar for editing, you notice that the orientation setting at the bottom of the Insert Navigation Bar is gone, so you cannot change the vertical or horizontal orientation. If you want to change this orientation, you have to delete the existing navigation bar and start fresh.

To edit a navigation bar, simply select Modify, Navigation Bar to open the Modify Navigation Bar dialog box. Because only a single navigation bar is allowed per page, the bar you've inserted is automatically selected. Make any changes and click the OK button. If you attempt to insert a second navigation bar, Dreamweaver reminds you that you can have only one navigation bar, as shown in Figure 16.4, and prompts you to modify the existing one.

FIGURE 16.4
Dreamweaver indicates that you can have only one navigation bar per page.

Inserting a Menu Bar

Next you explore inserting a menu bar into a web page using Dreamweaver's Spry Menu Bar object. There is a whole set of Spry elements, called the Spry framework for Ajax, which is built on a JavaScript library that you learn about in Hour 19, "Using AJAX Frameworks and Libraries." You will be able to successfully use the Spry Menu Bar object without understanding much about the framework.

The Spry Menu Bar object enables you to add three menu levels to either a vertical or a horizontal menu bar. Figure 16.5 shows a horizontal Spry menu bar with the menu levels displayed. Figure 16.6 shows a vertical Spry menu bar with its menu levels displayed.

FIGURE 16.5
This horizontal Spry menu bar displays multiple menu levels.

FIGURE 16.6
This vertical Spry menu bar displays multiple menu levels.

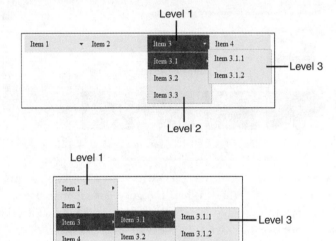

The Spry menu bar is created using CSS (Cascading Style Sheets) instead of images. So you can use your CSS-editing skills to modify the fonts, colors, sizes, and other attributes. After you insert the menu bar, you learn how to modify the CSS that Dreamweaver saves in an external style sheet.

To insert a Spry menu bar, do the following:

1. Create and save a web page (File, Save) before inserting a Spry menu bar.

2. Select Insert, Layout Objects, Spry Menu Bar. The Spry Menu Bar dialog box appears, as shown in Figure 16.7.

3. Select either Horizontal or Vertical as the menu orientation.

4. Click OK and the menu bar inserts into the web page.

5. Save your web page (File, Save) and Dreamweaver prompts you to copy dependent files as shown in Figure 16.8.

6. Dreamweaver creates a folder named SpryAssets within the folder where it saves your web page, and copies the dependent files into this folder. These files are images, external JavaScript files, and external CSS style sheets. Do not delete these files.

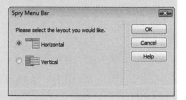

FIGURE 16.7
When you insert a Spry menu bar, you first must select the orientation, horizontal or vertical, of the menu bar.

FIGURE 16.8
Dreamweaver prompts you to copy the files that the Spry menu bar requires.

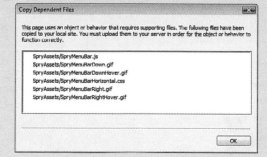

After you've created a Spry menu bar in a web page, Dreamweaver no longer needs to copy the dependent files unless you insert a different Spry object that requires additional files. The external JavaScript files work just like external CSS style sheets: You have to maintain only one file that can link to many different web pages. If you update that one file, you affect all the web pages attached to it.

When you test the web page in Live View or a web browser, you should have a fully functional menu. But now you have to add your text and links to the menu.

TIP

Multiple Menu Bars

Unlike navigation bars, you can have multiple Spry menu bars in a single web page.

To customize a Spry menu bar, follow these steps:

1. Select the Spry Menu Bar tab above the newly inserted menu bar to display the menu bar properties in the Property inspector, as shown in Figure 16.9.

▼ TRY IT YOURSELF

Customizing a Spry Menu Bar

continued

2. Use the Add or Remove Elements buttons to modify the number of elements in each of the menu sections. Use the Reorder Elements buttons to move elements up or down in the list.

3. Enter the text, link, and title for each menu element as shown in Figure 16.10. The Text value is the text displayed in the menu bar; the Link value is where visitors go when they click that menu element; and the Title value is a ToolTip that appears above the menu element and gives more information about it.

4. Repeat steps 2 and 3 until the menu is complete.

FIGURE 16.9
Select the menu bar to display the Spry menu bar properties in the Property inspector.

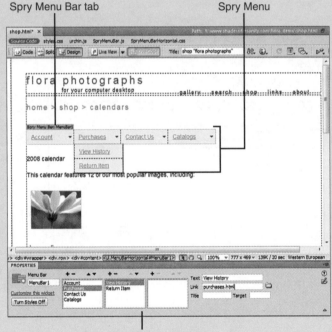

FIGURE 16.10
Enter the text, link, and title (ToolTip) for each of the menu elements.

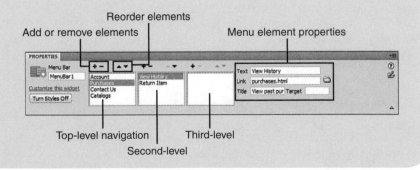

Editing the Menu Bar CSS

It's likely that you'd prefer the menu to match the design, fonts, colors, and other properties of objects on the web page. You can easily edit the CSS affecting the menu bar to make it fit with your design. You use what you've learned in earlier hours about CSS and apply it to the menu bar.

You edit the styles in either SpryMenuBarVertical.css or SpryMenuBarHorizontal.css, depending on the menu bar orientation you chose earlier. The style definitions appear in the CSS Styles panel, as shown in Figure 16.11. These are the styles in the external style sheet that you can modify to change the look of the menu bar.

External style sheet name —

Menu bar styles —

FIGURE 16.11
Styles affecting the Spry menu bar are stored in an external style sheet.

You might notice that all the styles in the external style sheet begin with ul. This is the tag for an unordered list (bulleted list) and that is how Dreamweaver implements the menu bar. The menu bar is simply an unordered list styled to look like a drop-down menu. You can actually see this by clicking the Turn Styles Off button in the Property inspector, as shown in Figure 16.12. Submenus are simply unordered lists that are nested.

You can easily bring up information about customizing the menu CSS by selecting the Customize This Widget link in the Property inspector. This link opens the Dreamweaver help specific to modifying the CSS for the menu. Use the tables in help to identify which styles you need to change to modify different parts of the menu.

FIGURE 16.12
Turn the styles off to see the actual unordered list structure.

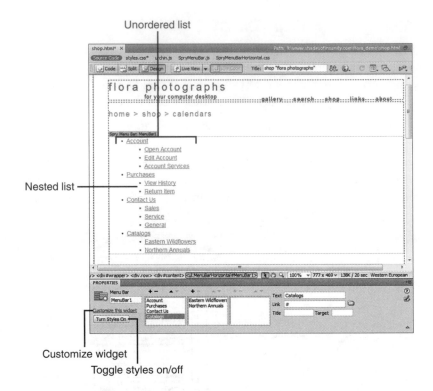

Changing the Font and Background of a Spry Menu Bar

To change the font and background colors for the menu bar:

1. In the CSS Styles panel, select ul.MenuBarHorizontal a or ul.MenuBarVertical a (depending on the orientation of your menu bar).

2. In the Properties pane at the bottom of the CSS Styles panel, edit the colors for the background-color and color properties, as shown in Figure 16.13.

3. Select ul.MenuBarHorizontal a:hover or ul.MenuBarVertical a:hover to modify the way the menu displays when the visitor's cursor is hovering over the link. This style is grouped in the same style with ul.MenuBarHorizontal a:focus or ul.MenuBarVertical a:focus.

4. Modify the colors in the Properties pane at the bottom of the CSS Styles panel.

You've been modifying properties of the unordered list tag (ul), but lists have another tag of interest. The list item (li) tag wraps around every individual list item, and an unordered list tag wraps around all the list items.

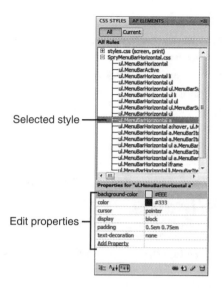

FIGURE 16.13
Edit the style properties directly in the lower pane of the CSS Styles panel.

The following steps show you how to modify the list item tag to change the dimensions of menu items:

1. In the CSS Styles panel, select ul.MenuBarVertical li or ul.MenuBarHorizontal li (depending on the menu bar orientation you selected earlier).

2. In the Properties pane at the bottom of the CSS Styles panel, edit the width, as shown in Figure 16.14.

TRY IT YOURSELF ▼

Changing the Dimensions of Spry Menus

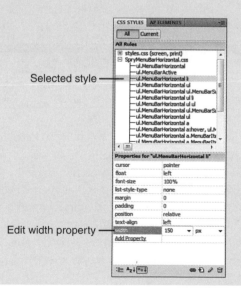

FIGURE 16.14
Edit the list item style to modify the width of the menu bar.

CAUTION

Use Help to Modify Properties

Resist the urge to guess about the purpose of properties in the Spry CSS. Refer to the tables in Dreamweaver help (select the Customize This Widget link in the Property inspector) to identify the correct styles. That way you won't modify properties unnecessarily or mess up other parts of the menu.

After you've modified the menu to the way you'd like it on all pages, you have to make sure that all the web pages link to the specific external style sheet that you modified. If you save new pages in the same directory as the original web page, Dreamweaver links the pages to the modified CSS style sheet. If you save pages to other directories, however, you might have to link to the external style sheet manually by using the Attach Style Sheet command in the CSS Styles panel.

Targeting a Link to Open in a New Browser Window

NOTE

What About the Other Reserved Names?

Three of the four reserved target names—_parent, _self, and _top—are mainly for use with frames.

One final navigational topic introduces you to how you can launch a new browser window with a link instead of loading a new page into the existing browser window. This technique is especially useful when linking to other, external websites. When visitors click the link, the web page with that link stays open and another browser window opens with the new web page. Both windows remain open until the visitor closes them.

When you select a hyperlink, the Property inspector has a drop-down box called Target. The _blank reserved target name, shown in Figure 16.15, is useful when you want to leave the current browser window open and have the link open a new browser window with the linked web page in it. Simply select _blank from the Target drop-down menu when you want a link to open a new browser window.

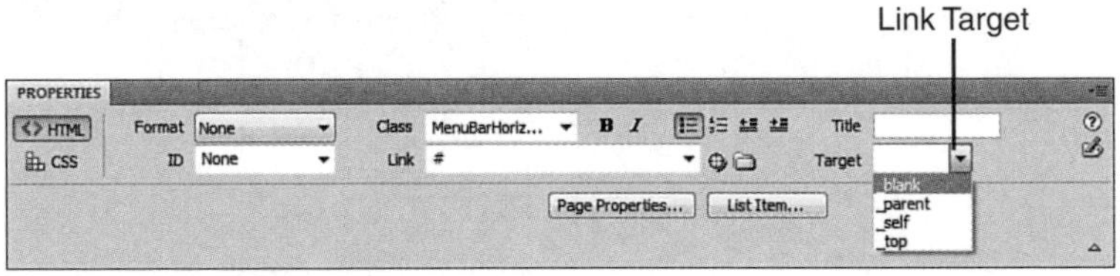

FIGURE 16.15
The **_blank** reserved target name in the Target drop-down menu in the Property inspector opens the link in a new browser window. The original document remains open.

Link Target

TIP

Tabs and Windows

Many browsers implement "tabs" to hold different web pages within a single window. Depending on a user's browser configuration, setting a target to open a new window *may* open a new tab instead.

Opening a new window is useful when you want to keep your original web page open but still allow the user to jump to other web pages. When the user closes the new window, the window containing your site is still open. It's nice to warn the users about this so that they do not become confused. You can add text to a link that opens a new window with a message that says something like link opens new window or close new window to return. In Hour 18, "Adding Interactivity with Behaviors," you learn how to use a Dreamweaver behavior to open a new window. You can use JavaScript to set the window size.

Summary

In this hour, you learned about various navigation objects you can add to your web pages and how to best organize navigation. You explored navigation bars created with different images, and menu bars created with CSS. You learned how to modify the CSS for Spry menu bars. You also learned how to open new browser windows with a link.

Q&A

Q. Do I have to use navigation or menu bars to create navigation in my page?

A. No, not at all. These are just shortcuts that speed up your development. You can use a combination of images, links, and CSS to create the primary and secondary page navigation. I use navigation and menu bars occasionally but produce a custom solution most of the time.

Q. Do I need to add all the button states (up, over, down, and over-while-down)?

A. You can add as many states as make sense for the website you are creating. I normally use at least the up and over states. The down button state disappears so quickly that it isn't essential. The over-while-down button is necessary only if you are maintaining one of the buttons in the down state (depressed) to signal that the visitor is in that section of the website. It's not commonly used.

Q. How do I open a web page in a new browser window without the toolbars and menus?

A. In Hour 18, you learn how to use the Open Browser Window behavior to create a link that opens a new browser window in a given size and without any of the browser navigation or menus.

Workshop

Quiz

1. What's the difference between primary and secondary navigation in a website?

2. How many Dreamweaver navigation bars can you have per web page?

3. What is the name of the JavaScript framework, included with Dreamweaver, that enables you to insert menu bars?

Quiz Answers

1. The primary navigation is the navigation that moves visitors around the major (and minor) sections of the website. The secondary navigation contains less frequently used items that are important to only a subset of visitors (such as those looking for privacy policy information or those who would like to apply for a job).

2. You can have only one Dreamweaver navigation bar per web page.

3. The Spry framework is the JavaScript framework that enables you to insert menu bars.

Exercises

1. Find images for buttons for all the states available in the navigation bar (up, down, over, over when down) or make them yourself in Fireworks (see Hour 9). Or use the free button generator at http://www.buttongenerator.com.

2. Create a vertical or horizontal Spry menu bar (or both!) and customize the CSS. Modify the font and background colors or the default menu display and the hover display. How do you think you could change the font for the whole menu?

HOUR 17
Using Dynamic HTML and AP Divs

Dreamweaver's AP (absolutely positioned) divs provide a way to control the placement of objects on the page with pixel-perfect accuracy. You can place items precisely where you want them, absolutely positioned on the page.

You don't have to pick between regular divs and AP divs. You can use both in a web page, taking advantage of the strengths of each. In Hour 13, "Using CSS for Positioning," you used div tags as containers for the web page content. You placed these divs relative to one another, stacked up like boxes in a store. AP divs are autonomous, can be moved individually, and can be placed anywhere on the page. In this hour, you experiment with AP divs and compare them to what you learned about div tags in Hour 13.

One of the great things about AP divs is that you can use them with Dreamweaver behaviors, which you learn more about in Hour 18, "Adding Interactivity with Behaviors."

What Is DHTML?

DHTML enables you to create an interactive experience for the web page user. DHTML isn't an official term; it's a term used by web developers to refer to a collection of technologies used to produce a more interactive web page. The two main components of DHTML are HTML Cascading Style Sheets (CSS; see Hour 6, "Formatting Web Pages Using Cascading Style Sheets") and JavaScript (see Hour 18).

DHTML allows greater interactivity without depending on interaction with a server. When people talk about DHTML, they usually mean the combination of HTML 4 (as defined by the W3C [World Wide Web Consortium]

WHAT YOU'LL LEARN IN THIS HOUR:

▶ What AP divs are, how they work, and how they are used

▶ How to add an AP div and position it on the page

▶ How to set the stacking order, background color, and visibility of an AP div

Web standards organization) and CSS. These elements work together through a scripting language, usually JavaScript.

Here's a short list of the types of things you can accomplish using DHTML:

- Insert hidden images that appear when the user clicks a button or a hotspot.

- Create pop-up menus.

- Enable the user to drag and drop an object around the screen at will.

- Cause text to change color or size when the user rolls her mouse over it.

- Repetitively load text into an area of the screen as feedback to the user. For instance, if the user clicks the wrong answer in a quiz, you can give feedback and then replace that feedback when the user gets the answer right.

In this hour, you experiment with **AP divs**, the containers that enable you to position items on the screen wherever you want. These elements are a critical part of the DHTML toolbox.

Adding an AP Div

AP divs are containers that you use to position content on a web page. The term *AP divs* is a Dreamweaver expression, and if you speak with other web developers who aren't using Dreamweaver, they won't know what you mean. *AP divs* is short for "absolutely positioned div," meaning a div tag that is positioned at a precise x and y position on the screen. As you learned in Hour 13, the div tag logically divides a web page into sections.

AP divs have two very interesting attributes:

- **Visibility**—This property enables you to hide all the content in an AP div and then trigger its appearance when the user performs an action on the screen. For instance, you can simulate a click on a menu in a software program. The AP div holding the menu image initially hides. When the user clicks a menu title on the screen, a script changes the visibility of the menu AP div from hidden to visible.

- **Z-index**—This property controls the stacking order of all the AP divs on the page. You can stack AP divs on top of one another (overlapping) and control which one is on top. This gives you the power to create complicated designs.

You can create an AP div in Dreamweaver in two ways:

▶ The simplest way is to select the Draw AP Div object from the Layout category of the Insert panel and drag the cross-hair cursor on your page to approximately the desired AP div size, as shown in Figure 17.1.

Drag handle   AP Div   Draw AP Div

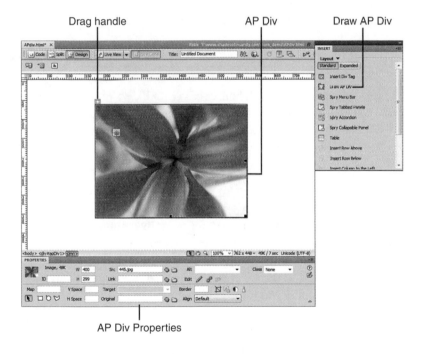

AP Div Properties

FIGURE 17.1
Selecting the Draw AP Div object from the Insert panel enables you to draw an AP div by dragging the cross-hair cursor.

TIP

Extensions to Dreamweaver

Dreamweaver contains many extensions that enable you to accomplish cool things with AP divs. (You learn more about extensions in Hour 24, "Customizing Dreamweaver.") There are extensions that make an AP div slide to a specified position and that make an AP div that doesn't scroll with the page. There are also several extensions to create drop-down menus using AP divs.

▶ Select Insert, Layout Objects, AP Div to insert an AP div.

The AP Elements category in the Preferences dialog box, shown in Figure 17.2, is where you can set default AP div values. You set the default visibility, width, height, background color, and background image. If you have a standard AP div size that you use often, you might want to set that size as the default in this dialog box. You can also enable nesting by checking the Nesting check box.

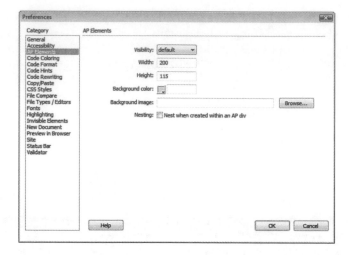

CAUTION

Unpredictable Placement of AP Div

You might be thinking, "Wow, AP divs are so easy to use. I should use them for the layout of my web pages!" Unfortunately, various browsers can display the position of AP divs differently, so it's difficult to perfectly calculate where an AP div should be placed when you're developing a web page.

You should also keep in mind that absolutely placed divs make assumptions about your users' browser sizes. Unlike relatively placed elements, AP divs cannot adapt to different screen sizes.

Stick to using relatively placed divs for page layout and use the occasional AP div for a special purpose.

FIGURE 17.3
Change the AP div name in the CSS-P Element box of the Property inspector. It's important to give AP divs meaningful names.

Notice resizing handles on each border of your AP div: You can drag these handles to make your AP div bigger or smaller. You can also set the width and height of the AP div in the Property inspector. The W and H properties in the Property inspector are the width and height, respectively, of the AP div. The default measurement unit is pixels.

It's always a good idea to name your AP divs. When you start adding behaviors, names help you identify specific AP divs. By default, Dreamweaver adds the name "apDiv" followed by a number; this obviously isn't very useful if you need to find a specific AP div among dozens. You can specify a name in the CSS-P Element box in the Property inspector (such as mapLegend), as shown in Figure 17.3. The name is actually a CSS ID, which can be used to specifically refer to that AP Div.

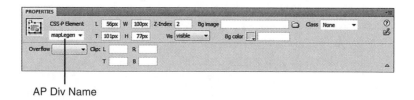

AP Div Name

TIP

No Punctuation in AP Div Names

Don't use spaces or punctuation in AP div names. If you later apply a behavior to the AP div, sometimes JavaScript isn't happy with spaces or punctuation in an AP div name. If you want to name your AP div with multiple words, you can use capitalization or underscores to make the name readable. For instance, CestLaVieBakery and Green_Grocer are possible AP div names.

You can also name Dreamweaver AP divs in the AP Elements panel. Double-click the name in the AP Elements panel ID column until it becomes editable and then type in a new name, as shown in Figure 17.4. Notice that when you select an AP div in the AP Elements panel, you select the AP div in the Document window also.

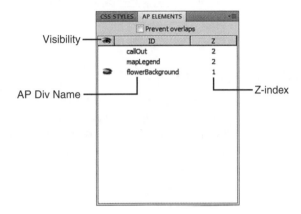

FIGURE 17.4
You can edit the name (ID) of an AP div in the AP Elements panel by double-clicking the name and changing it.

TIP

Use the Drag Handle

Get in the habit of moving AP divs by picking up the drag handle. It's very easy to accidentally move items contained in an AP div instead of moving the AP div itself. If you become accustomed to using the handle, you won't make that mistake. If you can't use the drag handle because the AP div is at the very top of the Document window, select the AP div in the AP Elements panel and use the arrow keys to move it. Alternatively, you can enter positioning values in the Property inspector.

Setting AP Div Positioning

An AP div has a drag handle in the upper-left corner. You can reposition an AP div by picking it up and moving it with this handle. To select multiple AP divs, hold down the Shift key while clicking AP divs to add them to the selection. You can also use the arrow keys on your keyboard to move a selected AP div.

Use the AP Elements panel to select one or many AP divs. The AP Elements panel enables you not only to select AP divs, but also to see and set some AP div properties. You learn about the two properties that you can set—the z-index and the visibility—in a few minutes. Notice that you can enable a check box at the top of the AP Elements panel to prevent overlaps. If you cannot place your AP divs on top of one another, you probably have to disable the Prevent Overlaps check box.

You can use the drag handle to drag an AP div anywhere on the screen, or you can use the Property inspector to set the AP div's exact positioning. The L and T properties stand for the left (the offset from the left edge of the page) and top (the offset from the top edge of the page). These positions are relative to the entire browser window. You can move an AP div by dragging it with its selection handle, or you can position it exactly by entering values in the L and T boxes, as shown in Figure 17.5.

TIP

Where Did the AP Div Properties Go?

If you don't see AP div properties in the Property inspector, it's because you don't have an AP div selected. You might have accidentally selected the contents of the AP div instead of selecting the AP div itself.

To select an AP div, click the outline or the drag handle.

FIGURE 17.5
Exactly position an AP div by entering values in the L (left) and T (top)
boxes of the Property inspector.

Left   Width

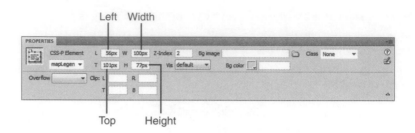

Top   Height

Adding a Background Color and Background Image

An AP div can have a background color, as shown in Figure 17.6. You can use the color picker or type in a color in the standard HTML hexadecimal format, preceded by #. Make sure that you leave the Bg Color option blank if you want your AP div to be transparent. If your page background is white and you make your AP div background white, your AP div seems as if it's transparent until you position it over something else!

FIGURE 17.6
An AP div can have a background
color or a tiled background image.

AP Div with background color

AP Div with tiled background image

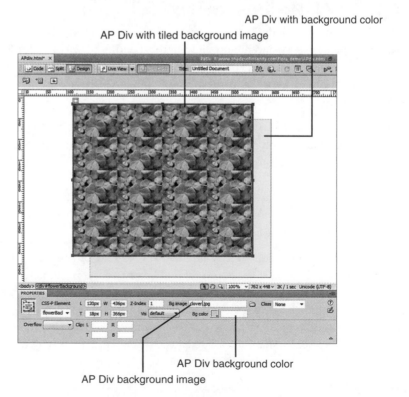

AP Div background color

AP Div background image

You can also place a background image in an AP div. The image repeats multiple times (called **tiling**) within the AP div if the AP div is larger than the image. Objects and text that you put within the AP div are on top of the background image. Click the Browse icon (the folder) beside the Bg Image box in the Property inspector and navigate to the background image file. Figure 17.6 also shows the Property inspector when a selected AP div contains a background image.

Exploring AP Div Stacking Order

Not only can you position AP divs in exact places on the page, but you also can allow AP divs to overlap one another. So which AP div is on top? The stacking order decides which AP div is on top of other AP divs. The **z-index** value, in turn, determines the stacking order. The z-index can be either a negative or a positive number.

The AP div with the highest z-index value is the one on the top. The term *z-index* comes from the coordinate system that you used back in geometry class—remember x and y coordinates? Well, the z-index is the third coordinate that is necessary to describe three-dimensional space. Imagine an arrow coming out of the paper or screen toward you and another going back into the screen or paper. That is the z-index.

Dreamweaver prefers to give each AP div a unique z-index value. In HTML, you can legally have multiple AP divs that have the same z-index. Remember, though, that if you reorder the AP divs, Dreamweaver renumbers each with a unique z-index. So why waste your time?

You can set the z-index in the Z-Index box in the Property inspector, as shown in Figure 17.7. The AP Elements panel displays the z-index to the right of each AP div's name. This panel displays the AP divs in order according to their z-index value, with the top being the highest z-index and the bottom being the lowest. You can easily rearrange the stacking order by selecting the AP div name in the AP Elements panel and then dragging and dropping it somewhere else.

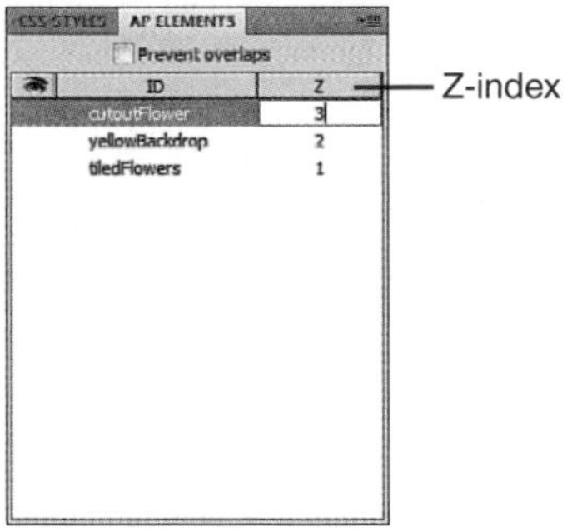

FIGURE 17.7
The z-index value represents the stacking order of AP divs. You can set the z-index (as either a positive or a negative value) in the Property inspector.

Changing AP Div Visibility

AP divs have a visibility attribute that can be set to Visible, Hidden, Inherit, or Default. The Vis drop-down menu, as shown in Figure 17.8, is in the middle of the Property inspector when you select an AP div. These are the visibility settings:

FIGURE 17.8
The Vis drop-down menu enables
you to set the visibility attribute for
an AP div.

Vis drop-down menu

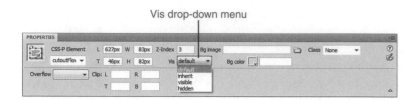

▶ **Default**—The Default setting is the same as the Inherit setting in
most browsers.

▶ **Inherit**—An AP div set to Inherit has the same visibility as its parent.
You learn more about nesting and parent AP divs in a few minutes. If
you set the parent to Hidden, and you set the AP div nesting within
that parent to Inherit, the nested element hides also.

▶ **Visible**—An AP div set to Visible appears on the web page at loading.

▶ **Hidden**—An AP div set to Hidden does not appear on the web page.
You can later make the AP div visible by using the Show-Hide Elements behavior.

Why you might want AP divs to be visible is obvious, but why might you
want them to hide? So that you can display them later, after something has
happened! You learn about using the Show-Hide Elements behavior in
Hour 18.

The AP Elements panel represents visibility with a picture of an eye. The
eye beside an AP div is open if you set the AP div to Visible. The eye is
closed if you set the AP div to Hidden. The Inherit setting does not have an
eye representation. The Eye icon is a toggle that moves through the Default,
Visible, and Hidden settings and then goes back to Default. You can set the
visibility characteristics of all the AP divs by clicking the Eye icon in the
header of the AP Elements panel.

CAUTION

**Don't Accidentally Click
the Eye Icon Column
Header**

Be careful when clicking the Eye
icon for your top AP div. It's easy
to accidentally click the header
instead and set all the eyes in
the column. You have to click in
the Eye column *beside* the AP
div for which you want to set the
Visibility property.

TIP

**Can't Draw? Check
Prevent Overlaps**

If Dreamweaver doesn't seem to
allow you to draw a nested AP
div by holding down the Ctrl key,
you probably have the Prevent
Overlaps check box enabled at
the top of the AP Elements
panel.

Nesting AP Divs

You can create an AP div within another AP div; the new AP div nests
within its parent AP div. If you move the parent AP div, the child AP div
moves with it. The child AP div also inherits its parent's visibility attributes.

To create a nested AP div, you place the cursor inside the parent AP div and
choose Insert, AP Div. You draw a nested AP div by using the Draw AP Div
object to draw inside an existing AP div while holding down the Ctrl key

(the Command key on the Mac). In addition, you can place an existing AP div within another AP div by picking it up in the AP Elements panel while holding down the Ctrl key (or the Command key on the Mac) and then dropping it into another AP div. The nested AP div appears indented in the AP Elements panel, as shown in Figure 17.9.

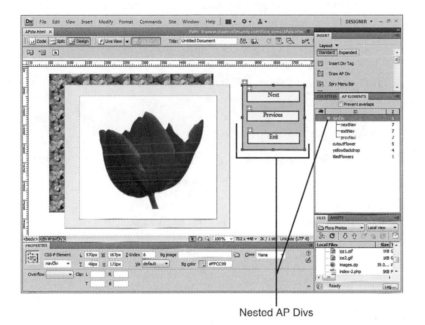

Nested AP Divs

FIGURE 17.9
An AP div nested within another AP div appears indented in the AP Elements panel.

CAUTION

Where Did the AP Divs Go?

Did your AP div disappear from the screen when you unnested it? When an AP div is nested, its position is relative to its parent. When you unnest the AP div, its position is then relative to the page. The AP div's coordinates might cause the AP div to be off the screen. To fix this problem, select the AP div in the AP Elements panel and give it L (left) and T (top) attributes that place it back on the screen.

The easiest way to unnest an AP div if you make a mistake or change your mind is to pick it up in the AP Elements panel and drop it somewhere else in the list of AP divs, as shown in Figure 17.10.

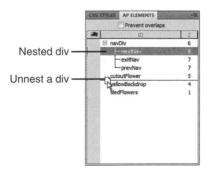

Nested div

Unnest a div

FIGURE 17.10
Pick up a nested AP div and move it to another position within the AP Elements panel to unnest it.

Animating an AP Div

In Hour 18, we take a look at how behaviors can be applied to divs and other elements to create effects. In earlier versions of Dreamweaver, a feature was provided that allowed you to create DHTML animations with your divs just by dragging them across the screen. While interesting, this feature wasn't widely used and produced complicated code. That being the case, let's take a look at how you can create animation on your own.

AP divs are unique because they are aligned to absolute coordinates. These coordinates can be manipulated through JavaScript to produce onscreen animations. By changing the top and left coordinates of a div, you can move it anywhere on the screen.

Follow these steps to create your own animated AP Div:

1. Add a new AP div to your web page and make sure that it is named apDiv1.

2. Add content to the div so that it is visible.

3. Switch your document to code view, and then add the following JavaScript code to the <head> portion of your document:

```
<script type="text/javascript">
var start=10;
var increment=10;
var stop=500;
var y=start;
function down() {
    object=document.getElementById('apDiv1');
    y=y+increment;
    object.style.top=(y+'px');
    if (y<stop) {
        timer=setTimeout("down()",20);
    }
}
</script>
```

4. Finally, add a link to the document that triggers the animation (for example, "click here to animate"). The link should point to `javascript:`
`down();`, which triggers the animation.

5. Save the file and switch to Design mode, Live View, or Preview in your browser. When you click the link, the AP div scrolls smoothly down the page.

Although the intricacies of JavaScript are beyond the scope of this book, this animation is very simple to understand. A single block of code, called a function, creates the animation. In this case, the function is called `down()` and is called when you click the link in the document.

To generate the moving div, the `down()` function simply increases the top (`object.style.top`) coordinate of the div from a starting point of 10px to a stopping point of 500px in increments of 10. As long as the stopping point hasn't been reached, the animation keeps running, pausing 20 milliseconds in between each move.

There are hundreds of DHTML JavaScripts that work with divs that you can add to your own pages. Googling "JavaScript Div animation" is a good place to start. Another excellent tutorial can be found on Apple's developer site at http://developer.apple.com/internet/webcontent/animation.html.

Summary

In this hour, you learned how to insert an AP div into a web page. You learned how to change an AP div's size, position, background color, and name. You explored setting the stacking order, or z-index, of AP divs and setting an AP div's visibility. You also learned how to create a simple JavaScript-based div animation.

Q&A

Q. How do AP divs differ from the div tags I use with CSS for page layout?

A. CSS defines box elements, which is what both AP divs and div tags are. When creating a page layout, you often leave the CSS properties applied to a div with the default positioning, which is relative. Relative positioning means that a div appears according to its position in the code; the div before it in the code appears above it on the page. AP divs have the positioning property set to absolute, which means that regardless of where the div tag appears in the code, the div and its content appear at a certain position—a particular number of pixels from the left and a particular number of pixels from the top of the web page.

Q. Why would I want to use AP divs in my web pages?

A. If you'd like to have some content overlapping or sitting on top of other content, you have to use AP divs and set their z-index values higher than the underlying content's z-index. Alternatively, if you want to hide an image or text on the screen and show it later by using the Show-Hide Elements behavior (see Hour 18), you have to use AP divs.

Workshop

Quiz

1. AP divs cannot be used to create animation. True or false?

2. What is the cross-browser tag used to implement AP divs?

3. The AP div with the lowest z-index is the one on the top. True or false?

Quiz Answers

1. False. AP divs, because they can be positioned anywhere onscreen, are ideal for animation effects.

2. The <div> tag implements AP divs in all modern browsers.

3. False. The AP div with the highest z-index is the one on top.

Exercises

1. Create a web page that has multiple AP divs. Experiment with inserting images and text into the AP divs. Change the background color of one of the AP divs. Be sure to make a few of the AP divs overlap so that you can see how the z-index works.

2. Create a banner and a navigation bar for a site by placing an AP div across the top of the site for the banner. Place individual AP divs with the text Home, Previous, and Next in them. You can make these hyperlinks if you like. Now convert these AP divs into a table.

3. Visit the website http://script.aculo.us/ to explore the Scriptaculous JavaScript framework for DHTML effects. Consider the different ways these effects could be applied to existing websites to improve or modernize the user experience.

Adding Interactivity with Behaviors

Dreamweaver behaviors add interactivity to web pages. Interactivity usually requires coding in JavaScript, but Dreamweaver adds all the JavaScript for you, so you don't have to understand scripting to use behaviors. Behaviors enable you to make something happen when the user clicks the mouse, loads a web page, or moves the cursor.

What Is a Dreamweaver Behavior?

When you add a behavior to a web page, Dreamweaver inserts JavaScript functions and function calls, enabling users to interact with the web page or make something happen. I like to think of a **function** as a little code machine—you send it some information, it processes that information, and it sends you a result or makes something happen. A **function call** is the code added to an object that triggers the function and sends it any information it needs to do its job. For instance, a popular Dreamweaver behavior is the Swap Image behavior. You actually used this behavior in Hour 8, "Displaying Images," because Dreamweaver adds the Swap Image behavior to your web page automatically when you use the Rollover Image object (Insert, Image Objects, Rollover Image).

When you insert a behavior, Dreamweaver writes a function in the head of the web page. The function that controls the Swap Image behavior is MM_swapImage(). Dreamweaver doesn't call the code in that function until some event on the page triggers it; until the event triggers the function code, it just sits waiting in the head. For instance, the MM_swapImage() function is usually triggered by the onMouseOver event—the event fired when the cursor is placed over whatever object the function is attached to. When the user rolls the mouse over an image with a behavior attached, the event triggers the function, which swaps the image source with another image.

A **behavior** is an action triggered by an event. Or you could look at it this way:

Event + Action = Behavior

Actions are the JavaScript code, the function, which Dreamweaver inserts into a web page. Browser events are user actions that the browser captures; for example, clicking a button on a web page triggers the onClick event.

Using the Reference Books

To learn more about individual events, use the Dreamweaver Reference panel (by selecting Window, Results, Reference). There are several reference books built into Dreamweaver.

TIP

Dreamweaver Terms: *Behavior* and *Action*

The terms *behavior* and *action* are specific to Dreamweaver and are not standard HTML terminology. These terms both describe prewritten JavaScript code that Dreamweaver makes available to anyone creating web pages with Dreamweaver. It works just like any other JavaScript code.

▼ TRY IT YOURSELF

Looking Up JavaScript Events

To find information about an event, do the following:

1. Open the References panel: Window, Results, References.

2. Select O'REILLY JavaScript Reference from the Book drop-down list.

3. Select an event name, such as onClick, onBlur, or onMouseUp, from the Object menu.

The Reference panel displays a description of the event, as shown in Figure 18.1, including which browsers support the event (in the upper-right corner) and typical targets for the event.

FIGURE 18.1
The Reference panel displays the JavaScript reference that includes descriptions of events.

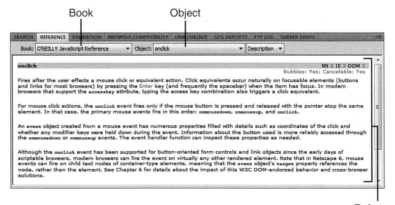

Book   Object

Reference
Information

To close the Results panel group that opens when you open the Reference panel, select the Close Panel Group command from the Panel Group menu on the far right of the panel group.

Exploring Dreamweaver Behaviors

Dreamweaver comes with many powerful behaviors that enable you to do some advanced web development without having to write JavaScript yourself. You access behaviors in the Behaviors panel (Window, Behaviors), as shown in Figure 18.2.

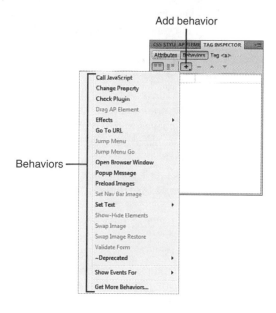

FIGURE 18.2
The Behaviors portion of the Tag Inspector panel displays a list of the behaviors you can attach to the object currently selected in the web page.

You explore attaching a behavior to an object on a web page by using the Add Behavior button in a few minutes.

Various behaviors come preinstalled in Dreamweaver. Table 18.1 lists these behaviors and gives a brief description of each one.

NOTE

Tag Attributes and Behaviors

Note that the Behaviors panel is really just a section within the Tag Attributes panel. Because it has its own Window menu entry and acts independently from the tag attributes, we refer to it as the Behaviors panel.

TABLE 18.1   Dreamweaver Behaviors

Behavior	Description
Call JavaScript	Specifies custom JavaScript code. You use this behavior when you want to add custom JavaScript code to an object in Dreamweaver.
Change Property	Changes an object's properties. This behavior enables you to change properties of absolutely positioned (AP) divs (such as the background color or the size), form objects, and images.
Check Plugin	Determines whether the user has a particular plug-in installed. You usually trigger this behavior by using the onLoad event of the body tag.
Drag AP Element	Makes an AP div draggable and defines a target to which to drag it.
Effects	Offers seven different effects you can apply to objects such as images and divs. The different effects are appear/fade, blind, grow/shrink, highlight, shake, slide, and squish. These effects, which are part of Dreamweaver's Spry framework, are covered in Hour 19, "Using AJAX Frameworks and Libraries."
Go to URL	Loads a URL into the browser when the behavior triggers.
Jump Menu	Edits a jump menu. You create a jump menu in Hour 20, "Creating a Form and Collecting Data." This type of menu enables users to jump to various URLs.
Jump Menu Go	Adds a custom jump menu's Go button. This button triggers the jump to the URL selected in the jump menu.
Open Browser Window	Opens a new browser window. Developers often use this behavior to open an additional window containing extra information.
Popup Message	Pops up a JavaScript alert box with text. This box contains an OK button that the user clicks to close the message.

TABLE 18.1   Dreamweaver Behaviors

Behavior	Description
Preload Images	Preloads images into the browser cache in the background. This behavior is often included with the Swap Image behavior. The image to swap is loaded into the cache so that it appears quickly.
Set Nav Bar Image	Changes the image in a navigation bar. You created a navigation bar in Hour 16, "Adding Navigation: Navigation and Menu Bars." This behavior enables you to set a button state.
Set Text of Container	Puts text (or HTML) into a container tag, usually a div.
Set Text of Frame	Puts text (or HTML) into a frame.
Set Text of Status Bar	Puts text into the browser's status bar.
Set Text of Text Field	Puts text into a text field in a form. You learn more about text fields in Hour 20.
Show-Hide Elements	Shows or hides a div or group of divs. This behavior changes the div or AP div visibility attribute.
Swap Image	Swaps the image source for another image source.
Swap Image Restore	Restores a previous image swap.
Validate Form	Validates the data in a form, enabling you to check whether the user has entered information into certain text fields and validating whether it is the correct type of information. You use this behavior in Hour 21, "Sending and Reacting to Form Data."

Some behaviors from previous versions of Dreamweaver use out-of-date methods or code, so Adobe deprecated them in Dreamweaver CS4. This means that you should not use the behaviors to create new objects. They have been included, however, so that you can edit existing pages created in previous versions of Dreamweaver that use these behaviors. Table 18.2 lists each deprecated behavior and gives a brief description of its use.

TIP

Want More Behaviors?

You can also download third-party behaviors, called **extensions**. You learn more about extensions in Hour 24, "Customizing Dreamweaver."

TABLE 18.2   Deprecated Dreamweaver Behaviors

Behavior	Description
Check Browser	Determines which browser the user has. This is useful when you create content that's specific to various browser versions. This behavior can redirect the user to different web pages based on the browser version in use.
Control Shockwave or Flash	Controls Shockwave or Flash movies. Can be set to Play, Stop, Rewind, or Go to Frame.
Hide Pop-up Menu	Hides a Dreamweaver pop-up menu (described later in this table, with the Show Pop-up Menu behavior).
Play Sound	Plays a sound file.
Show Pop-up Menu	Shows a Dreamweaver pop-up menu with links. This menu uses Cascading Style Sheets (CSS) to present a complex menu. Use this behavior only for editing existing pop-up menus. Use the Spry Menu Bar widget instead of this behavior to add new menus.
Go to Timeline Frame	Goes to a specific frame in a timeline. This is part of an animation function that is no longer included in Dreamweaver CS4.
Play Timeline	Plays a timeline.
Stop Timeline	Stops a timeline.

Exploring Events

One of the most frustrating problems with browsers is the lack of standard event support. You might write JavaScript that worked perfectly in Internet Explorer, only for nothing to happen in Firefox. Because of this, Dreamweaver enables you to select the events available to versions of Netscape and Internet Explorer, as well as "generic" HTML 4.01 events for the greatest compatibility.

Dreamweaver enables you to set the browser events that it presents in the Behaviors panel based on browser versions. The Show Events For drop-down menu, shown in Figure 18.3, enables you to target specific browsers and browser versions. Depending on the selection in this menu, different

events are available. To be compatible with the most users, choose the
HTML 4.01 setting. You access the Show Events For drop-down menu by
clicking the Add Behaviors (+) button in the Behaviors panel.

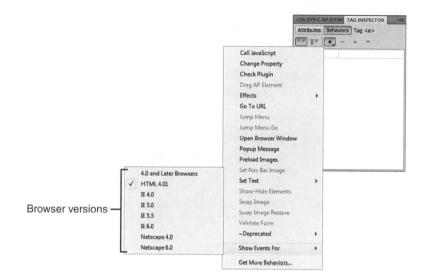

Browser versions

FIGURE 18.3
The Show Events For list enables
you to choose browsers and
browser versions. Only the actions
and events that work with the
browser and version you choose
are available.

Table 18.3 lists examples of common browser events available with the
HTML 4.01 setting. Although browsers capture different events, various objects also capture events. This is just a small sampling of the available
events, but luckily most of the events' names make their functionality obvious. The onDblClick event, for instance, is similar to the onClick event, except that the user clicks twice instead of once.

TIP

Which Event Setting Is Best?

You have access to the largest
number of events by choosing IE
6.0. However, the HTML 4.01
events offer a good standards-
based compromise between a
useful number of events and
compatibility with almost all
browsers, so you generally want
to choose the HTML 4.01 setting.

TABLE 18.3   Common Browser Events

Event	Description
onBlur	Triggered when an object **loses focus**; that is, it be-comes inactive. The body of a web page often cap-tures this event when the user switches to a different web page, or from a form object such as a text field or a check box.
onChange	Triggered after a user makes and commits a change to a form object, usually a text field, textarea, drop-down menu, or list. The user commits the change by leaving the form object, usually by putting the focus elsewhere on the web page.

CAUTION

What Happens When an Event Isn't Supported?

If you select an event that does
not work in a certain browser,
users with that browser either
will have nothing happen or will
receive a JavaScript error.

TABLE 18.3   Common Browser Events

Event	Description
onClick	Triggered when the user presses and releases, or clicks, a mouse button. Images or hyperlinks often capture this event.
onFocus	Triggered when an object receives focus; that is, it becomes active. For example, when a user clicks in a form object such as a text field, that field has received "focus."
onLoad	Triggered when an object or a web page finishes loading. The body of a web page often captures this event, but images occasionally use it.
onMouseDown	Triggered when the user presses a mouse button. Images or hyperlinks often capture this event.
onMouseOver	Triggered when the user places the cursor over an object. Images or hyperlinks often capture this event.
onMouseUp	Triggered when the user releases a mouse button. Images or hyperlinks often capture this event.
onSelect	Triggered when a user selects text within a form object, usually a text field or textarea.
onSubmit	Triggered when the user submits a form by using a submit button or an image button.
onUnload	Triggered when the browser unloads a web page—that is, when the user goes to a new URL or closes the browser. The body of a web page usually captures this event, which is often responsible for triggering those annoying pop-up windows that seem impossible to close.

Attaching a Behavior to an Object

You attach behaviors to objects in a web page. When you attach a behavior, Dreamweaver opens the appropriate behavior dialog box. After you've set up the behavior characteristics in the dialog box, select the event to trigger the behavior. Dreamweaver inserts the necessary JavaScript into the head of the web page. It also adds code to the object's tag to capture the event and call the JavaScript.

Every time you attach a behavior, regardless of which behavior it is, follow these general steps:

1. Create a web page and save it (File, Save).

2. Select the object on the web page that triggers the behavior—the object that the user clicks, for instance, such as a link.

3. Select the appropriate behavior by clicking the Add Behavior button in the Behaviors panel and selecting a behavior from the drop-down menu.

4. Set the behavior's properties in its specific dialog box and click OK.

5. Select the appropriate event in the Events column of the Behaviors panel.

TRY IT YOURSELF ▼

Attaching JavaScript Behaviors

You must attach behaviors to appropriate objects. Dreamweaver won't let you attach inappropriate behaviors; it grays out inappropriate behaviors so that you cannot select them. Likewise, you can't attach inappropriate events to certain objects.

You can tell which object you have selected in the Document window because the top of the Behaviors panel displays the tag's name, as shown in Figure 18.4.

In the rest of the hour, you explore in detail how to attach a sampling of the behaviors available in Dreamweaver. We don't have time to cover every behavior, but you look at enough different behaviors to get the idea of how they all work. In this hour, you explore the following behaviors:

▶ Show-Hide Elements

▶ Open Browser Window

▶ Popup Message

▶ Set Text of Container

▶ Go to URL

▶ Drag AP Element

Currently selected tag

FIGURE 18.4
The top of the panel displays the tag's name.

CAUTION

Different Behaviors

The Behaviors panel is not the same as the Server Behaviors panel. The Server Behaviors panel works with sites that use server-side scripting, such as PHP (a recursive abbreviation for PHP: Hypertext Preprocessor) and ColdFusion. The Behaviors panel uses JavaScript, which is client-side scripting and does not rely on a server.

Showing and Hiding Elements

Now you're ready to add your first behavior. The Show-Hide Elements behavior has a name that pretty much says it all: You can use it to show or hide an element on the web page, using a div or an AP div. You don't usually apply a behavior to the object that it affects, so you need to have another object on the page that triggers the behavior. For instance, you might create a hyperlink that triggers showing or hiding an AP div.

To begin, add an image or a hyperlink that captures the user's click and hides the AP div. Dreamweaver is smart enough to not display the Show-Hide Elements behavior in the Add Behavior drop-down menu if you don't actually have an AP div in the web page, so you have to add an AP div to the page before you add the behavior. It's important to name your AP divs when using the Show-Hide Elements behavior because the Show-Hide Elements dialog box displays all the AP divs on the page by name, so it helps for the AP divs to have meaningful names.

Creating a Null Link to Trigger the Behavior

Make sure that you've already defined a site in Dreamweaver and created a new web page. First you create a link to trigger the Show-Hide Elements behavior.

▼ TRY IT YOURSELF

Creating a Null Link

Follow these steps to create a null link:

1. Add text for a hyperlink somewhere on the web page. You could enter something such as **Show the AP Div**.

2. Instead of creating an active link, you add what's called a **null link**, which is a link to nowhere. This is just so that you create a clickable object that can trigger the behavior.

   Select the text you created in step 1 and enter `javascript:;` in the Link box of the Property inspector, as shown in Figure 18.5.

Null link

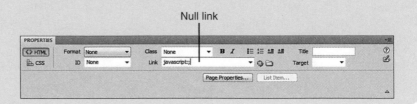

Creating a Hidden AP Div

Next you create the AP div to hide when the visitor clicks the null link you created earlier. After you've created the AP div, type some text into it or give it a background color so that you can actually see it in the browser. Check out Hour 17, "Using Dynamic HTML and AP Divs," if you need a refresher on how to insert an AP div and set its properties.

To create a hidden AP div, do the following:

1. Insert an AP div (Insert, Layout Objects, AP Div).

2. Enter some text in the AP div or give it a background color in the Property inspector.

3. Select the AP div and set its Visibility attribute value to Hidden by selecting Hidden from the Vis drop-down menu in the Property inspector.

TRY IT YOURSELF ▼

Creating a Hidden AP Div

Attaching the Show-Hide Elements Behavior

Now that you have both the object that you will show and the object that the visitor clicks to trigger the behavior, you are ready to attach the behavior.

To attach the Show-Hide Elements behavior, do the following:

1. Click anywhere within the null link you created.

2. Open the Behaviors panel (Window, Behaviors).

3. Make sure that <a> (the anchor tag that creates a link) is visible at the top of the Behaviors panel. This means that you have the correct object selected on the page.

4. Click the Add Behavior (+) button in the Behaviors panel, as shown in Figure 18.6. Select the Show-Hide Elements behavior. The Show-Hide Elements dialog box appears.

5. The Show-Hide Elements dialog box, shown in Figure 18.7, lists all the AP divs in the page. There are three buttons: Show, Hide, and Default. Highlight the correct AP div and click the Show button. The word *show* then appears in parentheses next to the AP div's name.

   You click the Show button to make an AP div visible, and you click the Hide button to make an AP div hidden. When an AP div is set to show, clicking the Show button again toggles show off (the same is true for the other buttons). The Default button restores an AP div to its default visibility (visible).

6. Click the OK button to save your changes.

TRY IT YOURSELF ▼

Attaching the Show-Hide Elements Behavior

NOTE

The Behavior Code

When you add a behavior to an object, Dreamweaver adds an attribute to the HTML tag, enabling the tag to respond to the event. The attribute includes a function call to the appropriate function inserted by the behavior. For instance, the code for an image tag with the Show-Hide Elements behavior attached looks like this:

```
<img src="button_up.gif"
width="80" height="35"
    onClick="MM_showHideAP
Divs('apDiv1','','hide')" />
```

When a user clicks the image, the AP div named apDiv1 hides.

FIGURE 18.6
The Add Behavior (+) button drops
down the Add Behavior drop-down
menu, with all the available actions
for the selected object.

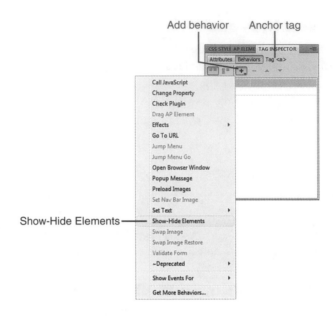

Add behavior   Anchor tag

Show-Hide Elements

FIGURE 18.7
The Show-Hide Elements dialog box
lists all the AP divs and enables you
to change their visibility attributes.

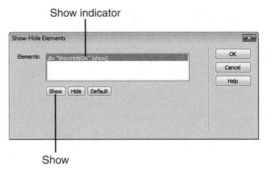

Show indicator

Show

Selecting the Event That Triggers the Behavior

At this point, you have selected half the behavior, but you also have to select the other half of the behavior: the event. When you selected the link, the Behaviors panel listed the Show-Hide Elements behavior under the Action column, and the Event column probably defaulted to the onClick event.

You could use the onClick event to trigger showing the AP div, but that's too easy! Try using the onMouseUp event instead:

TRY IT YOURSELF ▼

Setting a Trigger Event

1. In the Behaviors panel, drop down the Events list by clicking the arrow button, as shown in Figure 18.8. You have to click within the event for this button to be available.

Arrow button

Events ─

FIGURE 18.8
The arrow button beside the event drops down a menu containing the available events.

2. Select onMouseUp in the Events drop-down menu.

Now when users let up the mouse button, they trigger the Show-Hide Elements behavior.

Because you have set up the behavior (Show-Hide Elements) and the event (onMouseUp), you can now test your work! First make sure that the AP div you set to show with the behavior is hiding (if you didn't do this earlier). Preview the web page in the browser or in the Dreamweaver Live View. Click the hyperlink and your AP div should appear!

Editing the Behavior

If you made a mistake while setting up the Show-Hide Elements behavior, you can edit the behavior after it has been set.

To edit a behavior, follow these steps:

TRY IT YOURSELF ▼

Editing a Behavior

1. Select the object (probably a link) that has the behavior attached to it.

2. Double-click Show-Hide Elements in the Action column of the Behaviors panel.

3. This reopens the Show-Hide Elements dialog box where you can make changes. Make changes and click OK.

Opening a New Browser Window

Use the Open Browser Window behavior to open a new browser window and display a URL. This time you capture the user clicking an image to trigger the action. The onClick event fires when the user clicks the image. This then triggers the Open Browser Window behavior that opens a new browser window.

You can open a browser window at a specific size and with specific browser attributes. Browser attributes, listed in Table 18.4, control whether the browser window has controls that enable the user to navigate out of the window. You set up the browser attributes in the Open Browser Window dialog box.

TABLE 18.4   Browser Properties for the Open Browser Window Behavior

Attribute	Description
URL to Display	Sets the URL of the page that opens in the new window.
Window Width	Controls the width (in pixels) of the window.
Window Height	Controls the height (in pixels) of the window.
Navigation Toolbar	Contains the Back, Next, and other navigation buttons for moving to different URLs.
Location Toolbar	Displays the current URL.
Status Bar	Displays the status bar (the bar located at the bottom of the browser). The status bar displays the loading status of a web page as well as the URL of a moused-over link.
Menu Bar	Contains all the standard browser menus.
Scrollbars as Needed	Enables the user to scroll the browser window.
Resize Handles	Enables the user to resize the browser window.
Window Name	Specifies the optional window name. You can use this name with JavaScript to control the window, so you cannot use spaces and punctuation in the name.

TRY IT YOURSELF ▼

Using onClick to Open a New Browser Window

To have a new browser window open when the user clicks an image, follow these steps:

1. Save the web page. The Open Browser Window behavior needs the web page saved so that it knows how to build the URL that it loads in the new browser window.
2. Insert an image into this web page. Select the image, and make sure that the correct tag (the `<img>` tag) shows at the top of the Behaviors panel.
3. Click the + button in the Behaviors panel. Select the Open Browser Window behavior, and the Open Browser Window dialog box appears.
4. Fill in the URL that loads in the new window. You can use a web page that you created previously or load an external web page from any website.
5. Set the width and height of the window. Check the browser attributes (listed in Table 18.4) that you want the new browser window to have. Optionally, give the window a name.
6. The Open Browser Window dialog box should look something like the one shown in Figure 18.9. Click the OK button.

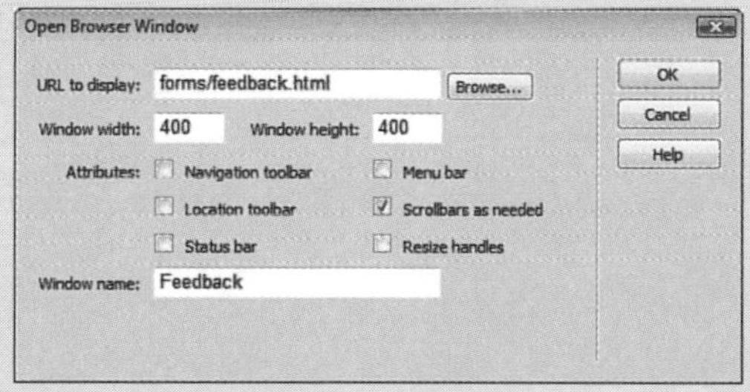

FIGURE 18.9
The Open Browser Window dialog box enables you to turn on or off various attributes of browser windows.

7. In the Behaviors panel, select the `onClick` event from the Events drop-down menu if it isn't selected by default.

Preview the web page you created in a browser. (It does not work with Live View.) When you click the image, your new window should appear.

Popping Up a Message

Next, you add an additional behavior—a pop-up message—to the same object you used to open a browser window. You can add as many behaviors as necessary to a single object. The Popup Message behavior displays a JavaScript alert box with a message.

To add the Popup Message behavior, follow these steps:

1. Select the object you applied the behavior to in the preceding section. You should see the Open Browser Window behavior listed in the Behaviors panel. Make sure that the appropriate tag appears in the title bar of the Tag panel group.

2. Click the + button and select the Popup Message behavior.

3. The Popup Message dialog box includes a text box where you type your message, as shown in Figure 18.10. Click OK after typing the message.

FIGURE 18.10
The Popup Message dialog box has a text box where you type the message that pops up for the user.

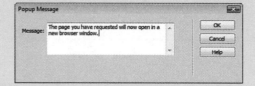

4. Select the onClick event as you did in the Open Browser Window dialog box earlier.

Attaching Multiple Behaviors to the Same Object

You can attach multiple behaviors to an object. One event can trigger several actions. In Figure 18.11, you can see that the onClick event triggers multiple actions. The actions happen in the order listed. You can change the order in which the actions occur by moving them with the up- and down-arrow buttons on the Behaviors panel.

Preview your web page with the two behaviors, Open Browser Window and Popup Message, in the browser. Does it work perfectly? It would probably be better if the message popped up and then the user went to the new

Arrow buttons (reorder)

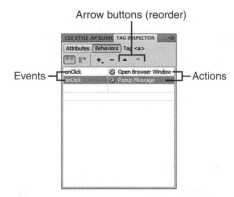

Events —[   ]— Actions

FIGURE 18.11
One event—for example, the
onClick event shown here—can
trigger multiple actions, and you
can have multiple behaviors attached to a single object in a web
page. You can change the execution
order of the behaviors by using the
arrow buttons.

window after clicking the OK button in the message box. You can change
the order of behaviors triggered by the same event.

To change the order of the behaviors, follow these steps:

1. Select the object to which the behaviors are applied. You should see
   both behaviors listed in the Behaviors panel.

2. Select the Popup Message behavior. Click the up-arrow button to move the
   Popup Message behavior above the Open Browser Window behavior.

TRY IT YOURSELF ▼

**Changing the Order of
Behaviors**

Preview your web page in the browser again. Now the pop-up message appears first. After you click the OK button on the pop-up message, the new
browser window should appear.

Setting Text in a Container

You can insert behaviors that write to various objects: frames, divs (containers, links, paragraphs, or other containers), text entry fields, and the
browser status bar.

To use the Set Text of Container behavior, follow these steps:

1. Add an AP div, a div, or another container to the web page and name it
   feedback.

2. Select an object on the web page to trigger the behavior. You can add
   this behavior to the same object you used earlier this hour or you can
   add a null link to an object on any web page.

TRY IT YOURSELF ▼

**Using the Set Text of
Container Behavior**

▼ TRY IT YOURSELF

Using the Set Text of Container Behavior

continued

3. Click the + button in the Behaviors panel. Choose the Set Text of Container behavior from the Set Text submenu—the menu that appears when you place your mouse over Set Text in the Add Behavior drop-down menu. The Set Text of Container dialog box appears.

4. Select the container named "feedback" from the drop-down menu.

5. Enter some text in the New HTML text box, as shown in Figure 18.12. Click OK.

FIGURE 18.12
The Set Text of Container dialog box enables you to enter text (and HTML) to display in the specified container.

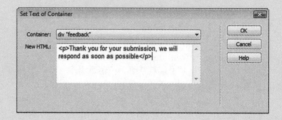

6. Select the onClick event from the Events drop-down menu in the Behaviors panel.

Preview the web page in your browser or in Live View. When you trigger the action, the text you entered appears in the container.

Using the Go to URL Behavior

The Go to URL behavior enables you to load a URL into the existing browser window. You might choose to use this behavior instead of simply using a link if you want to trigger other behaviors before the visitor goes to the link. For instance, you could first trigger a pop-up message telling users that they are leaving your website before linking them to another web page using the Go to URL behavior.

▼ TRY IT YOURSELF

Using the Go to URL Behavior

To use the Go to URL behavior, follow these steps:

1. Select that object that triggers the behavior. Make sure that the correct tag appears in the Tag panel group title bar.

2. Type **javascript:;** in the Link box in the Property inspector to create a null link.

3. In the Behaviors drop-down menu, select Go to URL.

4. The Go to URL dialog box opens, as shown in Figure 18.13. Enter a URL in the URL box.

FIGURE 18.13
The Go to URL dialog box enables you to load a new web page in the existing browser window.

5. Click OK to save the behavior settings.

6. Preview the page in a browser.

Adding Drag and Drop with a Draggable AP Div

The Drag AP Element behavior enables you to create AP divs that the user can drag around the browser window. You can even constrain the area within which the user can drag the AP div. This capability is useful for creating sliders, puzzles, dialog boxes, and other interactions.

You can use the Drag AP Element behavior to let users interact with objects on your web page. For instance, you might have an AP div that contains a map legend. You could make that AP div draggable so that the user can move it out of the way if it blocks part of the map. Or you could create a blank face and let people drag different noses, ears, eyes, and so on onto the face.

The Drag AP Element behavior enables users to drag an AP div. You have to turn on this behavior before a user can drag the AP div. This behavior can trigger when the web page loads by capturing the body tag's onLoad event. You select the body tag in Dreamweaver's tag selector. You should see <body> at the top of the panel group.

After you've created your Drag AP Element and given it a name, you're ready to apply the Drag AP Element behavior.

TIP

Check Out CourseBuilder

If you need to create complicated drag-and-drop interactions, you should investigate the CourseBuilder extension to Dreamweaver, which is available at the Adobe Exchange (see Hour 24 for information about extensions to Dreamweaver). The drag-and-drop interactions created by CourseBuilder have the capability to make an object return to its original position if dropped incorrectly.

NOTE

The <body> Tag Holds Everything Visible

You might notice that when you select the <body> tag, you also select everything in your web page. That's because the <body> tag is the container within which all the objects on your web page reside.

Creating a Draggable Div

To use the Drag AP Element behavior, follow these steps:

1. Add an AP div to a web page (Insert, Layout Objects, AP Div) and give it a name.

2. Select the body tag from the tag selector in the Dreamweaver status bar, as shown in Figure 18.14.

FIGURE 18.14
Select the body tag from the tag selector to trigger a behavior when the web page loads.

Body tag

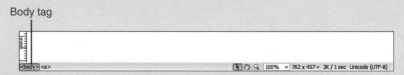

3. Click the Add Behavior (+) button in the Behaviors panel and select Drag AP Element. The Drag AP Element dialog box appears, as shown in Figure 18.15.

FIGURE 18.15
The Drag AP Element dialog box enables you to select the AP div you want to be draggable.

AP elements

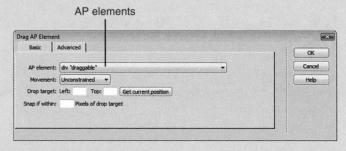

4. From the AP Element drop-down menu, select the name of the AP div to drag.

5. Click OK to save your changes.

6. Make sure that the onLoad event is listed in the Behaviors panel next to the Drag AP Element action. This means the Drag AP Element behavior triggers when the web page loads.

TIP

Can't Find the Behavior?

If you do not see the behavior attached to the <body> tag when you select it, you've applied the behavior to the wrong tag. You have to hunt down the object to which you applied the behavior and delete that behavior in the Behaviors panel. As you click objects in the Document window, look at the Behaviors panel to see which object has the behavior attached to it.

Check to see that the Drag AP Element behavior is working the way you want it to by previewing the web page in a browser. The correct AP div should be draggable.

Enabling Drag and Drop

A draggable AP div is, obviously, of questionable value on most web pages. To make things a bit more interesting, we can create a full drag-and-drop quiz using this same behavior. This is possible thanks to some additional options in the Drag AP Element behavior. Specifically, we can choose a "Drop Target" for the div. A Drop Target is a predefined location where the div should be dropped. We can also call some simple JavaScript if an object is really close to its Drop Target, making it possible to tell a user if they've successfully dragged and dropped a div.

Let's go ahead and try this now by making a simple three-item drag-and-drop matching game using words and definitions.

To create a simple drag-and-drop game, entirely in Dreamweaver, just follow these steps:

1. First, create an AP div with the definitions that serve as the "answers" to this exercise, as shown in Figure 18.16.

Creating a Drag-and-Drop Game

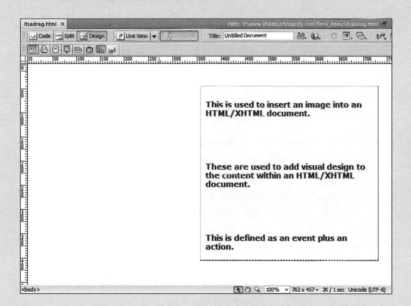

FIGURE 18.16
Create an AP div that holds the answers to your word-definition matching quiz.

2. Add three AP divs to your document. Within each div, place the word that should be matched with one of the definitions. Name each div using the word it contains.

3. Before doing anything else, position the three AP divs exactly where you'd like them to be when the user has successfully solved the puzzle—presumably right beside each definition. Your screen should look similar to that shown in Figure 18.17.

▼ TRY IT YOURSELF

Creating a Drag-and-Drop Game

continued

FIGURE 18.17
Set up your display so that it looks the way you'd expect if all the answers are correct.

4. Now you're ready to add the Drag AP Element behavior. As you did before, select the body tag and add the Drag AP Element behavior.

5. In the Drag AP Element configuration screen, select one of your AP elements.

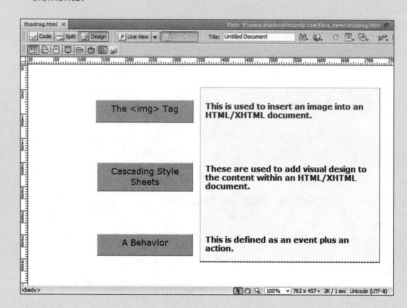

6. Click the button Get Current Position to enter the drop target. This indicates that this is the correct location for where the item should end up when the user is finished dragging it.

7. Enter a value of **50** in the Snap if Within field. This allows the user to be a little bit off in their drag. If they're within 50 pixels of the correct location, the element snaps into place. Your configuration should now resemble what's shown in Figure 18.18.

8. Now it's time to provide some feedback for a successful drag and drop. Click the Advanced tab in the Drag AP Element dialog box.

FIGURE 18.18
The drop target designates where the "correct" drop point is for an element. Providing a Snap if Within value allows your users to be a little sloppy.

Get current position

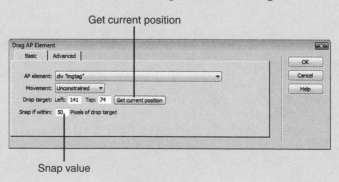

Snap value

9. In the line that says When Dropped: Call JavaScript, enter the text alert('**You are correct!**');. This simple function displays a message to the user.

10. Leave the Only if Snapped box checked—this ensures that the user dropped the item in the right place. The advanced settings should resemble those shown in Figure 18.19.

11. Repeat these same steps (4–10) for your other two AP divs.

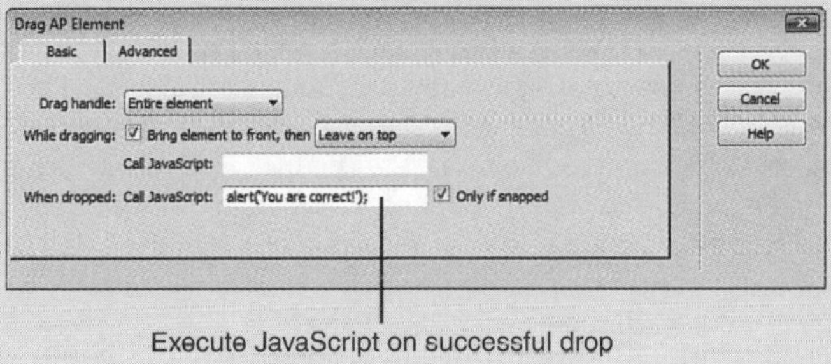

Execute JavaScript on successful drop

FIGURE 18.19
The advanced settings can be used to execute a JavaScript function if a successful drop takes place.

12. Now, the final (and fun!) step. Mix up the AP divs! Drag them anywhere on the page. This is their starting location.

Whew! It was a bit of work, but the end result is pretty cool! You can preview your page in a web browser or use Live View to try it out.

When the page loads, your AP divs are wherever you placed them in step 12. You can then drag each word so that it matches up with its definition. If you get close enough, it snaps into place and you see the pop-up message "You are right!" Apply this to activities in which users match images to names (state outlines to capitals, bird photos to names, and so on) and you are able to create compelling interactive online exercises.

Summary

In this hour, you learned that a Dreamweaver behavior consists of an event that triggers an action. You used the Show-Hide Elements, Open Browser Window, Popup Message, Set Text in Container, Go to URL, and Drag AP Element behaviors. You captured events from a hyperlink and an image. And you used the onMouseUp, onClick, and onLoad events as triggers for Dreamweaver actions.

Q&A

Q. How can I apply a behavior to a hidden AP div?

A. You can select a hidden AP div in the AP Elements panel. Switch to the Behaviors panel, without selecting anything else, and apply the behavior. Or you can temporarily make the AP div visible, apply the behavior, and then hide the AP div again.

Q. How can I create a button that triggers a behavior?

A. We cover forms and buttons in Hour 20. Basically, you place a button into the web page to trigger a behavior. You insert a button from the Forms tab of the Insert panel. If Dreamweaver asks whether you'd like to add a `<form>` tag, you can click Yes. The trick is to make sure that the button is not a Submit or Reset button. Select the None radio button in the Property inspector and then apply a behavior to the button.

Q. Where can I learn more about JavaScript?

A. You can learn JavaScript from some excellent resources and tutorials on the Web. You don't have to understand everything about JavaScript to use it. The short statements that you used during this hour should be easy to find in any JavaScript book or reference. You might want to start out with *Sams Teach Yourself JavaScript in 24 Hours, Fourth Edition*, by Michael Moncur; ISBN: 0672328798.

Workshop

Quiz

1. What is the equation that connects an event, an action, and a behavior?

2. You have the most behaviors and events available when you choose HTML 4.01 from the Show Events For submenu in the Behaviors panel. True or false?

3. What two events add up to an `onClick` event?

4. What is a deprecated behavior?

Quiz Answers

1. This is the equation that connects an event, an action, and a behavior:

   Event + Action = Behavior

2. False. You have the most events available when you select IE 6.0 as the target browser.

3. An `onClick` event consists of the `onMouseDown` and `onMouseUp` events.

4. A deprecated behavior is one that is provided for compatibility with pages created in older versions of Dreamweaver but that can't be used in new pages.

Exercises

1. Create a second hyperlink for the Show-Hide Elements example that you created earlier in the hour. Type **Hide the AP Div**, make it a hyperlink, and make clicking this hyperlink hide the AP div you created.

2. Try using some behaviors that are similar to the behaviors you used in this hour (for example, the Set Text of Status Bar behavior). What events are available for these behaviors? What objects must you have on the web page for these behaviors to work?

3. Create an AP div and make it draggable by attaching the Drag AP Element behavior to the body tag. Figure out how to constrain the AP div's movement to only horizontal (select Constrained from the Drag AP Element dialog box). Check the web page by previewing it in a browser. Then try constraining the movement to only vertical. Finally, constrain the movement to an area.

Using AJAX Frameworks and Libraries

You now know all the prerequisites necessary to understand AJAX and Dreamweaver's built-in AJAX library, Spry. These tools can be used to create dynamic website interfaces that look and feel like more traditional desktop applications. You actually used a little bit of this already when you created the menu bar in Hour 16, "Adding Navigation: Navigation and Menu Bars." In this hour, you learn more about AJAX, the Spry AJAX framework, as well as external AJAX libraries.

To effectively use the Spry AJAX framework, you have to understand a little bit about JavaScript and Dreamweaver behaviors (covered in Hour 18, "Adding Interactivity with Behaviors") along with an understand of applying CSS to div containers (covered in Hour 13, "Using CSS for Positioning"). Although Spry and AJAX in general are complicated pieces of code, even a Dreamweaver beginner can begin using these technologies on a web page.

Understanding AJAX

AJAX—Asynchronous JavaScript and XML—is a collection of technologies that create modern application-like interfaces on websites. Originally, AJAX was conceived as a way of dynamically updating portions of a web page (such as a div) using JavaScript and XML data exchanged with a server. A well-known example of AJAX is Google Maps (http://maps.google.com). You can zoom or drag the map to a different location while staying on the same web page.

Although dynamic updates are still the primary purpose of AJAX, its popular definition has been relaxed to include virtually any web elements that are dynamically generated or manipulated using JavaScript and CSS. Fancy

WHAT YOU'LL LEARN IN THIS HOUR:

▶ About the various AJAX elements available in Dreamweaver CS4

▶ How the external JavaScript and CSS files support the Spry AJAX framework

▶ How to apply Spry AJAX effects

▶ How to insert tabbed panels, collapsible panels, and accordions

▶ How to use XML and HTML as data sources for Spry AJAX elements

▶ How to use external AJAX libraries

menus (like those in Hour 16) are just the beginning of what is possible with AJAX.

As you might guess, AJAX isn't trivial to program. It requires an in-depth knowledge of how browsers structure their information (called a DOM, or Document Object Model), JavaScript, and CSS—at a minimum. More complex AJAX communicates with a server to send and receive information and update the browser display as the user works within the interface. In short, AJAX is daunting to learn and use from scratch!

The good news is that there are *many* different AJAX frameworks you can use to add effects to your pages without writing any code. In this hour, we look at Adobe's AJAX framework, Spry, and later we explore some other AJAX options, including an AJAX JavaScript library that creates a popular "lightbox" effect. You'll discover that you can do some amazing things with just a few clicks in the Dreamweaver CS4 interface.

Using the Spry Framework

Dreamweaver CS4 includes the Spry AJAX framework. All you need to do to access it is to insert one of the Spry widgets available in both the Spry category of the Insert panel and the Spry submenu of the Insert menu, shown in Figure 19.1. When you insert a widget, Dreamweaver either inserts the appropriate code into your web page or opens a dialog box if there are settings required for the widget.

Spry can be added to new or existing web pages. After you insert a Spry widget into your web page, you are prompted to save supporting files when you save that page. These supporting files are external JavaScript files that end in the .js file extension. Some Spry widgets also insert external CSS files that end in the .css file extension. These files are necessary for the Spry widgets to work and must remain in your website. The Spry framework enables you to accomplish the following five types of tasks:

▶ **Visual effects**—Several visual effects are available through the Behaviors panel. Users trigger these effects by interacting with an object on the web page (such as clicking a button or a link).

▶ **XML and HTML presentation**—These widgets enable you to present data extracted from an external XML (Extensible Markup Language) data file or HTML table in a web page.

▶ **Form validation**—These widgets are special form objects that can validate whether appropriate information has been selected or entered (covered in Hour 21, "Sending and Reacting to Form Data").

▶ **Navigation**—The menu bar widget creates a CSS-based menu bar that enables a visitor to navigate to sections of the website (covered in Hour 16).

▶ **Content presentation**—The Tabbed Panels, Collapsible Panel, and Accordion widgets enable you to present content in a condensed way. The ToolTip widget makes it easy to attach small pieces of helpful content to other objects.

An example of what you can do with the Spry framework is shown in Figure 19.2. This application was created by the Adobe Labs (check it out for yourself at http://labs.adobe.com/technologies/spry/demos/gallery/). It's a photo gallery displaying photos based on XML data. The small thumbnails on the left grow when you roll your mouse over them. Effects available in the Behaviors panel make this possible. When you click a link, the larger image appears on the right side of the page.

When you add a new image to the photo gallery, you don't open the page in Dreamweaver, add another thumbnail, and link it to a larger image. Instead, you add another record to the XML file listing links to all the thumbnail images and the larger version of that image. The Spry widget reads this

NOTE

Spry Is Client-Side

The beauty of the Spry framework, and the reason this book covers it, is that these advanced functionalities are client-side instead of server-side. Previously, web pages could accomplish complex form validation, navigation, and XML presentation only by interacting with the server using a server-side scripting language such as PHP.

FIGURE 19.2
A sample application of the Spry framework is found in this photo-gallery example from Adobe Labs.

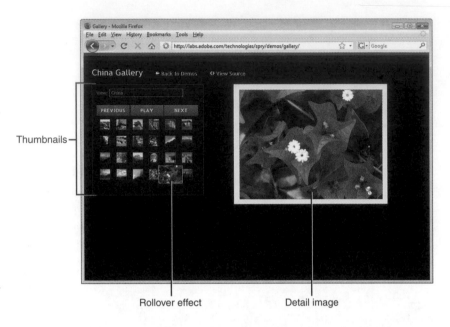

CAUTION

Spry Browser Requirements

Visitors have to be using one of the following browsers for Spry to work: Firefox, IE 6 and higher, Safari 2 and higher, or Opera 9 and higher.

TIP

No File Prompt?

If you aren't prompted to save the supporting files when you insert a Spry widget, it's because they are already present. Dreamweaver prompts you only the first time you insert the widget. Dreamweaver detects when the files already exist in your file structure and links to those existing files.

updated XML file, including the data about the new image, and presents all the thumbnails listed in the XML file.

External JavaScript and CSS Files

A library of JavaScript files is what makes the Spry framework widgets and effects work. Dreamweaver knows which external JavaScript files it must copy into your website; the files required depends on the widget or effect you are using. When you save the web page, Dreamweaver prompts you to copy dependent files, as shown in Figure 19.3.

FIGURE 19.3
Dreamweaver prompts you to copy dependent files, the scripts and images that are necessary for the Spry widget to work.

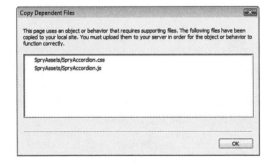

When you click the OK button, agreeing to copy dependent files, Dreamweaver creates a directory called SpryAssets in the root of your site.

It then copies the external JavaScript and CSS files into that directory. The Files panel, shown in Figure 19.4, displays these external files when you expand the view of the directory.

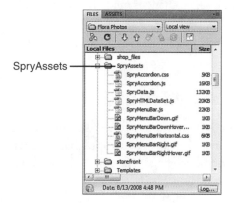

SpryAssets

FIGURE 19.4
Dreamweaver creates the
SpryAssets directory to hold the
external JavaScript and CSS files
necessary to use the Spry framework.

TIP

Refresh the Files Panel

If you just added a Spry widget
and do not see the SpryAssets
directory in the Files panel, click
the Refresh button to get
Dreamweaver to refresh the
view.

Dreamweaver also adds a link to the necessary external files in the head of the web page, as shown in Figure 19.5. The example in the figure shows a link to a single external JavaScript file using the script tag. There is also a link to a single external CSS file using the link tag. Some Spry widgets might require links to multiple files. Some of the Spry widgets might also insert JavaScript functions in the head of your web page.

External CSS file

External JavaScript file

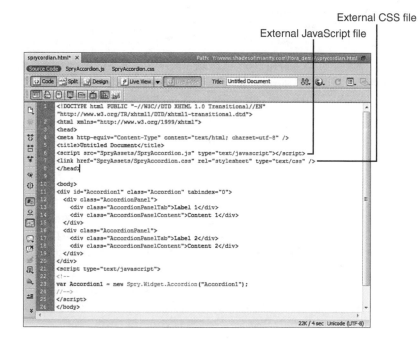

FIGURE 19.5
Dreamweaver creates links to the
necessary external files in the head
of the web page.

You really shouldn't modify the external JavaScript files. But you might want to modify the colors, fonts, and other properties contained in the external CSS files. Remember that because these files are linked to every instance of that Spry widget, changes made to the external CSS file apply to all instances. Because it's usually a good idea to have common colors and fonts for a website's user interface, this probably won't be a problem.

Adding Spry Effects

Let's start out with the Spry framework effects, the most fun items in my opinion. These behaviors enable you to apply visual effects to containers you've created on your web page. The containers are created using div tags or AP divs (covered in Hour 17, "Using Dynamic HTML and AP Divs"). The one catch is that all containers must have an ID in order to be used with Spry effects.

TIP

Other Effect Objects

You can apply Spry effects to a web page's other objects, such as buttons, form elements, and paragraphs. The examples in this hour involve divs because they are the most common container and applying the effects has a predictable result.

Here's a brief description of each of the Spry effects:

▶ **Appear/Fade**—This effect makes a container appear or fade. You can toggle this effect so that it goes back and forth between appearing and fading with successive triggering.

▶ **Blind Up/Down**—This effect collapses the container like pulling up a window blind and expands the container like pulling a window blind down. You can toggle this effect.

▶ **Grow/Shrink**—This effect shrinks a container, either to the center or from the upper-left corner, or grows the container if it has already been shrunk. You can toggle this effect.

▶ **Highlight**—This effect highlights the container with a fade-in of color. You can reverse the color fade by selecting the Toggle check box.

▶ **Shake**—This effect shakes the container from left to right five or six times.

▶ **Slide Up/Down**—This effect slides the container up, hiding the content, or back down, displaying the content. You can toggle this effect. Slide Up/Down differs from Blind Up/Down in that the container doesn't collapse but slides instead.

▶ **Squish**—This effect shrinks a container from the lower-right corner. It is similar to the Grow/Shrink effect but shrinks from the lower-right corner instead of the upper-left corner as with the Grow/Shrink effect.

Applying the Squish Effect

Let's begin by creating the supporting objects.

Follow these steps to create both an image that has the Spry effect applied to it and the link that triggers the effect:

1. Create a new web page (File, New) and save it (File, Save).

2. Insert an image into the web page (Insert, Image).

3. Wrap a div tag around the image by selecting the image and then selecting Insert, Layout Objects, Div Tag. The Insert Div Tag dialog box opens. Because you selected an object, Dreamweaver automatically sets Insert to Wrap Around Selection so that the div tag is wrapped around the image tag.

4. In the ID field, enter an ID for the div. A name such as `spryExample`, as shown in Figure 19.6, would be good.

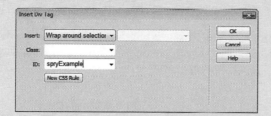

5. Click OK to add the div tag.

6. Type the text **Trigger the Effect** below the image.

7. Select the text and make it a null link by entering **javascript:;** in the Link box in the Property inspector. Press Enter to save the null link.

FIGURE 19.6
Wrap a div around an image and give it an ID before applying a Spry effect to the image.

Now you have the two elements necessary to apply a Spry effect: a container (the div with the image in it) and a link to trigger the effect.

Apply the Spry effect with these steps:

1. Select the link.

2. Open the Behaviors panel (Window, Behaviors). Confirm that the <a> tag shows in the top of the panel.

3. Click the Add Behavior button and select the Squish behavior from the Effects submenu.

4. Select the div you created earlier in the Target Element drop-down menu.

▼ TRY IT YOURSELF

Applying a Spry Effect to an Object

continued

5. Click OK.

6. Make sure that the onClick event is selected.

7. Save the web page (File, Save).

8. Click OK to agree to copy the dependent files, the SpryEffects.js file in this case. Dreamweaver won't prompt you for this step if the .js file already exists in the SpryAssets directory.

9. Preview the web page in Live View mode, or a web browser. Click the link and you should see the effect. Click the link again to reverse the effect.

Applying the Appear/Fade Effect

The Shake and Squish effects are very simple and have no properties to set. Next let's explore applying a slightly more complicated effect with properties for you to adjust. This example applies the Appear/Fade effect, but it works similarly to all the other effects. You should be able to apply the techniques used here to all the other effects available in the Behaviors panel.

You use the same elements you used in the previous example when you applied the Squish effect. Either re-create the earlier setup again or remove the effects from your existing file.

▼ TRY IT YOURSELF

Removing an Effect Behavior

To remove an effect from an element, do the following:

1. Select the element (in this case, the link).

2. Select the Squish entry in the Behaviors panel and click the Remove Event button (–).

Now you're ready to apply the Appear/Fade effect. Let's add the effect using the same link and div you created earlier.

▼ TRY IT YOURSELF

Adding the Appear/Fade Effect

To apply the Appear/Fade effect, follow these steps:

1. Select the link element in your document.

2. Click the Add Behavior button and select the Appear/Fade behavior from the Effects submenu.

3. Select the div you created earlier in the Target Element drop-down menu, as shown in Figure 19.7.

4. Set the effect properties: Effect Duration, Effect, Fade From, and Fade To. You can simply leave the defaults if you'd like.

5. Select the Toggle Effect check box.

Target element

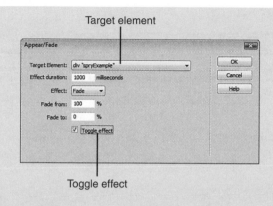

Toggle effect

FIGURE 19.7
Select a container in the
Appear/Fade dialog box. You can
also toggle the effect.

6. Click OK.

7. Save the web page (File, Save). Dreamweaver does not prompt you to
copy dependent files if you've already done so for a previous effect.

8. Preview the web page in the Live View or a web browser. Click the link
and you should see the effect. Click the link again to reverse the effect.

The other effects work similarly. The one slightly different effect is the
Highlight effect, which applies a colored highlight to the container instead
of making it appear and disappear.

Using Tabbed Panels, Collapsible Panels, Accordions, and ToolTips

The content-presentation Spry widgets enable you to creatively display
content on the page. These Spry widgets depend on the Spry framework
and, like the Spry effects, must copy dependent .js and .css files into the
SpryAssets directory to work.

Adding a Tabbed Panel

First we insert a tabbed panel using the Spry Tabbed Panels widget. This
widget inserts a set of divs that are styled with CSS. Each div can have
unique content and the user can switch between pieces of content by clicking tabs at the top of the widget. Figure 19.8 shows an example of a completed tabbed panel.

FIGURE 19.8
A tabbed panel displays tabs at the top. Clicking a tab presents you with the information contained on that individual tab.

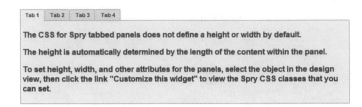

▼ TRY IT YOURSELF

Creating a Tabbed Panel

Follow these steps to add a tabbed panel:

1. Create a new web page (File, New) and save it (File, Save).

2. Select Insert, Spry, Spry Tabbed Panels.

3. Dreamweaver inserts a set of tabbed panels into the web page. Save the page (File, Save).

4. Click OK to copy dependent files (if prompted).

5. Click the blue tab above the tabbed panels to select the entire element. You should see the tabbed panels' properties in the Property inspector, as shown in Figure 19.9.

FIGURE 19.9
Select the tabbed panels to see their properties in the Property inspector.

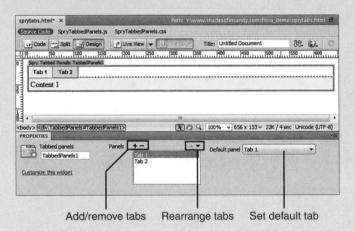

Add/remove tabs   Rearrange tabs   Set default tab

6. Add or remove tabs, rearrange the order, and set the default panel in the Property inspector.

7. Roll your cursor over the tabs in the Document window. Click the Eye button that appears to select the tab, shown in Figure 19.10, and change the tab's content. Rename each tab and add content to each.

8. Save the file (File, Save) and preview the web page in Live View mode or a web browser. Experiment by clicking each of the tabs and examining its content.

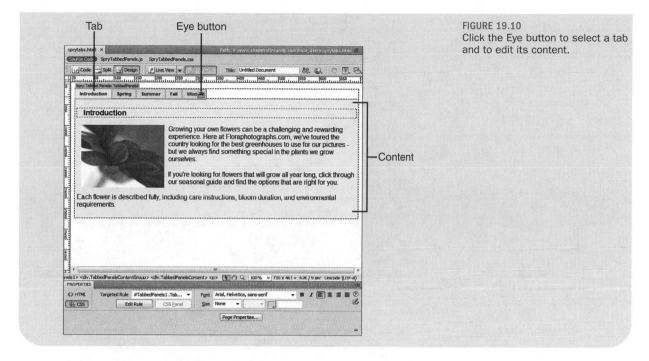

Tab   Eye button

FIGURE 19.10
Click the Eye button to select a tab and to edit its content.

Adding a Collapsible Panel

You create both the accordion and collapsible panel widgets in exactly the same way. The collapsible panel is just a single pane of content, unlike the accordion and tabbed panel widgets. After you've inserted this widget, you can modify in the Property inspector (shown in Figure 19.11) whether the content displays. You can also choose whether you want the panel to animate opening and closing by checking or unchecking the Enable Animation check box.

Adding an Accordion

No, we aren't talking about polka music in this section! **Accordions** are a set of collapsible panels that can store a large amount of content in a very small space. Web page visitors can delve into information by clicking the accordion panel tabs, which hides or reveals the information they'd like to see.

Again, you insert an accordion just as you did the tabbed panels earlier. Figure 19.12 shows an accordion with three panel tabs. The content in the top panel initially shows when you preview the web page in the browser. Simply clicking the panel tabs animates the opening of that panel's content.

FIGURE 19.11
Add content to a collapsible panel widget and set the widget's properties in the Property inspector.

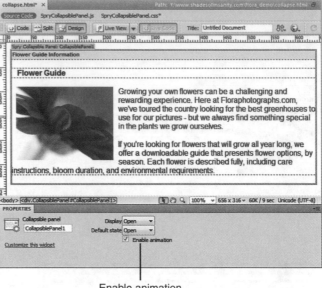

Enable animation

FIGURE 19.12
Add an accordion widget to insert a large amount of content in a very small space.

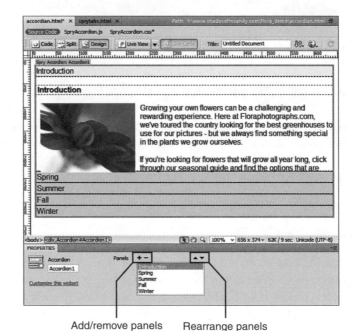

Add/remove panels   Rearrange panels

TIP

Fix Disappearing ToolTips

Sometimes it is useful for a ToolTip to contain links to information that a user can click on. Unfortunately, the ToolTip disappears as soon as the user moves the cursor out of the triggering element, so the user can't reach the link! To fix this problem, click the confusingly named Hide on Mouse Out check box in the ToolTip properties. This sets the ToolTip to hide only when the mouse leaves *it*, rather than as soon as it leaves the triggering element.

Adding ToolTips

ToolTips are short pieces of content that can be displayed when a user's mouse is over an object (such as a link or a div) within a web page. They typically display useful information to help the user understand the context of what they're looking at. Most applications, including Dreamweaver, use ToolTips to help describe the functions of toolbar icons. Spry ToolTips can contain any HTML content you want, including links, images, and, of course, text.

Let's try adding a ToolTip to an object on a web page:

1. First, create a new page (File, New) and add an object to it, such as a link or a div. Save the page (File, Save).

2. Next, select the object tag that you want to use to trigger the ToolTip.

3. Select Insert, Spry, Spry ToolTip from the menu bar.

4. Dreamweaver inserts a ToolTip content area into your document. Save the page (File, Save).

5. Click OK to copy dependent files (If prompted).

6. Click inside the ToolTip area and add content to the ToolTip. Use text, images, links—anything you'd like.

7. Click the blue tab above the ToolTip content to select the entire element. You should see the ToolTip properties in the Property inspector, as shown in Figure 19.13.

8. Use the properties to configure an effect for when the ToolTip appears and disappears (fade/blind). You can also choose whether there is a delay before it appears and disappears, if there is an offset (horizontal or vertical) from the user's cursor, and whether the ToolTip should follow the cursor.

9. Save the file (File, Save) and preview the web page in the Live View mode or a web browser. Experiment with the different property settings to get the ToolTip effect you want.

TRY IT YOURSELF ▼

Adding a ToolTip to a Page Element

CAUTION

Visitors Can't Easily Print Spry Content

Note that visitors to your web page will not be able to easily print the information available in the Spry content widgets. You must either provide CSS specifically for printing (see Hour 14, "Creating CSS for Mobile Devices and Printing") or present any information the visitor might want to print in a different way.

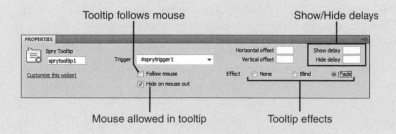

Tooltip follows mouse   Show/Hide delays

Mouse allowed in tooltip   Tooltip effects

FIGURE 19.13
ToolTip effects can be customized in the property inspector.

Editing the Spry Panel CSS

The background colors, fonts, and widths of Spry content-presentation elements are all controlled by CSS. When you open the CSS Styles panel in a web page with one of these elements inserted, you see a listing of styles under the name of the external CSS style sheet that Dreamweaver attached (see Figure 19.14). You edit these styles to change the way the Spry elements appear.

FIGURE 19.14
The CSS Styles panel lists the styles in the external CSS style sheet that affects the Spry elements.

External CSS file

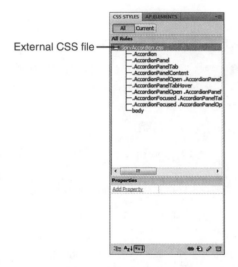

It's not hard to find the CSS styles, but it can be very confusing as to which styles are the correct ones to change. Luckily, Adobe has made that easy by adding a Customize This Widget link in the Property inspector when you select a widget. (You first explored editing the Spry CSS in Hour 16.)

Clicking Customize This Widget takes you to the Adobe Help website. The help topic displays several tables listing the appropriate style name of the property you'd like to change. For instance, in Figure 19.15, you see a table listing the styles to change if you'd like to change the way the text appears in an accordion widget. If you'd like to change the font for the entire accordion, simply edit the .Accordion style. However, if you'd like to change only the font of the text in the accordion tabs, you would modify .AccordionPanelTab.

By default, the Spry elements do not have a specified width, so they stretch the width of the web page or the container they are in. Adobe Help also lets you know which styles to edit to constrain the Spry element to a particular width. For instance, in an accordion panel, you would modify the width property in the .Accordion style.

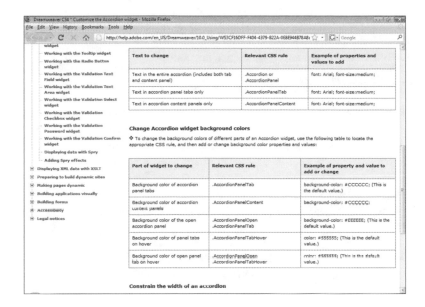

FIGURE 19.15
Adobe Help offers information on
the CSS styles to change to modify
the look of Spry elements.

Displaying XML and HTML Data in a Web Page

The final use of the Spry framework that you explore this hour is the presentation of information from an external XML file and a live HTML table in a web page. Before we start using the Spry Data Source widget, you get some background on XML. Lucky you!

What Is XML?

XML is a meta-language, that is, a language for creating other languages. XHTML, for instance, is an example of XML created for web markup. Another example is SMIL (Synchronized Multimedia Integration Language), which you can use to mark up content to trigger multimedia: text, audio, and video content.

The cool thing about XML, however, is that you can create your *own* language, a language describing the data that is important to you. For instance, if you make daily changes to a web page on your company intranet listing the menu items in the company cafeteria, you could store the menu items in XML instead. You simply save a new version of the XML file, and the web page that you embedded it in, using the Spry framework, automatically begins displaying the new menu items.

CAUTION
Carefully Create XML

When creating XML, be very careful that you type it consistently. XML is very particular that elements are correctly formed. It is also case-sensitive, so the element `<item>` is not the same as the element `<Item>`. You can validate your XML by selecting File, Validate, As XML.

NOTE
XML Usually Created by an Application

We are creating an XML file by hand in this example, but that's not actually what happens in the real world. In most cases, XML files are produced by other applications such as the MS Office applications (Word, Excel, and InfoPath), page layout applications (FrameMaker and InDesign), or database applications.

XML has two basic pieces: elements and attributes. **Elements** are the equivalent of tags in HTML and **attributes** are the same as in HTML. Elements have opening and closing tags. Here's an example:

```
<menu day="Monday"></menu>
```

The preceding example shows a menu element with the day attribute that equals "Monday". You can nest elements within other elements. So if you add items to Monday's menu, the XML might look like this:

```
<menu day="Monday">
    <item name="Lobster" />
    <item name="Corn" />
    <item name="Fondue" />
</menu>
```

Now there are three item elements nested within the menu element. This is a very simple introduction to XML and there are many other ways to use XML.

Create a new XML file so that you can use it in the examples in a few minutes.

▼ TRY IT YOURSELF

Create an XML File

The following is how to create an XML file in Dreamweaver:

1. Create a new file (File, New), selecting XML in the Page Type category.

2. Save the file (File, Save) as `menu.xml`.

3. Add XML to the file, following the menu example earlier. The finished file should look something like that shown in Figure 19.16.

FIGURE 19.16
Create an XML file with repeating elements and data.

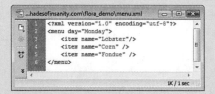

4. Save the XML file in a directory where you also save the pages linking to the information in the XML.

Displaying XML Using the Spry Data Source

To display XML on a web page, you first have to create an XML data set. This enables Dreamweaver to analyze and display the elements and attributes available in a certain XML file so that you can use the Spry elements to display it on the web page.

To create a data set, do the following:

1. Open or create a new web page where you insert the data from the XML file.

2. Select Insert, Spry, Spry Data Set. The Spry Data Set dialog box opens.

3. Make sure that the Data Type is set to XML, and then click the Browse button and load the XML file you created.

4. Select @name from the Row Element list, as shown in Figure 19.17.

Item attribute   Item   XML source

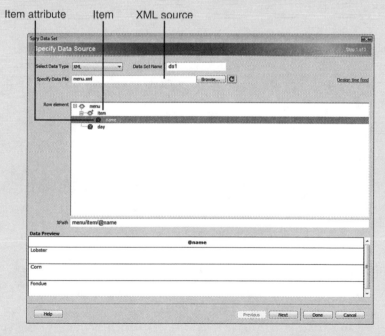

5. Click Done. Dreamweaver opens the Bindings panel (Window, Bindings), as shown in Figure 19.18, displaying the data available from the XML.

6. Save the web page (File, Save) and click OK to copy the dependent files, if prompted.

TRY IT YOURSELF ▼

Creating a Spry Data Set

FIGURE 19.17
The screen refreshes to display the structure of the XML data. Select **@name** from the Row Element list.

FIGURE 19.18
The Bindings panel displays the XML data elements.

Inserting a Spry Repeat List

The last step in displaying XML data in your page is to insert a Spry Repeat List to display the menu items held in the data set you created. The Spry Repeat List creates either an ordered (numbered), unordered (bulleted), or definition list with the data from the selected data set.

▼ TRY IT YOURSELF

Inserting a Spry Repeat List

The following steps show how to insert a Spry Repeat List:

1. Place the insertion point in the web page where you'd like the Spry Repeat List to appear.

2. Select Insert, Spry, Spry Repeat List. The Insert Spry Repeat List dialog box appears.

3. Select UL (Unordered List) as the Container tag and make sure that your data set and Display column are correct—it should be set to @name if you're using the sample XML created earlier this hour in the "What Is XML?" section. See Figure 19.19.

FIGURE 19.19
Select the type of list, the data-set name, and the data to display in the Insert Spry Repeat List dialog box.

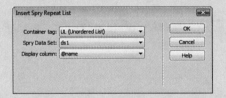

4. Dreamweaver prompts you to also add a Spry region. Click OK to agree with this.

5. Save changes to the web page and agree to copy any dependent files for the Spry framework. Preview the page in the Live View mode or a browser to see the information pulled from XML appear.

Reusing HTML Data with the Spry Data Set

XML is a great data format. It is cross-platform, nonproprietary, and easy to understand. Unfortunately, chances are, your fellow web developers are posting most data in HTML tables or lists. Amazingly enough, you can use this to pull existing data from a site and reuse it in your own! The only limitation is that the element you're reading information from must have an ID attribute.

Let's go ahead and try this on some live data. You can use this example without upsetting the website owner (me), so feel free to try this out as much as you want. We are using a table that displays the 25 newest flower photos posted to the Flora Photographs website. The page that contains this information is http://www.floraphotographs.com/25newest.php.

To collect and display HTML data using the Spry Data Set, follow these steps:

1. Open or create a new web page where you will insert the data from the HTML data source.

2. Select Insert, Spry, Spry Data Set. The Spry Data Set dialog box opens.

3. Make sure that the Data Type is set to HTML, and then enter the Data File of **http://www.floraphotographs.com/25newest.php**.

4. After a few seconds the web table appears; click in the upper-left corner of the table to select its data, as shown in Figure 19.20.

Element selector

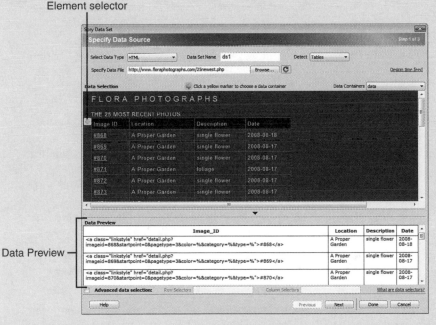

FIGURE 19.20
Choose an element from the page to capture data from.

Data Preview ─

5. The bottom of the screen refreshes to show the data that is being made available to you.

▼ TRY IT YOURSELF

**Creating and
Displaying an
HTML Spry Data Set**

continued

6. Click Next. Dreamweaver shows the data options for the HTML table you've chosen, as shown in Figure 19.21. Here you can choose what type of data is in a column.

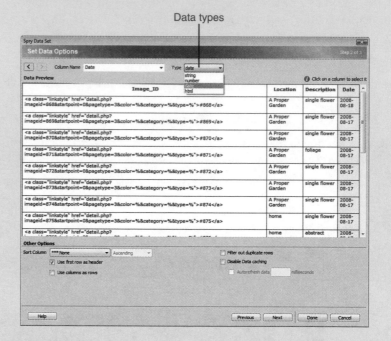

Data types

FIGURE 19.21
Choose what type of data is in each column

7. For example, the Image_ID column is obviously HTML, so use the Column Name pop-up menu to choose Image_ID and then select HTML in the Type pop-up menu.

8. Set the Date field to a Date data type.

9. Click Next. Dreamweaver now prompts for how you'd like the data to be inserted in your page, as shown in Figure 19.22.

10. For fun, choose Insert Table. This creates a table whose headings are clickable so that the content can be sorted. You can feel free to try the other options as well.

11. Click Set Up to choose which columns are displayed, the order in which they are be shown, and which ones are sortable, as shown in Figure 19.23. A description, for example, isn't very useful to sort on. Click OK to save your settings.

12. Finally, click Done. Dreamweaver inserts the necessary code into your page to generate the sortable table, as shown in Figure 19.24.

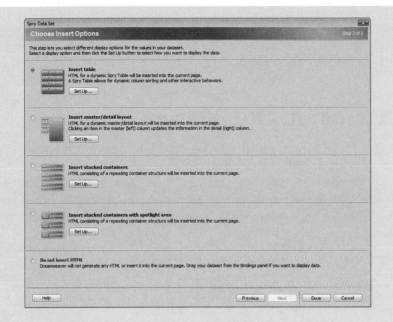

FIGURE 19.22
Dreamweaver gives you several ways to add the content to your page.

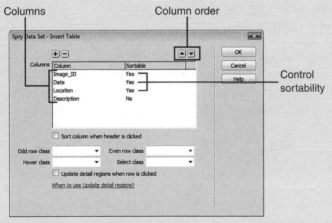

FIGURE 19.23
Choose which columns are displayed, their order, and whether they should be sortable.

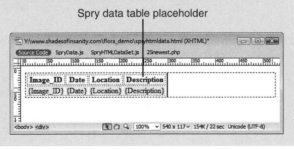

FIGURE 19.24
Dreamweaver inserts a placeholder for your new table with external data.

You can now preview this table in a browser or in the Live View mode. The end result is a new view of the data with clickable table headers for sorting, a content ordering that you specified, and styles that can be defined using the Dreamweaver tools to look like anything you want!

External AJAX Libraries

As I sat down to work through this hour, one of the things that I wanted to make sure was covered was the existence of other AJAX libraries and effects. There is a world beyond Spry that includes amazing tools and components that can be used in web pages. Some of these are complex, but as you grow more familiar with web development, you'll want them in your toolkit.

To get started, I'd recommend looking at the following:

> jQuery: http://jquery.com/
>
> MooTools: http://mootools.net/
>
> Script.aculo.us: http://script.aculo.us/
>
> Ext.js: http://extjs.com/

Each of these tools provides advanced JavaScript functionality for websites. AJAX development is happening quickly, so new options are popping up all the time. To conclude this hour, let's take a quick look at how to embed a popular AJAX effect called a "lightbox" into your existing pages.

Using Lightview

If you've used the Web in the past year or two, you've almost certainly seen a lightbox. This is the effect where you click a link, the background dims on your website, and new content appears in an overlay, as shown in Figure 19.25.

My favorite lightbox implementation is Lightview, by Nick Stakenburg, found at http://www.nickstakenburg.com/projects/lightview/.

Lightbox effect

FIGURE 19.25
Lightboxes are an attractive and effective means of providing additional content within a limited amount of space.

Installing Lightview

To install and use this tool, you need to download three JavaScript libraries:

> Prototype: http://prototypejs.org/download
>
> Script.aculo.us: http://script.aculo.us/downloads
>
> Lightview: http://www.nickstakenburg.com/projects/download/ ?project=lightview

Each of these downloads should unzip into several JavaScript files, an images directory, and a CSS file. The JavaScript should be placed in a common JavaScript directory, such as js within your site, and the CSS file, lightview.css (located in the css folder), should be placed within your site's css directory. Finally, the folder lightview in the images folder should be placed in the images directory within your site.

Next, you need to include three JavaScript files within the head content of a page that you want to use the lightbox effect. Assuming that the

NOTE

Pay for Your Code!

Lightview, although free to download, has a cost of about $4 for personal use. Please pay for the software if you use it! It's well worth the cost.

lightview.js JavaScript is in the js directory in your site, add these lines between the <head></head> tags of a page:

```
<script type='text/javascript' src='js/prototype.js'></script>
<script type='text/javascript'
src='js/scriptaculous.js?load=effects'></script>
<script type='text/javascript' src='js/lightview.js'></script>
```

Finally, you want to link the Lightview.css file into your site. Using the CSS Styles panel, click the Attach Style Sheet button, locate the Lightview.css file, and link it to your page.

Lightview is now installed and ready to use.

Adding a Lightview link

There are many ways that Lightview can be used to link to content—more than we can describe here. After you play with the library a bit, I urge you to read the full documentation on the Lightview website.

The most popular use for a lightbox is displaying an image over your page content.

▼ TRY IT YOURSELF

Linking an Image in a Lightbox

Let's look at how this can be accomplished with Lightview:

1. First, create the link to an image file, just as you would normally. Create some link text, select it, and then set the Link attribute to your image file, such as myimage.jpg.

2. Next, with the link selected, use the Class (or Targeted Rule) drop-down menu in the Property inspector to select Lightview.

3. That's it! You're done. The effect is best seen in a real browser, so save your page (File, Save) and then preview it in your web browser.

Lightview can be used to present image content, flash content, and even entire websites in a lightbox view—all by changing attributes to your <a> tags. You can check out all the different link styles and display customizations at http://www.nickstakenburg.com/projects/lightview/.

Summary

In this hour, you learned about AJAX and how to use the Spry AJAX framework to add Spry effects and Spry content containers such as tabbed panels, and to repurpose XML and HTML content. Finally, you also explored other external AJAX libraries and how to include the popular "lightbox" effect within your web pages.

Q&A

Q. I'm creating web pages for a government site and I want to use the Spry effects. Is that OK?

A. Considering that the Spry effects require modern browsers and a government site has to support all browsers, old and new, you probably should not use these effects. Have fun with them on your personal website instead.

Q. How can I reuse a tabbed panel (or another Spry element) on multiple web pages?

A. You can simply copy and paste the tabbed panel and paste it on the other page. Dreamweaver automatically inserts links to the supporting .js and .css files. Make sure that you have the entire element selected by looking at the tag selected in the tag selector.

Q. How can I use Spry data sets in a more complex way on my page?

A. You have to do some hand-coding to do more complex Spry elements on your web pages.

Workshop

Quiz

1. Are links to external JavaScript files contained in the body or the head of a web page?

2. How can you change the default colors and fonts of Spry elements such as tabbed or collapsible panels?

3. Name an example of a markup language that is a type of XML.

4. Spry is the only AJAX framework/library you can use in Dreamweaver. True or false?

Quiz Answers

1. Links to external JavaScript files are contained in the head of the web page.

2. To change the default colors and fonts of Spry elements, you modify the CSS that is applied to an element.

3. You've learned a lot about XHTML in this book and it is a type of XML.

4. False. Although Dreamweaver integrates Spry (because it's an Adobe product!), there are many, many other third-party libraries (such as MooTools, Ext.js, and jQuery) you can take advantage of.

Exercises

1. Try all the Spry effects available in the Behaviors panel by simply replacing the previous effect (deleting it) and applying a new effect to the same objects on the web page.

2. Download and install Lightview in a website. Create links that use the Lightview class. Remember to pay the author if you like the results!

Creating a Form and Collecting Data

In this hour, you create a form to collect user input. Dreamweaver gives you easy access to various form elements, including text boxes, radio buttons, check boxes, lists, drop-down menus, and buttons to capture user choices. We cover how to submit form data in Hour 21, "Sending and Reacting to Form Data."

With forms, you can collect information, such as comments or orders, and interact with your users. In your form, you can ask for your user's name and email address, have the user sign a guest book, or have the user purchase a product from your website. You can send this information back to the web server if you'd like. Dreamweaver enables you to validate information so that you know it's in the correct format for a script that accepts the form data.

Creating a Form

A **form** is a container for other objects, as well as an invisible element. When you add a form to a web page, Dreamweaver represents it as a red box if you have Form Delimiter checked in the Invisible Elements category of the Preferences dialog box (Edit, Preferences), as shown in Figure 20.1. Make sure you have this option selected so that you can see the outline of each form.

While you're creating a form, it is helpful to have the Forms category selected in the Insert panel, as shown in Figure 20.2. The first step in creating a form is to insert a Form object into your web page to hold all the form objects that collect user input.

FIGURE 20.1
The Invisible Elements category in
the Preferences dialog box enables
you to turn on and off the red box
that represents the form outline.

Form delimiter invisible element

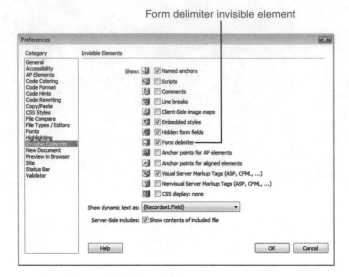

FIGURE 20.2
The Forms category in the Insert
panel presents all the form objects
you insert into your web page to
collect user input.

To add a form, follow these steps:

1. Create a new web page and place the insertion point where you want to insert the form.

2. Select Insert, Form, Form or select the Form object in the Forms category of the Insert panel.

3. A message box might appear, as shown in Figure 20.3, telling you that you will not be able to see the form unless you view the invisible elements. Click OK and then, if necessary, select View, Visual Aids, Invisible Elements.

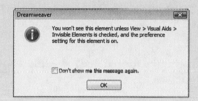

FIGURE 20.3
A message box might appear, telling you to view invisible elements to see the form you inserted into your web page.

4. A red box appears on the page, as shown in Figure 20.4. It represents the form.

Form delimiter

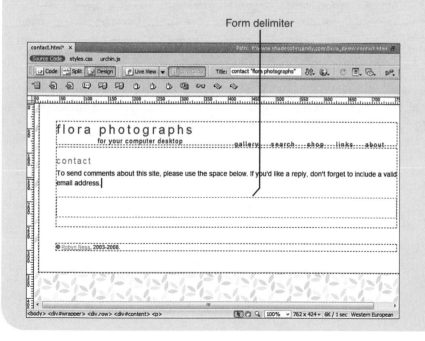

FIGURE 20.4
A form appears as a red box (a form delimiter) when invisible elements are turned on.

You can format the area within a form using tables, horizontal rules, text, and other items that would normally be in a web page. The only items that the form submits, however, are the names of the form elements and the data the user enters into the form. The form does not submit the text and formatting objects you place within it.

To select a form, click the edge of the form delimiter or place the cursor within the form and select the <form> tag in the tag selector. The Property inspector shows the properties you can enter for a form:

> ▶ **Form ID**—This property is necessary if you plan to apply any behaviors (or your own custom scripts) to a form. It's always a good idea to name your forms. Dreamweaver puts a default form ID in for you.

> ▶ **Action**—This property defines the URL of an application where the web page should send the form data. You explore more about the form action in Hour 21.

> ▶ **Method**—This property tells the application on the server how the data should be processed. Again, you explore this in Hour 21.

> ▶ **Enctype**—This property specifies the MIME (Multipurpose Internet Mail Extensions) encoding type for the form data. If you don't set a value here, the default value is application/x-www-form-urlencoded.

> ▶ **Class**—This property enables you to choose a CSS style that is applied to the form object.

Give your form an ID, as shown in Figure 20.5. Because you explore the Action, Method, and Enctype properties in the next hour, you can just leave them blank for now. Place your cursor inside the form to insert objects into it.

FIGURE 20.5
The Property inspector shows the attributes available to be set for a form.

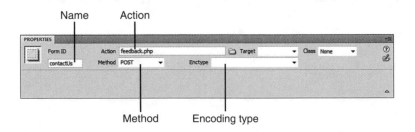

Adding Text Fields to Forms

As shown in Figure 20.6, forms commonly include text fields. Single-line text fields enable users to type in a name, a street address, a phone number, or other short pieces of text information. Text fields can also have multiple lines, called a **textarea**, suitable for comments or lengthy pieces of information.

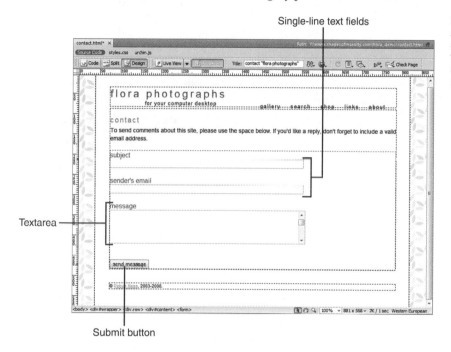

FIGURE 20.6
A group of text fields, a textarea, and a submit button collect user information on an order form that is submitted to the server and then processed.

Text fields are added using the Text Field object from the Forms category of the Insert panel. When you add a text field to a page, Dreamweaver prompts for accessibility information, as shown in Figure 20.7.

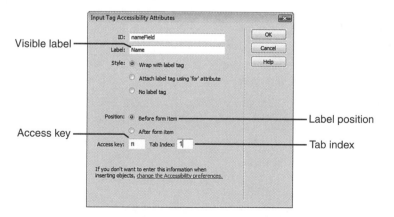

FIGURE 20.7
Make your forms accessible by completing the accessibility attributes.

TIP

Dreamweaver Asks to Insert a Form When You've Already Inserted One

If you get a dialog box asking you to insert a <form> tag but you thought you had already inserted one, you did not properly place the insertion point within the form. In that case, it's easiest to click No in the dialog box, delete the newly created object, reposition the cursor, and try again. If you are just beginning to create a form and forget to insert a Form object first, click Yes in the dialog box. Dreamweaver inserts a <form> tag around the form element you just created.

Provide the following information when you fill out the accessibility attributes:

▶ **ID**—A CSS ID that will be applied to the form element. This can be left blank if no CSS will be used.

▶ **Label**—A label that describes what the form element is for (a name, a street, and so on)

▶ **Style**—Defines how the label tag is applied. The default (Wrap with Label Tag) should be fine for most uses.

▶ **Position**—Choose whether the label will appear before or after the text field.

▶ **Access Key**—Choose a keyboard character that, when pressed with the Alt key (or Option on the Macintosh) will jump the cursor to the field.

▶ **Tab Index**—Choose a numeric value that represents the order in which the field will be selected if you press the tab key to move through the form.

If you're designing a form for the public, it is a wise idea to make it as accessible as possible. If you're creating the form for yourself or a limited audience, you can disable these accessibility features within the Accessibility category of the application preferences.

▼ TRY IT YOURSELF

Creating a Form

Now you continue creating your own form from scratch. Create a group of text fields designed to collect the user's first and last names, email address, and subject. Begin by inserting a single-line text field into your web page to collect the user's first name, and then follow these steps:

1. Click to add a new text field to the form. Enter a label of **Name:** in the accessibility attributes, leaving the rest blank.

2. Click OK. A text field with label appears in the form, as shown in Figure 20.8.

3. Add a new line (press the Enter or Return key), and click to add a new field. Label this one as **Email:**.

4. Add another new line (press the Enter or Return key) and another field, labeled **Subject:**. The form should appear as shown in Figure 20.9.

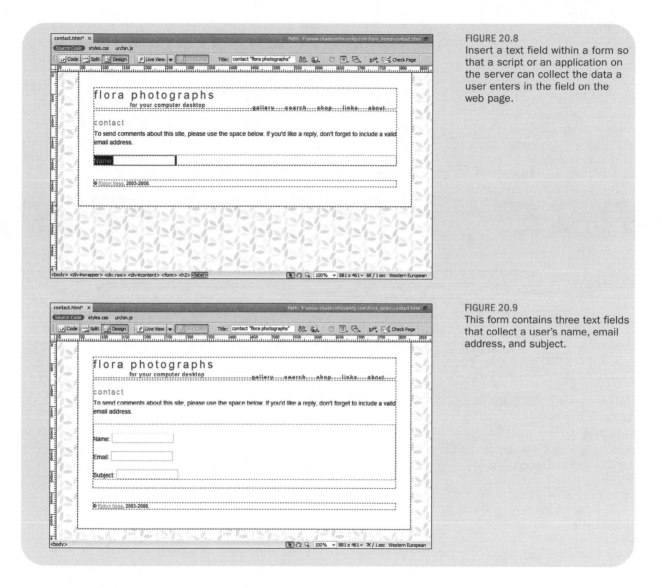

FIGURE 20.8
Insert a text field within a form so that a script or an application on the server can collect the data a user enters in the field on the web page.

FIGURE 20.9
This form contains three text fields that collect a user's name, email address, and subject.

Applying Text Field Attributes

When you have a text field selected, the Property inspector presents the text field attributes. Dreamweaver fills in a unique default name. Rename all the text fields in your form with meaningful and unique names, such as full-name, email, and subject. As when you're naming other Dreamweaver objects, it is a good idea not to use spaces and punctuation in the names of the

CAUTION

Don't Use *Name* as a Name

You have to name form objects carefully so that users don't receive JavaScript error messages. You should never name an object on the page with any HTML attribute name. So naming a text field *name* might be a logical choice, but it could cause JavaScript errors in some browsers because that is also the name of a tag attribute.

TIP

Using One of the Built-in Style Sheets

You can select File, New, Pages from Sample, and then select the CSS Style Sheets category to create one of the built-in style sheets that come with Dreamweaver. Select one of the Forms designs, such as Forms: Verdana, and click OK. Dreamweaver opens a style sheet file. Save this file with the .css extension and then attach the style sheet to the web page that contains the form. Using the Attach Style Sheet button at the bottom of the CSS Styles panel, select Link to link the style sheet you just created to the form you are creating. You should see the results immediately.

text fields. Some scripts and applications cannot deal with form element names that contain spaces and punctuation.

You can set both the size of the text field and the number of characters a user can enter into it. There are two width settings for a text field:

▶ **Char Width**—You use this setting to set the size of the text field and the number of characters visible in the field. If there are more characters in the text field than the width setting can accommodate, the form submits them but they won't be visible unless you scroll.

▶ **Max Chars**—You use this setting to limit the number of characters a user can enter into the text field. The user cannot enter more characters than the value of Max Chars. Setting Max Chars might be useful when you know the absolute length of the data the user should enter, such as a Social Security number, and do not want the user to enter additional characters.

You can set three types of text fields in the Property inspector:

▶ **Single Line**—These text fields are useful for collecting small, discrete words, names, or phrases from the user.

▶ **Multi Line**—This type of text field presents an area with multiple lines that enables the user to enter larger blocks of text. This is the same as the Textarea object, which is available in the Forms category of the Insert panel.

▶ **Password**—These text fields are special single-line fields that mask what the user types into the field, using asterisks or bullets to shield the data from other people. This doesn't, however, encrypt the submitted data.

You can select any styles in the Class drop-down list to apply a CSS (Cascading Style Sheets) style to the text field. You learned about CSS styles in Hour 6, "Formatting Web Pages Using Cascading Style Sheets." You can set the font, the background color, and other attributes of a text field by using CSS styles.

The first three fields in your form are single-line text fields. Create a new field on a new line with the label **Message:**, but this time use a Textarea object from the Insert panel (or Insert, Form, Textarea). This object is treated exactly like the TextField object in Dreamweaver, but it has the Multi Line property already applied, as seen in Figure 20.10.

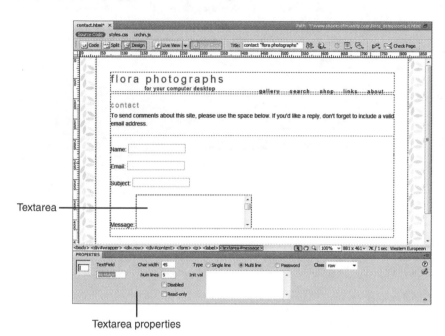

Textarea ——

Textarea properties

FIGURE 20.10
A textarea has a Num attribute, which you can set in the Property inspector. Num Lines sets the number of lines, or height, of the textarea.

NOTE

Change Char Width to Change the Size

You can't resize text fields by clicking and dragging their borders. You can change the size only by changing the Char Width property in the Property inspector.

TIP

Using the Autoclear Snippet

Dreamweaver includes some form elements, along with other items, in the Snippets panel (Window, Snippets). You drag snippets from the panel and drop them on your web pages. A useful snippet for your form might be Text Field Autoclear; this snippet places a text field containing default text into a form. When the user clicks the text field, the default text automatically disappears. You explore snippets further in Hour 24, "Customizing Dreamweaver."

The Textarea object includes a property that enables you to enter the height of the object (the number of lines in the textarea). Enter a value into the Num Lines property to set the height. There is no Max Chars setting for a textarea; you can control only the number of lines visible on the screen.

You can add some text that appears in the text field when the user views the form. This could be instructions on what to enter into the field or a default value that the users can change if they want to. Enter text into the Init Val box in the Property inspector, as shown in Figure 20.11, so that text is present when users initially load the form.

FIGURE 20.11
Enter text into the Init Val box in the Property inspector so that it appears when users initially load the form.

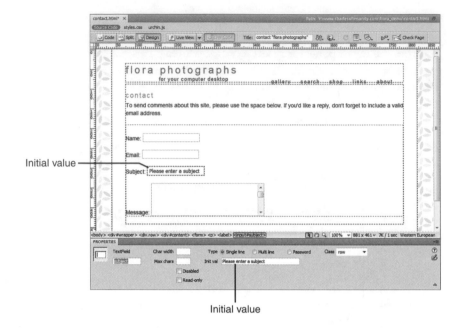

Initial value

Initial value

NOTE

Single Radio Buttons

Radio buttons can also be added one at a time from the Insert panel. Because radio buttons are of little use by themselves, chances are you'll want to use the Radio Button Group object rather than dealing with individual buttons. You still need this capability, however, to add new radio buttons to an existing radio group.

Keep in mind that if you do add new radio buttons one at a time, you need to name them to match other radio buttons that should be associated with them.

Adding Radio Buttons and Check Boxes to Forms

A radio button group is another type of form element you can use to collect user input. These elements allow a user to choose from one or more of a set of predefined values, rather than providing their own input like the text field and text areas.

Radio Button Groups

Radio buttons come in groups so that the user can select only one button of the group at a time (such as male or female); when the user selects a different member of the button group, the previously selected button is deselected. For radio buttons to compose a group, they all must have the same name.

To create a group of radio buttons, follow these steps:

1. Place the insertion point within a form where the radio buttons will be located. Type **How did you hear about us?** and press the Enter or Return key.

2. Select the Radio Group object from the Forms category of the Insert panel or select Insert, Form, Radio Group.

3. Enter the name of the radio button group in the Name box of the Radio Group dialog box.

4. Enter a label name in the Label column and enter the value of the radio button when it is checked (called the **checked value**) in the Value column, as shown in Figure 20.12. The label is simply the text that appears next to the button; it is not part of the form. Use the + and – buttons to add and remove radio buttons. At the bottom of the dialog box, select whether you want to place the buttons in a table or separate them with line breaks. Click OK to save your settings.

TRY IT YOURSELF ▼

Creating a Radio Button Group

FIGURE 20.12
Add a radio button group. Each button has a label and a value.

5. When you select an individual radio button, the Property inspector displays that button's properties. Choose whether the button will be checked or unchecked when the user first loads the form by selecting either the Checked option or the Unchecked option, next to Initial State.

Check Boxes

Check boxes collect user input when the user either checks or unchecks the box. They differ from radio buttons in that each check box acts independently. Radio buttons enable the user to select a single option, whereas check boxes enable the user to select any options that apply. Because check boxes are used to collect discrete pieces of information (like "check here to sign me up for the mailing list"), they are frequently added to forms individually.

Adding a Check Box to a Form

To add a check box to your form, follow these steps:

1. Place the insertion point within a form where the check box will be located.

2. Select the Check Box object from the Insert panel, or select Insert, Form, Check Box. Type **Receive Newsletter:** Into the Label accessibility attribute for the tag—leave the other accessibility fields alone.

3. Enter a name for the check box into the box in the far left of the Property inspector.

4. Enter a checked value into the Checked Value box. If you do not specify a checked value, the form sends the value On for the check box when the form submits its values. If there is an entry for the Checked Value setting, the form sends that value instead of On.

5. Choose whether the initial state of the check box is checked or unchecked in the Initial State setting.

6. Type a text label beside the check box. The settings should look as shown in Figure 20.13.

FIGURE 20.13
The check box settings are similar to the radio button settings.

Initial state

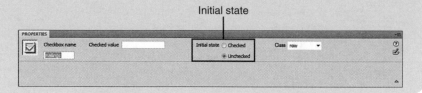

Check Box Groups

Starting in Dreamweaver CS4, you can now add groups of check boxes, just as you would add a group of radio buttons. This is useful for instances when you want a user to provide you with multiple different values for a single question, such as "What mailing lists do you want to subscribe to? Check all that apply."

Check box groups are added and configured just like radio button groups. Use the Checkbox object to add a new group to your document, as shown in Figure 20.14.

Use the + and – buttons to add or remove check boxes, editing their names and labels as needed. The up and down arrows can rearrange check boxes in the list. Finally, choose whether the boxes are laid out using simple line breaks (the most accessible means) or with a table. Click OK to add the check boxes to the page.

FIGURE 20.14
Check box groups can collect multiple values in a single response.

Adding Lists and Menus to Forms

Some form objects work better than others in certain situations (for example, selecting one of the 50 states for a United States address). If you allowed users to enter a state in a text field, some users might enter the full name, such as Washington; other users might enter the correct postal abbreviation, such as WA; and other users might enter something in between. Allowing the user to select from a drop-down menu helps you collect consistent data. In Dreamweaver, you add a drop-down menu by using the List/Menu object.

The List/Menu object inserts a list of values. You create the List/Menu object as either a list, displaying a set number of lines, or a menu, displaying all the list values. Figure 20.15 shows a list and a menu in a form displayed in a browser.

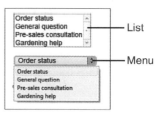

FIGURE 20.15
Lists display a certain number of values. A menu drops down when the user clicks it, allowing the user to select a value.

To create a list, follow these steps:

1. Place the insertion point within the form where the list will be located.

2. Select the List/Menu object from the Insert panel, or select Insert, Form, List/Menu. Type **Why are you contacting us?** into the Label accessibility attribute for the tag—leave the other accessibility fields alone.

3. Click the new list in the design view so that it is selected. Enter the name of the list into the box in the far left of the Property inspector.

4. Select the List radio button, and the Height and Allow Multiple attributes become active.

5. In the Height box, type the number of list items you want visible at one time (see Figure 20.16). If there are more list items than can be shown, scrollbars automatically appear. If the Height property isn't active, you selected Menu instead of List in step 4.

TRY IT YOURSELF ▼

Creating a List

▼ TRY IT YOURSELF

Creating a List
continued

FIGURE 20.16
You set a list's height and other properties in the Property inspector.

6. Check the Allow Multiple check box if you want to allow the user to select multiple values in the list. You might want to add instructions that tell users that they can select multiple entries by holding down the Ctrl key (or the Command key on the Macintosh) and clicking multiple selections.

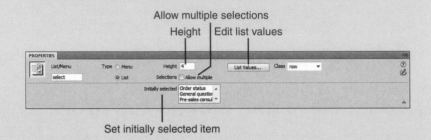

Set initially selected item

7. Set up the list values by selecting the List Values button. The List Values dialog box appears, as shown in Figure 20.17.

FIGURE 20.17
Select the + button in the List Values dialog box to add an item to the list.

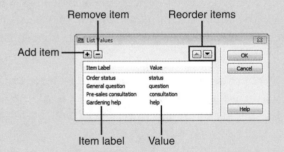

8. Enter an item label and a value for each item in the list. The item label is what the user sees and selects. The value is what the form sends back to a script on the server for processing. They can be the same, if appropriate. To add an item, click the + sign, enter the item label, tab to the Value field, and enter a value. You can press the Tab key to go forward or press Shift+Tab to go back. Use the − button to delete entries, and use the arrow buttons to rearrange entries. When you are at the end of the list, pressing Tab creates a new item label and value pair.

9. Click OK in the List Values dialog box.

10. Select an item from the Initially Selected box if one of the items should be selected by default. Otherwise, the first item appears.

Whereas a list can show a number of lines, a menu shows only one line until the user drops down the menu by clicking. Menus use less space than lists because a menu can drop down over other objects on the page when clicked, but it shrinks to only one line when it is inactive. Creating a menu is similar to creating a list, except that you don't set the height and you cannot allow the user to select multiple entries. You can turn a list into a drop-down menu by selecting the Menu option as the type in the Property inspector.

For a quick and easy way to add standard menus, such as menus for years, numbers, or months, use the Snippets panel. The Forms section of the Snippets panel contains prebuilt menus and form elements you can simply drag and drop onto your web page.

Adding Push Buttons and Image Buttons to Forms

You can add the following four types of buttons to forms:

- ▶ **Submit**—This type of button sends the data the user has entered into a form to a script or an application on the server. A submit button triggers the action that you set in the form's Action box in the Property inspector.

- ▶ **Reset**—This type of button erases all the data the user has entered in the form. It also reloads any initial values.

- ▶ **None**—This type of generic button has no automatic function. You can add functionality to a generic button by applying a behavior to it.

- ▶ **Image**—This type of button acts like a submit button. The form submits all the data it contains, and it sends the coordinates of where the user clicked.

The first three buttons are push buttons you create by inserting Dreamweaver's Button object. They differ in the way you configure them in the Property inspector. You create the fourth button, the image button, by inserting an Image Field object.

Adding Submit and Reset Buttons to Forms

In this section, you add submit and reset buttons to your form. Usually, the submit button is on the left and the reset button is to the right of the submit button.

To add a button to the form, follow these steps:

1. Position the insertion point and then select the Button object from the Insert panel, or select Insert, Form, Button. Because most buttons have their own labels, leave the accessibility attributes empty and click OK.

2. Highlight the button in your page, and then select Submit Form as the action for this button in the Property inspector. Type "Send Message" into Property Inspector value field.

3. Add another button to the right of the submit button.

4. Select Reset Form as the action for this button and a value of "Clear Form." The buttons should look like the buttons in Figure 20.18.

FIGURE 20.18
The submit button is usually placed on the left of the reset button. You need one submit button per form if you are sending this form to a script or to an application on a server.

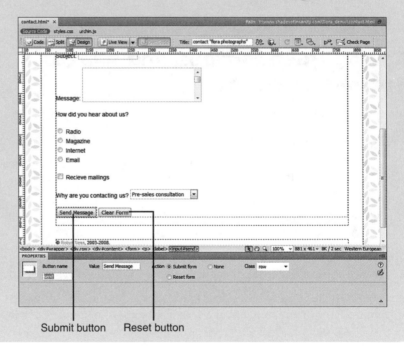

Submit button   Reset button

You can accept the default labels that Dreamweaver gives the submit and reset buttons or you can give them new labels. You can change the label of either button; a button does not have to say Submit to function as a submit button.

Many web developers like to give a submit button a label that actually describes what the button does, such as Enter the Contest or Send Comment. Each form must have a submit button to send the form data. The reset button is optional. You should have only one submit button per form with multiple text fields.

Adding an Image Button to Forms

You can replace a submit button with an image button. When the user clicks the image, the form submits its contents and the coordinates of the location where the user clicked the image button. Obviously, you do not need a submit button if you have an image button.

To add an image field to a form, first make sure that the insertion point is inside the form. Add an image field by selecting the Image Field object from the Insert panel or selecting Insert, Form, Image Field. The Select Image Source dialog box appears, enabling you to navigate and select a standard web image file. The Property inspector displays the name, source, alt text, and alignment attributes for the field. You set these attributes as you would for any image.

Adding Generic Buttons to Forms

Add a generic button by selecting the Button object from the Insert panel or by selecting Insert, Form, Button. Name the button, give it a label, and select None as the button's action. Now you can apply a behavior to this button that the user can trigger with a button click.

You might want to use a generic button if you aren't actually submitting the form to a script on the server (the topic for the next hour). You can use what's called a **client-side script**, that is, JavaScript contained in the web page that reacts to the form data. Submit buttons work only with server-side scripts, but a generic button can trigger a client-side script, via Dreamweaver behaviors or custom JavaScript. An example of this functionality would be a multiple-choice question in a web page. When users click the generic button, a client-side script triggers to check whether they picked the correct radio button and displays feedback for them on the web page.

TIP

Deleting a Form

Sometimes it is difficult to delete a form from the page. The easiest way to delete a form is to right-click the form delimiter to view the context menu. Then choose the Remove Tag `<form>` command. If the Remove Tag command does not say `<form>`, you have the wrong object selected. You could, of course, always select the `<form>` tag in the tag selector to delete the form.

Structuring a Form with Labels and Fieldsets

There are two other form elements you might want to apply along with the buttons and fields you've seen here.

The first, the `<label>` tag, provides a visible label for a given form field. These tags are inserted automatically if you use the label accessibility attribute when inserting a field. If you want to insert a label manually, just select the form elements that should be labeled, and then click the Label element inside the Forms category of the Insert panel. Dreamweaver inserts the `<label></label>` tags around your selection—it is up to you, however, to insert and style the text that composes the label between the two tags.

The second element you can use to create more structured and accessible forms is the fieldset. A fieldset separates a related group of fields and labels them as a distinct part of a form. For example, you may have filled in forms with areas for personal information, shipping address, and billing address—these could all be denoted as fieldsets within a form. It doesn't change how the fields work, but it does draw a box around them and provide a label to denote their purpose.

To add a fieldset to your form, first create the fields just as you have been doing throughout the hour. Next, select the fields that should be grouped together and click the Fieldset object in the Insert panel. You are asked to provide a "Legend" for the fieldset—this is just a label that describes what the fields have in common. Enter an appropriate value and click OK to add the `<fieldset></fieldset>` and `<legend></legend>` tags to your form.

Creating a Jump Menu to Navigate to Different URLs

A **jump menu** is a list of links that allows the viewer to jump to other websites or different web pages within the current site. Dreamweaver's Jump Menu object makes it easy to set up this type of jump menu. You can create a jump menu of email links, images, or any objects that a browser can display. The Jump Menu object uses JavaScript to redirect the browser.

Dreamweaver's Jump Menu object inserts a drop-down menu similar to the one you created a few minutes ago along with the JavaScript code contained in the Jump Menu behavior. You set up the list values in a special dialog box. The item labels appear in the drop-down menu, and the values contain the URLs to the web pages to which the user jumps. If you want to edit the jump menu after you have created it in the special dialog box, you have to brush up on the form skills you learned in this hour and the behavior skills you learned in previous hours.

To create a jump menu, follow these steps:

1. Place the insertion point on the page where you want the jump menu to appear. You don't need to insert a form because the Jump Menu object does that for you.

2. Either select the Jump Menu object from the Insert panel or select Insert, Form, Jump Menu. The Insert Jump Menu dialog box appears, as shown in Figure 20.19.

Menu items

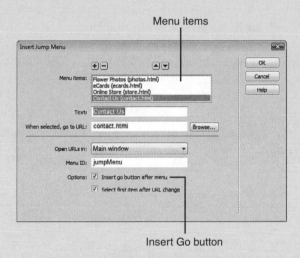

Insert Go button

FIGURE 20.19
The Insert Jump Menu dialog box enables you to create a drop-down menu where the user can select an item to which to link.

3. Type an item label for the first item in the jump menu in the Text box. The first item label highlights when you first open the Insert Jump Menu dialog box.

4. Enter the URL that launches when users select the item. You can either type it in or use the Browse button to navigate to a local file.

5. Click the + button to add another item.

6. Repeat steps 3–5 until you have entered all the items for the jump menu.

7. Give the menu a unique name in the Menu ID box.

8. Select the appropriate Options check boxes. Enable the Insert Go Button After Menu check box if you would like to have a button, with the label Go, which the user can click to jump. You can also enable the Select First Item After URL Change check box if you want the first item to be reselected after each jump selection.

9. When you finish selecting options in the Insert Jump Menu dialog box, click OK. Doing so inserts the jump menu within a form into your web page.

TIP

Add an Initial Value

A common way to create a jump menu is to have the first item be the text "Choose One..." and not to give it a link. Because you never want the user to select this item, the inability to select the first item in the drop-down menu won't be a problem. Then enable the Select First Item After URL Change check box so that the Choose One selection reappears.

FIGURE 20.20
You can create your own Go button by inserting a generic button into a form and applying the Jump Menu Go behavior.

You can edit the jump menu by editing the Jump Menu behavior. Select the List/Menu object that the Jump Menu command creates and double-click the Jump Menu behavior in the Behaviors panel. Add or remove list items by using the + and – buttons. Rearrange the list by using the up- and down-arrow buttons. You can enable or disable the Select First Item After URL Change setting.

You cannot add a Go button by editing the Jump Menu behavior. You can add one manually, however. Create a generic button by inserting a button into the form, giving it the label Go, and setting its action to None. Apply the Jump Menu Go behavior to the button triggered by the onClick event. When prompted, choose the jump menu ID from the Jump Menu Go dialog box, then click OK. The final behavior should resemble Figure 20.20.

Jump Menu   Jump Menu Go behavior

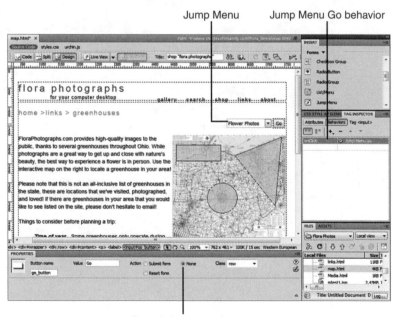

Generic button setting

Summary

In this hour, you learned how to insert and configure a form. You learned how to add text fields, radio buttons, check boxes, lists, and menus to the form. You learned how to add submit and reset buttons to the form and how to create a generic button. You learned how to use Dreamweaver's Jump Menu object to create a menu that consists of a bunch of URLs to which the user can jump.

Q&A

Q. I just want to email my form contents. I know that in the next hour I learn about CGI and other scripting methods, but isn't there a quick-and-dirty way to do this?

A. You can email form contents by using your email address as the action. You must preface your email address with `mailto:` so that it looks like this: `mailto:`*you@yourdomain.com.* In addition, you might need to type **text/plain** into the Enctype attribute in the Property inspector when you select the `<form>` tag.

This way of submitting a form might be fine for collecting form data about where your co-workers want to go to lunch on Friday. They all know and trust you (at least I hope they do), and they probably all have their email programs set up in a similar fashion to yours. An email program must be set up properly with the browser for this method to work. In addition, some browsers put up a warning when the user tries to submit a form in this fashion.

Q. Why can't I see my form elements?

A. If your form elements aren't showing up, they must not be inside the `<form>` tags. Some browsers hide form elements that are not inside a form.

Workshop

Quiz

1. What do you need to do to make a number of radio buttons act as though they are a group?

2. How do you create a generic button?

3. What's the difference between a list and a menu?

Quiz Answers

1. All the radio buttons in a group must have the same name.

2. After you insert a button into a form, select None as the action. You can then attach Dreamweaver behaviors to the button if you like.

3. A list displays a configurable number of items and might allow the user to select more than one item to submit. A menu displays only one line and drops down when the user clicks it so that the user can select an item. The user can select only one item at a time from a menu.

Exercises

1. Create a form to collect the user data of your choice. Format the form objects and labels with a table so that they line up nicely. Place the submit and reset buttons in the bottom row of the table and merge the cells so that the buttons are centered under the entire table.

2. Create a jump menu in a frame at the top of the page. Enter all your favorite URLs into the menu. Have the URLs load into a frame in the bottom of the page.

3. Experiment with using the form page designs and Snippets panel to quickly create forms. Create one of the built-in CSS style sheets that applies to forms and attach it to a forms page. Try modifying some of the styles in the style sheet.

Sending and Reacting to Form Data

In Hour 20, "Creating a Form and Collecting Data," you learned how to create a form. In this hour, you decide what to do with the data that the user enters into your form. You have to send the data to a script on the server for processing. The script on the server can store data in a database, send it to an email address, send results back to the browser, or process it any way you want (depending on your scripting abilities!).

The types of information you might want to receive in a form could include orders, feedback, comments, guest-book entries, polls, and even uploaded files. Creating the form and inserting form elements are usually the easy parts. The difficult part is installing and configuring the scripts that process the data.

Validating a Form's Data Using the Validate Form Behavior

Before you receive and process information from a form, it is a good idea to make sure that the information is complete and in the right format. Dreamweaver has a Validate Form behavior which can ensure that a user has entered data into a required field, check the validity of an email address, and verify that the user enters numbers correctly.

The Validate Form behavior requires the user to enter the form data correctly before submitting the data to a script or an application on the server. You can validate the form in two ways:

- ▶ Attach the Validate Form behavior to the Submit button to validate the entire form when the Submit button is clicked. The onClick event triggers the behavior.

WHAT YOU'LL LEARN IN
THIS HOUR:

- ▶ How to use the Validate Form behavior and Spry form validation elements
- ▶ How to set up a page to submit to a CGI script
- ▶ How to create secure web pages
- ▶ How Dreamweaver edits and displays ASP, ASP.NET, JSP, PHP, and CFML code

▶ Attach the Validate Form behavior to an individual text field to validate the data entered in that field when the user leaves it. The onChange event triggers the behavior when the user's focus leaves the field.

You must have a form with form objects in your web page before the Validate Form behavior is active in the + drop-down menu of the Behaviors panel.

▼ TRY IT YOURSELF

Creating a Validating Form

To validate a form, follow these steps:

1. Create a new form that has various text fields, or open the form you created in Hour 20.

2. Click the Submit button.

3. Open the Behaviors panel. Click the + button and select the Validate Form behavior.

4. The Validate Form dialog box appears. A list of all the text fields appears in the dialog box.

5. Set up validation settings for every text field that requires them.

6. Check the Required check box if the user must fill in an entry in the field.

7. Choose from among the four settings in the Accept category:

> **Anything**—Select this setting if the user has to enter data into the field but that data can be in any format. For instance, if you are asking for a phone number, you do not want to limit the user to entering only numbers because users often format phone numbers with other characters.

> **Number**—Select this setting if the user has to enter data that is numeric.

> **Email Address**—Select this setting if the user has to enter an email address. This setting checks for an @ symbol.

> **Number From**—Select this setting to check for a number within a range of specific numbers. Fill in both the low and high ends of the range.

8. Notice that your settings appear in parentheses beside the name of the text field in the Fields list (shown in Figure 21.1). Repeat steps 5–7 to validate all the text fields.

9. When you are finished making changes in the Validate Form dialog box, click OK. Select the onClick event if the Validate Form behavior is

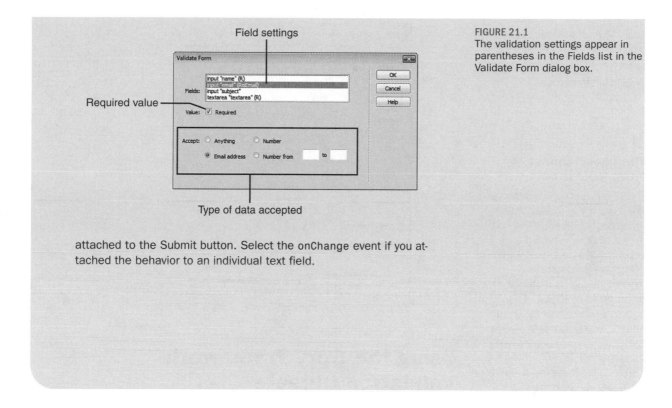

Field settings

Required value

Type of data accepted

FIGURE 21.1
The validation settings appear in parentheses in the Fields list in the Validate Form dialog box.

attached to the Submit button. Select the onChange event if you attached the behavior to an individual text field.

When the Validate Form behavior triggers, it checks the data in the form against the settings you entered. You should make sure that your form's labels and instructions clearly tell users what type of data to enter in each field and indicate which fields are required. You should give the users the information to fill out the form properly so that they don't get frustrated with error messages.

If the user enters incorrect data, the message box shown in Figure 21.2 appears. This message tells the user that errors have occurred, lists the text fields' names, and explains why the Validate Form behavior rejected the data. Here is another place where a meaningful name for a Dreamweaver object is important. If you are validating a form, it is a good idea to give a text field the same name as the label beside it so that the user can easily locate and change the field's data.

TIP

Required Form Elements

A standard way to signal that a form element is required is to place an asterisk next to its label. It's becoming more common to use a bold label to signal that a form element is required. You should tell your users somewhere on the page what indicates that a form element is required.

FIGURE 21.2
After the validation script is run, a form that has errors or omissions displays this message, indicating which fields the user either omitted or filled out incorrectly.

TIP

The Uncertainties of Form Validation

The Form validation behaviors are a great way to help a user enter correct input before data gets sent to a server. It should not, however, be the only type of validation that occurs. JavaScript can be disabled on a client browser, enabling users to submit *anything* within a form. Form validation should always happen both at the user side, using behaviors, and at the server side, using the scripting language you've chosen.

Using the Spry Framework Validation Objects

In Hour 19, "Using Ajax Frameworks and Libraries," you explored the Spry framework and learned how to insert Spry elements in a web page. Spry has several special form elements you can insert in a form to add automatic form validation: a Spry text field, select object (list or menu), check box, radio group, text area, and password.

Let's walk through inserting and setting up a text field as an example. All the Spry form elements work similarly.

▼ TRY IT YOURSELF

Setting Up a Spry Validation Text Field

To set up a Spry Validation text field, do the following:

1. Place the insertion point inside a form.

2. Select Insert, Spry, Spry Validation Text Field.

3. Click the tab above the text field to display the text field validation settings in the Property inspector, as shown in Figure 21.3.

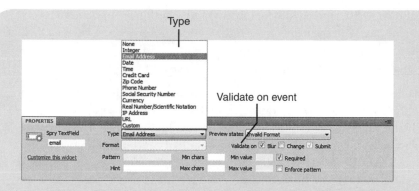

FIGURE 21.3
You can set up Spry validation properties by selecting the object and changing settings in the Property inspector.

4. Select the type of data that the text field should be. Is it a credit card? A number? A ZIP Code? A Social Security number? There are validation settings for all of these commonly collected pieces of data.

5. Select when the text field validates by choosing one of the Validate On selections. Select Blur to validate when the user clicks outside the form element. Select Change to validate when the content of the form element changes. Select Submit to validate when the user clicks the Submit button.

6. Save the web page (File, Save) and copy the dependent files if prompted. Preview the page in the browser or in Live View and test the validation.

The other Spry validation widgets work the same way. Simply insert the "Spry Validation" version of the form element that you want to use, and then select the blue tab that appears above it and configure the validation, default values, and so on accordingly. After you start using the Spry validation widgets, you'll probably hardly ever build a straight HTML-based form again.

NOTE

The Confirm Widget

One "strange" widget is the "confirm" widget. This is meant to be used along with a Spry Validation password widget. It provides a second password field whose contents must match the first password field.

Receiving Information from a Form

The standard way to process a form is to have on the server an application that parses the data and performs an action on it. **Parsing** data is the act of dividing and interpreting the name-value pairs that are sent to the server.

Each name-value pair contains the name of the form element created in Dreamweaver and the value that the user entered or selected for that field. A text field has a name-value pair that contains the name of the text field and the value entered into that field. A radio button group sends a name-value pair with the name of the radio button group and the value of the button selected when the user submitted the form. A list or a drop-down menu sends the name of the object and any items the user selected.

The web browser sends the name-value pairs to a server via an **HTTP request**. The web server software passes the request to the application server that handles the scripting language specified in the request, as shown in Figure 21.4. For instance, if the script is in PHP: Hypertext Preprocessor (PHP), the ColdFusion application server handles the request. Depending on the script, the application server might request data from a database or send a request to an email server to send a specific email message. The server can process scripts in many ways. The application server usually returns some sort of output, normally HTML, which the web server sends back to the browser. This all takes place in milliseconds!

FIGURE 21.4
The browser sends a request to a script on the server and receives a response. The script might control sending an email message or accessing and returning data from a database.

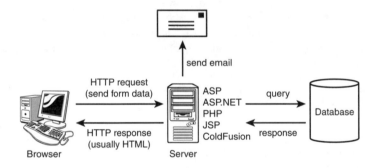

A common way of processing forms on a server is by using a CGI script. Developers usually write those scripts in Perl or another programming language. Later in this hour, you learn about other ways of processing forms, with Active Server Pages (ASP), ASP.NET, JavaServer Pages (JSP), PHP: Hypertext Preprocessor (PHP), and ColdFusion—proprietary processing systems that are powerful in creating web applications.

Luckily, there are various places on the Web to download already-written CGI scripts. Because programming CGI scripts is beyond the scope of this book, the examples in this hour use an existing script that processes form data and sends it to a specific email address.

CGI stands for **common gateway interface**, and it is the definition of the standard method of communication between a script and the web server. A CGI script resides in a specific directory on the web server. It is common for access to this directory to be limited to webmasters for security reasons. You can contact your webmaster and ask whether a script is already available on your server to do what you want to do or whether the webmaster installs one for you. You might have a directory within your own web directory that can hold CGI scripts. Often this directory's name is cgi-bin or has *cgi* somewhere in its name.

You should double-check that your hosting service, if you are using one, supports CGI scripts. Sometimes you can use only the scripts that the service has available; check that a form mail script is available. Carefully review the features of the type of account you are signing up for and ask questions, if necessary.

To prepare your form to send data to a script, first select the form. Next, enter the URL to the CGI script in the Action text box in the Property inspector, as shown in Figure 21.5. The documentation for the script tells you whether the script expects the form name-value pairs to be submitted via either the GET or the POST method.

The GET and POST methods differ in the following ways:

- The GET method appends form data via the URL, a URL that can be saved as a bookmark in the browser. Data submitted via this method is displayed in the address field of the browser after submission, and is limited to text-based data; file uploads won't work.

- The POST method packages and sends the data invisibly to the user; the output doesn't appear in the URL. There is no limitation on the amount of data that forms can send. In addition, the POST method allows uploading of files with forms.

TIP

Get Free Scripts on the Web

The Web is an incredibly generous place, and you can download all sorts of free scripts to use. If you don't know how to program CGI scripts and you are willing to process your forms generically, you can find a number of great scripts available from Matt's Script Archive (http://www.scriptarchive.com) and FreeScripts (http://www.freescripts.com).

TIP

Use a Form-Hosting Site

If you don't have access to CGI scripts, you might want to use a form-hosting site (search for "free form hosting" on Yahoo! or any other search engine). The site http://www.formmail.com enables you to build and host forms without advertisements for less than a dollar per month.

These sites allow you to create forms that the form-hosting sites process for you. You simply link to the page with the form located on the hosting service's server. The disadvantage of using these services is that they usually display advertising on your form page.

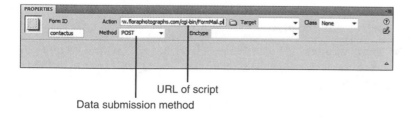

URL of script

Data submission method

FIGURE 21.5
With the form selected, enter the URL to the CGI script that processes your form in the Action text box of the Property inspector.

Using the FormMail Script

In this section, we look at a popular form of handling script that is written in Perl. This requires the use of a web server with Perl and CGI support. Even if you don't have access to these facilities, you might be interested in following along just to better understand the mechanics of form processing.

CAUTION

Web Server Operating Systems

Web server applications reside on various operating systems. UNIX and Windows Server are the most popular operating systems for servers. It's important that you know which operating system your web server uses. Developers write scripts to run on certain operating systems. For instance, Matthew Wright wrote the FormMail script to run on UNIX. Other people have translated the script to other operating systems. One additional caution: UNIX filenames are case sensitive, so you must be careful that you reference links and image files with the proper case.

Download Matthew Wright's FormMail script from http://www.scriptarchive.com/formmail.html to use with the rest of this hour. This script sends the contents of a form to an email address. The script can be configured in various ways. If you are going to test the script, you need to install it first. The script comes with a readme file that describes all the functions and parameters you can set in the script. The process of setting up and calling the FormMail script is similar to that of submitting a form to any CGI script.

To use the FormMail script, you must add to your form hidden fields containing parameters that tell the script what to do. Open the FormMail script in Dreamweaver or a text editor, such as Notepad, and you see instructions at the top of the file. The scripted processes are also contained in the file, so be careful what you change. You have to configure the following four variables at the top of the FormMail script before loading it onto the server:

▶ `$mailprog`—This variable needs to point to the UNIX server's sendmail program. Leave the variable set at the default; if it doesn't work, your webmaster can give you the path. You do not need this variable if you are running the Windows NT version of the script. If your hosting company provided the FormMail script for you, it has probably modified this variable for you. A common path to sendmail is `/usr/lib/sendmail` or `/usr/sbin/sendmail`; you have to read your hosting service's documentation or contact the service to determine what address you have to use.

▶ `@referers`—This variable contains the domains (usually one) allowed access to the script. This setting keeps unauthorized domains from using the script and the resources on your server. My domain is www.johneray.com, so that's what I would enter into this variable. This prevents people with forms in domains other than mine from using my script to process their forms.

▶ `@recipients`—This variable defines the email addresses that can receive email from the form. This deters spammers from using the form to do their dirty deeds.

▶ **@valid_ENV**—This variable is configurable by the webmaster in order to define environment variables. You don't need to worry about this unless your webmaster gives you information on how to change it.

Adding a Hidden Field to a Form

Hidden fields are sent along with all the other form fields. The users cannot change the contents of these fields, nor can they see the fields unless they view your HTML source. You should create hidden fields for the recipient of the emailed form data, the subject that appears in the email subject field, and the URL to which the script redirects the user after the form is filled out. You can explore many other settings on your own.

Set the form action to the URL of the FormMail script on your server. The FormMail script can accept either the GET method or the POST method for submitting the data. I suggest the POST method because it is typically considered better form (no pun intended).

To add hidden fields to your form, follow these steps:

1. Place the insertion point anywhere inside your form. It does not matter where the hidden fields are located.

2. Select the Hidden Field object from the Insert panel or select Insert, Form, Hidden Field.

3. Dreamweaver displays the Hidden Field symbol in your web page, as shown in Figure 21.6.

4. Enter **recipient** in the text box on the left side of the Property inspector and enter your email address as the value, as shown in Figure 21.6. The script documentation describes these name-value pairs.

5. Optionally, add another hidden field to the form and enter the name **redirect**. As the value of the field, enter the URL to which the script redirects the user after the form is submitted.

You can add a number of optional form fields to the FormMail script. Refer to the documentation to read about them. When the user submits the form, the script sends the name-value pairs to the email address specified in the hidden field named recipient. This is the simplest processing possible for a form. Other scripts can save data to databases, validate and process credit card information, and perform all sorts of other complex actions.

CAUTION

Type Carefully!

When you are naming your own objects in Dreamweaver, you can afford to occasionally make a typo or misspelling. Scripts and applications, however, are not forgiving of typos. Adding hidden fields requires you to enter the names exactly as they are listed in the documentation. It's often necessary that the letter case be exact as well because many servers are case sensitive.

TRY IT YOURSELF ▼

Adding Hidden Fields to a Form

FIGURE 21.6
The Hidden Field symbol appears when you insert a hidden field into a form. The Property inspector shows a hidden field name-value pair.

NOTE

Enabling Hidden Field Symbols

If you do not see the Hidden Field symbol, verify that you have Invisible Elements checked (select View, Visual Aids, Invisible Elements); also check that the Invisible Elements category in the Dreamweaver Preferences dialog box has the Hidden Form Fields checked.

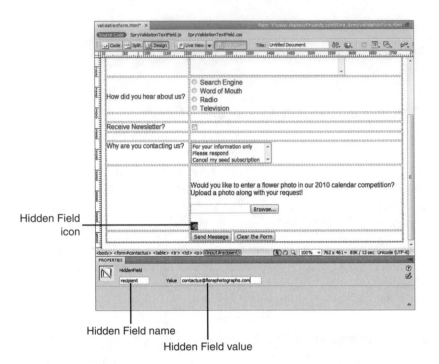

Hidden Field icon

Hidden Field name

Hidden Field value

Exploring Submission Security

When your users submit form information, it travels in packets across the Internet, along with millions of other packets. **Packets** are electronic bundles of information that carry data to the server. People who are along the path of the data and who understand how to intercept and reassemble data taken from the Web can intercept and read these packets of information. The only way around this problem is to create a secure site in which all packets are encrypted (scrambled) before they are sent from the browser to the server and vice versa. After you take steps to secure sensitive data, don't forget to assure users that their transactions and data are indeed secure.

Again, this is a web server issue. The web server on which your site is located must have SSL—the secure sockets layer—enabled. Many ISPs offer this service. Ask your webmaster whether you have access to secure web pages.

Users access a secure URL exactly as they would a regular URL. The only difference is that the protocol portion of the URL changes from http to https. As shown in Figure 21.7, the browser displays a Lock icon in the status bar when it is in secure mode.

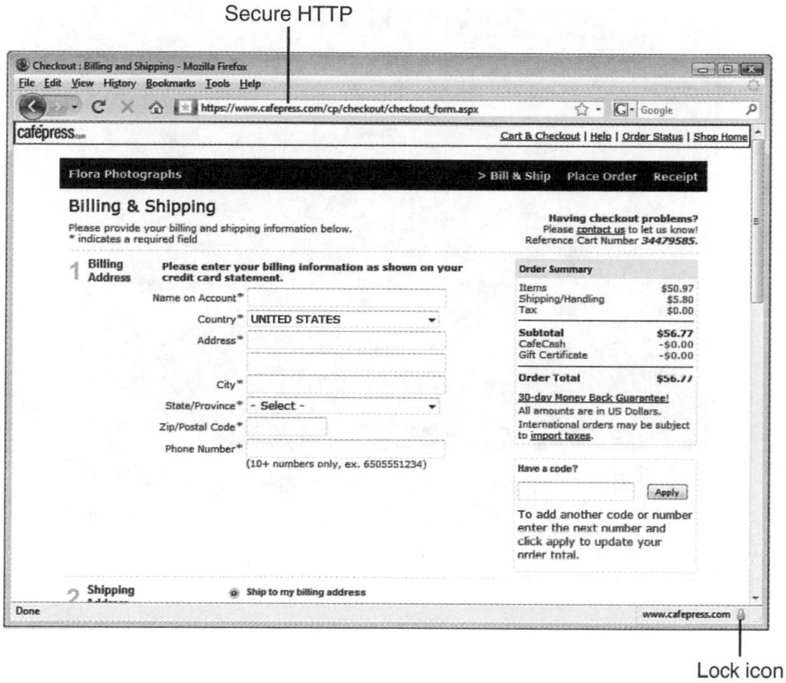

Secure HTTP

FIGURE 21.7
The browser displays a Lock icon in
the status bar when serving the
page via secure sockets.

Lock icon

You have to worry about secure submissions only when the user enters sensitive information, such as credit card numbers or other financial data. For public polls, guest books, or feedback forms, you don't have to shield the information from potential thieves. Customers expect you to protect only their sensitive data.

You need a server certificate to add security to your form submissions. A **certificate** is an electronic document verifying that you are who you say you are. You might be able to use your web host's certificate, or you might need to purchase your own. One of the major certificate vendors is VeriSign, and you can learn more about certificates at VeriSign's website: http://www.verisign.com/ssl/buy-ssl-certificates/.

Uploading a File from a Form

With the proper server scripts in place, you might have to add a **file field** that enables users to upload files. You can collect images, homework assignments, or any types of files that you want to have sent to you with a file field object. Users click the Browse button, shown in Figure 21.8, to select a file from the local drive. When a user clicks the Submit button, the file travels to the server.

FIGURE 21.8
Use a file field to enable a user to upload a file to the server. However, make sure that your server allows uploading before you create your form.

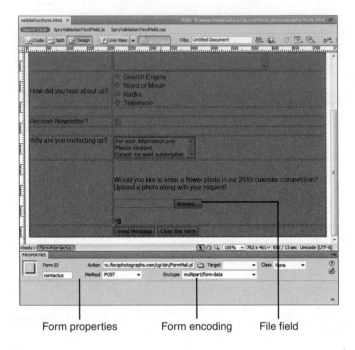

Form properties   Form encoding   File field

A file field has attributes similar to those of a text field, which you used in the preceding hour. You can set the size of the file field by putting a value in the Char Width box in the Property inspector. You can also set the Max Chars attribute and the Init Val attribute in the Property inspector. You must give the file field a unique name.

The important question you must answer before you use a file field is this: Does your server allow anonymous file uploads? You also have to select multipart/form-data from the Enctype drop-down list for the <form> tag so that the file encoding is correct. Also, you should use the POST method to submit your form; the GET method does not work with file fields.

Preparing a Page to Interact with ASP, ASP.NET, JSP, PHP, or CFML

In addition to using CGI scripts, there are other ways to process forms and create dynamic web applications. Like CGI scripting, these technologies interact with the web server to process web page information. Dreamweaver enables you to create dynamic web pages that incorporate server-side scripting. When you create a new web page, you choose from several different development platforms, as shown in Figure 21.9.

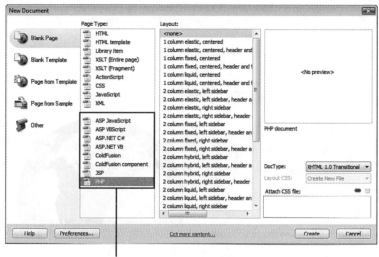

Supported server languages

FIGURE 21.9
You can create ASP, ASP.NET, JSP, PHP, and CFML pages with Dreamweaver.

Dreamweaver supports these five major server-side scripting technologies:

- ► **ASP**—Microsoft's legacy web development platform, ASP, combines client-side scripting with server-side processing to create dynamic web pages. Dreamweaver CS4 supports both JavaScript and VB-Script-based ASP development.

- ► **ASP.NET**—Microsoft's ASP.NET, released in 2002, is a server-side application platform that has replaced ASP in all but legacy applications. ASP.NET runs on Windows 2000 Server or later. Dreamweaver CS4 supports C# and Visual Basic .NET development languages.

- ► **JSP**—JSP is a Java-based way to dynamically process web pages. JSP scripts interact with a JSP-enabled server. The popular Apache web server and the free Tomcat JSP application server are available. For Microsoft IIS, Tomcat offers an IIS connector as well.

- ► **PHP**—PHP is a free, open-source server-side scripting language that sends dynamic web pages to the user after interpreting PHP code. PHP is the open-source movement's answer to ASP and is widely supported by free applications and scripts.

- ► **ColdFusion**—Adobe's ColdFusion server interprets CFML (ColdFusion Markup Language) to create dynamic web pages. The ColdFusion server application can run on many operating systems. CFML is

TIP

Intrigued? Want to Learn More?

Adobe Dreamweaver CS4 Unleashed (ISBN: 0672330393), by Zak Ruvalcaba, picks up where this book leaves off by introducing you to dynamic websites and scripting.

slightly different from the other scripting languages described here because it is a tag-based language, like HTML.

All these technologies accomplish the same thing: enabling a client-side web page to interact with the server by accessing data, sending an email message, or processing input in some way. They all have advantages and disadvantages, and each uses a different syntax to add code to web pages. That said, after you learn one, it's easy to pick up another.

You can embed ASP, ASP.NET, JSP, PHP, and CFML into your web pages, and Dreamweaver represents the code with special icons, as shown in Figure 21.10. When you define your site as one containing dynamic pages, your page looks slightly different from this. In a dynamic site, Dreamweaver displays a representation of the code; you can display actual data from the database by viewing the web page in Live View.

FIGURE 21.10
Special icons, in this case a PHP Script icon, appear when you're viewing invisible elements that represent code.

PHP script icons

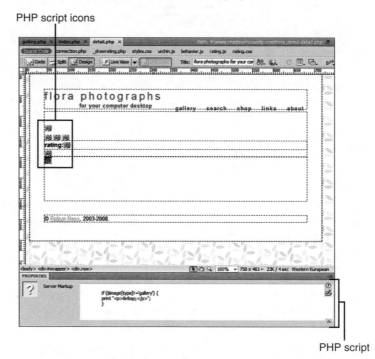

PHP script

You can use ASP, ASP.NET, JSP, PHP, or CFML scripts contained in an external script file to process a form. Such a script acts like the CGI script you used earlier this hour. You reference the script's URL as the form's action in the Property inspector. Again, the script's directory must have the proper permission set in order for the script to execute. Figure 21.11 shows a form submitting its contents to a PHP script.

When you define your site as a dynamic site, you can author dynamic web pages in Dreamweaver. Dreamweaver enables you to easily hook up your web content to databases. You can visually add PHP and CFML components, but visually building apps with other server languages isn't supported without third party software. Dreamweaver generates the code for you behind the scenes and displays the dynamic elements. You can even see how your web page will look with real data from the database within Dreamweaver.

Choosing a Dreamweaver CS4 Compatible Hosting Provider

If you choose to start exploring the scripting languages in Dreamweaver, you want to use a hosting provider that can support either PHP or ColdFusion scripting capabilities. The good news is that there are plenty of excellent (and cheap!) options for PHP. I'd also recommend PHP over ColdFusion because of the thousands of freely available applications that you can download, install, and run.

Two excellent PHP providers are HostGator (http://www.hostgator.com/) and DreamHost (http://www.dreamhost.com/). These systems provide a blossoming web developer with plenty of space and bandwidth, database access, PHP scripting, and other features for only a few dollars a month.

For ColdFusion hosting, Adobe maintains a list of partners at http://www.adobe.com/products/coldfusion/hosting/. These servers provide you with similar capacity as the aforementioned PHP hosts, but there are fewer ColdFusion resources available online. If you choose this route, I recommend visiting RIAForge for open-source software built on Adobe software.

TIP

Learn More with the Dreamweaver Tutorials

If you'd like to learn more about creating dynamic web pages, go through the tutorials that come with Dreamweaver.

Summary

In this hour, you learned how CGI scripts work and how form data gets to them. You learned how to use the Validate Form behavior and Spry form validation elements to validate the data that the user enters into your form. You inserted into a form hidden fields that contain a name-value pair. You set the action for a form and learned the difference between the GET and POST methods for submitting data. You learned about secure transactions. In addition, you learned how to call ASP, ASP.NET, PHP, JSP, and CFML scripts.

Q&A

Q. I know a PHP programmer who will help me with my web pages. What do I need to tell her about my web pages so that she can write a script to process them on the server?

A. She needs to know what you called the items in your form and how you want them processed. If she is sending the data to a database, she has to know what you call the items in your form so that she can parse the data into the correct place. She also needs to know whether you need any validation or processing applied to the data. For instance, you might need to have individual prices added together as one total price.

Q. Should I learn Perl, ASP, ASP.NET, PHP, JSP, or CFML?

A. It depends on what you want to do when you grow up! Do you have a knack for coding? If so, having skills in any of these technologies might be fun and look great on your resume. Find out which technologies are hot in the marketplace. ASP.NET, JSP, and PHP are a safe bet for those looking for a job in a web development field.

If you aren't very interested in coding but want to expand your web skill set, maybe it's a better idea to specialize in Dreamweaver—there's a lot to learn! On the other hand, you can always learn more about databases. If you don't really enjoy coding, it can be a real chore. Dreamweaver offers objects and server behaviors that make it much easier than before to code dynamic web pages.

Workshop

Quiz

1. What pair of items do users send when submitting a form?

2. What is a hidden text field?

3. What languages does Dreamweaver CS4 support for visual application development?

4. What does it mean when a URL begins with *https*?

Quiz Answers

1. Users send a name-value pair when they submit a form. This is the name of the form object and the value either entered or selected by the user.

2. A hidden text field contains a name-value pair that the user cannot change. Generally, the script requires this data to process the form properly.

3. PHP and CFML (ColdFusion) are the only languages supported out of the box in Dreamweaver CS4, although other languages may be supported as extensions downloadable from Adobe Exchange (http://www.adobe.com/cfusion/exchange/).

4. A URL beginning with *https* signals that the URL is secure using the Secure HTTP protocol.

Exercises

1. Add a Google search box to a web page. You'll be adding a form that contacts the Google servers and returns results to the web page. You can find the code at http://www.google.com/searchcode.html; paste this code in Dreamweaver's Code view and then change to Design view to examine and edit it.

2. Experiment with the FormMail fields that you did not explore in this hour. The script also offers validation functionality that you could use instead of using the Dreamweaver Validate Form behavior. You can find the documentation online at http://www.scriptarchive.com/readme/formmail.html.

3. Find a form on the Web and look at it critically. Select the View Source command to see the HTML. Does the form have any hidden fields? To what server is the form submitted? You should look for the `<form>` and `</form>` tags that contain the code for the form.

Uploading, Sharing, and Managing Website Projects

Finished websites reside on a web server where many people can access the web pages. While you are working on your websites, you want to move them onto a server for testing. At the end of the project, you have to move your web pages to a public server so that other people can look at them. There are different ways to move the files onto a server and different methods for ensuring that the version of the files is correct and not accidentally overwritten.

Enabling Server Connection

When you define a website in Dreamweaver, you define a local site that exactly mirrors the final, public website. **Mirroring** means that the local site contains an exact copy of the files on the final site. Dreamweaver calls your final site the **remote site**. You work on the files in your local site and then upload them to the remote site by using Dreamweaver's file transfer commands.

When working in Dreamweaver, you don't need additional file transfer protocol (FTP) software or any other software to move your files onto the remote server. Dreamweaver has this capability built in! It's more convenient to set up your remote site and transfer files while working in Dreamweaver than to jump to another application.

Adding Your Remote Site

You define a remote site by editing the website definition (which you get to by selecting Site, Manage Sites). Select a site and click the Edit button to launch the Site Definition dialog box for the selected website. In the Basic

WHAT YOU'LL LEARN IN THIS HOUR:

► How to configure a remote site

► How to move your site onto a remote server

► How to import an existing site

► How to use Check In/Check Out

tab, click the Next button until you reach the Sharing Files section of the Site Definition Wizard, as shown in Figure 22.1.

FIGURE 22.1
You set up the remote site definition in the Sharing Files section of
the Site Definition Wizard.

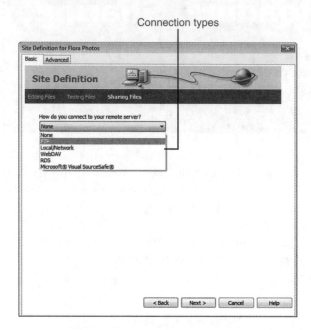

You can choose from among five transfer methods in the drop-down menu:

► FTP (including SFTP)

► Local/Network

► WebDAV

► RDS

► Microsoft Visual SourceSafe

The transfer method you select depends on where your remote site is hosted. The site might be at your ISP, the folks who provide you with an Internet dial-up service, or a web hosting service. In that case, you probably connect to its servers by using FTP or SFTP. The site might be on your company's intranet, and if so, you can transfer the local site to the remote site by using a LAN connection (the Local/Network option in the drop-down menu). WebDAV, RDS, and Visual SourceSafe connections are less common than the others, but professional web development environments sometimes use them.

Setting FTP Information

You should select FTP access, as shown in Figure 22.2, if you need to transfer files over the Web to a remote server. The server could be physically located in your building, or it could be on the other side of the world. You
must enter the name of the FTP server in the What Is the Hostname or FTP
Address of Your Web Server text box. Often the hostname is in the following format: ftp.*domain*.com.

CAUTION

No Protocol Necessary

Do not enter the server name
preceded by the protocol, as you
would in a browser (such as
ftp://ftp.domain.com).

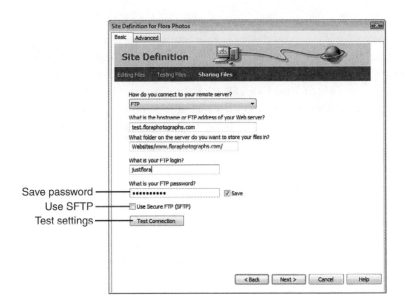

FIGURE 22.2
You have to set the FTP information, including the server address.

Enter the correct directory in the What Folder on the Server Do You Want to
Store Your Files In text box. You might have to get the path for this directory from your web or network administrator. If you are unsure what the
root directory is on the remote site, try leaving the What Is the Hostname or
FTP Address of Your Web Server box blank. The FTP server might put you
directly in the correct directory because your account might be configured
that way.

You must have a login and a password to access the FTP server. The standard anonymous login, often used to download files over the Internet,
probably does not work to upload files to a website. You need to log in as a
user who has access and permission to get and put files in the directories
that house your website. Dreamweaver saves your password by default. If
other people have access to Dreamweaver on your computer and you don't
want them to access your FTP account, deselect the Save check box.

Click the Test Connection button to make sure that you've entered everything correctly and are successfully connecting to the FTP server. You can troubleshoot FTP connection problems by first closing the Site Definition dialog box and then selecting Window, Results and clicking the FTP Log tab. The FTP log lists the reason you didn't connect successfully. For instance, if the log states that the password was incorrect or the directory you are targeting doesn't exist, you can change these settings in the Site Definition Wizard and try again.

If you are behind a firewall or using a proxy server, you might have difficulties with FTP. Consult the network administrator about which settings you need to choose when setting up FTP. The most common change you need to make is to enable passive FTP, which helps with most simple firewall issues. To enable passive FTP, click the Advanced button to switch to the advanced site settings, and then click the Remote Info category. Finally, click the check box beside Use Passive FTP, as shown in Figure 22.3.

FIGURE 22.3
Configure passive FTP to deal with the most common firewall issues.

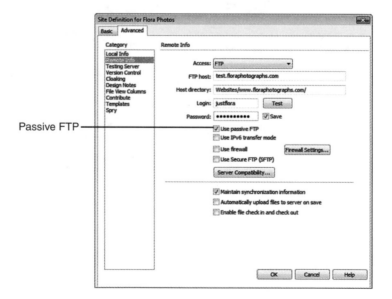

For more complex setups, you might have to configure the firewall port and host in the Site category of the Dreamweaver Preferences dialog box. If you have a slow connection to the Internet, the default FTP timeout might be too short, causing your FTP connection to time out too often. You can increase this time also in the Site category of the Preferences dialog box.

Setting LAN Information

Select Local/Network in the Site Definition Wizard, as shown in Figure 22.4, if the server is on a computer that you can connect to directly by using a network. If you can access files on the server the same way you access your hard drive, moving files to and from it with ease, you have LAN access. You must know the correct web-accessible directory; your web administrator should be able to give you that information.

FIGURE 22.4
Select Local/Network when the remote directory resides within your LAN.

Set up LAN access to the remote server by entering the path to the remote directory. Click the Browse icon to browse to the directory or type in the path. Checking the Refresh Remote File List Automatically might slow down Dreamweaver's performance a bit, but you always have an up-to-date reflection of the remote site.

Setting RDS Access

You use the RDS setting only if your remote site is on a ColdFusion server. ColdFusion is one of the server-side scripting languages that Dreamweaver supports. As when you select FTP, you enter a hostname (the server address), a username, and a password to connect to this type of remote site.

Setting WebDAV Access

WebDAV stands for "Web Distributed Authoring and Versioning." It is a popular extension to the standard HTTP protocol for reading and writing

TIP

Version Control and Dreamweaver

Both WebDAV and Visual SourceSafe *can* be used as version control systems. A version control system monitors changes to files and ensures that a full history of activity is maintained. It can even help combine changes made by two developers to a single file. Dreamweaver's implementation of WebDAV and Visual Source-Safe only allow for reading and writing from/to these systems— just like a normal file server. To gain access to *true* version control under Dreamweaver, you need access to a "Subversion" server. This is the only version control standard supported under Dreamweaver; it is discussed later in this chapter.

to remote file systems. It works through proxy servers and firewalls with relative ease—and is entirely cross-platform. Apple's MobileMe iDisk service, for example, uses this protocol to provide access on Mac OS X and Windows.

Select WebDAV from the drop-down menu in the Site Definition Wizard, and then fill in the URL of your WebDAV file server (usually your website address) and the username and password assigned to you.

Setting Microsoft Visual SourceSafe Access

For those working in pure Microsoft environments, you may use Microsoft Visual SourceSafe as your remote code repository. This system allows multiple people to work on a website simultaneously and tracks their changes. Unfortunately, it is available only on the Windows platform version of Dreamweaver, and does not allow full interaction with Visual SourceSafe.

Set up a Visual SourceSafe database as your remote site by selecting the Microsoft Visual SourceSafe choice in the Site Definition Wizard. Set up the Visual SourceSafe database by clicking the Settings button. The Open Microsoft Visual SourceSafe Database dialog box appears, as shown in Figure 22.5. Enter the database path, project, username, and password in this dialog box. You can get this information from your Visual SourceSafe administrator.

FIGURE 22.5
Enter the database, username, and password to connect to a Visual SourceSafe database.

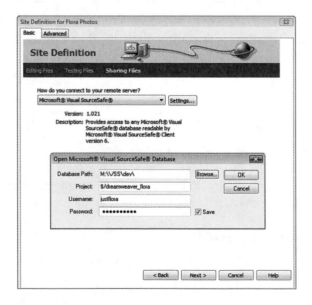

Using the Remote Site Advanced Tab

Click the Advanced tab of the Site Definition dialog box to see a different view of your remote site's settings. The Remote Info category, shown in Figure 22.6, displays the login information along with firewall and other settings. You can click back and forth between the Basic and Advanced tabs if you like.

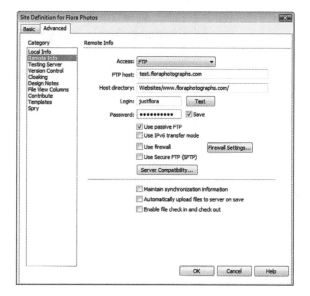

FIGURE 22.6
The Advanced tab shows all the remote site's settings.

Moving a Site onto a Remote Server

If your server is located on a LAN, you normally connect to the server when you log on to your computer and you stay connected all day. If you access the remote server over the Internet by using FTP, you connect while getting and putting files onto the server and then you disconnect. Even if you don't disconnect on your end, your connection will most likely time out on the server if you have been inactive for a period and you will have to reconnect.

The Files panel contains buttons, as shown in Figure 22.7, that enable you to transfer files to and from the remote site. You can transfer files to your local site by clicking the Get button, and you can transfer files to the remote site by clicking the Put button. In Hour 23, "Maintaining a Website," you learn about using the Synchronize command, which is a better way to transfer

TIP

Passive FTP and Other Settings

As mentioned earlier, if you are having problems connecting to the server when using FTP (you receive a message from Dreamweaver), you might want to enable the Use Passive FTP check box on the Advanced tab of the Site Definition dialog box. This often solves transfer problems, especially when you are transferring files from behind a firewall.

You can also click the Firewall Settings button from the Advanced tab of the Site Definition dialog box to quickly jump to the application's Site Preferences, or click the Server Compatibility button to enable options that may help Dreamweaver talk to nonstandard FTP servers.

files. The Synchronize command detects whether a local file (or remote file) is newer and transfers it only if necessary, thus saving transfer time.

FIGURE 22.7
The buttons at the top of the Files panel help you transfer files between the local and remote sites.

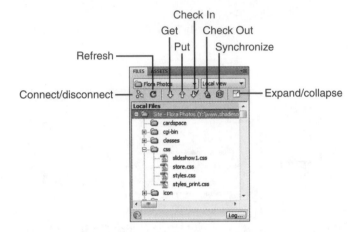

The buttons at the top of the Files panel are as detailed here:

> ▶ **Connect/Disconnect**—This button establishes a connection to an FTP server. The button has a little green light that stays lit when you have a connection to an FTP server. The light remains constantly lit when you have LAN access to your remote site.

> ▶ **Refresh**—This button manually refreshes the list of files in the Files panel.

> ▶ **Get**—This button retrieves files from the remote site and moves them to your local site.

> ▶ **Put**—This button places files from your local site onto the remote site.

> ▶ **Check In**—This button places files from your local site onto the remote site and marks them as "checked in" and accessible for other developers to edit.

> ▶ **Check Out**—This button retrieves files from the remote site, moves them to your local site, and marks them as "checked out" so that other Dreamweaver users can't modify them.

> ▶ **Synchronize**—This button triggers the Synchronize command that enables you to check which files are new and have to be uploaded to the remote site.

> ▶ **Expand/Collapse**—This button expands the Files panel into the Expanded Files panel.

Click the Expand/Collapse button on the far right of the Files panel to expand the panel, as shown in Figure 22.8. The expanded Files panel not only shows the local site, as does the collapsed Files panel, but also shows the remote site. A list of the files on the remote site appears when you are connected. When you want to collapse the expanded Files panel, click the Expand/Collapse button again.

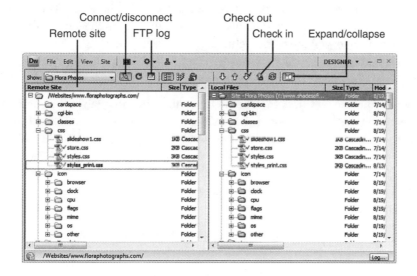

FIGURE 22.8
Use the Expand/Collapse button to expand the Files panel.

Understanding Dreamweaver's Website Management Capabilities

Dreamweaver's file management system is useful if you are creating web pages with other people. You use the Check In/Check Out tools in Dreamweaver to make sure that only one person is working on a file at a time. When you have a file checked out, no one else can check out that file until you check it in, just like when you have a DVD or video checked out from the video store. Dreamweaver marks the file as checked out by you so that your collaborators know who to bug if they also want to make changes to the file!

When you check out a file from the remote site, Dreamweaver retrieves a copy of that file from the remote server to ensure that you have the most up-to-date version of the file in your local site. When Dreamweaver gets the file, it overwrites the file that exists on your local drive. The checked-out file appears to Dreamweaver users with your name beside it on the remote server, signaling to your collaborators that you have the file checked out.

The file has a green check mark beside it in your local site, showing that you currently have that file checked out.

Enabling Check In/Check Out

After you define the remote site in the Site Definition Wizard and click Next, Dreamweaver asks whether you want to enable Check In/Check Out. Because you overwrite files when you transfer them from the local site to the remote site, you must be careful. You can use Check In/Check Out functionality so that you do not overwrite files that others have recently edited and uploaded to the remote site.

When you turn on Check In/Check Out on the Advanced tab of the Site Definition dialog box, options that enable you to configure this feature appear, as shown in Figure 22.9. Choose whether you want to check out a file (one not currently checked out, that is) when you open a file in your local site. I suggest that you choose to view the file as a read-only copy because then you can look at it without checking it out; if you want to edit the file, you can quickly check it out.

FIGURE 22.9
Enable Check In/Check Out so that you can control collaboration with others.

Enter a name and an email address so that others accessing the remote site can see who has the file checked out. They'll be able to click your name and send you an email message about the file you have checked out.

Transferring Files

When you check in a file to the remote site, Dreamweaver transfers the file back to the remote server to make it available for others to work on or view. Your name no longer appears beside the file's name.

Check In/Check Out is designed to help you manage a collaborative environment. The Check Out procedure forces you to download the most recent version of the file. While you have the file checked out, others cannot work on it. You can open the file after you check it in, but you cannot save any changes because Dreamweaver marks it as read-only.

Dreamweaver enables you to circumvent some of the Check In/Check Out safeguards. You can, for instance, override somebody else's checked-out file and check it out yourself. You can also turn off the read-only attribute of a file and edit it without checking it out. However, why would you want to do any of these things? Dreamweaver's Check In/Check Out process is fine for a small environment where you don't expect mischief. If you need tighter security and version control, you need to turn to Subversion, the version control system supported by Dreamweaver CS4.

You can still use Get and Put when you have Check In/Check Out enabled. The Get command moves a file from the remote server and overwrites the local file. The file is read-only on your local machine because you won't have it checked out. If you try to put a file that someone has checked out onto the remote server, Dreamweaver warns you that changes to the remote copy of the file might be lost if you go ahead and transfer the file. You can choose to do the action anyway or cancel it.

To get or put files, first make sure that you select the correct site in the Site drop-down menu of the Files panel or the Site window. If you access your site via FTP, click the Connect button. If you have already connected or are accessing the files on a LAN, skip this step.

TIP

The Synchronize Command

To get only the files that are more recent than the files on the local site onto the remote site, you use the Synchronize command, which we discuss in Hour 23.

NOTE

Dreamweaver's Locking Mechanism

Dreamweaver creates a file on the remote server with the .lck (for *lock*) file extension. This file contains the name of the person who has checked out the file. You don't need to worry about creating these .lck files, but I mention them because you might get questions about these files from others who examine the remote site without Dreamweaver.

TIP

Don't Leave Without Checking Your Files In!

Remember to check in files when you are finished with them! Don't go on vacation with a bunch of files checked out if you want your co-workers to happily welcome you back when you return.

TIP

Everyone on the Team Needs to Use Check In/Check Out

Your project works more smoothly if everyone collaborating on the project turns on the Check In/Check Out functionality for the site. Otherwise, it's too easy to overwrite a file that someone else updated. Check In/Check Out works only if everyone on the team uses Dreamweaver and enables the Check In/Check Out functionality.

▼ TRY IT YOURSELF

Getting or Checking Out Files

To get or check out files, follow these steps:

1. Select the files you want to transfer to your local site. You can also select an entire folder to transfer all of its contents.

2. Click the Get command, or click the Check Out command if you have Check In/Check Out enabled for this site.

3. Dreamweaver might display a dialog box, asking whether you would also like to download dependent files. **Dependent files** are images and other assets that are linked to the files you are transferring. You can disable this dialog box by checking the Don't Ask Me Again check box. I prefer to transfer the asset files manually instead of having Dreamweaver transfer them automatically.

TIP

Don't Transfer Dependent Files Multiple Times

Continually getting and putting dependent files slows down your transfers. Image files are usually much larger than HTML files and take longer to transfer. If the files haven't changed, you don't need to transfer them.

TIP

Dreamweaver and Content Management

Check In and Check Out are tools that were created for website developers. After a website is launched, maintaining the content is a task better suited for Adobe Contribute or Adobe's InContext Editing system. You can find out more about these systems in Hour 15, "Creating Library Items and Templates."

TRY IT YOURSELF   ▼

Putting or Checking In Files

To put or check in files, follow these steps:

1. Select the files you want to transfer to the remote site.

2. Click the Put command, or click the Check In command if you have Check In/Check Out enabled for this site. If you transfer a file that is currently open, Dreamweaver prompts you to save the file before you put it on the remote site.

3. Dreamweaver might display a dialog box, asking whether you would also like to upload dependent files. You can disable this dialog box by checking the Don't Ask Me Again check box.

Importing an Existing Website

When a website already exists at a remote site, you have to define the website in Dreamweaver, connect to the remote site, and download all the files in the site to work on it. Remember, you can edit only files that are located on your own machine. You can download and edit an existing site even if Dreamweaver wasn't involved in the site's creation.

Downloading a site for the first time might take some time, depending on how you are accessing the site and what your network connection speed is. After you initially download all the files, however, you should need only to download any files that change.

To import an existing website, all you have to do is mirror the existing site on your local drive. There is no conversion process, and the files remain unchanged in Dreamweaver.

To import an existing website, follow these steps:

1. Set up both your local and remote info in the Site Definition dialog box. You should use a local directory that is empty.

2. Connect to the remote site using the Connect/Disconnect button in the Files panel.

3. Select the top entry in the remote site of the Files panel, selecting the entire site. If you select a file instead, you get only that file and not the entire site.

4. Click the Get button to transfer all the files on the remote site to your local site. You are asked whether or not you are sure you want to get the entire site. Answer "Yes," and the transfer completes.

TRY IT YOURSELF ▼

Importing an Existing Website

You can also import and export a site definition, either to share with others or to back up your site definition. To do this, select Export from the Manage Sites dialog box (Site, Manage Sites). You can choose to either back up your site definition (saving your login, password, and local path information), or share the site definition with other users (without the personal information). Dreamweaver saves the file with the .ste extension. Select the Import command from the Manage Sites dialog box to import the site definition contained in the .ste file.

Subversion Version Control

In my mind, one of the most exciting new features of Dreamweaver CS4 is the integration of the Subversion version control system into the application. Subversion is true version control in that it enables multiple users to work on a project, make changes, and safely combine those changes back together. It can also revert files to previous versions and display a full history of what has changed in a file over time. Unfortunately, Subversion is also a very complicated topic that requires a Subversion server, so we can only touch on the basics here.

Understanding Subversion

Subversion works based on the idea that there is a central source code repository that all developers tie into. This repository exists on the Subversion server and is *not* located on your web server. Each developer downloads his or her own copy of the source code from the repository, called a *working copy*—this is your local copy of the site. As you make changes to the working copy, you *commit* them back to the Subversion repository, noting what has changed. Your fellow developers do the same. This builds a central location with all the latest changes and a full history of what everyone has done. You can easily retrieve and integrate your collaborators' changes into your own working copy automatically.

When you have a *working copy* that is ready for production, you transfer it to the remote server, just as you normally would.

Subversion is a unique system in that it allows developers to work on the same files at the same time, then attempts to combine the changes in a meaningful way when they are committed back to the Subversion repository. If this doesn't work for your group, you can even use a more traditional "check-in/check-out" method to prevent other users from making changes to files in the central repository. Unlike in Dreamweaver, you can't just override these settings because they're controlled by a central server.

Getting Started with Subversion

To get started with Subversion, you first need to establish a Subversion server and a repository for the project you are working on. You may want to check out "beanstalk"—which offers a free Subversion repository and a simple interface for setting it up: http://beanstalkapp.com/. Another option is Dreamhost.com, which provides Dreamweaver CS4 compatible hosting and Subversion support for a reasonable monthly price.

After your server and repository are established, you need to open the Version Control category within the Advanced site settings, as shown in Figure 22.10.

FIGURE 22.10
Configure the Subversion repository for a project.

You need to check with your Subversion provider for all the correct protocol and path settings—these can vary greatly between implementations. After you have the information you need entered, click Test to verify that the repository can be found.

Subversion Tools

After you've connected to your repository, you'll notice some visual changes take place in the Files local files view. First, a Repository button becomes active. This button, when clicked, shows all the files in the central Subversion repository, as shown in Figure 22.11. You can select the files to move into your working copy, then use Get, Put, Check In, and Check Out to work with the files just as you would on any other server.

FIGURE 22.11
Use the Repository button to show the files in the central repository, and then interact with the files just as you would with another remote server.

Repository view

Repository files

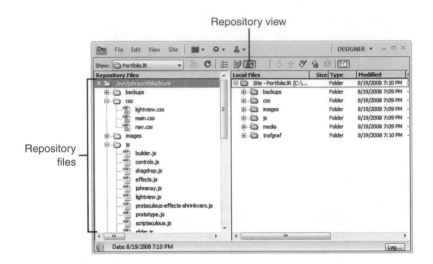

As you make changes to the files locally, you'll see symbols superimposed over the file icons in the Files panel. A plus symbol indicates that a new local file has been detected and should be transferred to the Subversion repository. A check mark shows that you've changed the file locally and need to commit it to the repository.

To send (commit) a file (or files) to the repository, just select it in the File panel, make sure the repository is also selected, and then click the Put button. You are prompted for a comment to post along with the files—this is tracked in the revision history.

To view the revision history, just right-click in the local files pane of the Files panel and choose Version Control, Show Revisions from the context menu. The revision history is shown in Figure 22.12. From this window you can even select a previous revision of your source code and click the Promote to Current button to revert to the state of the project at that time.

As you can see, Subversion is a powerful tool that any development team can take advantage of.

TIP

Version Control for Free!

Because the Subversion software itself is free (http://subversion.tigris.org/), there's nothing preventing even the smallest shops from using the technology. For a full picture of the software's capabilities, I urge you to read through the free online Subversion book at http://svnbook.red-bean.com/.

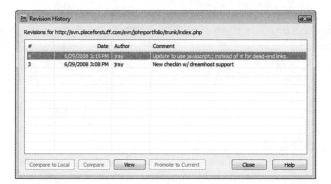

FIGURE 22.12
View all the changes in your site.

Summary

In this hour, you learned how to connect to a remote site and transfer files. You learned how to use the Advanced tab of the Site Definition dialog box and how to set up FTP, local/network, Visual SourceSafe, and WebDAV connections. You also learned how to use Dreamweaver's internal file conflict control feature, Check In/Check Out. You also learned about Subversion and how it can create a more managed and distributed development environment.

Q&A

Q. When is it appropriate to use Check In/Check Out?

A. There are two major uses for Check In/Check Out: for working in a small group and for working on a site from two computers. Check In/Check Out isn't designed for use by enterprise-type projects (those with many developers), but it is perfect for a small group of developers working on the same sites. I use it all the time when I work on a site with two computers (home and work computers, for instance). It helps me know whether I have uploaded my changes.

Q. Do you use the Site Definition Wizard or the Advanced tab of the Side Definition dialog box to define websites in Dreamweaver?

A. I usually define a site initially by using the wizard because it's fast, but I often tweak the site definition by using the Advanced tab.

Q. One of my co-workers left for a two-week vacation with a bunch of files checked out in his name. How can I work on these files while he is gone?

A. When you attempt to check out the files, Dreamweaver warns you that someone else has them checked out. It then asks you to override your co-worker's checkout. If you click the Yes button, Dreamweaver checks the files out to you. Just hope that your co-worker hasn't made any changes to the files and forgotten to move them onto the remote site.

Workshop

Quiz

1. When you're working in a collaborative environment and using FTP, it doesn't matter if everyone is using Dreamweaver's Check In/Check Out functionality. True or false?

2. Why do you have to define a remote site for a website?

3. What is Dreamweaver's most useful tool for troubleshooting a connection to a remote site via FTP?

4. What version control system does Dreamweaver fully support?

Quiz Answers

1. False. It's too easy for one member of your group to overwrite the work of another member if not everyone is using the Check In/Check Out functionality. The only time you don't need to use this functionality when working with a group is when you are using a third-party program to manage version control.

2. To put website files on a public server or share files with a group, you have to define a remote site in Dreamweaver.

3. Dreamweaver's most useful tool in this situation is the FTP log. The FTP Log tab in the Results panel enables you to read the error messages sent back by the server. Alternatively, you can select the View Site FTP Log button in the Expanded Files panel.

4. Dreamweaver supports Subversion as its primary version control system. Although WebDAV and Visual SourceSafe are offered as options for remote servers, they are used only as file storage.

Exercises

1. Define a remote site connection, using either the FTP setting or the Local/Network setting. If you don't have access to a remote computer, create a directory on your hard drive and name it **remote**. Pretend that this is a directory on a LAN and define it as a remote site. Try transferring files back and forth between the local and remote sites.

2. Turn on Check In/Check Out functionality for a defined site and connect to the remote site. What changes in Dreamweaver?

Maintaining a Website

Dreamweaver has various useful commands that can help you make sitewide changes. In this hour, you use commands that are very powerful and can save you time. You should be careful when changing items sitewide in case you make a mistake. But, of course, you could just fix such a mistake sitewide, too!

Managing the Local and Remote Sites

Let's get started by exploring the features for managing the site files that are stored on your computer (local), as well as the files on your web server (remote).

The commands that you apply to an entire site (such as the commands to transfer files) are available from the menus in the expanded Files panel. The expanded Files panel showing both the local and the remote sites has File, Edit, View, and Site menus. These same menus and commands are available from the Files panel menu, shown in Figure 23.1.

Synchronizing Your Files on the Local and Remote Sites

Synchronizing your files on the local and remote sites ensures that you have the most up-to-date files in both places. Dreamweaver has three commands that are useful in determining which site has the newer files: Select Newer Local, Select Newer Remote, and Synchronize.

If you want to check whether new files reside on the local site or the remote site, use the Select Newer Local and Select Newer Remote commands, respectively, from the Edit menu in the Files panel.

WHAT YOU'LL LEARN IN THIS HOUR:

▶ How to synchronize files on local and remote sites

▶ How to manage links

▶ How to add design notes to document your project and share ideas with others

▶ How to generate reports about a website

▶ How to track site usage statistics with Google Analytics

FIGURE 23.1
The Files panel menu gives you access to the same menus available when you expand the Files panel.

Files panel menu

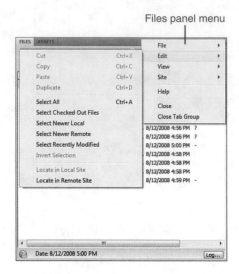

▼ TRY IT YOURSELF

Finding Updated Files on a Remote Server

To see which files are newer on the remote site, follow these steps:

1. Connect to the remote site by clicking the Connect button at the top of the Files panel (F8) if you are using FTP to access the remote site.

2. Select either the root directory or a section of files in the local site.

3. Select Edit, Select Newer Remote from the Edit menu.

Dreamweaver searches the files on the remote site to see whether any are newer than the same files on the local site. It then selects all the files that are newer on the remote site. If files that don't exist on the local site exist on the remote site, Dreamweaver selects those, too. With all the files selected, you simply get the files from the remote site to update your local files. To select files that are newer on the local site, you follow the same steps, except you use the Select Newer Local command in step 3.

You select the Synchronize command to automatically synchronize files between the local and the remote sites, bringing both sites up to date with the most recent files. When you synchronize files, Dreamweaver analyzes the files on both the local and the remote sites and gives you a report on which files it has to copy to synchronize the sites. You have total control over the process and can deselect any files you do not want transferred. Dreamweaver also tells you whether files are completely up to date and whether there is a need to synchronize.

To use the Synchronize command, you must have synchronization enabled in the site definition. Make sure that you checked the Maintain Synchronization Information check box in the Remote Info category of the Site Definition dialog box, as shown in Figure 23.2.

Remote info category

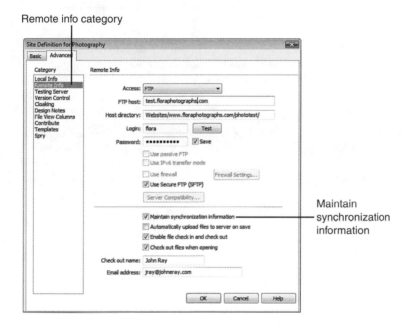

Maintain synchronization information

FIGURE 23.2
The Maintain Synchronization Information check box turns on synchronization functionality for the site.

TRY IT YOURSELF ▼

Synchronizing Local and Remote Files

To synchronize the files in the local and remote sites, follow these steps:

1. Make sure that the site you want to synchronize is open in the Files panel. Select a different site from the Site drop-down menu if necessary.

2. If you want to synchronize only certain files or folders, select those files or folders.

3. Select Site, Synchronize from the Site menu. The Synchronize Files dialog box appears, as shown in Figure 23.3.

4. In the Synchronize drop-down menu, choose to synchronize the entire site or only the files you have selected.

5. Select how you want to transfer the files in the Direction drop-down menu. You can transfer the newer files to the remote site, get the newer files from the remote site, or get and put newer files in both directions.

▼ TRY IT YOURSELF

Synchronizing Local and Remote Files

continued

TIP

Synchronize When Collaborating

Because I often collaborate with groups of people on websites, I am usually interested in which files are newer on the remote site. Others on the team might have changed files and uploaded them while I was doing something else. I like to make sure that I'm looking at the most recent files in the project by synchronizing to get the newer files from the remote site.

FIGURE 23.4
The Synchronize dialog box lists the files to synchronize.

FIGURE 23.3
The Synchronize Files dialog box enables you to select which files to synchronize.

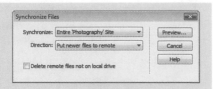

6. Check the Delete Local Files Not on Remote Server check box if you want to get rid of any extraneous local files or the Delete Remote Files Not on Local Drive check box if there are extraneous files in the remote site. Careful! Someone else might have recently uploaded the files to the site.

7. Click the Preview button. If your files are up to date, you get a message saying no synchronization is necessary and asking whether you want to view a list of files to synchronize manually. Dreamweaver displays the Synchronize dialog box, shown in Figure 23.4, if files require synchronization. The Synchronize dialog box lists all the files that must be transferred for the local and remote sites to be in sync.

8. When you are ready to transfer the files, click OK.

Caution —
"skipping" files
will break connections.

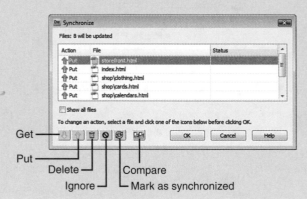

Get — Put — Delete — Ignore — Compare — Mark as synchronized

CAUTION

Delete Files Carefully

Be very careful about checking the Delete Local Files Not on Remote Server check box because you don't want to delete files you need later. When you select this check box, you are deleting the files from your hard drive. If the files do not exist anywhere else, you can't restore them. Checking this box is a quick way to clean your local site of files that are not used.

Several buttons at the bottom of the Synchronize dialog box enable you to modify the list of files to transfer. The following buttons help you fine-tune the synchronization process:

- ▶ **Get**—This command marks the file to be downloaded from the remote site to the local site.

- ▶ **Put**—This command marks the file to be uploaded from the local site to the remote site.

- ▶ **Delete**—This command marks the file to be deleted.

- ▶ **Ignore**—This command marks the file to be ignored by the synchronization process.

- ▶ **Mark as Synchronized**—This command marks the file as already synchronized.

- ▶ **Compare**—This command opens the file in a file comparison utility. You specify a file comparison software program in the File Compare category of Preferences (Edit, Preferences).

While updating and editing files on a live website, you will probably use the Synchronize command many times. It's a quick and mechanical method of deciding which files have been updated and, therefore, you have to upload to the server. When you are collaborating with others, the Synchronize command is useful for helping you decide which files have been updated on the server and have to be updated on your local site. This saves you the trouble of downloading the entire site when only a few files have been updated.

Managing Your Links

Dreamweaver automatically updates links when you move or rename a file within the current website. When you define the website, make sure that you create a cache to speed up the update process. The cache is on by default, and it's best that you do not turn it off in your site definition. When you move or rename web pages, Dreamweaver displays the Update Files dialog box. As shown in Figure 23.5, the dialog box displays a list of linked files. Click the Update button to update all the links or select individual files to update.

FIGURE 23.5
When you move or rename web
pages, the Update Files dialog box
appears, allowing you to update all
the links to that file.

FIGURE 23.5
When you move or rename web
pages, the Update Files dialog box
appears, allowing you to update all
the links to that file.

Use the Change Link Sitewide command to change the URL of a certain
link throughout the site. For instance, if you displayed a link in your site for
each day's menu in the cafeteria, you would need to change the link to a
new web page every day. On Tuesday morning, you could select the Monday web page and then select Site, Change Link Sitewide. The Change Link
Sitewide dialog box, shown in Figure 23.6, enables you to enter the old link
and then select the path for the new link.

FIGURE 23.6
Use the Change Link Sitewide command to change all the links to a
certain web page.

You can use the Link Checker, shown in Figure 23.7, to check all the links in
your site. To open the Link Checker, select Site, Check Links Sitewide from
the Files panel. The Link Checker displays three categories: broken links,
external links, and orphaned files. **External links** are links that
Dreamweaver cannot check. **Orphaned files** are those that do not have any
files linking to them.

FIGURE 23.7
The Link Checker displays broken
links, external links, and orphaned
files.

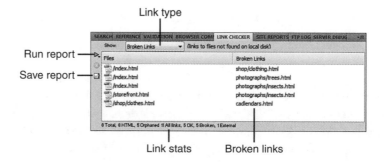

Broken links need to be fixed. Fortunately, Dreamweaver makes that easy.
You just select the broken link displayed in the Results panel group, click
the Browse icon, and navigate to the correct file to fix the link.

The Link Checker opens in the Results panel group, located directly below the Property inspector. You can hide the panel group by clicking the arrow to the left of the panel title (Results), or you can close the panel group by selecting the Close Panel Group command from the panel menu, the menu in the upper-right corner of the panel.

Adding Design Notes to Pages

Design notes enable you to add notes to your web pages. You can use design notes to document your design process, share information with others, and keep any extra information that would be useful. Because design notes are not actually part of the web page, you can use them to record sensitive information you might not want people who view the web page to be able to read.

You can add a design note to any file in a website, including templates, images, and movies. You might want to add a design note to each image to list the name and location of the original image file. To add design notes to files in your site, you must enable design notes in the Design Notes category of the Site Definition dialog box, as shown in Figure 23.8. Edit the site definition by double-clicking the site name in the Site drop-down menu of the Files panel.

Maintain Design Notes

FIGURE 23.8
Enable design notes in the Design Notes category of the Site Definition dialog box.

Adding a Design Note to a File

To attach a design note to a file, follow these steps:

1. When a file is open in the Document window, select File, Design Notes. Alternatively, you can right-click a file in the Files panel and select the Design Notes command.

2. The Design Notes dialog box appears, as shown in Figure 23.9. Select the type of design note you want from the Status drop-down menu.

FIGURE 23.9
You select the type of design note you want from the Status drop-down menu.

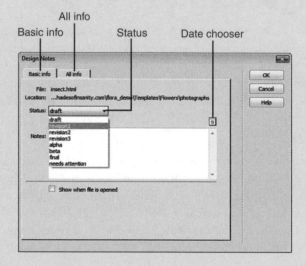

3. Click the Date icon to insert today's date in the Notes field. Type a note in the field after the date.

4. Check the Show When File Is Opened check box if you want this design note to appear the next time someone opens the file.

5. Select the All Info tab in the Design Notes dialog box to see a list of the information in the current design note, as shown in Figure 23.10. Add a record to the list by clicking the + button, entering a name, and entering a value.

6. When you are done making changes in this dialog box, click OK.

TIP

Record the Author

When you are in a collaborative environment, a useful name and value data pair to add to a design note is the name of the author of the note. To do this, you select the All Info tab in the Design Notes dialog box and click the + button. Name your new record **Name** and enter your name in the Value field.

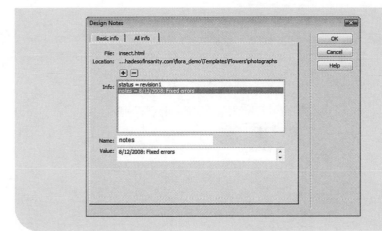

FIGURE 23.10
You can add data to design notes
by selecting the All Info tab.

A design note remains associated with a file even if it is copied, renamed, moved, or deleted. Dreamweaver saves your design notes in a directory called notes in your site root. This directory doesn't appear in the Site window. Notes are saved with the name of the file plus the .mno extension.

Generating Reports About a Website

The reports that come with Dreamweaver enable you to compile information about your site, such as when files were created or what errors you've found in your site. These reports are useful for examining, troubleshooting, and documenting your website. You can also save and print the results of the reports. The following reports are available in Dreamweaver:

- ▶ Checked Out By
- ▶ Design Notes
- ▶ Recently Modified
- ▶ Combinable Nested Font Tags
- ▶ Accessibility
- ▶ Missing Alt Text
- ▶ Redundant Nested Tags
- ▶ Removable Empty Tags
- ▶ Untitled Documents

CAUTION

Contribute Uses Design Notes

Adobe Contribute, a companion product to Dreamweaver, uses design notes to facilitate tracking revisions to a file. If you are working in an environment where some users are using Contribute, don't delete or modify any of the design notes Contribute has created.

Running a Website Report

FIGURE 23.11
Many reports are available to give you information about either your current document or an entire site.

To run a report, follow these steps:

1. Select Site, Reports (in either the Files panel or the menu bar). The Reports dialog box appears, as shown in Figure 23.11.

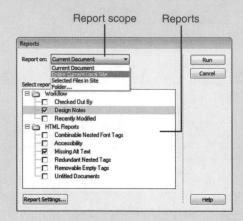

Report scope   Reports

2. Select what you want to report on (the current document, the current site, the selected files, or a particular folder).

3. Select one or more of the reports. Some reports have additional settings you can make to refine the search. If the Report Settings button is active at the bottom of the dialog box, additional settings are available for that report.

4. Click the Run button to run the report.

5. A Results panel group appears with a list of files. You can save this report as well as open the individual files that it references.

Generating Website Statistics with Google Analytics

After you've created your site and uploaded it to a production server, you probably want to start tracking your visitors. Dreamweaver provides plenty of reporting options, but none of them can tell you who is visiting your site, where they're located, or which pages are the most popular. To get information like this, you need to use a web statistics package. Web statistics packages often rely on special software that reads web server log files from the server. One of the best statistics options, however, is Google Analytics, a powerful analysis package that doesn't require any additional software to be installed on your server.

Google Analytics, pictured in Figure 23.12, works anywhere, on any website that you create. All you need to do is set up a free Google Analytics account and insert a small piece of code into your web pages.

FIGURE 23.12
Google Analytics provides free enterprise-grade statistics without requiring any additional software.

To get started with Google Analytics, set up your free account at https://www.google.com/analytics/. After you've activated the Google Analytics service on your account, add a new website profile to the account, as shown in Figure 23.13. A website profile uniquely identifies your site by its domain. Enter your domain name, and then click Finish to create the profile.

Google Analytics provides you with Tracking Code, as shown in Figure 23.14. The tracking code is a simple piece of JavaScript that must be inserted into the <head> content of your page so that Google can start collecting statistics for your site. If you're using templates, simply insert this into your template's <head></head> tags to quickly propagate the changes to your entire site. Alternatively, you can use Dreamweaver's find and replace feature (Edit, Find and Replace) to search for the <head> tag, and then replace it with <head> plus the tracking code.

CAUTION

Don't Share Tracking Code!

Tracking code is unique for each web profile you create. If you share tracking code between sites, their statistics are combined! Always remember to create a new profile and use the custom tracking code for each website you're publishing.

FIGURE 23.13
Create a new profile for each site
you want to track.

Profiles should be unique for each domain.

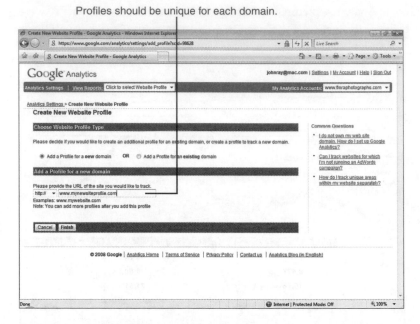

FIGURE 23.14
Google's Tracking Code is inserted
into each page in your site and
communicates traffic statistics
back to Google's servers.

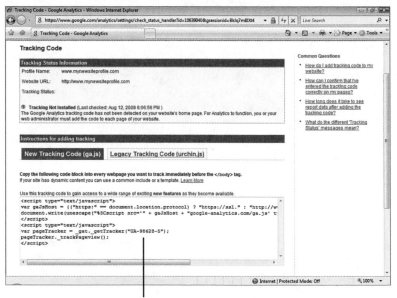

Tracking code

After the tracking code is installed, Google immediately starts collecting data as visitors view your website. Reports become available within a few hours of the first data coming in. Google's reports range from simple graphs of how many visitors you're receiving in a given day to maps of the world that highlight specific regions and cities where your visitors are located. Google is continually refining the reports to provide new features and an improved interface.

By monitoring how your site is used, you can identify which portions of your site are popular and which aren't. This gives you an opportunity to improve or remove sections of the site and focus your attention on the content your viewers want.

Summary

In this hour, you learned how to synchronize files between local and remote sites and how to manage links in a website. You also learned how to create site maps that visually represent the relationship between the files in a website. You learned how to add design notes to capture extra information about files in a website and how to run reports on a website. These skills are important when you need to manage websites and all the files they contain.

Q&A

Q. Am I really going to goof up my files if I use the Synchronize command?

A. Using Synchronize can be a little scary. You might want to run the Select Newer Local and the Select Newer Remote commands first. Jot down the filenames that Dreamweaver selects. Then, when you run Synchronize, check to see whether that command comes up with the same filenames. This should reassure you that you can confidently use the Synchronize command in the future!

Q. Why does Dreamweaver list some of my files as orphaned files when they really aren't?

A. Dreamweaver checks whether files link to other files. However, behaviors might use the files that Dreamweaver lists as orphaned. For instance, you might have a web page loaded with the Open Browser Window behavior. Because the file is not actually linked to another file, Dreamweaver shows it as orphaned.

Workshop

Quiz

1. How can you tell which images in your entire site are missing alt text?

2. Dreamweaver can attach a design note to any file in a website, whether it's a web page or another type of file. True or false?

3. What software do you need to purchase to use Google Analytics?

Quiz Answers

1. Run the Missing Alt Text report on the entire site.

2. True. Dreamweaver can attach a design note to any file in a website.

3. None. Google Analytics is provided free and runs on Google's servers.

Exercises

1. Create a website profile in Google Analytics and attach the tracking code to your website. Monitor the statistics for a few days and try to identify trends in your visitor traffic. What pages are the most popular? Where are most of your visitors located?

2. Run the Link Checker on a site you created or imported. Do you have any broken links? If so, fix them. Do you have any orphaned files? If you no longer need those files, delete them. If your site has external links, you should periodically check to verify that they are still valid.

Customizing Dreamweaver

Developers skilled in JavaScript create Dreamweaver behaviors, objects, and commands—extra functionality for Dreamweaver—that you can download free from the Web. Adobe provides a site—the Adobe Exchange (http://www.adobe.com/exchange)—that collects these extensions. From that site, you can download extensions for not only Dreamweaver but also Flash, Fireworks, ColdFusion, and other Adobe products. When Dreamweaver doesn't seem to have a behavior, an object, or a command for what you are trying to accomplish in your web page, search Adobe Exchange and you might find just what you need.

There are also ways you can customize Dreamweaver yourself by creating reusable objects stored within Dreamweaver for easy access. In this hour, you explore creating snippets and custom commands to help speed up the creation of web pages. In addition, you learn how to save searches to reuse or share with others.

Creating a Custom Snippet

Snippets are bits of code that are available from Dreamweaver's Snippets panel. You can use any of the multiple snippets available when you install Dreamweaver. You can also create custom snippets from code you use repetitively. This can speed up development of web pages as well as maintain consistency in your code.

First, let's explore the existing snippets available in Dreamweaver. Some of these snippets might not interest you, but some might speed up your daily work in Dreamweaver. The lower half of the Snippets panel (Window, Snippets) displays categories of snippets along with descriptions of what the snippets do (you might have to enlarge the Snippets panel to see the

---

WHAT YOU'LL LEARN IN THIS HOUR:

- ► How to create and organize Dreamweaver snippets and custom snippets
- ► How to record custom commands and save history steps as commands
- ► How to use the Extension Manager to install third-party extensions to Dreamweaver
- ► How to modify Dreamweaver's keyboard shortcuts
- ► How to add your favorite objects to the Favorites category of the Insert panel
- ► How to use and save Dreamweaver searches

descriptions). The upper portion of the Snippets panel gives you a preview of the selected snippet. The default Snippets panel, shown in Figure 24.1, has the following categories:

FIGURE 24.1
The Snippets panel has several snippet categories and displays a preview of the selected snippet.

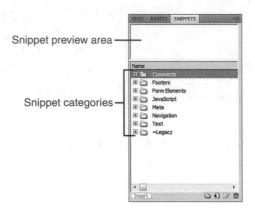

Snippet preview area

Snippet categories

- ▶ Comments
- ▶ Footers
- ▶ Form Elements
- ▶ JavaScript
- ▶ Meta
- ▶ Navigation
- ▶ Text
- ▶ ~Legacy

TIP
Shortcuts for Snippets

You can create keyboard short-cuts so that you can insert your favorite snippets into a web page with just a couple of key-strokes. You learn how to add keyboard shortcuts to Dreamweaver and how to modify the existing shortcuts in the "Editing the Keyboard Shortcuts" section, later in this chapter.

CAUTION
Don't Use the Legacy Snippets

The ~Legacy snippet folder con-tains snippets that use depre-cated code—basically, code that uses tags that are no longer part of HTML standard tags and that may stop working in future browser releases. You should avoid using these snippets.

You can create a new snippet out of an object or some code you use often. You can create a new snippet within an existing category, or you can create a new folder for your own personal snippets. To create a new snippet folder to hold your custom snippets, click the New Snippet Folder button (see Figure 24.2). Give your new folder a name. Now you can store new snip-pets in this folder or move existing snippets into the folder for easy access.

Click the New Snippet button (refer to Figure 24.2) at the bottom of the Snippets panel to begin creating a snippet of code. In the Snippet dialog box that appears, as shown in Figure 24.3, you enter a name and a descrip-tion for the snippet. You can select either the Wrap Selection radio button or the Insert Block radio button. The Wrap Selection setting divides the dialog box into two halves; this setting causes the insertion of the top half before the current selection, and the insertion of the bottom half after the current selection. The Insert Block setting inserts the snippet as a block of code instead of wrapping it around other objects.

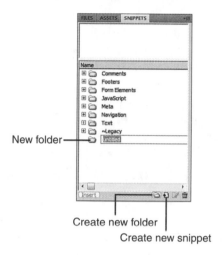

New folder

Create new folder

Create new snippet

FIGURE 24.2
You can create a new snippet folder and new snippets in the Snippets panel.

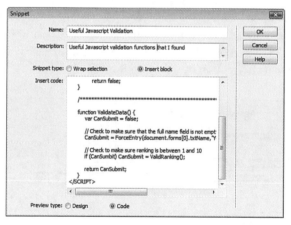

FIGURE 24.3
You can create a new snippet that either inserts a block of code (as shown) or wraps code around the current selection.

When you're using the Insert Block option, your snippet content goes into the Insert Code text box. The easiest way to insert code into a snippet is to create the code in Dreamweaver first, in either Design or Code view. When you select the New Snippet command with the code selected, Dreamweaver automatically places the code into the Insert Code text box. You can select how you want the snippet preview to appear in the Snippets panel by selecting either the Design radio button, which presents the snippet preview in Design view, or the Code radio button, which presents the

TIP

My Favorite Snippet

I use several snippets on a semi-frequent basis, but the snippet I use most is the Text Field, Autoclear snippet from the Form Elements category. This snippet adds a text field with a default initial value that is automatically cleared when the user clicks in the field. This is nice because you can enter an initial value in the field to give users some guidance as to what to put there, but they don't have to take the extra step to delete that text when they are filling in the form.

snippet preview in Code view. These radio buttons are located at the bottom of the Snippet dialog box.

If you select the Wrap Selection radio button when creating a snippet, you must enter code into two text boxes: Insert Before and Insert After. When you apply the snippet to an object on the page, Dreamweaver adds the code in the Insert Before text box before the object code, and adds the code in the Insert After text box after the object code. You need to create this type of snippet to package an object within the code you create in the snippet. For instance, if you want an object to be within a hyperlink, you have to add tags before and after the object, and you have to create a snippet with Wrap Selection selected to get the Insert Before and Insert After text boxes.

Editing the Keyboard Shortcuts

You can edit all the keyboard shortcuts in Dreamweaver by using the Keyboard Shortcuts dialog box, shown in Figure 24.4, which you can open by selecting Edit, Keyboard Shortcuts. Instead of modifying the existing set of keyboard shortcuts, you should create your own set. Drop down the Current Set drop-down menu to see the existing keyboard shortcut sets: Dreamweaver Standard, BBEdit, Dreamweaver MX 2004, and HomeSite. If you are used to the keyboard shortcuts of any of these other web editors, you can use that shortcut set by selecting it in this menu.

FIGURE 24.4
You can edit and access keyboard shortcut sets in the Keyboard Shortcuts dialog box.

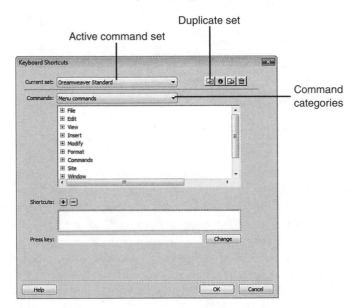

You cannot modify the Adobe Standard keyboard shortcut set because you might need to revert to it later. Instead, you need to create your own version of that keyboard shortcut set by duplicating it; you do this by clicking the Duplicate Set button. Give your new set a name and select it in the Current Set drop-down menu. Then you are ready to customize any of the keyboard shortcuts you want.

While editing keyboard shortcuts, you select commands from several categories in the Commands drop-down menu: Menu Commands, Files Panel options menu, Site Panel, Code Editing, Document Editing, Site Window, and Snippets. Select one of the categories and then select a command from the list. If the command already has a keyboard shortcut, it shows up in the Shortcuts list at the bottom of the dialog box. You can either modify the existing keyboard shortcut for that command or add a shortcut by clicking the + button.

To add or edit a keyboard shortcut, place the cursor in the Press Key text box at the bottom of the dialog box and press the key combination you want to use for the keyboard shortcut on your keyboard. The Press Key text box records the keystrokes. If that shortcut already exists for another command, you see an error message, as shown in Figure 24.5. You should press different keys until you come up with a unique keyboard shortcut for the command. Click the Change button to apply the shortcut to the command.

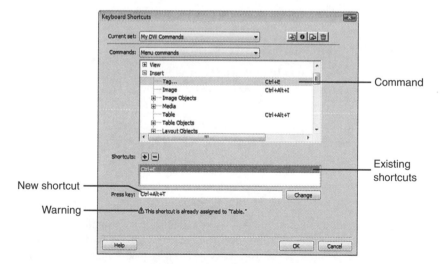

FIGURE 24.5
Press the keys on your keyboard to record a keyboard shortcut for a command.

Command

New shortcut

Warning

Existing shortcuts

Click OK to save your custom keyboard shortcuts. Be sure to test the shortcuts to ensure that they work the way you want them to. You can always

TIP
Print a List of Your Keyboard Shortcuts

When you make changes to the keyboard shortcuts available in Dreamweaver, you should document those changes to remind you while you are working. Click the Export Set as HTML button at the top of the Keyboard Shortcuts dialog box to create a web page listing every command and its corresponding keyboard shortcut. Give the web page a name in the Save as HTML File dialog box and save it to your hard drive. You can open this file in Dreamweaver and edit it if necessary. Preview this file in the browser and then print it out to have a paper copy of your shortcuts.

NOTE
Record Reproducible Steps

Dreamweaver keeps you from recording steps that are not reproducible by Dreamweaver. For instance, Dreamweaver cannot reproduce selecting text on the page, so you cannot save that as a step. Dreamweaver warns you if you cannot save a particular step.

▼ TRY IT YOURSELF

Recording and Playing Back a Command

open the Keyboard Shortcuts dialog box and edit your shortcuts later if needed.

By the way, did you notice that you can give keyboard shortcuts to any of the custom snippets you created earlier this hour? Snippets is one of the command categories you can select to apply keyboard shortcuts. Select Snippets in the Commands drop-down menu and the Keyboard Shortcuts dialog box displays all the Snippets categories. Expand the categories until you find the name of the snippet you want to add a keyboard shortcut to, and then add the shortcut as you did earlier.

Making a Menu Command

Dreamweaver enables you to record and save a step or set of steps as a command. These recorded commands are like macros created in other applications, such as Word and Excel. **Commands** enable you to save a complicated set of steps to apply whenever you have to accomplish a repetitive task. The following are two ways to accomplish this:

▶ Record a set of steps as you perform them and then play them back.

▶ Select a step or set of steps from the History panel and save them as a command.

Recording a Command

Dreamweaver enables you to record a set of steps and then play them back. Dreamweaver can record only a single set of steps in this way. When you record a new set of steps, it replaces the previous set. You can use a recorded set of steps again and again until you either record a new set of steps or close Dreamweaver. This functionality is useful when you're carrying out the same set of steps repeatedly in Dreamweaver.

To record a command for playback, follow these steps:

1. Choose the type of object to which you will apply your steps. If you've created a command that modifies text, you have to apply the command to text; it does not work if you apply it to a dissimilar object. You can't select objects while recording because Dreamweaver cannot record the selection step.

2. Select Commands, Start Recording—the cursor changes into a little cassette icon.

3. Perform the steps you want to record in the Dreamweaver window.

4. Choose Commands, Stop Recording.

5. Select an object to apply the recorded steps to.

6. Choose Commands, Play Recorded Command. Dreamweaver performs the steps you previously recorded.

7. You can continue to use this command until you either replace it with another command or close Dreamweaver.

You have to perform an additional step if you want to save the recorded command to use after you shut down Dreamweaver. To save a command, select Commands, Play Recorded Command. Right-click the final Run Command step in the list, and choose Save as Command, as seen in Figure 24.6. When the Save as Command dialog box appears, enter a name for the command.

Saving a Command from the History Panel

In addition to things you've recorded, the History panel, shown in Figure 24.7, displays *all* the steps you've performed on the current document since you opened it. You can launch the History panel from the Window menu. The History panel enables you to undo certain steps, copy steps to the Clipboard and apply them to different web pages, and save a set of steps as a command.

The History panel lists the steps in the order in which you performed them, with the most recent step at the bottom of the list. You can undo steps by moving the slider up, as shown in Figure 24.8. Notice that the steps dim after you undo them. To redo the steps, move the slider down.

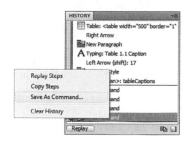

FIGURE 24.6
The History panel includes the Run Command step so that you can save and use your recorded command during future Dreamweaver sessions.

FIGURE 24.7
The History panel records and displays all the steps you've performed on the current web page.

TIP

Change the Number of History Steps Recorded

You can set the number of steps Dreamweaver displays in the History panel in the General category of the Dreamweaver Preferences (Edit, Preferences) dialog box. The default value for the Maximum Number of History Steps setting is 50.

FIGURE 24.8
Move the slider up in the History panel to undo steps. The steps dim when they are undone. Move the slider down to redo the steps.

Clear the History Panel Steps

You can clear all the currently listed steps by selecting the Clear History command from the History panel drop-down menu.

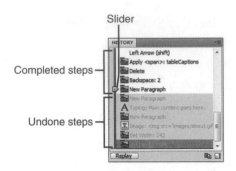

You can save a set of steps from the History panel as a command. Select the steps in the panel by dragging the cursor over them. Click the Save Selected Steps as Command button. When the Save as Command dialog box appears, name the command.

Using and Managing Commands

When a new command is created, it automatically appears at the bottom of the Commands menu, as shown in Figure 24.9. To run your custom command, select it from the Commands menu.

FIGURE 24.9
Custom commands that you create appear at the bottom of the Commands menu.

To rename or delete a command, Select Commands, Edit Command List. This opens a new window where you can click the command labels to edit them, or select a command and click Delete to remove it from the system.

Adding Favorites to the Insert Panel

You explored the Insert panel in Hour 2, "A Tour of Dreamweaver," but postponed discussion of one of its categories—Favorites—until this hour. **Favorites** is the Insert panel category where you store your own custom group of Dreamweaver objects. You can add, group, and organize a list of specific objects to display in the Favorites category.

To begin adding objects to your Favorites category, right-click in the Insert panel with the Favorites category selected and choose Customize Favorites, as seen in Figure 24.10 to display the Customize Favorite Objects dialog box.

FIGURE 24.10
Select the Customize Favorites command by right-clicking on the Favorites category of the Insert panel.

Select objects from the Available Objects list on the left side of the dialog box, which shows all the objects listed in the Insert panel. Select an object in the Available Objects list and click the arrow button in the middle of the dialog box to move that object to the Favorite Objects list on the right side of the dialog box. Use the up-arrow and down-arrow buttons to reorder the Favorites Objects list. Add a separator to the list, as shown in Figure 24.11, by clicking the Add Separator button; the separator is added below whatever you have selected in the Favorite Objects list.

After you click OK to save your list of favorites, those objects appear in the Favorites category of the Insert panel. Clicking OK does not delete the objects from their original categories, it simply duplicates them in the Favorites category so that you can access them easily from a single category. You might modify your favorites from time to time, depending on the type of projects you are working on.

Available objects   Favorites

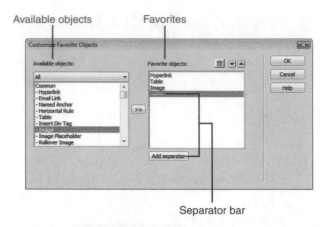

Separator bar

Extending Dreamweaver by Using Third-Party Extensions

You can easily install third-party extensions to Dreamweaver by selecting Commands, Manage Extensions. This command launches Adobe Extension Manager, which enables you to automatically install and uninstall extensions packaged in a standard Adobe extensions format. Many extensions are available to extend Dreamweaver's functionality; check out the Adobe Exchange at http://www.adobe.com/exchange.

Extensions can be commands, objects, suites, or behaviors. The Adobe Exchange, shown in Figure 24.12, lists categories of extensions. You can also search for a certain type of extension at this site. When you select an extension from the list, the site shows you a description of the extension's functionality and a link to download it. Many extensions are free, but some of the extension developers charge a small amount for their work. Sometimes you can try the extension free for a limited amount of time. Most extensions that carry a charge are well worth the money spent because they usually provide functionality you could not create, they speed up your development enormously, and they often have support documentation available.

You have to create a free account to download extensions. After you download a Dreamweaver extension, you use the Adobe Extension Manager to install it to Dreamweaver. Adobe Extension Manager installs automatically when you install Dreamweaver. It manages the extensions to all the Adobe applications you have installed. You launch Adobe Extension Manager by selecting Help, Manage Extensions.

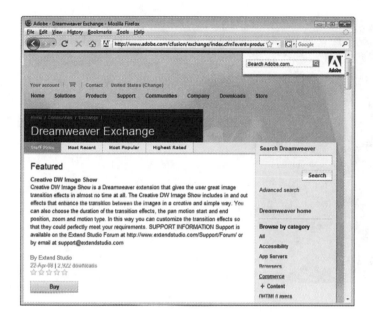

FIGURE 24.12
The Adobe Exchange enables you to view and download extensions to Dreamweaver and other Adobe projects. Select the link to the Dreamweaver Exchange to see only Dreamweaver extensions.

To install a third-party extension, follow these steps:

1. Download an extension file from the Dreamweaver Exchange website. An extension file has the .mxp file extension.

2. Launch Adobe Extension Manager.

3. Click the Install button in Adobe Extension Manager. The Select Extension to Install dialog box appears.

4. Browse to the directory where you saved the file you downloaded. Select the file and click the Open button, as shown in Figure 24.13.

5. Accept any disclaimer by clicking the Accept button.

6. The extension installs into Dreamweaver. The appropriate icons and commands are added automatically.

TRY IT YOURSELF ▼

Installing a Dreamweaver Extension

You can disable an extension by unchecking the check box next to the extension's name under the Enabled column of Adobe Extension Manager. This does not delete the extension but simply makes it unavailable in Dreamweaver. To delete an extension, select the extension name and click the Remove button to the far right of the name.

TIP

Double-Click to Install

You can install most extensions automatically just by finding their icon on your computer and double-clicking them!

FIGURE 24.13
Adobe Extension Manager enables you to easily install third-party extensions into Dreamweaver.

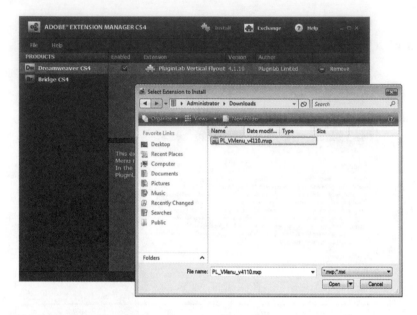

NOTE

Extensions Available for All Studio Products

Adobe Extension Manager manages extensions not only to Dreamweaver but also to Flash, Fireworks, Director, Authorware, and ColdFusion. If you use any of these other products, you can also download and install extensions for them via Adobe Extension Manager.

FIGURE 24.14
The Find and Replace dialog box enables you to search the source code, search the text, or search for a specific tag.

Using, Saving, and Sharing Searches

Dreamweaver has powerful find and replace capabilities. The Find and Replace command is under the Edit menu and it launches the Find and Replace dialog box, shown in Figure 24.14. You can run a search on the current document, all open documents, a certain folder, or an entire current website. You can search the source code, search the text, or search for a specific tag by using the selections in the Search drop-down menu.

To conduct searches, you enter a pattern of text or code into the Find text box. Click the Find button to find the next instance of the pattern or click the Find All button to display a list of all instances of the pattern, as shown in

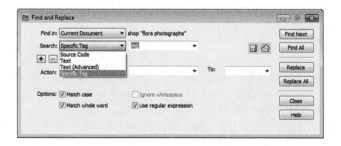

Figure 24.15. The Search panel of the Results panel group under the Property inspector displays the list.

Search results

FIGURE 24.15
The Search panel displays the results of a Find All search.

The Text and Source Code search categories are self-explanatory: You search for text within the web page by using a Text search, and you search for code within Dreamweaver's Code view by using a Source Code search.

The Specific Tag search is a little more complicated, however. You use the Specific Tag search to find HTML tags in your code and modify the tag, modify an attribute of a tag, or strip the tag out of the code completely.

If you have old web pages, you might want to search your website for font tags because Cascading Style Sheets (CSS) styles, the more modern way of formatting page display, have replaced these tags. The following steps show how you can use a Specific Tag search to accomplish this task:

1. In the Find and Replace dialog box, set the scope of your search in the Find In drop-down menu.

2. Select Specific Tag from the Search drop-down menu.

3. Select Font from the list of tags directly to the right of the Search drop-down menu.

4. If you are looking for font tags with a specific attribute—for example, the `face` attribute or the `size` attribute—enter the search characteristics in the Attributes section. Add and subtract attributes by using the + and – buttons. If your tag search has no attribute, click the – button to delete the initial attribute listed.

5. Set what happens to the font tags by using the Action drop-down menu. To simply strip all the tags out of your site, use the Strip Tag action, as shown in Figure 24.16. To replace the font tags with a CSS style, use the Change Tag action and select Span from the drop-down menu to the right.

6. Click the Find All button to display all the search findings.

7. Fine-tune your search by selecting the Find and Replace command again. Dreamweaver retains your search parameters. If your search returns the correct findings, select the Replace command or the Replace All command.

TIP

Search for Text Within Tags

Use the Text (Advanced) Find and Replace commands to search for text within specific HTML tags.

TRY IT YOURSELF ▼

Using Search and Replace to Remove Font Tags

CAUTION

Find Before You Replace

Never click the Replace or Replace All button before confirming that your search returns the correct findings by using the Find Next or Find All buttons.

▼ TRY IT YOURSELF

Using Search and Replace to Remove Font Tags

continued

8. In the Search panel, double-click each of the entries to apply a CSS style to the selection.

FIGURE 24.16
Select the replacement tag when doing a Specific Tag search.

If you've created a complicated search that you want to reuse later or share with others, you can save the search as a Dreamweaver query file. To do this, click the Save Query button to save the current query in the Find and Replace dialog box. Dreamweaver prompts you to browse to a location and then save a file with the .dwr file extension. To load this query, click the Load Query button (refer to Figure 24.14). You can share these .dwr files with others so that they can run the query, too.

Summary

In this hour, you learned techniques and tips for customizing Dreamweaver the way you want it. You learned how to use Dreamweaver snippets and to create and organize your own snippets. You also learned how to modify and create keyboard shortcuts if you are the type of user who prefers to use the keyboard rather than select commands from menus. You learned how to record commands and save commands from the History panel. You used Adobe Extension Manager to load third-party extensions into Dreamweaver. In the final section of the hour, you learned how to use the Find and Replace command and how to save a custom query to reuse or share with others.

Q&A

Q. What's the difference between snippets and Dreamweaver's library items?

A. A snippet simply places objects or code into a web page, whereas a library item maintains a link to the library that enables you to update each instance of the item by updating the original.

Q. How can I remove items from the Favorites category of the Insert panel?

A. Select the Customize Favorites command by right-clicking (Control-clicking on the Mac) the Insert panel. The Customize Favorites dialog box appears. Select the favorite you want to remove and then click the Remove button at the top of the dialog box (the small trash can).

Workshop

Quiz

1. What is the name of the application installed with Dreamweaver that facilitates loading third-party extensions into Dreamweaver?

2. Where do you change the number of steps maintained in the History panel?

3. What are the four searches you can do in the Find and Replace dialog box?

Quiz Answers

1. Adobe Extension Manager installs with Dreamweaver and facilitates loading third-party extensions into it.

2. You change the number of steps maintained in the History panel in the General category of the Dreamweaver Preferences dialog box.

3. You can do these searches in the Find and Replace dialog box: Source Code, Text, Text (Advanced), and Specific Tag.

Exercises

1. Use the Find and Replace command to search for a specific tag in your website. Click the Find All button to view the Search panel. Save the query to your hard drive.

2. Explore the Adobe Exchange and identify an extension that you think is interesting. You have to create a login before you can download an extension from the Adobe Exchange. I like some of the extensions that automatically create a calendar in a web page. If that interests you, use the search functionality to search for calendar extensions in the Dreamweaver Exchange.

INDEX

Symbols

<> (angle brackets), 19

* (asterisk), 12

. (period), 114

(pound sign), 114

/ (slash), 98

A

Absolute Bottom image alignment (Property Inspector), 165

Absolute Middle image alignment (Property Inspector), 165

absolute paths (hyperlinks), 94-96

accessibility

alternate text, 162

definition of, 161

forms, 404

long descriptions, 162

tables, 248-249

Accessibility settings (Table dialog box), 248-249

accessing Spry framework, 374

accordions, 383

Acrobat Reader, 213

Action property (forms), 402

actions, 348, 357

Active link color option (Page Properties dialog), 102

ActiveX controls, 208

Add Separator button (Insert bar, Favorites category), 481

Add to Favorites button (Assets panel), 235

Adobe Bridge, 198

Adobe Dreamweaver CS4 Unleashed (Ruvalcaba), 434

Adobe Exchange website, 473, 482-483

advanced handhelds, 295-297

Advanced tab (Site Definition dialog box), 445, 448

AIFF file format, 208, 215

AJAX (Asynchronous JavaScript and XML), 373

definition of, 373

external AJAX libraries, 394-396

overview, 373-374

Spry framework

accessing, 374

accordions, 383

capabilities of, 374-376

collapsible panels, 383

data sets, creating, 389-394

effects, 378-381

external JavaScript and CSS files, 376-378

Repeat Lists, inserting, 390

Spry panel CSS, editing, 386

tabbed panels, 381-382

ToolTips, 384-385

alerts, 142

Align menu (Property Inspector), 164

X

Y-Z

FREE Online Edition

Your purchase of **Sams Teach Yourself Adobe Dreamweaver CS4 in 24 Hours** includes access to a free online edition for 45 days through the Safari Books Online subscription service. Nearly every Sams book is available online through Safari Books Online, along with more than 5,000 other technical books and videos from publishers such as Addison-Wesley Professional, Cisco Press, Exam Cram, IBM Press, O'Reilly, Prentice Hall, and Que.

SAFARI BOOKS ONLINE allows you to search for a specific answer, cut and paste code, download chapters, and stay current with emerging technologies.

Activate your FREE Online Edition at www.informit.com/safarifree

> **STEP 1:** Enter the coupon code: AXSFJGA.

> **STEP 2:** New Safari users, complete the brief registration form.
> Safari subscribers, just log in.

If you have difficulty registering on Safari or accessing the online edition, please e-mail customer-service@safaribooksonline.com